THE RISE, CORRUPTION AND COMING FALL OF THE HOUSE OF SAUD

THE RISE, CORRUPTION
AND COMING FALL OF
THE HOUSE OF SAUD

SAÏD K. ABURISH

ST. MARTIN'S PRESS
NEW YORK

THE RISE, CORRUPTION AND COMING FALL OF THE HOUSE OF SAUD
Copyright © 1994, 1995 by Saïd K. Aburish

ISBN 0-312-12541-0

Library of Congress Cataloging-in-Publication Data

Aburish, Saïd K.
   The rise, corruption and coming fall of the House of Saud / Saïd
K. Aburish.
        p. cm.
   ISBN 0-312-12541-0
   1. Saudi Arabia—History.   I. Title.
DS244.A26 1995
953.8—dc20   95-10197
                                                        CIP

First published in Great Britain by
Bloomsbury Publishing Limited, 1994.

First St. Martin's Edition: June 1995
10 9 8 7 6 5 4 3 2 1

In memory of my friend Saud Ibrahim Al Muammer, who was tortured to death by the House of Saud, and of my mother, who mourned him as much as I did.

Contents

Acknowledgments

This list is incomplete. Thirty-four of the people who were interviewed for this book did so on condition of anonymity. Others allowed me to mention their names but did not want specific facts or ideas attributed to them. Moreover, it should be stated that some of those interviewed disagreed with my approach and my conclusions. Indeed the opinions expressed in this book, like its shortcomings, are mine alone. These provisions aside, I nevertheless owe a huge debt of thanks to the following:

Jamil Mroeh, journalist; Abdel Barri Attwan, newspaper editor; Ghassan Zakkaria, magazine editor; Robert Fisk, news correspondent; Jean Diah, journalist and historian; Suleiman Firzli, journalist; Farid Al Khatib, journalist; Toby Odone, journalist; Murray Gart, journalist and editor; Kassem Ja'afar, journalist; David Boardman, television producer; Rosie Waterhouse, journalist; Pierre Salinger, journalist and former press spokesman for President Kennedy; Mohammad Kabardai, journalist; Maria Kelmas, journalist; Helga Graham, journalist; David Gardner, journalist; Steven Timewell, editor; Professor Mousa Mazzawi, authority on Sharia law; Dr Muhammad Faisal, editor; David Helier, television writer; Khaldoun Solh, publisher.

Rosemary Hollis, Royal United Services Institute; William Quandt, Brookings Institution; James Akins, Harold Cutler and Hermann Eilts, former US Ambassadors to Saudi Arabia; Robert Komer, former member of the National Security Council; Eric Roulu, former French Ambassador to Syria and Iran.

Tewfiq Al Sheikh, Abdel Ameer Mousa and Hamza Al Hassan, Saudi opposition members; Sa'ad Al Bazzaz, Iraqi Government official; Dr Gholamhussein Ra'ad, former Iranian Government official; Paul Parker, former banker; Bob McCarthy, banker; Ziad Beidoun, geologist; Sue Arnold, former employee of the Military Hospital, Riyadh.

Among the names missing for reasons of anonymity are one member of the House of Saud, two former British diplomats, three

CIA agents, five bankers, including some with the World Bank and the International Monetary fund, seven journalists who still visit Saudi Arabia and three businessmen with interests there. The rest are academics, think-tank members and others who have worked in Saudi Arabia.

Also, as in all book-writing endeavours, there were relatives and friends who provided much-needed companionship and comfort without involvement in my purpose as a writer. In this regard, thanks are due to my father, Abu Said, my cousins Khalil and Ghuleb, my nephew Nasser and my friends Kate Beck, Sa'ida Nusseibeh, Laura Sandys, Sue Taylor, Jan Cushing, Elke Bryer, Gene Etchevere, Henry Elewell, James Exelby, Gregor MacKinnon and Samir Chourbaji.

THE RISE, CORRUPTION
AND COMING FALL OF
THE HOUSE OF SAUD

1

Blood, Oil and Cynicism

'British Aerospace Wins Huge Saudi Defence Contract'; 'King Fahd Forms Consultative Council but Retains Absolute Power'; 'Saudi Arabia Maintains Lower Oil Prices – Pressure Mounts on Other OPEC Members'; 'Saudi Arabia Appears Set to Replace Saddam'.

The above newspaper headlines concerning Saudi deeds and misdeeds appeared during one month in 1992 and vividly demonstrate the extent of the economic and political powers wielded by that country. They also hint at attempts to respond to the winds of change. If we add two unreported events – 'Thousands Languish in Saudi Prisons' and 'King Fahd Marries – for the 100th Time' – then the picture of contemporary Saudi Arabia becomes clearer still.

What Saudi Arabia represents, and the disproportionate power it wields, cannot be considered acceptable in the modern world. Fortunately, I am not alone in viewing this situation with alarm, and whether or not Saudi Arabia should continue in its present form is an emerging question which the Saudi people and the international community cannot avoid answering for much longer. The perceived new world order and the dynamics of social change within the Middle East and Saudi Arabia itself have produced a clear response unencumbered by the historic separation of ideology from politics. No longer will people overlook the Saudi Government's backward ways because of its oil-based friendship with the West. The House of Saud's ability to maintain itself and wield regional and international power through the use of the 'oil weapon' remains strong, but most of the constraints which protected and absolved the world's most absolute feudal monarchy are no more.

Nonetheless, the conclusive answer suggested by these worldwide, regional and internal developments is not as clear-cut as it would appear. A realistic answer can only be provisional and has to take into consideration the circles of power within which Saudi Arabia operates. The country exercises power and

1

influence inside permanent identifiable spheres, but the way they interact is constantly changing, and this has permitted the House of Saud to continue an elaborate and very successful balancing act aimed exclusively at perpetuating its rule. As the world's leading autocracy, the House of Saud runs the country as a family fiefdom, so that Saudi Arabia and the House of Saud are one and the same. For the purposes of this book, therefore, the terms are used interchangeably.

Broadly stated, Saudi Arabia's policies and internal politics have varying effects on its own people, the Arab world, the Muslim world and the world in general. The country's influence is based on two main factors: its position as the world's leading producer of oil and site of the largest oil reserves; and its important though exaggerated position as the home of Islam's holiest shrines. In the absence of a Soviet-based communist threat, Saudi Arabia's strategic position, formerly another source of power, has lost most of its importance.

The contradictions in the way Saudi Arabia skilfully nullifies the established policies of the countries with which it deals are best demonstrated through a simple example of how it uses the power oil gives it. The West is dependent on Saudi Arabia for oil at a low price, but the very same West, though it has shown a remarkable reluctance to talk about the issue, would like to see a more sensible internal and regional sharing of the oil wealth.

The House of Saud undermines the West's wish for a more equitable sharing of wealth by making it dependent on its ability to pump more oil than it needs, thereby keeping the price of oil low. This places the West in a position of dependence which varies with economic conditions. Afraid to upset this beneficial arrangement, the West forgoes its commitment to a more equitable distribution of the oil wealth. This both allows the House of Saud to continue to view the revenues from oil as a private family income and leads the West to ignore its moral commitment to the introduction of political reforms within the country.

There are even simpler examples. The Saudi money which goes to help the Arab and Muslim countries is given on the basis of a divide-and-rule policy. Saudi Arabia gives money to Syria to balance the growing power of Egypt – and vice versa – and this makes them compete, keeps them apart and renders them weaker. It supports Muslim fundamentalists in the occupied territories of the West Bank and the Gaza Strip in order to undermine the PLO's Yasser Arafat while opposing freely elected Muslim fundamentalist groups in Algeria for fear that a militant Muslim Algeria might challenge its Arab policies. The central purpose of all these policies is to promote regional discord and retard democratic progress in other countries of the Middle East. This situation serves to ensure the continuance of the House of Saud, since regional harmony could produce competitors and democratic progress in neighbouring countries might prove to be infectious.

For the first time, however, Saudi Arabia's self-perpetuating policies are now being challenged by international, regional and local developments which are converging and gaining momentum. Nothing that the rulers of the country are doing suggests that they are able or willing to undertake the steps necessary to evolve a new political approach which would help maintain their position and influence on world affairs on a more sensible basis. In fact, during the past five years the two governmental departments whose budgets have continued to increase are the royal household and the Ministry of Defence – the ruling family and its protectors.

In addition to the already mentioned diminution of the strategic importance of the country, there is an explicit desire by the advocates of the new world order to eliminate the sources of friction and future upheavals in the Middle East. For Saudi Arabia this would mean the introduction of measures to bring the abuse of internal and regional power to an end. Eliminating internal abuse goes beyond the House of Saud's sharing of the country's natural wealth with the average Saudi to protecting human rights and giving its citizens a voice in the affairs of their country.

The awareness that Saudi Arabia cannot continue to ignore the economic plight of its neighbours and survive unmolested means that future Saudi help to Arab countries must be directed at raising the standard of living of the people and not at the pockets of rulers who follow a regressive Saudi line. Surrounded as it is by poor neighbours, Saudi Arabia must deal with those who suffer this poverty, the people. (Saddam Hussein's justification for the invasion of Kuwait, buried as it is in the tide of rhetoric which followed it, called for the distribution of Kuwait's oil income among all Arabs.)

Regional developments have added to the pressures on the House of Saud to change its ways. Syria and Egypt have become outspoken in their demands for more help in return for affording the Saudis military assistance and protection. Their basic complaint resembles Saddam's: Saudi Arabia has too much and they have too little. Jordan has a functioning parliament and many of its members are critical of Saudi Arabia's wasteful policies. They, too, demand more help. The Yemen has decided that it finds the Saudi use of money to reduce it to a tributary country objectionable and has challenged Saudi attempts to stop it from enacting populist measures aimed at democratizing its institutions and satisfying its people. Muslim Iran represents an even greater challenge because it espouses a militant Islam which frowns on the idea of monarchy and questions the Saudi way of expressing it. Saudi Arabia needs to develop policies to respond to these pressures.

In addition to worldwide and regional developments, the third source of pressure for change comes from within. The Saudi people are beginning to object openly to the monopoly of power exercised by the ever-increasing members (35–40 more males monthly) of the House of Saud. The number of educated people has risen dramatically beyond the country's ability to absorb them and this means that the House of Saud is no longer able to bribe all educated Saudis with good jobs. The tribal system, which constituted a questionable power base for the House of Saud, is disappearing, making way for the permanent settlement and growing sophistication of a previously scattered people incapable of joint action. The religious leaders, afraid that they might be pre-empted by a grassroots militant Islamic movement, are demanding changes aimed at reducing the power of the royal family before it is too late. Even the heavily financed and Western-equipped army is unreliable and a future coalition of these forces or parts of them seems inevitable.

The House of Saud's response to these pressures has been nothing more than the creation, after 30 years of waiting and dozens of false starts since it was first promised, of a consultative council to be appointed by King Fahd himself. It is safe to assume that the people appointed by the King will not act against his wishes and his family's interests, and Fahd has already undermined the council's future by making it clear that he is solidly opposed to the introduction of anything resembling a democratic system. The powers of the council will be limited to debating minor issues as directed by the King. In reality, the most important aspect of the consultative council may very well be its creation, underlining as it does the explicit acceptance by King Fahd of the need for change.

Apart from this highly publicized, though flawed step, the House of Saud shows no signs of understanding the world's and the Western powers' desire for it to change. It hides behind an untrue claim that Muslim countries are different and incapable of adopting democracy, and it sees all calls for a more equitable sharing of the wealth and the protection of human rights as nothing more than interference in its internal affairs. (People still disappear in the middle of the night and others are imprisoned for years without trial, not to speak of public floggings and executions.) The House of Saud refuses to accept that the disappearance of the Soviet threat has made it 'fair game' and that it is no longer immune to criticism and pressure. Unpopular as its oil policies are with its people and fellow OPEC members, the House of Saud continues to believe that providing the West with cheaper oil will protect it.

Regionally, the policies of the House of Saud are an extension of its internal attitude. Not only do its members ignore the explosive regional imbalance created by the difference of living standards between them and their neighbours but, more critically, they see money spent on programmes which raise the standard of living of the average Arab as nothing less than dangerous. To the House of Saud all this does is educate the beneficiaries into demanding more money and more rights. This is why it concentrates on supporting corrupt regimes whose leaders follow its example in stifling democracy and retarding progress. This superficial ability to control things gives it a feeling of safety which it covets above all else. And it is this same need to feel safe which makes it sponsor moves against budding parliamentarianism in Jordan, Bahrain, Kuwait and the Yemen. The House of Saud also opposes other progressive moves, including a free press, in neighbouring Arab countries. Years ago, this yearning for safety led it to try to assassinate the Arab world's leading advocate of change, the late President Nasser of Egypt.

However, it is within the kingdom itself that the problems of the House of Saud show most. The pace of social change, with all the destruction it can wreak, has a positive aspect to it. The Saudi people are not as docile as they used to be. The educated young, the merchant class, the religious leaders, the genuinely liberal and committed, the rare few who have an optimistic yen for political power, and even members of the armed forces, have become opposed to the dictatorial and profligate ways of the royal family. Locally produced audio cassettes and books carrying anti-House of Saud political messages (even the hitherto elusive number of the King's wives is now documented) have become bestsellers.

Religious leaders, including Sheikh Abdel Aziz bin Baz, the leading official imam of the country, have petitioned King Fahd, demanding a political system which would allow greater power-sharing.

The merchant class's complaints become louder with every passing month; they want a share in the governance of their country and object to the increasing numbers of the royal household who use their influence to monopolize trade and relegate others to a secondary position. Except with the royal family itself, its lackeys and a tiny group of believers in feudalism, the House of Saud has become very unpopular. Conservative estimates place the number of people arrested for 'political crimes' since the Gulf War at 8000, although most were released after a short stay in prison.

The nature of the internal and regional pressures on Saudi Arabia, anchored as they are in the progress of the common Saudi and the average Arab, renders them irreversible. The gap between the demands of the advocates of change and the antiquated, insensitive ways of the House of Saud is widening. The latter appears to have made a decision that these forces matter considerably less than the influence of the oil-dependent countries, particularly the USA and Europe. Instead of mollifying the cries of discontent of its own people and fellow Arabs, it is making itself more dependent on Western support. This trend has extended to its open acceptance of Western military protection, not against a superpower threat, but against its own people and its unhappy neighbours.

The simple matrix shown below, which compares the policies of the House of Saud with those of Saddam Hussein and Libya's Colonel Qaddafi, the two Arab leaders least accepted by Western governments, press and people, demonstrates this practical though morally questionable Saudi–Western relationship. King Fahd is not only the criminal equal of the Iraqi and Libyan leaders, but is much worse in important aspects of his personal conduct and in his support for despotic regimes.

	FAHD	SADDAM	QADDAFI
MURDER	X	X	X
DENIAL OF POLITICAL FREEDOM	X	X	X
CORRUPTION	X	?	X
NEPOTISM	X	X	?
RELIGIOUS AND/OR ETHNIC INTOLERANCE	X	X	–
SUPPORT FOR DESPOTIC REGIMES	X	–	–

UNACCEPTABLE PERSONAL BEHAVIOUR	X	–	–
HIGHER OIL PRICES	–	X	X
ENMITY WITH WEST	–	X	X

The Saudi position is very clear: the only relevant area where King Fahd and the House of Saud come out ahead is their overall relationship with the West. Judged qualitatively, they murder and stifle political dissent the way the others do; they are guilty of nepotism and lechery; they support despotic regimes; they suppress their Shia minority as violently as Saddam suppresses the Kurds and his Shias; and they are infinitely more corrupt than the others. When we add the fact that the Saudi people would rather have higher oil prices and place their own welfare above that of the West – I have been told this by Saudi labourers, taxi drivers, teachers, businessmen and former Oil Minister Yamani, whose moderate oil-pricing policies made him the most unpopular man in his country – the picture is complete. The House of Saud is beholden to the West more than it is to its own people.

For its part, the West will have to try to salvage the deteriorating situation in Saudi Arabia through striking a better balance between deriving economic comfort from cheap oil and making a commitment to human rights and regional stability. So far the governments of the USA, the United Kingdom and France, and indeed their press and people, have sacrificed principle to expediency. They demonstrate no willingness to stop seeing the House of Saud as the cornerstone of their Middle East policies, but their short-sighted cynicism may come back to haunt them. After all, in a parallel situation, their inevitable inability to protect the Shah of Iran against the anger of his own people cost them a great deal.

Is it desirable for the House of Saud as we know it to continue? The simpler answer is no. The behaviour of members of the royal household and its more than 7000 members represents the lowest common denominator of twentieth-century life and Arab tradition. This book began as a documented plea against the House of Saud in the hope of convincing the press and the people of the West to mobilize their governments to take a stand against this ugly abuse of power. Somewhere along the way my attitude changed: now it is an appeal to the West to make plans to contain the damage which will follow the coming turmoil in Saudi Arabia or to pre-empt events by engineering a palace coup which would change the very nature of the rule of the House of Saud and reduce its kings to figureheads.

A revolution in Saudi Arabia could to lead to disruption or stoppage of its oil production. Such a stoppage, even a short-lived one, could lead to a depression, a West–Muslim confrontation or both. There is no way to replace the production of nine million barrels of oil a day and the machinery of the industrialized world would grind to a halt. The most obvious response, occupying the oilfields, even if it were militarily feasible, would mean occupying Muslim holy soil and that would lead to a jihad – a holy war – against the infidel West.

2

In the Shadow of the Tent

I will begin with the popular image and then reveal the real man. I do not want to present the naked truth about Ibn Saud without an attempt at explaining why most readers brought up in the West think he was the greatest Arab of the twentieth century and among the greatest Arabs of all time.

Forty years ago the eccentric Orientalist-agent Harry St John Philby described Abdel Aziz Abdel Rahman Al Saud (1870–1953), the first king and founder of today's Saudi Arabia (commonly known as Ibn Saud), as 'the greatest Arab since the Prophet Mohammad'. Were Philby alone in this demonstration of adoration, it would be dismissed out of hand, the view of someone who was praising a friend to whom he had been an adviser for over 30 years. (The British Government sent Philby to assist Ibn Saud, perhaps to play kingmaker, in 1917 and, except for a brief absence in Jordan in the 1920s, he was part of the Saudi court until the King's death.) But dozens, if not hundreds, of others who have written on the subject before and after Philby tend to agree with him – most without being totally carried away, however. Even when these writers try to moderate their misrepresentation of facts, their documented attempt to elevate an unworthy man to the status of a great Arab and Muslim leader, they still settle for weighty statements such as 'the man who unified and brought Arabia into the 20th century' or 'the founder of modern Arabia and the leader of the Muslim world'.

While more than a few among the historians, journalists, businessmen and even CIA agents who have written books and articles about Ibn Saud allude to some of his unattractive traits such as public beheadings, amputations and floggings, his childish dependence on a full-time interpreter of dreams and his financial maintenance of hundreds of wives, they insist on seeing them either as necessary to govern the Arabs or as a source of outright amusement. There is a disturbing absence of judgement, moral or practical, which ignores the abuse of his wives, slaves and concubines. Overlooked are the fact that he roared with laughter when he told stories about hacking his enemies to death; his abuse of his personal drivers and domestic servants to the extent of regularly using the stick on them in the presence of guests; how he squandered his country's wealth and used much of it to corrupt that same country's age-old tradition of giving and receiving; and even how he used the same wealth to divide and weaken the rest of the Arabs.

The image of Ibn Saud which has filtered through to the ordinary reader is of a progressive, benevolent, wise and fun-loving autocrat who early this century unified Arabia in stages and gave his people what was best for them. Even the simple fact that the Saudis became better off under him than they were before is implicitly attributed to him. One would think some of the writers believe he discovered or invented the oil.

Ibn Saud's true record tells a different story from what Philby and others invented. Progressive, wise, benevolent and fun-loving were not words that applied to the man, and even the accounts of his more ardent supporters reveal a lecher and a bloodthirsty autocrat and Bedouin chief for hire who did not see far, did not represent his culture and set the smallest of his personal pleasures above the welfare of his people. For example, not a single school for girls was opened during his reign whereas many were started in poorer Arab countries which had become aware of the value of educating women. Nor is there a record of a single visit to a school or of the building of one hospital or clinic during Ibn Saud's more than 30 years of rule, and he turned down the request of his son Tallal to build a hospital by admonishing him to 'do something useful instead'. In fact, there is a deliberate de-emphasis by his admirers of the significance of other unpalatable facts and a pretence that they were the norm of the day. These include public beheadings and amputations, the fact that he begat 42 boys and an unknown number of girls (the latter he refused to educate at all) and that, despite the oil wealth, he was in debt for most of his life and died in that graceless state. To the long list of forgiven sins and an abysmal record of internal governance can be added his subservience to outside powers at a time when the Arabs, including the people of Saudi Arabia, wanted to be independent and free.

Unlike the rest of this book, which relies on a substantial amount of original research, this chapter is mostly dependent on the sources that were used by the people who carried the torch on behalf of his late majesty. This raises the question of why my conclusions differ dramatically from those of the loyal herd.

It boils down to the different ways we view the circumstances of Ibn Saud's rise to power and his governance. Those who celebrate him, his Western and equally guilty Arab apologists (in both cases their books depended on interviews with princes and ministers and their ranks included many of his former officials and people paid by the family to praise him), saw and continue to see the Arab as ungovernable and hence undeserving of anything except a dictator's whip to mould him into an exemplar of the false modernity practised by Ibn Saud and his family. This overblown vision of the modern world was exemplified by a fondness for gold bathroom fixtures, a preponderance of Cadillacs and an untraditional attachment to Black Label whisky, diamond rings and gold watches. Furthermore, there was an absence of social and charitable institutions (Saudi Arabia has no Red Crescent, charity organizations or professional associations and certainly no effective national health system or family planning network).

I judge Ibn Saud by a different yardstick. By this measure, the Arabs undeniably deserved better, particularly when you take into consideration the fact that better-qualified people were available to govern Arabia and that Ibn Saud did not meet the most basic requirement of a hero, that of being an expression of his culture. Indeed he represented a serious step backwards: it was a case of the uneducated Bedouin stunting urban-led progress. (Sadly but tellingly, most Arab leaders who have been accepted by and celebrated in the West are often rejected by their own people, and this includes those who were violently eliminated: the former kings of Libya and Tunisia, Anwar Sadat of Egypt and Prime Minister Nuri Said of Iraq.) Perhaps I am a romantic dreamer, but I enjoy closing my eyes momentarily to see an Arabia that never was, a place where oil wealth was used to benefit most of the people.

If I may cite the distinguished Palestinian–American man of letters Edward Said: 'Formally the Orientalist sees himself as accomplishing the union of Orient with Occident, mainly by asserting the technological political supremacy of the West. History in such a union is attenuated if not banished.' Said goes on to show how Western historians see the Arabs as 'childish and primitive'. While many of the people who wrote about Ibn Saud were not historians, they all pretended to be providing footnotes to a history which saw them ignore most of the Arabs of the Peninsula in favour of the antics of a noble Bedouin savage.

They manifested the same flawed Western attitude of which Said speaks.

A direct application of Said's eloquent statement yields an Ibn Saud who is indeed romantic, wise and wonderful if the Arab is nothing but a nomad who is 'childish and primitive' and incapable of producing better leaders. This view is totally unacceptable, however, if the Arabs are seen for what they really are: the possessors of a proud culture of great historical depth and eminently able to pass judgement on their leaders, including Ibn Saud.

I hasten to add that my seemingly radical view is quite innocent. I am not a rabid Arab nationalist nor am I a Muslim fundamentalist. I belong to both East and West and am a firm believer in Arab–Western cooperation. But I maintain that only through proper understanding can such cooperation produce positive results for both sides. Such an understanding would eliminate the subordination of history to a dramatic portrayal of a romantic desert figure regardless of his merits. It would preclude comparing Ibn Saud with Muhammad and it would eliminate the often violent misunderstandings which continue to bedevil Arab–Western and Muslim–Western relations to the disadvantage of both parties.

Now we should turn to the man himself and how to judge him. The time for the revisionist historian to play detective has come. It is time to examine Ibn Saud's early qualities as propounded by his advocates: his familial claim to the leadership of modern Arabia, his possession of a superior far-seeing mind and his fame as a military leader who united the Arabs.

It is true that by the time Ibn Saud became its leader early this century, the House of Saud had been around for some time. It had been a thorn in the side of the Arabian Peninsula's body politic since the eighteenth century, but whatever it had achieved, it was never an accepted, established monarchy recognized by other countries or an expression of the idea of a nation-state. One might compare the House of Saud to the Kurds and their periodic success in attaining autonomy. Though twice successful in controlling vast tracts of today's Saudi Arabia and capable of causing trouble for the Sultanate of Turkey which ruled it, the House of Saud accepted Turkey as the empire within which it operated and Ibn Saud himself wrote to the Sultan of Turkey, 'We've always been servants of the crown.'

The members of the House of Saud belonged and still belong to the puritan Wahhabi sect. The religious beliefs and small numbers of this sect stood between them and the attainment of permanent power in a part of the world which has always attached great importance to religious affiliation and the numbers of a tribe and its followers. In fact, while they had been on and off rulers of Nejed and the city of Riyadh, the House of Saud was never totally accepted by the majority of Muslims and it was its religion-based, warlike qualities rather than its popularity, the legitimacy of its claim or its sound governance which was responsible for its notoriety. Its rule depended on a special application of force, terror, and even its own tribe, the 'Ennezza, never totally accepted it. Two of Ibn Saud's uncles and many other relatives died as a result of family and tribal feuds which originated in questions about the application of Wahhabi doctrine, what to do to become acceptable to more people and stop what one of Ibn Saud's uncles described as 'consistent bad behaviour', namely the killing of all non-Wahhabis.

From 1902 to 1925 Ibn Saud waged wars in which he defeated three more established and popular families who ruled large areas of what is now known as Saudi Arabia. He made himself king, and sometime during the 1930s sought to remedy his lack of a solid base or royal background. In an attempt to gain legitimacy and acceptance by the people through appealing to their religious instincts, he hired an Egyptian religious sheikh by the name of Muhammad Tammimi to fabricate a family tree which showed him to be a direct descendant of the Prophet. The sheikh's handiwork was sent back several times until it satisfied the upstart king. This claim has never been seriously accepted by the true descendants of the Prophet and later the same family-tree maker was hired by King Farouk of Egypt to invent a religious lineage for him. It is worth noting that Ibn Saud was friendlier towards the corrupt and lacking-in-background Farouk than any other Arab king or head of state. The sheikh obliged both status-seeking monarchs and died a relatively wealthy man, having made his fortune acquiring holiness for all those who could afford it.

But Ibn Saud's inferiority complex over his origins continued well after Tammimi's laughable efforts. In the 1940s the Arabian–American Oil Company (ARAMCO), hardly a disinterested party, sponsored a massive study of the history of the House of Saud which produced results similar to those of the Egyptian cleric. Though this study is used by most writers about Saudi Arabia to this day, the true descendants of the Prophet, the Hashemites, the family of King Hussein of Jordan, have steadfastly refused to intermarry with the House of Saud despite their poverty and the obvious financial benefits.

If the proper family, tribal and religious backgrounds were lacking, what then of Ibn Saud's reputation as a warrior and leader of men? It is pure fabrication. Even Philby admits that until he was afforded British military aid and advice, Ibn Saud's military achievements were questionable and hardly glorious. That he was a master of the *ghazzu*, or raid, is essentially true, but the ensuing larger reputation he gained is only acceptable if one overlooks the nature of his exploits and how he conducted himself in this narrow sphere of warfare. He was backed by the religious zealots of the Wahhabi sect, who had little regard for life but sought death in the hope of martyrdom and ascent to heaven. Ibn Saud was never a gentleman warrior even in the *ghazzu*.

During this time the major respectable tribes of Arabia, most certainly the other contenders for its leadership, were moving towards modernity and respect for individual property. They were settling and farming, and most tribal sheikhs lived in towns, but Ibn Saud was still in the business of raiding other tribes to steal their camels, sheep and grain. Despite the existence of a serious etiquette for this activity, which forbade the killing of the people of the raided tribe, he prided himself on never taking prisoners. He murdered all the men of the raided tribe to prevent future retaliation.

Ibn Saud's political emergence began in 1902 when he reclaimed Riyadh, the city where his family had been local sheikhs in their own right or sheikhs appointed by the local emirs. His first merciless act was to terrorize the population by spiking the heads of his enemies and displaying them at the gates of the city. His followers burned 1200 people to death. When conducting a raid, he and his followers were very much in the habit of taking young maidens back to enslave them or make gifts of them to friends. That is how Ibn Saud and his people lived at the turn of the century, before he became king and when he was a mere head of a large tribe.

Ibn Saud's insistence on continuing the *ghazzu* came close to getting him ejected from Kuwait, where he had taken refuge from the emirs of eastern Arabia and where the ruling Sabbah family, themselves Bedouin sheikhs who are in power to this day, frowned on the unwholesome and dishonourable activity. Western historians' presentation of the *ghazzu* as the norm of the day is totally untrue, and the heads of the major Bedouin tribes, who claimed hegemony over large tracts of land, did not practise it. Even if the institution was not totally unknown, the way it was practised by Ibn Saud was contrary to all Arab and Muslim traditions of generosity to the vanquished, the revered notion of a victor's mercy which went back to the Prophet.

According to the same blinkered historians and fellow-travellers, the third of the elements which distinguished Ibn Saud's youth, after his family background and natural military talent, was his wisdom despite a lack of education. There is good reason to believe the man was only semi-literate, though this is a point which is ignored by Western writers, who ascribe to him some sort of 'mysterious' desert learning and dwell on his ability to recite the Koran, poetry and Bedouin sayings. In reality, these were very ordinary attributes common to the simplest of Bedouin sheikhs.

Ibn Saud's father was definitely illiterate and at best he learned to read and sign his name (most of the documents I have seen indicate he used a seal, but some handwritten ones were simple enough for his meagre talents). For most of his life he thought all Americans were Red Indians and he died insisting that the world was flat and without learning the difference between a Catholic and a Protestant. His ignorance also extended to matters which affected the conduct of his country's internal and external policies. In the late 1940s he complained about the undue influence of the Jews on American foreign policy and attributed it to the presence of 5000 Jews in New York City.

While I do not scoff at Bedouin learning, there was in Ibn Saud very little evidence of the type of wisdom which results from it and he certainly failed to maintain a judicial system in areas which once had one. He destroyed the existing governmental structures by taking all things into his hands and encouraged slavery by personally owning hundreds of slaves. He surrounded himself with unintelligent yes-men, an insult to an established tradition which celebrated the wisdom of advisers, as recorded in many of the sayings of the Prophet. Well into the 1940s, each of Ibn Saud's sons had a young slave-entertainer attached to him known as an *akiwaya*, or 'little brother'. In reality they were hostage playmates.

If Ibn Saud lacked wisdom except such as appealed to the Orientalist, with his prejudices against the Arab people and wish to create romantic figures where none existed, then it is more appropriate to judge him by his obviously limited horizons. His lack of a formal education was a serious reflection on his family's status and social development and affected his ability to manage the affairs of what was at that time the biggest independent Muslim state. Literacy was sought by Bedouins and their chiefs – certainly members of the ruling families who opposed him were educated – and its absence among the members of the House of Saud and Ibn Saud's repeated refusal to send his children to school provide further confirmation of his lack of appreciation of what really mattered.

So Ibn Saud's oft-mentioned major attributes during his early years, the justifications for his eventual success – his family back-ground, qualities as a military leader of men and native wisdom – are suspect, if not simply non-existent. Western historians would have us believe that he was a true hero, that the way Ibn Saud expressed these qualities was superior to the ways they were expressed by others, that they were rare qualities unavailable elsewhere. Most of this reputation rests on his ability to recite simple maxims known to most people of his time. (My own grandfather was fond of repeating 'the hand you can't bite, kiss it' and 'it is a wise man who says little and listens a great deal', two of many sayings wrongly attributed to Ibn Saud.) The same chorus of supporters shy away from conducting the necessary comparative analysis which would prove their admiring statements, and very little is said to detract from the image of the larger-than-life figure they create for their protagonist. As a matter of fact, most supporters of Ibn Saud are so outrageously prejudiced that they praise some qualities in him which they condemn in others.

At the outbreak of the First World War, beyond the already established emirates along the Gulf, there were three other families trying to replace the Ottoman Empire as governors of the Arabian Peninsula. They were the Hashemites in the western part of the peninsula, the religiously important Hijaz where the Muslim holy cities of Mecca and Medina are located, the Ibn Rasheeds, who were the enemies of the House of Saud and co-claimants to Nejed, the middle of the country, where Riyadh is situated, and the Idrissis in Asir, the highlands which neighbour the Yemen, a mountainous area with many fertile spots and a relatively high standard of living. The eastern part of the country along the Gulf, which contains Saudi Arabia's oilfields, was controlled by Turkey until May 1914 and though there were no local leaders of note most of the people there were Shias and anti-Wahhabi.

The Hashemites were the most important dynasty and, because of their undeniable historical importance, Ibn Saud's advocates are forced to afford them full if unsympathetic treatment. They had been the guardians of the Muslim holy places of Mecca and Medina for hundreds of years. They were and are the accepted descendants of the Prophet, educated people who spoke several languages and who were full of genuine Islamic gentility and generosity. Even their women were tutored and many busied themselves with social work. I met several of them in the 1960s – they were quite elderly by then – who spoke elegant Arabic, Turkish, English and French and discoursed freely on affairs of state and social problems. Ibn Saud's abominable treatment of women aside, they would have viewed the *ghazzu* and its consequences as practised by Ibn Saud with total abhorrence. It is difficult to imagine a Hashemite sharing a meal with Ibn Saud or to conceive of a Hashemite ordering summary executions, as Ibn Saud did on a large scale and with relish. (He personally executed 18 rebellious tribal chiefs and spoke proudly of how he kissed the sword covered with blood after beheading one of his tribal enemies, Ubyade Ibn Rasheed.)

The Ibn Rasheeds, who vied with the Al Sauds for the same fiefdom, were also settled folk with a lineage which went back several centuries and, while querulous in nature and always feuding, they too scoffed at the *ghazzu* and did not see the Al Sauds as their equals. The Ibn Rasheeds belonged to the noble tribe of Shamar, too big and too proud to depend on raids in the Ibn Saud fashion. They were educated people refined enough to sign friendship treaties with the Sultanate of Turkey, and ample evidence exists that they conducted their court affairs in a civilized manner. To establish the difference between the Ibn Rasheeds and the Al Sauds, all one has to do is examine contemporaneous pictures of the former looking regal and romantic and compare them with pictures of the dishevelled Ibn Saud and his barefoot children, including one of the present King Fahd looking desperately dusty and in need of a bath.

The Idrissis, though accepted as sharifs or descendants of the Prophet, were simpler people who lacked the stature of Hashemites or the Ibn Rasheeds; in fact there is no more to the present inclusion of them as a potential ruling family of Arabia than the fact that they were there. Still, they were educated people who lived in accordance with an Islamic tradition which preached equality, kindness and the rule of law, and they were people full of goodness and hospitality and opposed to illiteracy and violence.

So it was not a combination of rare qualities which elevated the most backward of available rulers, Ibn Saud, to the leadership of Arabia. The simple, undeniable fact behind Ibn Saud's rise to power was Britain's interest in finding someone to deputize for it on the eve of the First World War, when it was trying to wrest control of the Arabian Peninsula from Turkey's hands, and later, when the other Arab leaders were not as forthcoming. Ibn Saud's ascendancy coincided with the growing British interest in the Gulf region. It is true that the Hashemites in western Arabia cooperated with the British at the same time, but their cooperation was non-subservient and conditional, based on their historical claim and desire to become kings of all the Arabs and their belief that the British would help them achieve this aim. The Ibn Rasheeds were allied to Turkey and hence an enemy of Britain and the Idrissis were not up to the task. Ibn Saud, homeless and hungry, was there for the asking, cheap and willing to accommodate any sponsor. So great was his need for outside help that on at least two occasions he wrote to the Sultan of Turkey offering his services. For a while they were accepted, but eventually the Sultan turned him down; he considered him a nuisance.

The first contact between Britain and the House of Saud goes back to 1865, to the time of Ibn Saud's grandfather. There was an unenforceable treaty, similar to many the British were fond of signing then ignoring, with local tribal chiefs, between Faisal Al Saud and a certain Colonel Lewis Pelly. The historical record is unclear as to whether Britain was the direct or indirect sponsor of Ibn Saud's raid on Riyadh, though his use of camels and equipment beyond his means seems to suggest a mysterious source of support. That aside, no substantial contact followed until 1904, when, according to Philby: 'Ibn Saud became convinced of the value of an understanding with Great Britain.' As usual, Philby's words contain an exaggeration; Ibn Saud was not a statesman seeking a friendship with another country – all he needed was money and support against his tribal enemies.

Still hopeful of reaching an agreement with Turkey to avoid war, the British maintained discreet contact with Ibn Saud while advancing him very small sums of money to keep him in reserve. By 1911 the prospect of war was real enough to increase that contact and the accompanying subsidies. Whether he was following his own instincts or obeying instructions is unknown, but Ibn Saud used much of this money to mould the Bedouin into a bloodthirsty monster, to expand and subsidize the loss-making colonies of soldier-saints of the Ikhwan, or 'brothers'. The latter were fanatics of the Wahhabi sect to which Ibn Saud belonged, who were to provide the backbone of his conquering forces and whose savagery wreaked havoc across Arabia. Traditionally committed to individual freedom and achievement, the rest of the Muslims found the idea of the colonies and the fanaticism they produced totally unacceptable. The extremism preached there contributed to that much-exaggerated and frowned-upon Muslim belief in going to heaven when dying fighting for the right cause.

The years 1911–14 reveal how the British supported Ibn Saud and his fanatics against Turkey and all other sheikhs and princes of eastern Arabia. His success against his enemies, particularly the defeat of the Ibn Rasheeds and the occupation of the Turkish-controlled eastern part of the Arabian Peninsula, was in reality a British success. 'With Ibn Saud in Hasa [the Gulf coast of Saudi Arabia], our position is strengthened,' wrote a British official in the Gulf. Later Sir Percy Cox, the British Resident in the Gulf, openly encouraged Ibn Saud to attack the Ibn Rasheeds' remaining territory to divert him from helping Turkey. Most of the other sheikhs, including the Ibn Rasheeds, had the misfortune of adhering to their treaty obligations with Turkey, the hated and crumbling outside power which, directly or through local chiefs, controlled most of Arabia at the turn of the century. Ibn Saud alone had the benefit of British financial aid, arms and advisers, initially Captain William Shakespeare and Sir Percy Cox and later none other than the famous distorter of truth Harry St John Philby, whose spy son Kim must have inherited similar unendearing characteristics.

Even the famous diarist and letter writer Gertrude Bell, a woman Orientalist-agent attached to British officialdom in the Middle East who figured more prominently in the history of modern Iraq, was occasionally with Ibn Saud to render advice and help. The nature of the Ibn Saud–British relationship which led to a friendship and cooperation treaty in 1915 can best be seen through her irreverent insistence on calling him by his first name, Abdel Aziz. The hastily prepared treaty may have elevated him to the role of a British-sponsored ruler of central and eastern Arabia but no self-reliant, self-respecting Arab sheikh or emir would have tolerated the use of his first name from any man, let alone a woman. Bell herself was much more circumspect when dealing with the Hashemites and others.

As luck would have it, soon after they helped him master eastern Arabia in 1917, the British found a similar use for Ibn

Saud. Having afforded him help to conquer his and their Turkish and pro-Turkish enemies, they were now embroiled in a dispute with their hitherto western Arabian protégés, the Hashemites. The background to the British–Hashemite dispute is simple. The Hashemites, with whom the legendary T. E. Lawrence had worked to provide Britain with much-needed anti-Turkish support, wanted Britain to live up to its First World War promises to grant them independence and a free hand in most of the Arab countries and they objected to British plans to provide the Jews with a national home in Palestine. It was not only that the British could not get the Hashemites to accept British policies on either point, but also that the Hashemites' independence of mind and plans to create a large, powerful Arab country under their leadership threatened Britain's growing interests in the Middle East. These interests included not only the entrenched wish to play colonizer but also the desire to control the Gulf to protect the oil of Iran and the routes to the Indian subcontinent.

In 1924 this British–Hashemite confrontation was exacerbated by the hasty declaration of an Islamic caliphate by King Hussein of the Hijaz, clearly an attempt to serve notice that, with or without British consent, his family's claim and the Arab march towards independence would continue under an Islamic flag. As expected, the ensuing negotiations in Kuwait to settle the problems between the Hashemites and Ibn Saud over territorial disputes came to naught and, unsurprisingly, Ibn Saud began his thrust into western Arabia. The British ostensibly cut off aid to both sides, but the Darea Treaty of 1915 guaranteed and protected Ibn Saud's domain, so that he was fighting a war he could not lose. Many historians claim that aid to Ibn Saud was never stopped and believe that the British continued to afford Ibn Saud and his merciless Ikhwan small but crucial amounts of money and arms while London was shamefully denying these to the Hashemites. Certainly, some of the military equipment he used in his attack was expensive and he would not have been able to afford or obtain it without outside help, or indeed to use it without instructors. In the background, some British officials were explicit enough about the reason for their support to prompt Sir Arthur Hirtzel of the British India Office to state: 'The feeling is growing that it would be good if Ibn Saud established himself in Mecca.'

So the British guaranteed the victory of Ibn Saud. In 1925 the Hijaz fell to his army and the more advanced settled part of Arabia was occupied by the Bedouin hordes. As had been feared,

Ibn Saud's Ikhwan followers killed hundreds of males, including children, ransacked an untold number of houses, murdered non-Wahhabi religious leaders who opposed their brutal ways and destroyed whole towns. (The words of one of their favourite war songs ran: 'The winds of paradise have blown, where are you dissenters?') It was as if the Moonies had turned violent and taken over the whole of America.

Western historians, notwithstanding the role played by the merciless sword, would have us believe that Ibn Saud was welcomed wherever he conquered. This calls for a reassessment of the later, commonly accepted reputation of Ibn Saud, the one he acquired as a result of his British-sponsored conquests: that of the unifier of the Arabs. The vital question is whether Ibn Saud had any interest whatsoever in unifying the Arabs. There is not a single reliable report to suggest that the idea of Arab unity ever interested the man and, according to many diarists of the time, including his one-time minister and ambassador to London, Hafez Wahbeh, he always waited for British sanction before he proceeded.

After Riyadh, Ibn Saud's first conquest was of Hassa, the eastern area where the oil was later discovered, but at that time its only importance was its strategic proximity to British interests and its people were Shias, the Wahhabis' dreaded enemies, who were hardly welcoming. His war with the Ibn Rasheeds was nothing more than a tribal blood feud, but they were allied to Turkey and thus the enemies of the British. His subsequent invasion of Hashemite territory was prompted by fear of their substantial claim to Arab leadership, something the British opposed to such an extent that Lord Crewe blatantly announced: 'What we want is not a united Arabia, but a disunited Arabia split into principalities under our suzerainty.' Indeed a truly independent, united Arabia under the rightful claimants to leadership would have relegated Ibn Saud to a secondary position. (The Hashemites in fact saw him as a minor player who should have recognized their supremacy.)

Unlike others who were truly interested in Arab unity, Ibn Saud knew very little about the Arabs in other countries and had no contact with them or appreciation of their political or social structures – even the moderately advanced ways of Hijaz did not sit right with him. His membership of a minority sect who believed that other Muslims, the great majority of the people of the Arabian Peninsula, were heretics who should be punished for their supposed apostasy stood in the way, as did his belief that Arabs beyond the Peninsula, the Iraqis, Syrians and the rest, were city people who were not to be trusted. A belief in big or small Arab unity would have been strange for members of a sect who, dangerously small and hence vulnerable where they were, would have been rendered much too weak to govern a greater entity. A belief in Arab unity would presuppose a belief in the idea of a nation-state and Ibn Saud never saw or governed his kingdom as anything except one big tribe. We must conclude that his conquests were no more than raids which, through British support, assumed a permanent nature.

There is the implicit suggestion by some Western historians that the other leaders of the time were not interested in Arab unity. This is patently untrue. The Hashemites never wavered from their wish to unify the Arabs in one big, strong country but, as already noted, it was this very wish which landed them in trouble with their erstwhile allies the British. As the true proponents of Arab unity, they responded to the challenge to the Arab position in Palestine and opposed it whereas Ibn Saud was totally unaffected by it. The latter's indifference offended the sensibilities of Arabs and Muslims who worried about the loss of Arab territory and Jerusalem, Islam's third holiest city, to the Jews. Indeed the Hashemite vision of Arab unity extended beyond Palestine to include Iraq, Syria and Jordan.

The real story of Ibn Saud's conquest of the country which he named after himself is much simpler. He represented a fanatical group of fighters and this minority, threatened by its lack of a broad popular base and committed to the idea of the *ghazzu*, joined outside powers to assume power in the land. (British and French colonial rules, in the Middle East and elsewhere, are full of examples of this extension of the divide-and-rule policy and they used the Alawites and Druze in Syria and continue to use the Kurds in Iraq in the same manner.) To repay the British for their assistance, Ibn Saud signed a lopsided friendship and cooperation treaty with them in 1927 which the Hashemites had turned down in a better version, and, among many others, the historian, and perhaps greatest authority on Arab unity this century, George Antonius, speaks of the Hashemite King Hussein thus: 'There is little doubt that if he had signed the treaty he would have retained his throne.' Ibn Saud signed it and it made him dependent on Britain. He ceded the external affairs of his country to Britain to oversee and Britain did not send him an ambassador for years, just a Resident, a title reserved for His Majesty's colonial officers.

The treaty also guaranteed that Ibn Saud's minority would never indulge in deviationist policies, like the ones which eventually wrecked the Hashemite–British alliance, to threaten their masters' interests. Overall, his aims remained a reflection of British strategy and David Howarth, author of the unusually balanced *The Desert King* and probably Ibn Saud's only critical British biographer, delivers the judgement: 'Not even Ibn Saud could say where he would have been without British help, protection and advice.'

The substantial record of British financial and military support for Ibn Saud is there for all to see. And in 1915, well before he assumed the titles King and Sultan, the British gave him the title Sir, which they bestowed on no other Arabian chief except Sheikh Mubarek of Kuwait, and again in 1935 he was awarded the Order of the Bath. (He looks utterly ridiculous wearing the sash and dangling over his Arab dress the jewelled star of a Knight Commander of the Indian Empire which goes with the title.) As for Britain's official claim that it was unable to restrain his attacks and conquest of the Hashemite part of Arabia, the Hijaz, among others the British press of that time complained bitterly about the British Government subsidizing the Arabs to fight each other. And, even when all claims that the British undermined the Hashemite war effort are dismissed, the British Government itself did a great deal to prove this claim false. Before and after his conquest of the Hijaz it prevented Ibn Saud, on occasion by using the RAF against him, from marching into Iraq and Jordan; to George Antonius, 'They had restrained Ibn Saud in the past.' But then it was more convenient for the British to stop him attaining total hegemony over all of the Arab countries, another indication that unifying the Arabs, even under a subservient ruler, was against their interests.

The false allegation that Ibn Saud was a great unifier suggests that the people in the areas he conquered supported such a union under him. Given the very simple fact that tolerance was against Wahhabi teachings and traditions and the Wahhabis' consequent behaviour against others, particularly the Shias, the historians who claimed and continue to claim that are indulging in a ridiculous day-dream. To subdue the population of Ibn Saud's conquered realm, the fanatical Wahhabi Ikhwan committed serious massacres in Taif, Bureida and Al Huda among other places, but, when their brutal ways remained unchecked, they went further and tried to destroy the tomb of the Prophet and remove the domes of major mosques because of their anti-Wahhabi ostentation. For the same reasons, they even desecrated the Mecca graveyards of the Sunni Muslims, to which religious persuasion the majority of the people of the country belonged. This is not to detail their genocide against the Shias of the eastern part of today's Saudi Arabia; to the Wahhabis the Shias were especially unacceptable and had to be eliminated.

The religious problem aside, Ibn Saud's supposedly excellent relations with the Bedouin tribes were hardly that and there is little to praise on that score. Between 1916 and 1928 there were no fewer than 26 anti-House of Saud rebellions by the Bedouins and each of them ended with the Ikhwan-led forces of Ibn Saud indulging in mass killings of mostly innocent victims, including women and children. (Ibn Saud's cousin Abdallah bin Mussalem bin Jalawi beheaded 250 members of the Mutair tribe and he himself set an example for his followers by personally beheading 18 rebels in the public square of the town of Artawaya.) The tribes of Ajman and Najran show the after-effects of these massacres to this day, for there is a gap of a whole generation. The Shammar tribe suffered 410 deaths, the bani Khalid 640 and the Najran a staggering 7000. And the cities were not far behind. Muhammad Tawil and Muhammad Sabhan organized two city-based conspiracies to rid their people of the scourge of the Arabs, and the cities of the Hijaz suffered the consequences. It was an atmosphere where the sword of the executioner had a recognizable name, the *rakban*, or 'necker', and it was as well known and feared as the guillotine during the French Revolution. It is used to this day and apologists for the House of Saud still report this fact with the minimum of comment.

To General Sir John Baggot Glubb, Ibn Saud 'used the massacre to subdue his enemies'. But 'Glubb Pasha' stops short of citing the recorded statistics and events produced by the Saudi campaign to subdue the Arabian Peninsula. No fewer than 400,000 people were killed and wounded, for the Ikhwan did not take prisoners, but mostly killed the vanquished. Well over a million inhabitants of the territories conquered by Ibn Saud fled to other countries: Iraq, Syria, Egypt, Jordan and Kuwait. The political parties of the Hijaz disappeared never to resurface, the more advanced people of the Hijaz were denied the right to hold public office, the huge Shammar tribe was driven to Iraq, and the educated were deemed dangerous and the target of harassment. Even the animal life of the country suffered when Ibn Saud, disregarding the traditional Bedouin respect for game and its preservation, proceeded to take his cronies on hunting trips on which they sat in the back of cars using relays of rifles to kill hundreds of animals at a time. Hence the disappearance from the region of the ostrich and oryx and several rare birds.

As if these divisive and brutal moves within the territory under his domain were not enough, the picture is completed by Ibn Saud's relations with the rest of the Arabs and Muslims. As already mentioned, he tried to invade Jordan and Iraq; he conducted a quarrel with Kuwait over their common frontier; he broke off diplomatic relations with Egypt over a simple incident concerning the colourful way the Egyptians sent their annual delegation to the Muslim Hajj; and he waged a war on the Yemen in an attempt to annex some of its land and stop it claiming Aden from Britain. In the larger Muslim world, his dispute with the Muslims of India and others over doctrine culminated in his ordering one of their visiting delegations to leave his country, an undiplomatic move which flew in the face of traditional Arab hospitality and was a clear denial of the right of every Muslim to be near his or her holy places. In fact an Islamic conference objected to Ibn Saud's assumption of the un-Islamic title of King (liberal Islam maintains that there is no Majesty but Allah's). Unsurprisingly, the only Muslim support he ever got was from some British colonies, and even that was lukewarm.

Ibn Saud's internal, Arab and Muslim policies were total failures, hardly the stuff to create unity. In short, the only thing he had going for him was his relationship with Britain. The latter played along to serve its own interests, including not wanting Islam's holiest shrines to fall to an unfriendly ruler. Thus, rather than acting as unifier of the Arabs, Ibn Saud afforded an outside power, Britain, the comfort of keeping the Arabs and Muslims divided and protected its commercial and political interests, which opposed the presence of a unifier at the Arab helm.

Ibn Saud grew up in a tent. Instead of adapting to his new status as a peer of the British Empire, the Sultan of Nejed and King of the Hijaz (the name Saudi Arabia was coined later, in 1932), he took the tent with him. The tent and, in this case, the mentality it represented – a total lack of organization and appreciation of what a country is, desert picnics, the harem, hunting and spending time gabbing with his cronies, telling them the same tales of his exploits in different versions because the original stories were fundamentally untrue – took precedence over all semblances of modernity and sensible governance.

In 1925 the guards at the gates of the fort-like structure that was Ibn Saud's palace belonged to the fanatical Wahhabi Ikhwan, a fearsome-looking band armed with swords or daggers, bandoliers and old muskets. There was nothing decorative or friendly about them; they were dusty warriors and they looked as if they were guarding someone who was out of place and perhaps afraid for his life. Inside, in the diwan or stateroom, Ibn Saud ruled supreme. He always began his day in that room with the reading of the Wird, the Muslim rosary. This was meant to imbue the atmosphere with the right Muslim spirit. A huge beige and gold room, the diwan was lined on three sides by ordinary wicker chairs divided by cushions of heavy brocade, while the floor was covered with mats and Persian carpets. Ibn Saud reclined on a bench on his elbow in front of a bay window, something no sensible Arab ruler in the twentieth century would have done, and took time to make himself comfortable.

He would begin the court proceedings with a saying, most of the time a statement aimed at explaining what he and the place he inhabited were all about, an attempt at self-justification which smacked of protesting too much:

'The Arab understands two things only: the Word of Allah and the sword. Compared with His word the accepted Arab notions of loyalty, brotherhood, hospitality, honour and beauty amount to very little. And the imported ideas of freedom, equality and representative government do even less. The word of the Koran is supreme; all is derived from it and everything is subordinated to it. The sword is how the Word is carried out.'

Whether these exact words, which pervert the tenets of Islam and its commitment to justice and individual rights, were used on more than one occasion or how Ibn Saud varied them was immaterial; the message was always the same. His daily justification of his rule was tantamount to the constitution of the land, and given the fact that until he conquered it in 1925 the Hijaz had had an elaborate constitution which incorporated Islamic teachings in a sensible manner, the enormity of Ibn Saud's regressive homilies becomes clear. It was the application of the sword or its equivalent which held sway and which was new.

Ibn Saud had no organized army to underpin his supremacy, but he depended on the Ikhwan and his family and felt safe. His huge country, the size of the United States east of the Mississippi, had been divided into districts or emirates under the control of his relatives and in-laws. Their parochial supremacy was an extension of his and in addition they used local Bedouins to enforce their ways. And to remould the relatively advanced cities of the Hijaz Ibn Saud created the Ikhwan-run Committee for the Advancement of Virtue and Elimination of Sin (CAVES).

Typical of the areas placed under the governance of Ibn Saud's relatives was the mostly Shia eastern province of Hasa, which fell under Abdallah bin Mussalem bin Jalawi, a cousin and comrade-in-arms who figured brutally in the occupation of the city of Riyadh and the killing of all members of the defending garrison who surrendered. Most of the people in the province belonged to anti-Saudi tribes and the majority were Shia Muslims. Philby wrote of the effects of the rule of bin Jalawi, in his uncritical book *Arabian Jubilee*: 'the province never again troubled the central government.' But as usual, the chief creator of the legend of Ibn Saud said nothing as to why. In reality bin Jalawi executed thousands of people, amputated the arms of the poor for stealing bread and mercilessly settled old scores, the chiefs of the anti-Saud tribe of Hazzami disappeared, and he violated the most fundamental Arab code of honour and executed someone who came to see him to negotiate a settlement.

Other provinces were run by Al Shaikhs and Al Thunyans, also cousins and fellow Wahhabis, the Sudeiris, Ibn Saud's favourite in-laws, and Ibn Saud's own sons. Not a single outsider attained the position of province governor, nor was there a single educated governor among those appointed by Ibn Saud, not even in accordance with Islamic ways. In fact the province governors were selected for their loyalty and ability to suppress dissent and proceeded to institute a reign of terror and add to the heavy toll of Ibn Saud's seemingly endless wars. By the time they had subdued the country, they had carried out 40,000 public executions and 350,000 amputations, respectively 1 and 7 per cent of the estimated population of four million.

In the cities, CAVES ran riot. Equipped with sticks to administer on-the-spot justice, its puritan Ikhwan members flogged its victims at random. People were punished for wearing Western clothes, gold, perfume or silk, for smoking and the men for not wearing a moustache or a beard. Singing was completely forbidden, the work of the chief devil, flowerpots were too decorative and were destroyed, and the Ikhwan occasionally tapped their sticks on people's windows to remind them of the time for prayer. A man's home, sacred according to Muslim tradition, provided no protection, and the Saudi writer Nasser Al Said remembers how CAVES zealots broke into his grandmother's house and flogged him in her presence when he was a boy of eight. Naturally nobody dared turn down a proposal of marriage by a CAVES member, and as a result people took to keeping their women indoors.

To establish Ibn Saud's idea of justice it is enough to cite four unrelated examples of how he himself administered it. He continued to dabble in the smallest things to prove that his justice was uniform and that the province governors and CAVES were not acting on their own. Sometime during the early 1930s, Ibn Saud's 24 drivers went on strike for higher pay. While their salaries and what they demanded are not known, it is safe to assume theirs must have been a desperate situation to drive them to this dangerous action. Ibn Saud reacted by firing every one of them, revoking their driving licences for life and deporting those among them who were not Saudis. On another occasion the palace electricians organized a work stoppage because they had not been paid for three months, and they too were fired. And on a third occasion Ibn Saud responded to a case of alleged buggery by ordering a summary execution of the three accused without a thorough investigation. (Islamic sharia, or religious, laws are so profound and exact that they have been adopted by many legal systems in the world and they require four eye-witnesses for conviction.) In the fourth incident, which Philby, Wahbeh and others would have us accept as a sign of benevolence and justice, he had a thief imprisoned instead of having his arm amputated. According to them, Ibn Saud ordered the family of the thief, who stole because of poverty, to provide the man with food while he was in prison.

Despite the existence of Islamic law courts to deal with minor crimes between insignificant people, there was clearly no law in Saudi Arabia under Ibn Saud. He and his Wahhabi followers applied their harsh justice with little respect for the religious and other ways of most of the people. The highly developed legal system which had existed in the Hijaz was destroyed; the civil courts, which were modelled on the eighth-century ones of the Abbasid caliphate, were disbanded and replaced by Wahhabi-administered religious ones; and the tribal law which prevailed in other parts of the country was replaced by the much stricter tenets of the Wahhabi sect. The source of justice in the country worked in accordance with a simple progression: Ibn Saud, his family and the Wahhabi sect, the latter a collection of fanatics who decreed that the only reading matter permissible was the Koran and religious scripts. The Arabs of the desert, perhaps the greatest exponents of lyric poetry in history, had to do without such writings.

But the backward way in which Sharia law was interpreted and justice was administered, essentially licence for the few and repression of the many, was not an isolated reflection of the overall step backwards that the rule of Ibn Saud represented. The ways he dealt with the rest of the affairs of state from his Diwan were equally telling.

The head of the treasury, now referred to by most writers as the Minister of Finance, was one Abdallah Al Suleiman. A strange little man who had been an accountant with a small trading firm in India, Al Suleiman had two qualities which endeared him to Ibn Saud. The first was his lack of threatening tribal connections – he was a nobody – and the second was his unwholesome ability to play court jester and overlook his master's cruelty. Physically unimposing and effete in manner, he was on the receiving end of Ibn Saud's crude jokes about sexual prowess. Ibn Saud never missed a chance to allude to his Minister of Finance's lack of sexual vigour and the latter took the barbs meekly, with a benign smile, and continued to provide his employer with his services even after the latter killed his brother with his stick in a characteristic fit of anger.

But more important than who Al Suleiman was and how he was abused was his deliberate or unintentional willingness to initiate the tradition that reduced the treasury to nothing more than the guardian of a huge, disorganized, highly questionable family business. He dealt with the debts of members of the family, often squeezing and threatening the creditors until they wrote them off. He also prevailed upon many wealthy merchants to advance money to His Majesty in return for commercial concessions and favours, even when there were none to be offered. As we will see later, even after oil wealth changed the financial character of the country, Al Suleiman still continued to place the insatiable needs of Ibn Saud and his family above the needs of the country. In 1950 the funds for important projects, including the building of bridges, were held up so that the family could afford a lavish simultaneous wedding for six of Ibn Saud's sons. This is why Al Suleiman was jokingly referred to as the 'Minister of Everything', including procurement.

Indeed there was nothing resembling a ministry of anything beyond finance, though this concerned Ibn Saud very little and he accepted it because he enjoyed tormenting Al Suleiman. Not even foreign affairs or defence merited organized ministries, and, as we have seen, the interior, justice and Islamic affairs were administered in Ibn Saud's inimitably reprehensible Wahhabi fashion. Again it is important to remember that the Government of the Hijaz had had a senate whose members indulged in open, healthy debate, and indeed a cabinet. Indeed the last cabinet to exist before the Saudi conquest had as members people who belonged to thriving political parties who advocated specific policies aimed at improving the lot of their people.

Under Ibn Saud what appears to have mattered more than a senate or a cabinet and the implied responsibility to the people which goes with these was the new invention of an ad hoc council of advisers. Philby was a member of this inner circle, as were Abdel Rahman Al Damulgi, Hafez Wahbeh, Rashad Pharoan, Yusuf Yassin and Fuad Hamza – an obvious Englishman, an Iraqi, an Egyptian, two Syrians and one Lebanese. The council had not a single Saudi member and the attributes of its alien members were highly questionable, to say the least. Beyond the dubious contributions of Philby, Yusuf Yassin appears to have specialized in the procurement of young blondes from his native Syria.

In all this there is something strange which recalls the ways of Hitler. The Führer depended on a group of butchers to enforce his policies and his inner circle was made up of outsiders, mostly territorial Germans, who were isolated from the mainstream of his country and had no connection with the traditional sources of power and guidance, Germany's General Staff or the Church. Likewise, Ibn Saud's advisory group were hardly tribal and spoke with accents the Saudis did not understand.

And as with Hitler and other dictators, Ibn Saud dealt with his inner circle on a one-to-one basis, and its members were never organized and did not constitute a body which could be held responsible for its actions. Ibn Saud was in the habit of seating whoever had something to discuss with him next to him and the affairs of state were conducted in whispers and reflected the opinions of outsiders whose main concern was the maintenance of their position. Interestingly, two of the advisers, Damulgi and Rashad Pharoan, were doctors of medicine like Hitler's Dr Morell, people who had greater access to Ibn Saud than most, and they and the many medical men who followed them as advisers administered virility potions, particularly the aphrodisiac Orston, to enhance his legendary sexual appetite. (The father of arms dealer Adnan Khashoggi was among Ibn Saud's personal doctors and Ghaith Pharoan, the son of Dr Rashad Pharoan, became a billionaire and is presently wanted for questioning in connection with the

BCCI scandal and the family of Dr Midhat Sheikh Al Ard are still connected with the House of Saud.)

If Ibn Saud's court and the way he conducted himself in it seem strange, isolated and unresponsive, then the way he managed his own family is even more bizarre. There were too many children for him to afford them the love or fatherly care for which the Arabs are known and he took no steps to educate them. Even if we play his game and ignore female members of his brood, there is no record that any of his sons went to college either; certainly none of the four sons who succeeded him on the throne had ever attended a university, their schooling having come to an end during their early teens. The 42 sons and unknown number of daughters (some estimates place their number at over 125) were left to their mothers to rear and their status was often a reflection of their mothers' positions and they were called after them. Prince Tallal was the son of an Armenian, Fahd was important because his mother was a tribal Sudeiri and ones whose mothers were slaves did not matter at all.

'I've never had a meal with a woman.' 'Learning does not become women.' These two statements indicate the attitude of Ibn Saud to women. To him a woman was no more than a combination of a source of pleasure and a breeding machine, an exchangeable commodity, and his response to a complaint about keeping his harem in a windowless basement was to state that 'windows let lovers in'. A good example of this attitude is the history of his marriages to Hassa Al Sudeiri. Ibn Saud married her then divorced her and she married his brother. He later wanted her back, prevailed on his brother to divorce her, and remarried her. She produced seven sons, including the present King Fahd. Later Ibn Saud married a number of her cousins and relatives.

As a matter of fact Ibn Saud turned sex into an instrument of policy, and perhaps the only way he tried to unify Arabia was in bed. At any one point he had four wives, four concubines and four slaves to satisfy his desire, but he replaced the groups of four regularly, and importantly he married into over 30 tribes and used these links to get closer to them and gain their support. Even when they were inclined to refuse him, the tribes were too afraid to do so and the present Crown Prince Abdallah's mother belonged to the Shammar, Ibn Saud's old tribal enemies. One could say with truth that most of Saudi Arabia is related to the House of Saud by marriage. Ibn Saud was not only a lecher, but a show-off too, and when a tribe spread rumours that he was losing his virility he paid them a surprise visit and 'shamed' them by deflowering one of their girls.

But it was pure, non-political sex that was uppermost in Ibn Saud's mind. He confided to Philby and others that he had had several hundred virgins and he was in the habit of deflowering young girls then giving them away as presents. Philby was on the receiving end of this largesse; nor did his Westminster and Oxford education stand in the way. (I myself saw one such 'present' looking completely lost, waiting for Philby in the lobby of the St George Hotel in Beirut while he sat in the bar drinking with the *Sunday Times* correspondent John Slade-Baker.) Indeed, beyond not recognizing his national anthem and not knowing what to do when told what it was, the only memorable comment attributed to Ibn Saud during his one visit to Egypt, except for his exile in Kuwait the only time he journeyed outside Arabia, amounted to an expression of his preoccupation with sex: 'This country is full of pretty women and I would like to buy some of them and take them back home. How about £100,000 worth of them?'

Other results of Ibn Saud's personal backwardness and inadequacy add to this picture of a careless parent and a lecher. During his lifetime his sons took to emulating him and marrying dozens of women each and Philby referred to 'the youngsters going wild every time they went away'. Not only did they abuse people openly, but the use of the stick became a family tradition, and one of them, Prince Mishari, went as far as assassinating the British Vice-Consul in Jeddah for not giving him more whisky. Prince Nasir distilled some poisonous stuff at home and killed four of his guests, while another son thought all European girls clad in bikinis were for sale, just like meat in a butcher's shop, and a third returned home from a foreign trip to tell his father of the most amazing thing in the world: a restaurant where he could watch girls swim under water.

Ibn Saud confirmed that all Western women were for sale, wanted to know more about the dazzling underwater restaurant and forgave Nasir. In response to the murder of the Vice-Consul, he paid the widow £70,000 and released the family drunk after a prison term of a few months – in all likelihood the same month saw the execution, imprisonment and flogging of dozens of people for the mere possession of alcohol – and both the release of the Prince and the execution of others did not get the attention they merited from the Western press and governments. Indeed Britain forgave the Prince and frowned on journalists who attempted to investigate the murder.

Towards the end of his life, his doctors' potions made Ibn Saud absent-minded and repetitive. Talk about sex seemed to take an even greater amount of his time and he regretted his inability to produce more children even when many of his sons were roaming the globe in the company of prostitutes, leaving behind stacks of unpaid bills and distributing like calling cards gold watches with the picture of their father on the dial. The institutionalization of lechery and ignorance was well on its way.

The tide of corruption that flowed all around Ibn Saud felt suffocatingly pervasive. As a result, the role of the Ikhwan came to an end in 1929. Like all groups which act as a dictator's instrument of suppression during his rise to power, they fell victim to Ibn Saud's quest for respectability. The Ikhwan had become dizzy with power and success. Not only did they behave like a state within a state and ignore the central government, but they had their military colonies and their own code of honour. With Saudi Arabia subdued, Ibn Saud no longer needed them and they became an embarrassment.

The seemingly inevitable confrontation between Ibn Saud and the Ikhwan reached a climax not over their brutal and stupid internal policies, arbitrary executions, murder, amputations and the fact that they regularly cut telephone lines because the telephone was an instrument of the devil, but because they accused him of subservience to the British and their ways and demanded an end to his pro-British policies. Indeed there were many signs of this subservience: Britain continued to provide him with a subsidy of £60,000 a year, the equivalent of two thirds of the country's annual income, and the important business of settling the new kingdom's boundaries was exclusively in British hands. Above all, Philby, who had undergone a suspect conversion to Islam and donned the clothes of the Arab of the desert, was always at Ibn Saud's side, and when not there he was in London to consult with the Foreign Office over ways to consolidate the rule and extend the influence of its friend. In fact, Philby and to a lesser degree Churchill, wanted to make Ibn Saud King of the Arabs in return for furthering British policies which included acceptance of a Jewish state in Palestine. When the suggestion was made to President Roosevelt, he turned it down because America was uncomfortable with the role of king-maker.

Ibn Saud set his relationship with his sponsors above his connection with religious zealots for whom he no longer had any use. As usual in these situations and as with Ernst Röhm and the SA in the Night of the Long Knives what triggered the bloodbath is not very clear, but, with Philby there to advise Ibn Saud, a vicious battle between the Ikhwan and the loyalists took place at the village of Sabila and was followed by others. Ibn Saud had the benefit of British-supplied equipment, including armoured personnel carriers, and this proved too much for the Ikhwan leader, Faisal Duwish, and his followers. Five thousand Ikhwan were killed, and the rest, including Duwish, fled to Kuwait and then Iraq. They were pushed out of Iraq and the RAF bombed them, forcing Duwish and a few hundred survivors to surrender. Duwish, according to H. R. P. Dickson in *The Arab of the Desert* 'the man who did more than anyone to put Ibn Saud in power', died in prison a year and a half later, in mysterious circumstances.

In the period which followed there was little need for the type of mass killings that had been practised by the Ikhwan, but the House of Saud still found it convenient to follow a policy of selective suppression and elimination. In the religious domain, the Shias had to pay a special tax because they were heretics. Among their personal targets were some of their old enemies, such as the Ibn Rasheeds, and the methods they used were despicably un-Arab. In 1946 Abdallah bin Mutaib bin Rasheed was invited to dinner in the palace of Ibn Saud's son Nasir (who later poisoned his guests with bad booze) and killed there. And very early in 1953 Muhammad bin Tallal bin Rasheed was killed in his home. In both cases the victims were unarmed and rather helpless and there was no investigation of either murder. The Idrissis of Assir disappeared altogether, after Saudi pressure drove them from the Yemen, and members of Duwish's tribe of Mutair were killed in groups of twos and threes. The Hashemites had escaped the country, but some of their old loyalists met sudden unexplained accidents or were imprisoned for life, and death by poisoning in a crude, painful way became a common occurrence. So much for the Arab tradition of protecting those living under your roof.

The Saudi attempt to neutralize all potential sources of political opposition had another, indirect aspect to it. So long as they did not threaten him, Ibn Saud abetted all disputes between the tribes and allowed them to turn into blood feuds while he sat on the sidelines until it became convenient for him to intervene and make both sides beholden to him. The very important anti-Ibn Saud merchant class in the relatively developed Hijaz was undermined, and favours went to foreigners who were politically unconcerned and reliable. The Ali Rezas, Iranians; Sharabatlis, Egyptians; Salha, Lebanese; bin Mahfouz, Yemenis; Philby (who became the agent for Ford), British; and Turkuman and other traders became wealthy and rose to prominence in a way which recalls the composition of Ibn Saud's circle of advisers.

But these internal acts of a Bedouin police state aside, from the time he completed his conquest of Arabia until the discovery of oil in commercial quantities in the late 1930s, Ibn Saud relied on the British subsidy and revenues from the Muslim Hajj to support himself (nothing was done for the country). Then suddenly there was oil.

The first oil concession was granted to Britain's Eastern General Syndicate in 1923. The company paid Ibn Saud a few thousand pounds, spent two years prospecting, confirmed the existence of 'some' oil and then did nothing. From the late 1920s until 1933 Philby unsuccessfully tried to interest others in taking over the concession. When the depression affected the number of Muslims making the Hajj, reduced Ibn Saud's income and drove him deeper into debt, the concession was auctioned and, despite last-minute attempts by Ibn Saud to get a British company to make a sensible offer, Standard Oil of California won it for $250,000.

On signing one of the many interim agreements which led to the ratification of the final concession, the original American representative, one Charles Crane of the bathroom fixtures family, presented Ibn Saud with a present. The box of Californian dates which Crane gave Ibn Saud was a measure of how the world viewed the man. It was not simply carrying coals to Newcastle, but represented a stunning statement about the limited horizons of the recipient, the same man who years later fell asleep while signing the final concession agreement with Lloyd Hamilton of Standard Oil of California.

It took time to produce oil in commercial quantities, and in 1935 Dhahran, the base for the American prospecting operations, had one car. Even in 1939, ARAMCO (the Arabian–American Oil Company, a consortium of Standard Oil of California and three other companies) still used 700 camels to do much of its work. But by then, the company was beginning to realize the colossal potential of its concession. The oil of eastern Saudi Arabia was (and is) present in huge quantities and located at shallow depths in flat lands with no vegetation in them and very near the water for transportation. It was and remains the cheapest place to produce oil in the whole world.

The value and importance of Saudi oil assumed greater significance during the Second World War. The USA's Secretary of the Interior, Harold Ickes, saw Saudi oil as the solution to the coming dependence of America on foreign sources. For strategic reasons which included difficulty of transporting it, a production ceiling was placed on Saudi oil for most of the war, but the US Government, worried that poverty might endanger the stability of a country which held an important key to its future, saw fit to make substantial direct and British-managed contributions and grants to Ibn Saud. All the money went into his pocket, but if the 1933 oil agreement was the beginning of America's invasion of the country, then the payments made by its Government represented the transfer of Saudi Arabia from the British to the American sphere of influence. To realize the full significance of this move, one has to remember that America withheld its recognition of Saudi Arabia until 1934; it took place shortly after Crane's famous gift was made.

At the end of the war Saudi Arabia was producing 300,000 barrels of oil a day and America's direct financial assistance was no longer needed. Ibn Saud had been helped through a difficult time and the Americans' commitment to support him was sealed when he met President Roosevelt in February 1945 in Egypt, the only Arab leader to be so honoured. (For the trip he took 200 live sheep with him and one of the ship's officers discovered a sackful of aphrodisiacs in his room.) All his obvious shortcomings were dismissed, and Roosevelt made it clear that the USA was committed to Ibn Saud as the primary Arab leader and made statements about safeguarding the territorial integrity of Saudi Arabia, something which was confirmed and elaborated by President Truman. Interestingly, Roosevelt, a chain-smoker, refrained from indulging in the habit in the presence of Ibn Saud, whereas a few days later Churchill refused to abstain. This simple act of accommodation and respect has determined the behaviour of American presidents in the presence of Saudi monarchs ever since: they always treat them with considerable, if almost naive, deference.

In terms of world affairs, the Saudi Arabia which emerged from the Second World War was a radically changed place. Financially self-sufficient for the first time since its creation, it was given by the Cold War and the emerging Arab–Israeli problem a strategic and political importance it had never had and, in particular, Soviet moves to befriend the Muslims enhanced the value of the country's holy places.

Two questions need to be answered at this point: why the Americans managed to snatch the oil concession from British hands and place the country under American hegemony, and whether this development made any difference to the direction Ibn Saud took in running the country. Amazingly, the question regarding the oil concession is shrouded in some mystery. British lethargy was undoubtedly part of the reason the Americans managed to get it, but it is hardly the whole reason. Some argue that the British had enough oil in neighbouring Iran, Iraq and Bahrain (Kuwait followed later), but, though true, this cannot be the whole reason either. In all likelihood, a third factor was the more aggressive approach by the American oil companies, who foresaw their country's need of foreign oil, were willing to pay for it and convinced their government of the importance of Saudi Arabia's reserves. So, as in many other instances, the American companies went in first and were followed by their government. But neither of them, nor the slow-acting British, realized the vastness of the Saudi oil reserves or their eventual importance.

There was nothing new in the reasons for America's adoption of Saudi Arabia, oil, strategic and Arab positions and the Muslim holy places, but America's emergence as a replacement for Britain was part of a larger global realignment. Britain came out of the Second World War tired and weakened and faced a considerable number of colonial problems. As with many other countries which were too important to 'release', the USA moved in to fill the vacuum.

While one can only theorize about what might have happened had Saudi Arabia remained under Britain's umbrella, there is a traceable major way in which America's involvement made a difference. For the most part, Britain had no reason for direct involvement in Saudi Arabia's internal affairs except when they affected its interests, and limited itself to influencing the country's direction in accordance with a policy aimed at protecting Britain's position in the Gulf and keeping a single Arab country from becoming powerful enough to threaten this regional stance. There was nothing beyond the presence of Philby-type advisers to warrant dictating special internal policies as long as they contributed to the elements already mentioned and as long as the consolidation of Ibn Saud's brutal rule went ahead unthreatened and unimpeded. (See The Trivialization of Everything.)

But in countries where the British ran the oil industries the picture was different: Britain's policy was an extension of its paternalistic colonial outlook. In Iran, Iraq and the rest the British prevailed upon the local governments to use some of their oil income for education and development projects, mostly to avoid future trouble. This is where America's attitude differed dramatically, for its traditional anti-colonial policy stood between it and telling Ibn Saud what to do with the oil income. As a result, serious British diplomatic attempts to steer Saudi Arabia towards using some of the oil money wisely were hotly and successfully resisted by the Americans. It was not the first time American oil companies had dictated their country's foreign policy and exploited countries with little regard for the welfare of their people; they had had a long history of supporting South American dictators. The Americans played right into Ibn Saud's hands by allowing him to see the oil revenue as his own private income.

The difference between the policies of Britain and the USA showed in many ways, even in the field of education. For example, the British saw to it that Iraq sent students to be educated overseas and most were selected on merit and placed under an obligation to perform well and repay the money spent to educate them. Ibn Saud sent fewer students to be educated overseas and they tended to be his relations and sons of tribal chiefs, and there was no requirement for them to do well or repay the costs of their education. Not only did the Iraqis achieve much better results from their overseas student missions, but in 1936 in their country they had 50,000 students to Ibn Saud's 700.

The overall results of America's hands-off policy were disastrous. There was not a single American hint as to how the huge oil revenues should be spent and not a penny of the $400 million paid to Ibn Saud between 1946 and 1953 was used for development. In 1946 the country's record of expenditure showed a mere $150,000 for building schools and $2 million for the royal garage. And Ibn Saud's sons followed his ways. The Crown Prince built a palace for $10 million then razed it when he disliked the way it looked and built one for $30 million. Another prince drove a Cadillac until the petrol ran out then gave it away and bought another with a full tank. In terms of the way he ran the country, Ibn Saud himself appeared to be as oblivious to what could be done with this sudden wealth as the rest of his family and he ordered ARAMCO, even then the country's largest employer, to double the salaries of all its employees, an act which led to an inflationary spiral. In one year alone he gave away 35,000 gold watches which carried his likeness on their dials and, against the advice of all around him, ordered the building of a railway because he liked the idea. Even the aeroplane, that expression of modernity which finally penetrated his kingdom, was subject to his archaic whims and all aircraft required his permission to land and take off, while those travelling from Jeddah in the west to Dhahran in the east had to make a stop in Riyadh, just in case His Majesty or members of his family needed them.

By 1950, Dhahran, the Saudi oil centre, was the biggest American city between Paris and Manila. Two aeroplanes, crudely called *Camel* and *Gazelle*, shuttled oil workers and executives in and out of Saudi Arabia. America's Strategic Air Command had built a huge airbase to protect the oilfields, chewing gum and wearing jeans had become fashionable and American steaks and potato chips had invaded the country. Meanwhile, Ibn Saud, a firm believer in djinn and *afreet* (spirits), was receiving a huge income which allowed him to indulge his ignorance, lack of understanding and vulgarity.

The number of Ibn Saud's advisers increased, but still there was not a single Saudi among them and none of them had an interest in anything beyond his pocket. (He never had an official American adviser, though Colonel William Eddy, a close friend of Roosevelt's and the USA's first Minister to Saudi Arabia, knew him well enough to proffer advice.) Ibn Saud's talk about sex became exceptionally base and he bragged about never seeing the face of a woman whom he bedded. The number of doctors whose job it was to keep him virile had now increased to about 10 per cent of all the doctors in the country. His profligate ways continued: he bought 40 Packards (the most vulgar car of the 1940s) at a time, built palaces, including one with the biggest air-conditioning system in the world, and gold fittings and fixtures and Paris perfumes began to appear in his bathrooms. And, as with the sons of South American dictators, ARAMCO hedged its bets by taking Ibn Saud's sons on foreign trips and introducing them to wine, women and song. Outside of his immediate entourage the country remained poor and there was at least one incident when beggars who tried to accost his motorcade to ask for money were beaten to death.

Ibn Saud's family and relatives continued to run the country in his name. Their salaries depended on how much there was in the treasury. The tribal chiefs were bribed into allegiance, and Ibn Saud persisted in abusing the Shias, favouring outsiders and frowning on girls' education. As with Hitler and the SA, he felt secure enough to reintegrate the Ikhwan by creating the White Guard (later the National Guard), an all-Bedouin and Wahhabi force to protect himself and his family. In the background cholera, blindness and syphilis were rampant and strikes were outlawed (funnily, he heard about this activity at second hand and banned them, not because there was a threat, but because he disliked the idea).

Within the Arab world, with the exception of Farouk, Ibn Saud still got along with no one. He joined the Arab League but refused to participate in any moves towards closer Arab cooperation while loudly stating that the only real unity among a people is brought about by the sword. Indeed his only forays into the field of inter-Arab politics were divisive. To weaken his neighbours and maintain his position, he paid Syria to quarrel with Iraq, and Egypt to feud with Syria, and claimed for himself some oil-rich areas which belonged to the United Arab Emirates and Oman (the Bureimi oasis). Saudi Arabia was the only Arab country which did not send army units to fight in Palestine – whether rightly or wrongly to the outside world is immaterial – a definitely un-Arab stance.

When Ibn Saud died in 1953, and despite the oil income and the huge monetary advances (to keep him in debt) made by the oil companies, his country was in a state of financial and administrative chaos for which he and Abdallah Al Suleiman, his 'Minister of Everything', bore responsibility. The total number of Government employees was around 5000, no infrastructure to cope with the country's new status existed and his eldest son and heir was a simpleton – at 52 he had married 100 times. Nor was there a Saudi cabinet during his lifetime; the first one was created a few months after he died.

Ibn Saud was not the greatest Arab since the Prophet Muhammad, the greatest Arab of his age, or even a good Arab. His personal and political qualities placed him well behind the Arabs of his time and many of his actions resembled those of Hitler. His connivance with Britain and allowing America to exploit his oil may have endeared him to them and the rest of the West, but he stood against Arab culture and traditions and any acceptable judgement of the man inevitably touches on his Arabness and his relationship to his people. His un-Arab behaviour included cruelty to the vanquished, the defenceless and the poor, lack of respect for the religion of others, abuse of women, vulgarity, celebration of ignorance, and the unsatisfactory way he brought up his children. The one word which clings to all his unwholesome acts is 'corruption'; in terms of its scale and its dependence upon outside powers to protect its source, it was an original corruption the like of which the world had never seen. In short, Ibn Saud was one of the most corrupt people of all time and his legacy consists of the immorality of his family and the sanctioning of official theft.

3

The Trivialization of Everything

With the death of Ibn Saud, even the unrepentant Philby, who spoke of 'the passing of a brilliant chapter in the history of the Arabs', had doubts about the future. His fears were aroused because of the rapid changes in the internal development of the country and its growing importance as a regional and world power which were brought about by oil money. By 1955 Saudi Arabia's income had reached $2 million a day, compared with $500,000 a year in 1935, an increase of 140,000 per cent. There was enough money for some of it to filter through to the people and improve their education and start a construction boom. Equally importantly, the predictions of Roosevelt's Secretary of the Interior Harold Ickes and many American oilmen were coming true: the dependence of America and the West as a whole on Saudi Arabia as the world's leading oil reservoir was becoming a palpable reality.

But, although its income exceeded the needs of the royal family, and money was finding its way into development projects and a consumer economy was emerging, Saudi Arabia had not really become a country. Ibn Saud's ways and his highly personal rule had eliminated the potential for social development and the evolution of a sensible system of government. In the 1950s the immense oil surplus became the motor behind the changes in the lifestyle of the people and the physical appearance of the country, which was beginning to resemble a vast construction site. But the House of Saud, though prepared to allow people to eat better, was unwilling to permit them to think better, and there were no parallel moves towards greater social cohesion and a working governmental system.

Most writers who have chronicled the effects of the oil wealth and have suggested that there was a government which merited analysis are guilty of serious exaggeration. Though superficially different from the days of Ibn Saud and considerably wealthier, Saudi Arabia remains substantially the same to this day. It is still the world's leading expression of feudal absolutism.

It is easy to trace the way this feudal system has worked so far through the various kings who followed Ibn Saud. He was succeeded by his eldest living son, Saud, who was pronounced king by an ad hoc family council (whoever felt strongly enough about the problem of succession joined the committee). To give this unorganized family affair the semblance of legitimacy, the perfunctory support of the religious leaders (who all belonged to the minority Wahhabis) was sought and obtained. But in reality the opinions of the religious people counted for little. Until their recent politicization, the Wahhabi religious ulemas were used for added support but ignored when their opinions contradicted the will of the family.

Saud ruled from 1953 until he was replaced by his younger brother Faisal in 1964. Nobody has anything nice to say about Saud, not even his own family, despite their legendary tolerance of familial misdeeds. Outsiders' judgements aside, according to the official history of Saudi Arabia, Saud is a non-person and his 11 years as king are treated as if they never were. In government offices the pictures of the various kings of the realm are hung for everybody to see but Saud's is conspicuously absent and until recently no street, building or institution was named after him.

What prompted Saud's dethronement and his relegation to oblivion reveals a lot about the family's inherent fears. Ostensibly it was the result of his personal, financial and moral corruption, nepotism and ignorance of statecraft. He squandered tens of millions of dollars on foolishnesses such as the use of 25,000 light bulbs in the garden of his palace, which he called 'Little Paradise'. He married more times than his father, appointed his ignorant children to ministerial posts, including the important portfolios of defence and the interior, and could not even run a diwan properly because he was always at a loss for words. He failed to impose himself on the country the way his father had, and his people, the Arabs, Muslims and the West never took him seriously.

All this was true, but Ibn Saud too had been guilty on all these counts, with the exception of running the diwan. Ibn Saud's criminal nepotism included naming the incompetent Saud his crown prince. What actually happened was that Saud's deplorable lack of finesse and his simplicity were revealed at a time when Nasser of Egypt was popular with the Saudi people and something more imaginative to counter the Nasser challenge was required. Saud never learned the present official Saudi method of pretending to do something while standing still. These shortcomings, all of which occurred when most Saudi people were enamoured of Nasser's Arab unity schemes, exposed the vulnerability of the family and its absolute rule and generated among its ranks a fear of being toppled.

Saud was much more lenient in dealing with the Saudi people than his father had been; he certainly showed no inclination towards eliminating local political enemies. This led to the emergence of political groups such as Young Nejed, the Peninsula Liberation Front and even a small communist party. He could not find it in himself to pressure merchants and others into subsidizing his profligate ways, even when he needed to do it to avoid exposure to debts. In the Arab arena, he was inconsistent: he switched sides between conservatives and progressives too many times and botched a Saudi-sponsored attempt to assassinate Nasser. In the wider Muslim world, he was not inclined to foment trouble, divide the Muslim world and impose the will of his country on others, even if they would have listened to him.

Towards the West, Saud cultivated an ambivalent policy which contained the seeds of independent thought and along with his occasional support for Nasser this threatened the traditional friendships with Britain and America, the backbone of the regime. Even when matters of policy and finance were under control, his personal behaviour was utterly deplorable (for example, the palace used 4000 eggs, 200 chickens and 30 lambs daily) and the family saw the CIA's willingness to procure boys for him as a sign of weakness because it left him open to blackmail. (I find it utterly appalling that Miles Copeland and other CIA agents knew about this and wrote about it with the minimum amount of moral misgiving.)

That Saud was rotten is beyond question, but he was an inherently simple, if not stupid, man and what mattered to his family, who deposed him, was not the principle of his rottenness, most of which they shared, but how unintelligently merciful, corrupt and ineffective he was. Eventually, the family became genuinely alarmed when ordinary people expressed admiration for Nasser and began thinking about politics. They acted because such permissiveness and Saud's refusal to wield the sword undermined the foundations of the Saudi state.

Essentially what the elimination of Saud meant was that a family will to protect and preserve the continuance of the House of Saud could emerge to replace the individual will of an ineffective king.

But even to this day, much like everything else in the country, this family will does not manifest itself in an organized fashion. There are no specific family groups to take care of these things, but there are coalitions which come into existence to deal with specific crises. The group which forced Saud to step down had no name; it was merely a collection of princes, 72 out of 1500 at that time, whose success or failure depended on the force of personality of the participants. In this case, they were led by Muhammad 'Twin-Evil', one of the elder brothers about whom we will hear more later, an alcoholic whose violent way earned him his uncomplimentary nickname and a real Bedouin with an instinctive attachment to absolutism. The whole episode of Saud's role could be reduced to one brief proposition: determined to continue its absolute rule, the House of Saud acted to guarantee that future kings would behave in the best way to retain such power.

Saud was replaced by Faisal, the second eldest brother and until 1964 the country's perennial Foreign Minister. Faisal was seen as more capable of continuing the ways of Ibn Saud and the family while giving them an aura of respectability. In the words of the Saudi historian Anwar Abdallah: 'He eliminated obvious corruption and continued the subtle variety.' His most memorable pronouncement on the essence of his rule was: 'What does man aspire to? He wants good. It is there in the Islamic Sharia. He wants justice. It is there in the Sharia. He wants security. It is also there. Man wants freedom. It is there. He wants propagation of science. It is there. Everything is there, inscribed in the Islamic Sharia.'

Goodness, justice, security, freedom and the propagation of science were nowhere in Saudi Arabia, but superimposing the family's view on the ways of Islam and perverting a most just religion was a better way of expressing state policy than Ibn Saud's pronouncement regarding the use of the sword. (Faisal's statement recalls Hitler's exploitation of the concept of the *Volk*.) This type of disguise was what Faisal was good at. He was a subtle manipulator who was extremely adept at concealing his misdeeds, regardless of their enormity and immorality, behind a veil of phoney correctness. His ability to create this cover was enhanced by a relative worldliness gained during his years as Foreign Minister. Unlike his brothers of similar age, he had travelled extensively and mastered the art of compromise, a skill which allowed him to appear capable in the eyes of the world.

Faisal ruled for 11 years, until he was assassinated by an irate nephew for non-political reasons in 1975. Despite the strictly familial reasons behind the murder, the simple facts that the murderer had acted to avenge a brother whom Faisal had ordered killed for objecting to 'non-Muslim ways' and that he himself was later beheaded publicly are a confirmation, if one was needed, that the ways of the House of Saud were anchored in an ancient past.

During his lifetime, Faisal made much of four deliberate acts. The first of these was his marriage for most of his life to one woman, Iffat, his fourth and last wife and a distant cousin who had been educated in Turkey. In fact, when it came to indulging his fancy, Faisal was hardly the puritan he pretended to be. Robert Lacey, among other historians of the House of Saud, speaks of Faisal leading 'a wild youth' and his abstinence from the family sport of marrying dozens of women was the result of Iffat's strength of character rather than his disapproval of the tradition. Though apologists for the House of Saud would have us accept that marrying a mere four times is a considerable virtue, little is said about why Faisal did nothing to contain or discourage the overindulgence of his brothers and relatives, for which the state paid. (A Saudi writer estimates that Ibn Saud's 42 sons married 1400 women – as good an estimate as any.)

The second source of Faisal's self-proclaimed reputation as a principled reformer was his freeing of the slaves in 1962, when he held power prior to his eventual accession to the throne. Once again there is less to this than meets the eye. In 1932, as his country's Foreign Minister, Faisal conducted a major diplomatic altercation with Britain and demanded the recall of the British Ambassador, Sir Andrew Ryan, because the latter helped free one of his father's slaves in accordance with the terms of the 1927 treaty between the two countries. It was Faisal who renegotiated the treaty in 1936 and produced one in which the only change was the elimination of a clause obligating Saudi Arabia to abolish slavery. For years after that, most of the world, a number of UN committees and unforgettably Nasser, were making noises against the institution of slavery in the country to the extent of threatening concrete anti-Saudi action. The UN condemned it, President Kennedy pointedly brought it up when he met Faisal and Egyptian radio beamed special broadcasts to Saudi Arabia to attack the practice. These messages were well received by most of the Saudis, whose thinking was already ahead of that of their rulers. As a result, after a long period of denying the existence of slavery in his country, Faisal acted under pressure, particularly from Kennedy. Even when the slaves were finally freed, most of the 4000 people who qualified remained where they were, totally unable to lead normal independent lives.

The slave-freeing act ordered by Faisal prohibited the open trade in slaves. But it did nothing about the new enslavement of foreign workers and the purchase of wives, something which his family practised and which still flourishes – members of the House of Saud have special scouts who do nothing else. Faisal cleverly turned this overdue act into a triumph and paid millions of dollars to Lebanese journalists and others to sing his praises. Yet they were under orders to say not a word about his own record or about how his father's kingdom had failed to sign any international conventions outlawing slavery and had declined to sign the United Nations Declaration of Universal Human Rights because it was seen as too liberal.

The third celebrated act attributed to Faisal concerned his supposed introduction of controls on the royal purse. If his other acts were exaggerations, then this one was no more than a blatant propaganda lie. What Faisal did was to find other ways of compensating his family and friends in callously corrupt but more subtle ways. The biggest new method did not completely replace the old one of outright treasury payments, but it perpetuated and expanded the ways of the family while acting to ease direct pressure on the treasury – and it was more difficult to trace.

Until Faisal dealt with it, the question of the ownership of public land, estimated at between 92 and 95 per cent of the country, had never been decided. True, it was assumed that like the land where the oil is, it belonged to the Government and hence to the House of Saud, but nothing had been done with it except the occasional building of a palace or establishment of a farm. Faisal cleverly decided to use public land to compensate his family and friends without 'abusing' the treasury. Ever committed to appearing magnanimous, he stopped short of expropriating all of it and settled for making 80 per cent of Saudi Arabia 'Aradi Emeria', land which belongs to the emirs or the rulers. Blatantly, like all things in the country, the confiscated land was arrogantly named after members of the family, Faisaliah, after Faisal, Khalidia, after Khalid, and Sultania, after Sultan. He used what remained to placate the people.

With oil income increasing at a rate faster than Saudi Arabia could absorb and the family well taken care of, business was booming and the country suffered from a huge dose of inflation which affected the price of land more than most things. Faisal began giving away huge parcels of land to those around him. The chief beneficiary was his wife Iffat, who was given vast tracts of land around the city of Jeddah worth an estimated $2 billion (almost $5 billion today). The only Saudi non-royal to achieve the status of a household name, the legendary Oil Minister Sheikh Ahmad Zaki Yamani, admitted to his biographer, Jeffrey Robinson, that he owns over $300 million worth of Faisal-given land. Bedouins were settling and people were building large houses and when a prince had his eye on a specific piece of development land, all he had to do was to liaise with the appropriate authority, the municipality or the province governor, and arrangements would be made for him to obtain ownership. Often this happened even when the land had an owner. It was taken away as a Royal Claim for Public Purposes, then handed to His Highness. While it is impossible to determine it with any accuracy, my attempts to assess the value of land given away by Faisal produce a figure between $35 billion and $50 billion. Naturally, the kings who have followed him have perpetuated this system and most of the give-away land has gone to members of the family.

Of course, some members of the family, including former King Saud, still needed treasury cash. Saud alone spent $10 million in one month while in exile in Athens. Faisal accommodated Saud. Not only that, but Faisal, more than anybody else, encouraged members of his family to go into business to capitalize on the huge opportunities the oil wealth was creating. This tradition led directly to what exists now. According to *Who's Who in Saudi Arabia* and other sources, members of the House of Saud and their relatives and in-laws are chairmen of 520 Saudi corporations. In many cases these titles mean simply that they have lent their names to corporations financed and run by the Government or by others who use the royal names and the influence which goes with them to win Government contracts. Beyond the massive number of chairmen, many princes of the House of Saud are 'silent partners' in corporations. They promote the business of companies and individuals without attribution and receive huge sums of money in return. Doing serious business in Saudi Arabia without a royal partner is a rare thing indeed.

The fourth of Faisal's celebrated acts was to appear as a champion of women's education and it is true that he ordered the opening of the first girls' school in the country. However, in view of the fact that it was never followed by any concrete efforts to improve the lot of women, there is good reason to suspect that it was instigated by his wife, Iffat, to educate members of their family. It was Faisal himself who exposed the limits of his so-called liberation of women. Many years after the girls' school was opened he responded to a question about when he was going to grant women rights by saying: 'When we grant them to men.' This meant never, and he never made any moves towards either. In fact, despite the many promises of political reform (see The Brutal Friendship) he had made while trying to oust Saud, his first political move on assuming total power was to dismiss the reforming cabinet of promising young men, average age 39, his brother had appointed to attract popular support.

By the time Faisal died, members of the royal family occupied half of the cabinet posts, all of the province governorships and 11 deputy ministerships. Several of them were generals in the Army and Air Force while still in their twenties and thirties and 32 others held key posts such as Director of Intelligence, or were ambassadors or chiefs of protocol. Faisal used members of the family to control all public and private aspects of the country, including his personal creation, the dreaded internal security apparatus, which he entrusted to his brother-in-law, Kamal Adham. Says Saudi opposition member Abdel Ameer Mousa: 'The things we most remember him for are the number of people he imprisoned and the initiation of torture. In this regard, he was the worst one of them all.'

In the 1960s Faisal used his questionable achievements to try to give Saudi Arabia a new image and this affected its relations with the Arabs, the Muslims and the West. The country's wealth allowed him to stand up to the external threats of Nasser and the progressive Arab forces and eventually to try to wrest the leadership of the Arab world from their hands. He supported an antiquated monarchy in the Yemen with funds and arms and ensnared Nasser in its civil war, which sapped the energies and financial strength of the Egyptian President's government and undermined his popular attempt to unify the Arabs. He continued the tradition of supporting backward Arab regimes without overtly demanding obedience – a simple case of bribing them into adhering to Saudi ways. He also systematized Saudi Arabian attempts to pervert the Arab press by buying the loyalty of newspapers and journalists throughout the Arab world – and many journalistic establishments had been free and effective until then. (See The Last Line of Defence.)

Above all, because the Muslims were less of a threat to the House of Saud than the awakening Arabs and Saudis, and also because control of Islam's holy shrines gave it a Muslim edge, Faisal pushed his country towards an Islamic identity at the expense of its Arabness. He encouraged conservative Muslim movements everywhere because they balanced the Arab threat against him and conservative Islam held governments back. Examples of this policy included supporting the Pakistani army and its Chief of Staff General Zia Al Huq against their country's legitimately elected Prime Minister, Ali Bhutto, which led to the latter's overthrow and execution. Bhutto was his own man, very much concerned with modernizing Pakistan, and what Faisal needed was a tributary country. In addition, as far back as 1959, when Faisal was Prime Minister, the Egyptian magazine *Al Musawar* had published a detailed report of how a CIA group under the guidance of one James Russell Barracks cooperated with Saudi Arabia to create Muslim political groups within the country as a counterweight to Nasser and pan-Arabism.

As would be expected, Faisal's change of direction extended to his country's relations with the West. He used his stand against Nasser and progressive Arab movements to get more Western support and to create a Saudi-led, Islam-based conservative camp. He blunted early Arab pressure on him to use his oil wealth against the West's support of Israel by espousing an incredibly unsound policy aimed at pleasing both sides. He claimed that communism and Zionism were evil and were one and the same, and this led to Arab acceptance of his condemnation of Zionism and Western support for his attack on communism.

In 1973, fearing Arab pressure and a nationalist uprising in support of Egypt after it attacked Israel and started the October War, Faisal briefly shut off oil supplies – seemingly an Arab move at the expense of the West. This very complicated move, which will be examined later, enhanced Faisal's Arab standing, but he rescinded the decision as soon as possible and hurried to mend fences with the West. In fact, despite this tactical shut-off of oil, he saw his fate and that of his country irrevocably linked to America. In 1975 he confirmed this to *Time* correspondent Wilton Wynn, saying, 'US relations are a pillar of Saudi policy.'

Faisal carried this approach forward and initiated the destructive and far-reaching policy of supporting American foreign policy with Saudi funds. The first demonstration of this common purpose was in the Horn of Africa, where conservative forces were supported at the expense of progressive ones. Later his brothers extended this policy to Afghanistan, where backward warlords were presented to the world as freedom fighters, and other countries and situations followed. (See Brotherhood is Selective and The Brutal Friendship.)

That Faisal was clever is beyond doubt, and clever men in the service of bad causes are more dangerous than stupid ones in the same role. According to dozens of Saudis interviewed for this book, Faisal's unmerciful ways eliminated all internal opposition. The liberal political movements in the Arab world and the Arab nationalist movement were broken and have never recovered. The West accepted Saudi Arabia as its deputy in the Arab world. Still Faisal never wavered from the unsound beliefs that his family could do anything so long as it was done cleverly, that Wahhabism and its strict ways were the path to salvation and, above all, that the average Saudi was not entitled to enjoy the fruits of the oil wealth. (In 1962 the uneven distribution of wealth left the average Saudi undernourished: the calorific intake was 83 per cent of what was needed to survive, compared with 100 per cent in Lebanon and 92 per cent in Jordan.) Faisal was a champion of absolutism who ensured that Saudi Arabia belonged to the House of Saud lock, stock and barrel. This is why his successful efforts to improve the country's image were not matched by benefits for the average Saudi and why many Saudis still cringe at the mention of his name.

Khalid, the man who became king after Faisal, did not even want the job. He had to accept it because his refusal would have led to a widening of the emerging divisions within the royal family and a consequent reversion to the tradition of blood feuds. Although he was much more interested in falconry than kingship, Khalid's years on the throne (1975–82) were marked by some of the most far-reaching developments in the history of the country.

The most serious development was the emergence of a strong family of full and devoted brothers within the larger Saud family. The Sudeiri seven, or Al Fahd as they are also called, are the seven sons of Hassa Al Sudeiri, the woman Ibn Saud married, divorced, allowed to marry his brother and then married again. Three of them, Fahd, Sultan and Nayef, occupied ministerial positions for some time and the rest were governors and deputy ministers. Through sheer wile and their connection to the powerful Sudeiri tribe, Fahd became Khalid's crown prince, while Sultan continued as Minister of Defence and Nayef as Minister of the Interior, and Salman assumed the important governorship of Riyadh.

The Sudeiri seven, with Fahd in the lead, became the power behind the throne and proceeded to take steps to eliminate or restrict the power of other groups within the family. In the process they undermined the seniority system (by prevailing on older brothers to forgo their slots) and the family council, the two authorities in the succession process. The sons of their brother, the late King Saud, were denied jobs in the Government and obstacles were placed in their way to prevent them attaining any positions of importance. The sons of King Faisal were allowed to occupy official positions, even that of Foreign Minister, but the Sudeiris saw to it that they were denied any real power. They were so successful that even the Foreign Minister, Prince Saud bin Faisal, was reported to have complained to King Hussein of Jordan that he was no more than an office boy. Of course, the sons of Fahd, Sultan and the rest of the Sudeiris became merchants, ambassadors, governors and generals. In total, the Sudeiris and their sons held 63 key government positions.

Eventually, the Sudeiri coup within the family, for that is what it was, ran into unexpected obstacles which thwarted a complete take-over. The line of succession which appointed Fahd Crown Prince to Khalid stipulated who should follow him, and Prince Abdallah and Muhammad Twin-Evil stood in their way and would not let them push the rest of the family too far and Abdallah was made next in line to the throne. Muhammad wanted Abdallah, and his bloodthirsty ways appealed to many of the tribes, with the result that the Sudeiris were always fearful that he might raise the rest of the family and the tribes against them.

The second major development affecting Khalid's years was a regional event, the accession to power of a Muslim fundamentalist movement in neighbouring Iran. Ayatollah Khomeini was an immediate problem. Because of Faisal's Muslim policies, the basis of Khomeini's appeal could not be denied and it reached beyond his Shia co-religionists, who represented 15 per cent of the Saudi population. Other Muslim groups were encouraged by his movement and were ready to emulate him. In response, Khalid, with total family backing, imprisoned hundreds of Shias and Muslim fundamentalists and the House of Saud was in a state of panic.

Unable to confront Iran directly, but determined to undermine the huge threat to its security, Saudi Arabia opted for an indirect assault on the Muslim revolution in that country. Saudi Arabia encouraged Iraq to start the Iran–Iraq War. The Saudi support for this move, which is discussed later, was recorded in the Arabic magazines *Al Tadamun* and *Al Dastour* and many Western newspapers and the country's controlled press admitted this without going into details. In fact, Saudi Arabia bankrolled Saddam Hussein of Iraq to the tune of a staggering $30 billion. The determination of the House of Saud to follow a divide-and-rule policy, in this case of Arab against Muslim, reached unprecedented levels.

The third development during Khalid's years was summed up by a former chargé at the American Embassy in Saudi Arabia, Marshall Wylie: 'We need their oil and they need our protection.' America's growing dependence on Saudi oil made it set aside all other considerations, including Jimmy Carter's commitment to human rights. Simultaneously, internal, Arab and Islamic funda-mentalist pressures started gathering strength and the country's inherent inability to fend for itself forced the House of Saud to seek the military protection of America more than ever.

Despite the consistency of the House of Saud and its unchanging ways, an important shift in the way its members reveal themselves has taken place under King Fahd and it is full of portents for the future.

The undoubted success of the House of Saud against all internal attempts to eliminate it or force it to change; the defeat of Arab and Muslim challenges and the neutralization of their sources; and the ever-increasing dependence of the West on Saudi oil and the so far consequent extension of uncritical support have merged to create an arrogant House of Saud whose members feel secure in their ways. This false security, based as it is on obliviousness to their surroundings, has led to a bad situation becoming totally absurd. Under Fahd, the House of Saud, unafraid and without pretence, has come into the open. This move has trivialized everything, even corruption.

Now King Fahd can play Saud without provoking the family's displeasure. He feels no need to go through Faisal's elaborate cover-ups. His coercion of Arab and Muslim countries through the use of money is crude and his dependence on the West is seldom offset or balanced by real or cosmetic internal or regional moves. As it is, the man stands for nothing or everything. Perhaps a new word has to be coined especially for him; nothing which exists describes him, though people have tried. To former British Prime Minister Margaret Thatcher, 'He has nothing to say for himself.' But Nihad Al Ghadiri, a Syrian journalist who watched him very closely for years, endows Thatcher's observation with appropriate angry Arab rhetoric: 'He's an empty hulk, a mountain of nothingness. Even his evil deeds don't reflect him; he's achieved the impossible, people don't take what he and his family do seriously. Nobody talks about corruption in Saudi Arabia any more; they take it for granted.'

The judgements of Thatcher and Ghadiri say a lot, but they are not enough. The man is still King of Saudi Arabia, the sole maker of the policies of an extremely important country. Even if Fahd is undoing Saudi Arabia, even if he turns out to be its last king, he deserves greater analysis than is contained in Thatcher's and Ghadiri's appealing generalities. But to me and many others the man is a mystery, almost beyond analysis. Says the editor of a major Saudi-sponsored Arabic newspaper in London: 'Before he came to the throne I was one of his leading supporters. Now I don't know what to say about him – he is the biggest single disappointment in the history of the country.' This is very close to my opinion, but the complexity or utter simplicity of the man makes a single opinion dangerous and, instead, I will take the reader from Fahd's beginnings to where he is now.

Fahd was not one of his father's favourites nor was there anything in his early years to single him out. He pursued his elementary education at the Princes' School in Riyadh, but did nothing else to broaden his horizons. Even his bedroom English remains elementary after years of wandering around Europe in pursuit of blondes. We do not know of a single personal interest he has which is not questionable – nothing like Saud's fascination with photography, Faisal's commitment to his children's education or Khalid's love of falconry.

The one thing common Saudis, princes of the household, oilmen, foreign diplomats and Western statesmen agree on is Fahd's laziness. By all accounts, every single book about the modern history of the kingdom alludes to his appalling laziness. He is supposed to have been a lazy student, an uninterested lover – even in his twenties – a lazy and careless minister of health, education and the interior. He used to leave his country for months at a time to play after he became crown prince and now, as king, cannot bring himself to read even the most important of documents. 'The documents, and some of them are very important, pile up on his desk for weeks, then he gets tired of looking at them, summons one of his aides and asks him to take them away without reading a single one. I have never seen anything like it, a total absence of interest in anything.' The speaker is a builder who worked on Fahd's $3-billion Jeddah palace, Al Salem, and had a chance to observe him at close range.

Beyond being lazy, there are four other unsavoury aspects to Fahd's character which are universally acknowledged. He is a womanizer, but interestingly – perhaps because he has no need to endow his womanizing with respectability – he does not have to marry to do it. I have seen pictures of him with European women who look beneath the dignity even of a Bedouin royal and he frequented Régine's discothèque in Paris, where he often picked up a socialite for the night. In addition to dozens of second-hand stories attesting to his playboy status, I have first-hand knowledge of one. Fahd was enamoured of the wife of a Lebanese acquaintance of mine, and conducted a five-year affair with her while favouring her husband with concessions and pieces of business. The couple are extremely wealthy now, and there are many similar stories.

There is little which is new in Fahd's womanizing and his sexual proclivities do not match those of his father or his brother Saud. On the other hand his gambling is unique and it takes up much of his time. Years ago, he used to spend a lot of time in Lebanon's casinos, and regularly lost hundreds of thousands of dollars. But it was in Monte Carlo in 1962 that his gambling reputation was established. According to the German magazine *Stern* and other publications, he lost DM 20 million in one evening. He was recalled to Saudi Arabia by his brother Faisal and scolded, but he was not cured. Now, even at home, he is always in search of poker parties and they definitely take precedence over the piles of documents he refuses to peruse. One way for an ambitious Jeddah businessman to get ahead is to join Fahd's gambling circuit, and, according to a Lebanese witness to one gambling party, Fahd has his servants pay his losses in cash which is carried in Samsonite suitcases. Often what is left in the suitcases is given to the servants.

Fahd has a drinking problem, like many of his brothers, a number of whom have died of it. *Time*, the *New York Times* and many other publications have alluded to this habit or mentioned it outright. His drinking is a twofold curse. He has been known to go on binges for days at a time, and even after he became king his drinking led him to neglect other affairs and forget state functions. But he suffers from severe diabetes and therefore drinking is a potential killer. When, as at the time of writing, he stops drinking for long periods of time, Fahd loses a considerable amount of weight and his pictures show a more alert man, but all this does is make him a better poker player. He still does no work.

Fahd's fourth characteristic is his love of money and his ability to spend it. This was always so, and he squandered millions of dollars as a young man, but now, except by the Sultan of Brunei, his wealth may be unmatched in history. He has seven huge palaces in Saudi Arabia and a conservative estimate of their value would be $11 billion. In addition to the palaces in his own country, he has a 100-room palace in Marbella, another fitted out for eighteenth-century French kings outside Paris, a third with 1500 telephone lines in Geneva and a huge house near London which cost £30 million to refurbish. Of course there is his flying palace, a Boeing 747 fitted with a sauna, a lift, chandeliers and gold bathroom fixtures, and his equally lavish $50-million yacht. He uses gold-plated toothbrushes and his beach buggy is a Rolls-Royce Camargue converted for the purpose by the British firm of Wood and Barret. Fahd's personal wealth, excluding the palaces, is estimated at $28 billion.

There is little new in the things Fahd does except their scale. As long as the family's ways remain intact, this will continue as a natural extension of their control of the oil income of the country. The fact that Fahd no longer cares to hide his money-wasting inclinations means that he will invent new ways to fritter it.

Before addressing the important points of how Fahd's behaviour affects his family, his people and the internal affairs of his country (relations with the West, Arabs and Muslims are addressed separately), it is important to ask why someone so meagrely endowed became king. According to the seniority system, which is based exclusively on age, he was not in line to succeed; his brothers Nasir and Sa'ad are older. Equally interesting is why he was groomed under Faisal, the shrewd specialist in disguises. More than anything else, it is Fahd's assumption of the throne which exposes both the pro forma way in which the House of Saud governs and its Western-approved failure to modernize the country and give it the necessary lasting institutions which would guarantee its survival.

The major reason for Fahd's accession to the throne is the simple fact that the basis for succession has not been settled. The kingship was passed on to Saud by his father and Faisal was designated crown prince in accordance with the seniority system. But, under stress, seniority gave way to perceived talent. The move from Faisal to Khalid bypassed Muhammad Twin-Evil, in recognition of his shortcomings and in favour of his younger full brother. Then from Khalid it went to the supposedly talented Fahd, bypassing Nasir and Sa'ad. In this case, while the House of Saud stresses the talent factor, what matters most in the improvised succession process is neither seniority nor talent but who is going to protect the unity of the family. Unlike the retiring Nasir and Sa'ad, Fahd represented a clan within a clan, the seven full brothers of Hassa Al Sudeiri, the Sudeiri seven, and there was no way to deny them the throne and keep the family united. They would have dissented and their numbers and relationship to the powerful Sudeiris would have led to trouble. They acted like a cohesive group, more of a family than the larger Ibn Saud one, and, amazingly, Nasir and Sa'ad had less to offer than Fahd and there was no block within the family capable of helping them.

As stated before, the Sudeiri seven's assumption of power was tantamount to a coup. But they worked to achieve it for a long time, and in the process, in an attempt to justify it, they endowed Fahd with a non-existent talent. For the most part, everybody, including journalists and outside powers, believed them, or, in the case of the latter, wanted to believe them. This is why Fahd is a disappointment to many thinking Saudis and, conversely, what prompts people like *Time*'s Wilton Wynn to describe him as 'amiable and talented', *Newsweek* to call him a 'workaholic' and other journalists to resort to the epithets 'modern and liberal-thinking'. This is why the assumption of power by someone with such small talents and a huge public relations apparatus was based on a lie and why the result, Fahd, has produced confusion among those who believed that lie.

Having said enough about Fahd's regressive personal inclinations to document his shortcomings, it is necessary to show how his inadequacy has affected Saudi absolutism at this critical point in the country's history.

The strangeness and lack of character revealed by Fahd's personal ways goes beyond his love of money, women, gambling and alcohol to affect the way he runs the Government. Despite an attempt to deflect regional and internal Islamic fundamentalist pressure by adopting the title Guardian of Islam's Holy Shrines and shedding the Islamicly unacceptable title of king, he is addressed in more ways that denote supremacy than any man alive. 'Majesty' is still used and so is 'King', as well as the official 'Guardian of Islam's Holy Shrines'. But he is also Al Muathem, the one endowed with greatness; Al Mufada, the one who deserves sacrifice; Moulana, the holder of ultimate authority: Saydna, our master; Walye Al Amr, the decider of all things. There is no end to the improvisations and variations; nor does he discourage any of it.

But if the average Saudi and Government officials who address Fahd have to go through the indignity of using the most sycophantic words the Arabic language can afford them, the demands of Fahd's ego impinge on even foreign heads of state. He is always late for appointments. In 1987 he was 45 minutes late for a Buckingham Palace lunch with the Queen and he has appeared late for meetings with President Bush, King Hussein and Japanese Prime Minister Fukuda. In a striking incident, his insulting constant lateness prompted Argentine President Menem to cut short his four-day visit to Saudi Arabia and leave after two days. And in 1992, visiting Kuwait after the Gulf War, he kept the Emir of that country waiting to receive him in the airport lobby for a whole hour while taking a nap in his plane. Fahd shows no signs of changing his ways and this self-importance has led to the issue of several ministerial directives as to what pictures of him to use in newspapers (he is extremely worried about a lazy eye and complains to the Minister of Information about uncomplimentary photographs).

Within Fahd's own country, this arrogance shows particularly in the way he dismisses those in high positions. Ahmad Zaki Yamani, the famous former Oil Minister, heard the news of his own dismissal on television (see Servants of the Crown). Muhammad Abdo Yamani, Minister of Information; Ghazi Al Ghoseibi, Minister of Health; Abdallay Al Jazairi, another Minister of Health; Ahmad Ali Abdel Wahab, the Head of the Royal Court; Abdel Munir Al Otteibi, the Chief of Staff; and Abdel Hadi Taher, the head of the Petromin – all were fired the same way. They heard the news second-hand or somebody told them to stay at home. Fahd's nephews, Prince General Khalid bin Sultan, Chief of the Saudi Air Force and Commander of the Arab Forces during the Gulf War, and Prince Fahd bin Salman, Deputy Emir of the Eastern Province, left their positions unexpectedly and are presumed fired. In early December 1992, in a politically more significant move, Fahd fired seven members of the extremely important Council of Ulemas because they would not issue a decree against people who criticized some Government actions and pleaded for political and social reforms to be enacted. Here it is important to state that Fahd's insensitive treatment of ministers, princes and religious leaders is original and that former Saudi kings fired people in much gentler Bedouin ways, just in case they needed their services again.

The reasons behind these undignified dismissals differ and range from matters of policy to unhappiness over the smallest of personal details.

In the case of the talented Ghoseibi, it was because he had written a poem complaining that the King was not seeing him, while others were fired because of equally trivial matters. Two other examples, one concerning what Fahd expects from his ministers and showing how little it would take to dismiss them and another of his general lack of care, are worth reporting.

One of the best known and more important Lebanese newspaper editors was visiting the Saudi Minister of Information, Ali Al Shaer, in his office at ten at night when Shaer's private telephone rang. This was his side of the conversation:

'Yes, sir.'

'I am extremely sorry, sir, I had no idea.'

'I will stop it right away, sir, immediately.'

Al Shaer hung up, looked at the puzzled Lebanese editor and dialled another number.

'Listen, if I told you once, I've told a you a million times: His Majesty doesn't like Indian films,' he said.

'I don't care if you're half-way through the film – stop it and put on an American film instead,' he insisted after hearing what the other person had to say.

As the Minister of Information gratuitously explained, Fahd had called him to complain that one of the television channels was showing an Indian film in the slot reserved for *Film of the Day*. He did not like it and ordered Al Shaer to stop the broadcast right away. That was the minister's order to the head of the station. How the rest of the viewers in the country reacted to this interruption is not known, but conceivably Al Shaer saved his job by acting with alacrity.

On another occasion Fahd telephoned the people building his Al Salem Palace in Jeddah to tell them of his wish to visit the site. In accordance with Islamic custom, sheep are butchered on these occasions, and 1000 sheep were slaughtered in anticipation of his arrival. Fahd did not show up, but telephoned to say that he would come the following day. The sheep-slaughtering exercise was repeated and again there was no Fahd. He made a promise to appear a third time, with the same result. Three thousand sheep had been slaughtered for nothing.

As usual, family behaviour follows the personal behaviour of the King. In this regard, Fahd is closer to Saud's ways than he is to those of Faisal and Khalid. Most of his sons are uneducated and many of them are in the Government. Muhammad is the governor of the oil-rich Eastern Province and he is heavily involved in commerce, a partner in the huge Al Bilad Trading Company, and besides involvement in selling oil on the open market (see Oil, OPEC and the Overseers), rumours persist that one of his companies managed a $10-billion contract to install a joint Bell of Canada and Philips of Holland telephone system throughout the kingdom. Faisal, Fahd's eldest son, is head of the Youth Welfare Organization, a job which carries the rank of minister. Many writers have accused another son of being a drug addict and rumours have it that he shot his male lover when the latter left him. Yet another son, Saud, is the deputy head of intelligence, a post growing in importance by the day. But it is the favourite son, Abdel Aziz, who represents another gross departure by Fahd.

When Abdel Aziz was young, a fortune-teller, almost certainly noticing the affection his father had for the child, advised Fahd to take him with him everywhere or else he, Fahd, would die. That is why when he came to Britain on a state visit in 1987, Fahd brought Abdel Aziz with him but, without knowing the background to his presence, the press treated the infirm 14-year-old gently. Towards the end of his stay in London, Fahd had meetings with members of the Arab press. This is part of what he voluntarily told journalists Haj Ahmad Al Houni and Ghassan Zakkaria during their royal audience: 'Young Azoouzi [Abdel Aziz's pet name] overspends. But Allah gave us wealth and we are glad to share it with our son. I've just transferred $300 million into his personal account to meet his needs.' Houni and Zakkaria looked at each other and had nothing to say. To this day, Zakkaria cannot tell the story without his eyes bulging. The same disastrous official trip saw him take Abdel Aziz wherever he went, even when the child was not invited. Fahd on his own was enough of a show; the step of the royal carriage had to be reinforced so as not to break under his weight, and he left on his personal Boeing 747, followed by another for his entourage and three 707s to carry the royal party's luggage, and four custom-made, armoured-plated cars.

Naturally enough Fahd's 'liberal' attitude towards his children extends to the rest of the family. Eleven years ago, hearing that some of the late King Saud's sons were in need, Fahd gave each $15 million to build 'a house'. But it does not stop at gifts and Fahd is quite explicit about his approval of the family's 'commercial' ways. The family's involvement in commerce is so total that they have begun to compete with each other. Because of their numbers and the depth of their involvement, a company sponsored by Prince X competes with another sponsored by Prince Y and perhaps Princes Z and W. Often, with little regard to competence or which companies are involved, the princes meet and decide how to split the pie, but occasionally commercial competition turns into a family feud. Either way, the money they get or share is so colossal that Ghassan Zakkaria insists that no fewer than 50 members of the family are billionaires. (See Big Deals and Dangerous Games).

Fahd's sanction of the use of commerce to make money goes beyond his family and extends to his in-laws and friends. He himself is a partner in several firms, though their Saudi registrations place libel constraints on naming them because the names of their owners could be easily changed and backdated. His favourite in-laws, the Ibrahims, are heavily involved in influence peddling and some of them manage the interests of young Prince Abdel Aziz, their nephew, who has been forced on some major Saudi trading houses as a partner. Even oil, the country's main resource, is not immune from royal dabbling and Fahd has used a Greek shipping friend to sell it on the open market. (See Oil, OPEC and the Overseers.)

The total laxity with which Fahd views his family's, friends' and officials' misdeeds and the freedom to misbehave afforded them by his attitudes came together in 1986 to produce one of the most bizarre episodes in the annals of corruption, a profound example of how a small story grew into a larger one which mirrored the condition of the whole country.

Beginning in August 1986, the *Washington Post*, *Washington Star*, *New York Times*, *Philadelphia Inquirer*, *San Francisco Chronicle*, ABC News and many other media organs carried the story of one Sam Bamieh, a resident of San Mateo County, California, who was suing for conspiracy, slander, libel and invasion of privacy the then Chief of the Saudi Royal Court and his predecessor, Muhammad Suleiman and Muhammad Imran. Bamieh demanded $50 million in compensation.

Bamieh produced a tale of horror to support his claim. In documents filed with the District Court of Northern California, he alleged that the two associates of King Fahd had held him captive in Jeddah for a period of 133 days between March and

August 1986. Bamieh, the head of a small Californian trading company, Industrial Development Corporation, claimed that he had gone to Saudi Arabia to collect money owed him from the commissions on contracts he transacted with the accused. There they had taken away his passport and held him hostage until he wired his solicitors in California, dropping all claims against them in return for a payment of $400,000. He further claimed that the King, whom he had met before, knew about his claim and detention.

The original allegations made so much press noise that the Saudi Embassy to the United States, Congressional Committees and the Secretary of State were soon involved. There was a question as to whether the Saudi Embassy would accept the service of writs on behalf of the accused and whether they had acted in an official capacity, on the instructions of Fahd. Congressional Committees wrote letters of protest and held hearings to discuss the denial of an American citizen's rights and this opened the door to the press, who proceeded to produce examples of other US citizens who had been denied their rights without recourse. There were cases of American mothers who had lost their children to Saudi fathers who had kidnapped them to Saudi Arabia and who were afforded protection by the Saudi Government, which ignored the American mothers' rights. There were also cases of executives who had been cheated out of money by important Saudis and others who had been imprisoned without trial.

At first the Saudi Government denied the original claim of detention and attributed the whole story to Bamieh's desire for publicity and his greed. Later, when he persisted, he began receiving threatening telephone calls. When he refused to be frightened into dropping the suit, the Saudis denied all official involvement and described it as a totally personal matter which should be resolved as such. It should be settled in Saudi Arabia in accordance with Saudi law, they insisted.

At this point, Bamieh broadened his attack. He claimed that some of the money owed him was paid to the defendants by Fahd's son Muhammad for business done with Bechtel Corporation, that Adnan Khashoggi, whom he described as a friend of the King, was another person who paid money to the defendants, and then he involved John Latsis, the King's Greek friend and renowned oil merchant. The rest of Bamieh's long list of the people involved read like a who's who in Saudi Arabia and included the former head of intelligence, Kamal Adham of Bank of Credit and

Commerce International (BCCI) fame, Fahd's brother-in-law Abdel Aziz Ibrahim and 44 others.

Though the case was moving through the courts, the slowness of the proceedings gave an angry Bamieh ample time to wage a thorough anti-Saudi campaign. In a change of direction aimed at exposing the rottenness of the whole country, Bamieh produced documents and details to support allegations that Saudi Arabia was funding the Nicaraguan Contras and the anti-communist forces in Angola. Soon this list was expanded and Bamieh provided information on how the Saudis were behind anti-communist movements in Afghanistan, Somalia and the Sudan.

Bamieh's relentless anti-Saudi attacks and his ability to afford a complicated legal suit, the interest the press and Congress took in the case and the obvious though muted US Government displeasure over the whole thing, eventually led to an out-of-court settlement which satisfied Bamieh. But nothing could be done to repair the publicity damage to Saudi Arabia generated by the case.

The Bamieh case showed that, in Saudi Arabia, the people who 'belong', the royal family and their friends, operate along sinister lines. The various branches of the system cooperate with each other to make money in complicated ways which outsiders cannot decipher and those involved band together for protection. The fact that two of the King's cronies imprisoned a senior American businessman for such a long time shows how far they have gone in disregarding the ways of others. Even after the case started, the Saudi Government was willing to try to protect two of its own because they were well-placed members of the team. The involvement of the King's son in commission-bearing business deals was confirmed. Saudi–American cooperation over Saudi financing of anti-communist activity all over the world was documented. And Bamieh produced evidence of how arms dealer Adnan Khashoggi dealt with the high and mighty of the Republican party and administration – for example, White House Chief of Staff Robert McFarland of Iran–Contra fame – and suggested American connivance in suppressing unpleasant news about Saudi Arabia. When the dust settled, one newspaper spoke of a Saudi finger in every pie and a member of Congress lamented the fact that America has never given Saudi Arabia any incentive to respect human rights.

Even though it was settled out of court and Bamieh has been 'rehabilitated', the case may be the ultimate expression of Saudi disregard for the opinions of others. An equally important indicator of this disregard is the growth of Saudi involvement in international scandals and their commitment to protecting the participants. Under King Fahd and when he was crown prince and strong man, the Saudis have been involved in many of the major scandals of our time. (See Big Deals and Dangerous Games and Servants of the Crown.) 'If the scandal is big enough, then look for the Saudi connection,' is the way the Lebanese journalist Suleiman Al Firzli describes the situation.

This phase began with the Lockheed scandal, when huge payments were made to Fahd's friend Adnan Khashoggi, and when the ensuing investigations suggested royal involvement. This was followed by the AWACS deal, the payment in oil for surveillance aircraft, a transaction which flooded the international market with oil and undermined the OPEC pricing system. It produced huge commissions for those who handled the oil sale and manipulated the price. Saudi Arabia was also a major player in the Iran–Contra scandal. By financing covert activities in Nicaragua it helped the executive branch of the US Government to circumvent congressional controls on aid to outside forces, a hugely dangerous precedent. The 1991 BCCI scandal revealed a substantial Saudi involvement in the persons of Kamal Adham, Ghaith Pharoan and Hamad bin Mahfouz, who have been accused of realizing hundreds of millions of dollars from illegal transactions. (Bin Mahfouz denied all charges strenuously then settled out of court in late 1994.) The Saudi participants are all friends of Fahd and while Adham has tried to exonerate himself by paying back $115 million, Ghaith Pharoan has been given official Saudi protection even though he is wanted for questioning in the UK and America. There were also important non-Saudi participants in the BCCI scandal, such as former Undersecretary of State Clark Clifford, who had been seduced by Saudi money. And the almost-forgotten silver scandal, the attempt by the Hunt brothers to corner the silver market, had a substantial Saudi aspect to it and the Fustuck in-laws of the House of Saud were involved. Now we have serious revelations of the Westland Helicopter scandal, the possible use of the US firm United Technologies' British associate to make payments to important Saudis to overcome the hurdles placed in its way by SEC and anti-corruption laws. (See Big Deals and Dangerous Games.)

These deeds demonstrate that Saudi corruption is international and infectious. America's laws and Congress are being undermined, the commodities market is revealed as vulnerable, an oil market controlled by Saudi Arabia is unreliable and American and British corporations and highly placed citizens are corruptible.

Under Fahd, when the Saudi throne is not directly involved, it is indirectly implicated through friends.

While it cannot be said that Saudi corruption and its consequences exist in an organized form, they continue to be the by-product of an atmosphere created, knowingly or through stupidity, by those in power. This is why, very often, some acts are discovered to be no more than the actions of lowly officials who wish to please their unknowing masters. One of the new ways this wish to please expresses itself is in the relatively recent kidnappings and violence perpetrated by operatives of branches of the Saudi Government.

In 1979, before Fahd became king but when he ran the day-to-day affairs of the country, the Saudis kidnapped the well-known Saudi writer Nasser Al Said from Beirut and took him to their country. They paid an associate of the PLO's Yasser Arafat $2 million to facilitate the kidnapping. As reported earlier, Al Said's fate is unknown, but the kidnapping was a clear violation of Lebanese sovereignty, provoked by Al Said's constant documentation of House of Saud crimes against its people. In 1984 the *Observer*, *Sunday Times*, *Washington Post* and the London-based Arabic weekly *Sourakia* reported the arrest at London's Gatwick Airport of one David Martindale. According to these reports, Martindale was carrying an Uzi automatic pistol and had come to London to assassinate the leader of the Muslim Sophist sect and Saudi opposition personality Shams Eddine Al Fassi. Martindale admitted receiving money to do the job (the figure changed several times) and was deported to the USA, where he was sentenced to 21 years in prison. Nothing was done about those he accused of paying him.

In another incident in late 1991, Muhammad Al Fassi, son of the already mentioned Shams Eddine, a Saudi citizen who openly opposed the Gulf War, was handed over to Saudi Arabia by the Jordanian authorities. Human rights organizations have protested about the illegal hand-overs, but to no avail. The appeals for his release produced a stark example of Saudi attempts to infiltrate the press and corrupt it (see The Last Line of Defence).

The use of these methods began under Fahd and has had an impact on the behaviour of Saudi and other journalists, writers and politicians opposed to the Saudi regime. Many of them have left the Arab countries where they had taken refuge because the Saudis are capable of kidnapping them or exerting pressure on the host countries to surrender them. Even in London, Saudi opposition people are afraid to give their telephone numbers and addresses and some of them used elaborate methods to determine that I was not a Saudi plant trying to assassinate them. The situation is brutally summed up in the words of Saudi writer Abdel Rahman Munif, the author of the monumental *Cities of Salt* trilogy: 'Exile doesn't guarantee safety.'

It is only fair to state that voices have been raised in objection to this massive, unprecedented and growing exercise in corruption. In addition to increased activity by Saudi opposition groups, former US Ambassador to Saudi Arabia James Akins has spoken and written about all this. And even the conservative former British Ambassador Sir James Craig wrote a two-hundred-page official critique which was leaked to the British press and provoked Saudi ire. Within the family, Foreign Minister Prince Saud Al Faisal has warned of the dire consequences of lack of reform. Of course, there are smaller voices, but the results of making a stand against corruption can be considerable. Protesting has not done Akins and Craig any good and it is one of the reasons behind the relegation of Prince Saud Al Faisal to a powerless functionary.

The concern of the objectors to life under Fahd is the overall deteriorating situation of the country. Recently, Fahd's imperious and unstoppable permissiveness has led him to divide and destabilize the House of Saud as never before. Because he flagrantly favours his children over other members of the family, he has crystallized the existence of several clans within the family as a whole and lost the support of his full brothers, the six who with him made up the Sudeiri seven. There are serious indications that Fahd wants his son Muhammad to succeed him and this is revealed in the most important and novel article in his proposed Consultative Council (Majlis Shura) charter which gives the King the right to appoint – and dismiss – his crown prince.

This blatant attempt to create a House of Fahd has not escaped his brothers Abdallah and Sultan (a Sudeiri), respectively the two people next in line to the throne. Abdallah is strengthening his National Guard power base and forming his own family group. Sultan is doing the same through his position as Minister of Defence. The late Faisal's sons are unhappy about the relegation of their brother Saud to a nonentity. King Saud's sons are also around and they have never forgiven Fahd for voting against their father.

These divisions in the ranks of the family weaken it and perhaps work against any family moves against Fahd. But they still strengthen the hand of the growing class of educated Saudis who are opposed to absolutism, the various Muslim fundamentalist movements and the Army in spearheading a change in government, through forming alliances among themselves or by using willing, disaffected members of the family as a front. In addition to the long list of abuses of the country by the House of Saud, there are new indisputable facts which suggest that this situation cannot continue for much longer:

- Despite its huge oil income, Saudi Arabia has run a budget deficit for 12 years and has begun to default on some internal and external contracts (bin Laden and Blount of the USA). The need to satisfy the countries which supported Saudi Arabia in the Gulf War will make this situation worse.
- Expenditure on defence uses 36 per cent of the country's income. Existing contracts to buy more military hardware will maintain it at this level, or higher, for the foreseeable future.
- All province governors are still members of the House of Saud or their Sudeiri in-laws.
- The demands of the family on the national budget are increasing because of the huge increase in their numbers and their insatiable appetites. Their growing involvement in commerce, and the Government support behind it, gives them an advantage which is adversely affecting the merchant class and alienating its members.
- Thirty per cent of the people still do not attend school. The budgets of the Ministries of Education and Health have been affected by a budgetary squeeze which has not affected expenditures on defence and the family.
- Little is being done to solve the problem of the water shortage which will develop early next century. The situation is so bad that it prompted Prince Tallal bin Abdel Aziz, the King's brother, to write to him warning of 'a disaster in the making'.
- The religious ulemas, aware of the people's unhappiness, have begun to object to the ways of the monarch and the monopoly on power and commerce held by his family and, in strong, uncompromising language, have petitioned him to change them.
- Afraid of Army-based conspiracies against him, Fahd has ordered the disarmament of all Saudi Air Force planes and the doubling of the number of security agents in all the armed forces.

As can be seen from this brief historical review, the basis of Saudi rule has changed little over time. To this day, the King rules supreme; the only change from the time of Ibn Saud is the potential for family interference to strengthen his will and the extent (but not the nature) of the assistance he gets from his relations. It is an unremarkable change forced by the existence of the potential for change, the greater numbers of family members and the remarkable increase in the country's wealth. (Having made my point, I see no substitute for using the word 'country'.)

The King of Saudi Arabia, in order of the importance he assigns to each of his functions, is head of the Al Saud family, the Prime Minister and chief executive of the Central Government, the Supreme Religious Imam, the Commander-in-Chief of the Armed Forces and the Chief Justice. With this type of unchecked control, the country's huge oil income is totally in Fahd's hands. Apart from the perfunctory need to appease the religious leaders, there are no executive, legislative or judicial authorities to questions his decisions. And because he controls the country's income and his position as head of the family comes first, describing Saudi Arabia as the world's largest family business becomes axiomatic. In 1984 each prince received a monthly salary of $20,000 and if he held a job or several then his official salary was an addition to his princely one, and both were additional to his commercial one if he was the head of a corporation. Naturally, the figure quoted was for lowly princes; important ones received considerably more. Also, the designation prince or princess applied to all members of the family, so an ordinary prince with ten children and two wives received $260,000 a month, and the top ones who were in the public eye and supposed to perform real or imaginary functions got as much as $100 million a year.

Although promises of major and minor reform have been made repeatedly since the death of Ibn Saud in 1953, very little has been done about it. Except for the influence of members of their family, all the powers inherent in the titles attached to the kings have a literal meaning and they do dismiss judges, generals and religious imams without having to justify their actions. It is well to remember that when confronted by an attempt to curtail his powers, King Saud, the one who succeeded his father only to be deposed by his family later, snapped back, 'I am not Queen Elizabeth – I am the King of Saudi Arabia.'

A brief examination of the qualifications of the Saudi kings to exercise the powers they assigned themselves is in order. When it comes to being the head religious figure, though members of the House of Saud observe most Islamic practices, none of the men who became king was trained to be an imam, a function requiring a high level of education and considerable intelligence. In addition, two of them drank heavily, something forbidden the average Muslim let alone a cleric. None of them would ever undergo the rigours of officer training or study military matters to become Commander-in-Chief. Three of the four kings were terribly overweight and all were quite sickly. And indeed their knowledge of the Sharia and Islamic justice was very shallow, rendering highly questionable their ability to preside over the judiciary or to appoint judges. (And Sharia laws are extremely elaborate.)

What Kings Saud, Faisal, Khalid and Fahd brought to the job were patterns of family behaviour bequeathed to them by their father and amended by their considerations of the family's increasing numbers and needs and the established tribal attitudes of the fanatic Wahhabis. Saud's wavering notwithstanding, whether what resulted from exercising power in accordance with these antiquated ways amounts to an extended individual rule, a family rule or a tribal rule, did not and does not alter the absolutism it produced. In fact family and tribal rule eventually became one and the same; the numbers of the House of Saud became big enough to make it a tribe.

Yet these absolute and obsolete family/tribal ways in which the House of Saud continues to govern are vulnerable and subject to change because they are not adequate to control the results of oil wealth and an evolving country. Tens of thousands of Saudis have received or are receiving higher education; there are three and a half million foreigners with infectious ideas working in the country and a citizen can buy a satellite dish and pick up television signals full of eye-opening information from all over the world. This is not to speak of ideological developments in neighbouring countries, the fact that the Middle East is full of Muslim fundamentalist and socialist ideas whose danger is made worse by the natural receptiveness of the Saudi people and the fact that some countries deliberately export such ideas to Saudi Arabia.

So far, despite the many pressures for change, what has prompted variation in the way the most valuable piece of personal real estate in the world is run has not been the desire of the kings or the family for it, but because no way has been found to protect against it. Many internal and outside stimuli for change have reached the point where they became impossible to resist. Totally opposed as they still are to any reduction in their control, the members of the House of Saud have resorted to accepting changes which are essentially cosmetic in nature. The aim is to ease the pressures by pretending change has taken place while obtaining the same old results through new or amended means.

On the external front, occasional pressures and fear of regional destabilization appear to have forced the House of Saud to extend aid to other Arab countries without regard to their political inclinations. But the budgets of Saudi Arabia have invariably revealed that much of the aid money allocated for 'pure', unselfish reasons with no strings attached has never been spent. The House of Saud has always managed to attach unacceptable conditions to them which amount to interference in the internal affairs of the recipient countries. It has often reneged on its supposedly humanitarian aid programme; in the case of aid to Lebanon and the Palestinian refugees, it has kept allocated funds because it could not find recipient organizations which would provide it with publicity and obey orders. On both the internal and external fronts, respectively creating a quasi-parliamentary consultative council and providing aid, what the House of Saud has managed to achieve is the semblance of doing something.

This type of superficial propaganda has gone beyond pretence. The House of Saud's present claim that it flies thousands of Muslims to do the Hajj at the King's personal expense is true only if his personal expense is different from the country's treasury. And it has given a lot of money to building mosques in the Arab and Muslim countries and in London, Brussels, Washington and Rome. Sponsoring the Hajj and building mosques have propaganda value and are not threatening – unlike building schools, something which the House of Saud has done considerably less of than other Arab oil producers. Even the aid money which has reached its targets has had a questionable, selfish reason behind it. The Saudis gave money to the Palestinians to stop them from veering left and to the Lebanese Christians to help them fight their radical Muslim fundamentalists, who frown on Saudi Arabia's Islamic veneer.

This conflict between pretence and fact makes it impossible to segment the 'governmental system' in terms of how it functions. What is 'analyzable' is what the country has purported to do, but what has actually happened is subject to constant change and has been motivated by a narrow self-interest which has expressed itself in the exclusive wish to preserve the household. All pretence aside, we are back to Ibn Saud.

It is because the House of Saud has constantly fabricated ephemeral responses to internal, Arab, Muslim and world pressures, that I find it difficult to assess its unwieldy 'policies'. The diversity and prospects of the pressures it has faced have been too wide and so have the improvised responses it has produced. The potential of encompassing what might happen and what the responses to them would be is impossible to reduce to a comprehensible analysis. To use realistic examples, a simple change in the government of a neighbouring Arab country could lead to a total change in the Saudi approach to Arab and regional affairs. For example, the emergence of an Islamic, radical and threatening Egypt could lead Saudi Arabia to re-befriend the presently detested Saddam Hussein of Iraq and the assassination or death of the present crown prince could open wide a contest for succession which could lead to civil war. With this in mind, the safest and soundest way to appreciate how the country has functioned and its prospects is to assume that the House of Saud has been in the business of self-protection and has held back progress and development and to look at the people who have run the country and how it has worked under them. In other words, to examine how the kings who followed Ibn Saud have tried to achieve the same goal of maintaining the place as a personal/family fiefdom through different means. Dangerous as it is, I leave it to the reader to think of all the things that could happen within and outside Saudi Arabia and the possible responses to them. A few examples are *coups d'état* in Arab countries producing threatening new regimes, a member of the family joining forces with the armed forces to eliminate corruption, a popular Islamic uprising against the unIslamic behaviour of members of the family. (Some of this speculation is detailed in Brotherhood is Selective.)

It is worth repeating that except for the presence of oil and Islam's two holiest shrines, in Mecca and Medina, Saudi Arabia still qualifies for the Roman name 'Arabia Deserta', a huge stretch of arid land that on a map of the world is a ghastly blank covered by shades of brown which denote barrenness. Historically, it was a land steeped in mystery, but the way its sources of importance have been used has generated enough interest to demystify it; oil and Islam are commodities whose importance has increased. The time for seeing the country as a remote little place with, in the words of Princess Alice of Athlone, 'attractive little chaps with tea towels on their heads', is no more. Even for those who still think of the Arab as simple and naive, there is enough at stake to warrant a close and critical look at Saudi Arabia.

What most of the world knows now is the country's unattractive face, the House of Saud as it is seen through cocktail-party stories, the wealthy, vulgar, corrupt people who run or own the place or both. The power of the image created by the everyday behaviour of members of the family, and the few others who have benefited enough from oil wealth to emulate them, is so total that the non-expert knows very little about the rest of the people of the country, not even their number. When the people of that huge expanse are thought about, they are reduced to abstractions with no face, and we are back to Princess Alice and her blinkered description.

There exists something of a conspiracy of silence regarding the people of Saudi Arabia; one in which their own government deliberately participates. Until a recent, highly questionable one whose results were undoubtedly exaggerated was conducted, the only population census in the history of the country was carried out in 1976. The complicated job cost about $100 million because of the vastness of the country and the use of aerial photography to track unsettled Bedouins who were on the move with the seasons. But the money paid to conduct the census was wasted. The House of Saud has never published the results of this huge and sophisticated effort. The reason is simple: the census produced a smaller figure than had been anticipated or estimated. To the House of Saud, a small population – and there is reason, based on word-of-mouth reports by Saudi officials, to believe the census produced a figure of seven million people – meant a vulnerable country which could not defend itself, supposedly an inherent weakness which might have encouraged anti-House of Saud forces within and outside its borders.

Fear also stood in the way of publishing any figures of the number of people who belonged to the ruling minority Wahhabi sect and of the downtrodden but considerably larger Shia community who continue to suffer the fate of 'heretics' – 20 and 15 per cent, respectively. And in fact it is Western fear of upsetting and eventually undermining the House of Saud, the people who control and supply the oil, which still stands in the way of the rest of the world giving a thought to the people in Saudi Arabia as a whole, or in terms of some particularly suffering parts.

It was a similar fear of what the native Saudis and others might say which prompted the House of Saud not to publish the 1991 budget, the one which would have exposed the records of the vast sums of money, at least $60 billion, they paid out to get other countries to join them in the Gulf War (to eliminate the fear of Saddam Hussein). And it was this same fear which prompted the family to cover up the many coups and assassination attempts against them except when such attempts became too widely known to ignore. Then they had to respond to the stories by successfully presenting their highly doctored versions of events which create the image of a country full of happiness. But while fear has been behind everything the House of Saud has done, including hiding the figures of the family budget, it has not had to be real and it has often resembled the reaction of someone who suspects the worst because he is insecure. For example, in today's Saudi Arabia, nobody can object to a policeman issuing him a traffic ticket without being accused of belonging to a subversive political party, reading French books is definitely frowned on and simple worship by Christian workers produces incredibly stiff prison sentences. (All political parties are subversive and banned, the French are regarded as degenerate and those in power are determined to outdo the Muslim fundamentalists, who object to all Christian presence in the country.) It is a paranoid family rule, insecure in its ways.

The House of Saud has committed itself and the enormous wealth of the country to continue what it has maintained for most of this century. In this regard, a cursory review of the recent reports of the human rights organizations Amnesty International, Article 19 and Middle East Watch confirms the continued use of the most brutal methods to maintain barriers against change.

Internally, there is no freedom of the press and criticism of the royal family, the Government and religious figures is against the law. As will be discussed later, the Government's control of the press is so tight that it took two days before it allowed newspapers to report the Iraqi invasion of Kuwait. Not for the first time, the people of Saudi Arabia were confused by international media reports which spoke of something which the Government concealed. (See The Last Line of Defence for a detailed analysis of how the authorities handle the Saudi and Arab press.)

Saudi women do not have the same rights as men, and they are not allowed to drive cars, travel alone or be secretaries. A woman is essentially a non-person and, engagingly, her husband is responsible for her behaviour, including her debts, even if the couple are separated. A number of female college professors, many of them with PhDs, who in 1991 conducted a group drive to protest against the laws which forbid them to be licensed to do it legally, lost their jobs and some were arrested, tried and imprisoned. In some cases, their husbands were threatened with physical violence. The husband's responsibility goes further and the estranged wife of one of my relatives ran up bills of hundreds of thousands of dollars which my brother was unable to stop but had to pay.

Political parties are illegal and so is the right of peaceable assembly. Members of CAVES (Committee for the Advancement of Virtue and Elimination of Sin) have been known to walk in on dinner parties to determine whether the guests, even when their numbers are no more than four or five, are indulging in political discussion. The people look over their shoulders and mention the King and members of his family in whispers and referring to them without affixing respectful titles can lead to stiff jail sentences.

All non-Muslim religious manifestations, including wearing a crucifix, are against the law and foreign workers, who represent one in four of the population, have very few rights: American and British citizens have been arrested for celebrating Christmas and Yemeni and Pakistani workers accused of minor crimes have disappeared in Saudi prisons without trace. There is no academic freedom and question-and-answer sessions between teachers and students are deemed dangerous and have been known to lead to the arrest of both. Although the Koran is the constitution of the land, even this wide, inexact and basically generous method of determining things is restricted further by the fact that the Wahhabi interpretation of the Koran is the only one acceptable. Among many others, a 40-year-old woman, Zahra Al Nasser, died in detention for carrying a Shia prayer book. Ali Salman Al-Ammar, 16, was detained for two years for the same reason, and a Shia religious student, Sadiq Al Illah, was executed for heresy. Even a book called *Development of Arab Family Structures* is banned and during the Gulf War *Time*, *Newsweek*, the *Independent*, *Le Point*, *Le Monde* and dozens of Arabic newspapers and magazines and ones from Muslim countries, including titles sponsored by and beholden to the House of Saud, were banned.

The House of Saud's attitude towards fellow Arabs is not a subject to be documented by human rights organizations except insofar as it affects Arabs living in Saudi Arabia when, like all foreigners, they are not afforded whatever meagre rights are accorded Saudi citizens. As will be seen in the following chapter, some have been deported for not being respectful enough in the presence of a lowly but full-of-himself bureaucrat, women have been beaten with sticks for not dressing modestly and others found themselves without residence visas because their Saudi employers objected to their asking for salary increases.

In addition, Saudi Arabia materially opposes the existence of political parties, parliaments, a free press, the granting of rights to women and the ownership of pets (most are profane and owning them is against Islam). Official pressure was exerted on Kuwait and Bahrain to stop them holding parliamentary elections; the Saudis threatened to cut off aid until the Lebanese Government imprisoned some critical journalists; Arabs working in Saudi Arabia are discouraged from having their wives join them there for fear they might teach Saudi women a thing or two and pressure has been applied to ban alcoholic drinks on all Arab airlines. The darkness which envelops Saudi Arabia is being geographically extended through the use of money to influence other Arab countries.

Violations of any of these unwritten rules governing Saudi Arabia's relationships with other Arab countries are considered dangerous because what others do is deemed infectious. Such offences to the Saudi Stone Age sensibilities have been met with unjustified and mostly unannounced retaliatory actions which have included the cancellation of aid programmes and the refusal to grant citizens of the 'guilty' country entry visas and work permits. The Yemen's refusal to accommodate Saudi pressure to support their Gulf War stance led to the deportation of 800,000 Yemeni workers and the near destruction of the Yemeni economy.

When the Saudi Government tries to justify its actions, it consistently resorts to substitute reasons acceptable to the international community and the rest of the time it gives no reason whatsoever. But a good way to judge how angry Saudi Arabia behaves with a fellow Arab country is to examine how it limits the number of visas issued to its citizens to work in Saudi Arabia and the amount of 'allocated' aid which is never remitted.

The Saudi treatment of the Muslim countries resembles that given to the Arab countries. Recently the House of Saud has taken to pressuring the Muslim countries into banning drink – curious when you remember that most members of the House of Saud, including Fahd, drink heavily. The Saudis also try to induce fellow Muslims to curtail the educational curriculum for women. Certainly anything which includes sports is disapproved of, but naturally the House of Saud has swimming pools where its female members indulge regularly and hold parties. Again, this is no more than a demonstration of Saudi Arabia trying to hold back Muslim countries because changes in them might be emulated by its own increasingly unhappy people.

In the larger international arena, particularly in terms of its special relationship with America and Britain, the House of Saud's policy is again to hold the line against change. This means attempting to maintain the blind support which it has traditionally received from its 'allies'. Neutralizing the sources of Arab and Muslim pressure automatically increases the importance of maintaining Western support. Here again the Saudis use their wealth to perpetuate the inclination of America and other Western countries to ignore their misdeeds, though in this case mostly in an indirect way. The House of Saud is willing to provide the world with cheap oil and political support in their problems with the Arabs and Muslims in return for the elimination of all criticism. It goes further and uses the awarding of huge defence contracts for the same purpose. (See Big Deals and Dangerous Games.) In reality, the twin policy of using oil and awarding defence contracts is no more than blackmail; they protect the Western economies from high oil prices and buy their arms in return for silence. (I cannot unearth a single public statement by a Western leader about the country's abominable human rights record and only Kennedy objected to it, and that secretly.)

In its internal behaviour and relations with all outside powers, the House of Saud's policies are negative, an attempt at protecting their piece of property, an improvised response to fear. Realistically, even the low price of oil and the huge defence contracts are only possible at the expense of the greater and obviously pressing needs of the people. (Among other problems, the Saudis suffer from the second-highest rate of blindness in the world.) Here, a simple formula is necessary to explain why the very ordinary Saudi, who is often illiterate, is for increasing the price of oil. If the present price of oil is $20 a barrel and the personal expenses of the House of Saud (estimated at over $7 billion a year) and defence costs use half of that, then a $5 increase in the price of oil increases what is left for the people by 50 per cent and not by the purely mathematical 25 per cent. But the House of Saud would rather keep the West as friends and protectors than satisfy its own people.

In return for keeping the price of oil down and resisting all OPEC pressure to do the opposite (see Oil, OPEC and the Overseers), America has supplied Saudi Arabia with F-15 fighters, C-130 transports, AWACS, Harpoon, Stinger and Patriot missiles, M-60 and Abrams tanks, as well as less sophisticated pieces of military hardware and military training. To protect against internal unrest, the House of Saud was supplied with an elaborate electronic monitoring system which records every single telephone call in the country (the problem is to decide which ones to recall and decipher). Major CIA agents were seconded to the country to occupy sensitive positions which would allow them to monitor developments at close range. And all these acts were encapsulated in unconditional statements of support by Nixon, Carter, Ford, Reagan and Bush, as well as Kissinger and Baker, guaranteeing the national integrity of the country.

What had existed before, a relationship of interdependence, was elevated to an unratified but open and unconditional alliance underwritten by presidential guarantees. Any internal or external attempts to change the Saudi Government without its approval would be met with the military might of the United States. Except for situations which cannot be defeated by America's armed might, the House of Saud became totally secure and set in its ways.

After 11 years of King Fahd, the transformation of the country is complete. The multi-function family controls everything inside the country. America is there to deal with outside problems and to apply its talents to all things the House of Saud cannot handle. The change from Ibn Saud has not affected the political fate of the people of the country and his ways have been extended to cover new questions (such as expatriate labour). The new sword in the hands of the House of Saud is made in the USA.

4

A Place Like No Other

The British call them lords; the French, Belgians and others prefer counts; the Poles and Spaniards favour dukes; regular Arabs have sheikhs and Turkey and Iran have their agas, beys, pashas and the rest. Saudi Arabia's notable contribution in the field of titles is to call one of their princes Muhammad Twin-Evil, in Arabic Muhammad Abu Sharain.

He died in 1988, the sixth of Ibn Saud's sons, and his nickname was so apt that it was used by members of his own family. The twin evils which earned him his reputation were booze and violence. He was an alcoholic who, in a rare moment of recognition, gave up his right to the throne in favour of his younger brother Khalid. So violent was his temper that he instilled fear in the hearts of members of his family, including all his brothers who became kings.

Twin-Evil's first memorable act happened in 1929. He personally machine-gunned dozens of Ikhwan rebels after they surrendered to his father. Afterwards his individual acts of violence continued unabated. In 1936, in London to attend the coronation of George VI, he slapped a bar girl so hard that he knocked out some of her teeth. (Naturally, there was a cover-up). Later, in 1945, he accompanied his father and the American Minister to Saudi Arabia, William Eddy, on the USS *Murphy* to meet President Roosevelt. On hearing that the ship had some risqué films, he asked to see them and insisted on watching them all the time. When Eddy objected, Twin-Evil's response was to ask him whether he would like to be killed immediately or chopped in small pieces bit by bit later. Eddy smiled and accommodated him.

In the years which followed, the family overlooked Twin-Evil's murderous ways. When his older brothers died, this thug was elevated to the role of elder statesman of the family. He was the one who delivered the demand to his brother Saud to step down, and he did it by throwing the piece of paper in his face. Later he figured considerably in the succession process – again by issuing personal threats. He was a law unto himself and regularly demanded, and got, several hundreds of thousands of barrels of oil to sell on the free market to meet his expenses. And, following the maxim of like attracts like, he used ignorant people to carry his offers to international markets without knowing their significance. (See Oil, OPEC and the Overseers.)

Throughout all this, the local press was helpless and the Arab press feared that criticizing an important Saudi royal would affect their countries' relations with Saudi Arabia, while Western reporters and 'historians' maintained their conspiracy of silence. Then, out of nowhere, we got to know him. Twin-Evil ordered the execution of his own granddaughter.

The film *Death of a Princess* did more to expose the corruption of the House of Saud than any article, tract, book or documentary this century. It depicted the love affair and tragic end of Princess Mishaal, Prince Muhammad's granddaughter, and one Muhammad Al Shaer. The Princess had been educated in Beirut and exposed to modernity, and then was 'given away' in marriage to a first cousin at the early age of 17. The cousin, in the true fashion of the House of Saud, proceeded to ignore her and, when she protested, divorced her. Travelling in Europe, the Princess fell in love with a young Lebanese whose family has solid Saudi connections (his uncle is the present Saudi Minister of Information).

When the Princess's family refused to grant her permission to marry her lover, she tried to escape the country disguised as a boy. She was recognized and brought home. Sometime later, her lover managed to enter the country and she met him in a Jeddah hotel using a pseudonym. They were caught and, on the orders of her grandfather, imprisoned.

Twin-Evil demanded that his brother, King Khalid, sentence the girl and her lover to death. Khalid demurred. Twin-Evil turned to Jeddah's head imam and demanded that he issue a sentence of death. The imam wanted to conduct an inquiry into the case but Muhammad lost all patience and issued a personal order to have his granddaughter executed. When the executioner expressed doubts about the procedure, claiming that he needed the order of a religious judge, Muhammad again acted on his own: he ordered his own guards to do the job.

It was July 1977 and Jeddah was obscured by haze, the heat and dust of the desert. Princess Mishaal was pushed into a square at the edge of town. Her lover, hands tied behind his back, followed her.

To the surprise of the spectators who flocked to what people in Jeddah call 'Chop Square' to get the morbid satisfaction of seeing the justice of the House of Saud carried out, the unknown young girl was shot dead while her lover looked straight at her. A moment later, the young man was beheaded and dismembered. Shooting a person and dismembering a dead body were unusual, but nobody knew who they were and nobody cared. Two days later the royal family, without fanfare, announced that Princess Mishaal had died in a drowning accident.

Rosemary Beacheau, Princess Mishaal's German nanny, knew everything, including the fabricated drowning story. She had loved her little ward and in one of those blessed triumphs of the human spirit, she vowed to do something about her death. Beacheau found a kindred spirit in the estranged wife of one of the princes, an educated Lebanese woman with wide connections. They went to work.

Early in 1980 news began circulating in London of a mysterious diplomatic crisis between Britain and Saudi Arabia. Soon the crisis had a name: the television company ATV was planning to screen a film called *Death of a Princess*. The princess did not have a name, but the Saudi Government was applying diplomatic and economic pressures to stop the airing of the film.

When requests to the British Foreign Office to stop the televising of the film met with the usual response about Her Majesty's Government's inability to interfere with the freedom of the press, the Saudis approached the film's producer, Anthony Thomas. He screened the film for them, refused an offer of money to kill it and would not even entertain editorial suggestions. Even so, he tried to keep the peace and never discussed the Saudi pressure and offers until the situation got completely out of hand.

The Saudis' frustration and ignorance drove them to foolish action. They recalled their ambassador to the UK and asked it to recall its ambassador, Sir James Craig. They threatened economic retaliation, including the cancellation of defence contracts and a boycott of British companies. When the British press took exception to its high-handedness, the House of Saud spent tens of millions of dollars sponsoring Arab and Muslim press attacks on Britain. There were headlines such as 'A Snake Called Britain', 'A Film Full of Lies', 'A New Crusade Against Islam', 'A Racist Attack on the Arabs' and the whole mud-slinging match reached a new low. One Arabic newspaper claimed that the British were a nation of thieves and said that the contents of the British Museum were all stolen, while another hinted that all female members of the British royal family were tarts.

Simultaneously the Saudis continued to exert diplomatic pressure. They prevailed on the Arab ambassadors in London to make a joint diplomatic protest. The General Secretariat of the Islamic Conference and other Muslim organizations lodged more protests, claiming the film was an insult to Islam, a sponsored Pakistani film director spoke of making a film about the life of Princess Margaret and the number of Saudi tourists to London fell by 70 per cent.

The film was shown on London's Independent Television on 9 March 1980. When plans to show it in the Netherlands, America and other countries were announced, Saudi Arabia mounted fresh efforts to stop it. It threatened to stop shipping oil to Rotterdam, and in America, Mobil Oil suspended its donations to the Public Broadcasting System and ran a six-page advertising campaign criticizing the film and lamenting its effects on American–Saudi relations. Predictably, the Saudis lost the war of the film, though some local American affiliates of the Public Broadcasting Corporation shamefully refused to carry it for fear of alienating the Saudis and causing an increase in oil prices.

It is worth examining the results of the execution and the consequent battle of the film. The Saudis demonstrated their ability to influence, or more accurately 'buy', Arab and Muslim private and public support. The prospect of economic pressure made the Arab countries afraid not to support Saudi Arabia and the Arab press followed a totally Saudi line. The Muslim countries and press were not far behind. With the Arabs and Muslims in harness, the Saudis tried to extend their influence to the Western press through the use of some sponsored Western journalists, economic blackmail and the influence of the oil companies.

It was one of the most expensive failures in the history of Saudi Arabia. A Lebanese journalist friend estimates that the payments to the Arab and Muslim press exceeded $50 million. Another source estimates at $300 million payments made to Arab and Muslim governments to gain their support. The partial break in trade relations with Britain was costly for the Saudis, and sending delegations to lobby against the film all over the world was not cheap either. The various Arab and Muslim film makers who threatened retaliation pocketed Saudi money and did nothing. By the time the episode was over, *Death of a Princess* had cost the Saudis a minimum of $500 million and exposed their brutal ways.

But the way the House of Saud behaved over the film was in character and, as chance would have it, it soon demonstrated that its members are people who never learn. Eight months after the airing of *Death of a Princess*, another prince approached King Khalid asking approval to have his adulterous daughter executed. The King, fearing a repeat publicity scandal, turned down the request, but suggested to his brother that he should handle the matter himself. The brother obliged. He took his daughter swimming in the sheltered pool of his palace and drowned her. The House of Saud claimed it was another accident. The murdering father has been married 36 times. The only attaché at the American Embassy to talk about it was told to shut up.

On 4 June 1992, in a more typical incident involving money, the wire services carried a terse announcement by the Diners Club Division of Citicorp. According to this announcement, the Diners Club was ceasing to operate in Saudi Arabia forthwith and the reasons given alluded to financial instability in the country. Everybody who read the announcement gasped with amazement, until they discovered the reason for it and gasped even harder.

The prince behind this incident was Walid bin Tallal, holder of 4.85 per cent of the outstanding shares of Citicorp, which he had purchased for a staggering $585 million. The problem between the corporation and its major shareholder was simple: His Highness, who had been appointed an agent for Diners Club, refused to honour $30 million worth of charges in his country. Citicorp's response was equally simple: Prince Walid was responsible for these charges and they had to be paid.

Behind the Prince's response was typical House of Saud thinking. He stated that he had distributed a number of Diners Club cards to members of his family as a promotion and that the recipients proceeded to use them without knowing that they had to pay for their purchases. They bought everything in sight. Prince Walid, in sympathy with the ways of his relatives, for a long time felt no obligation to pay.

There is very little Diners Club can do except cease to operate in the kingdom. Suing the Prince in Saudi Arabia is useless: 'Saudi law' governs the agreement.

There are other startling examples of how this state-sponsored immunity from prosecution works. I am in possession of documents which reveal a new twist to the old game. Prince Muhammad bin Saud borrowed over $4 million from a French company to build the Nassaria Hotel in Riyadh and then sold it profitably, but decided not to repay the loan. The lawyer for the French lender and French Government guarantor, Crédit Industriel et Commercial and Coface, had no recourse but to appeal to senior members of the family for settlement of the debt. Despite years of pleading, the creditors have so far got nowhere and Prince Muhammad is alive and well in Saudi Arabia.

On another occasion which documents the spread of this protection racket to include family friends, Prince Ahmad bin Abdel Aziz, the Deputy Minister of the Interior, used the power of his office to absolve one Muhammad Kaid, a Saudi businessman who had borrowed money from Lloyds Bank in London under false pretences and again over $4 million were lost to outside creditors. Kaid used phoney bank guarantees originating in Saudi Arabia to do the same in France. These are not isolated incidents and big and small examples of officially protected irresponsible behaviour abound. Some border on the unbelievably flagrant.

Two years ago, a sister-in-law of King Fahd bought £40,000 worth of knickers from a shop in London's Knightsbridge and had them delivered to her hotel suite. She proceeded to evade the shop's owners, who were demanding payment. They got their money only after a strongly worded complaint to the Saudi Embassy which raised the matter with His Majesty, who agreed to act as a knickers problem solver and paid the money. In 1986 in Paris, Princess Nouf, the daughter of the late King Khalid, and her entourage caused several million dollars' worth of damage to the St Régis Hotel which the Saudi Government paid. Some of these acts of extravagance represent an official approach to things, and in 1986 the *Washington Post* reported that Prince Bandar, the Saudi Ambassador to the USA, gave a party that cost $500,000.

In Saudi Arabia itself, a province emir demanded a payment of $3 million from the Saudi agents of a Swedish building contractor because the company was doing good business in 'his territory'. When the agents objected, claiming that their total profit from dealing with this company amounted to $2 million, the emir told them that refusal to pay meant forcing the owner of the company to leave the country. The demand was met.

Today, in as contradictory a statement on human behaviour as is conceivable, it is the very few well-behaved members of the royal family who are pointed out as exceptions and who earn comments like, 'He's a Saudi prince but he's polite' or 'He's a Saudi prince but he doesn't gamble.' But the majority of them are covered by the sick joke of a Saudi businessman who told me: 'I am for executing adulterers – it's the surest way of getting rid of the whole royal family.'

There are other seemingly innocent manifestations of this overall royal lack of concern which are plentiful within Saudi Arabia and are not presently newsworthy, but which are full of unhappy auguries for the future. The maternity ward of the King Faisal Hospital in Riyadh has turned away emergency delivery cases because it was busy handling dozens of new arrivals of the House of Saud who have priority regardless of the seriousness of other cases. More interestingly, the females of the royal household, who usually occupy a background position, have come into their own as expressions of the royal malaise. Not only are they the pioneers of telephone sex, but according to doctors and others who have served in the kingdom they suffer from severe psychosomatic illnesses. Dr Seymour Gray, who practised in Saudi Arabia for several years, attributes their mental maladies to general boredom, insecurity because their husbands are always marrying additional women, sexual frustration and the closed nature of a society which forbids them to do anything – even social work. Dr Gray and others support a suggestion made in the film *Death of a Princess* and claim that many princesses take lovers from among their servants. There are other men who service them for money. A greater number of the princesses live on coffee and tranquillizers and some react to male neglect by turning lesbian. Most of this is caused by the maltreatment they suffer from male members of their family, who educate them and then expect them to become vegetables.

Perhaps a more important aspect of the lives of the princes and princesses of the royal household has to do with their education. Their parents follow family fashion and have them tutored but their tutors are afraid to ask them to study or to apply any discipline. In the words of a former tutor: 'How do you tell one of them to study harder and keep your job – or your head?' The results of this undisciplined education are obvious: the level of learning among members of the House of Saud remains appallingly low, and many foreign universities turn them down when they discover how ill-prepared for higher education they are. (Suspicion lurks that the level of education among the royal family is lower than that of Saudi Arabia as a whole.)

Personal behaviour is only one facet of how the Saudi royals manifest the inherent unsoundness of the 'system' over which King Fahd presides. Their official behaviour, though more subject to exposure, is unashamedly the same. Every House of Saud minister or province emir has a diwan in which he conducts a majlis, a royal court in which he dispenses justice once a week. Naturally, the King's diwan is the largest in the land, but the others have adopted this institution to enhance their status. An examination of how they conduct themselves in their open houses reveals a great deal.

Most diwans are the same, physically and in character and function. Most of them are 30 feet wide and 60 feet long and, with an abundance of chandeliers, they resemble what Ibn Saud started. The average number of people who come to a majlis is 150 and they attend to air their grievances and seek redress from the prince. The only things he cannot handle are some small commercial matters and things which go to whatever courts exist automatically. Otherwise, there are no limitations on his power as judge.

Some of the princes who administer this judicial power are in their twenties and thirties and their lack of experience is matched by a lack of education. One province prince who now plays judge was my classmate for a while, until he got stuck in the same form for four years and failed to finish high school. Another never went to school. These deficiencies do not seem to matter. Belonging to the family is the only qualification required.

In 1986 the general manager of a major Saudi hotel, part of an international chain, went to see the local province prince regarding one of his employees, a Filipino bellboy, who had been arrested by members of CAVES. The manager entered the diwan and sat down until his turn to speak came. He handed over a piece of paper containing his name and occupation and a statement about the case, but stood up and made an oral presentation which elaborated the paper's contents.

'May you live long, one of my employees, a poor Filipino boy of 17, was arrested by members of the Mutawa [another name for CAVES] three months ago for wearing indecent clothes. I do not question their right or judgement, but my initial enquiries indicated that he would be released in four weeks. My subsequent enquiries produced similar promises, but nothing has happened. May you live long, I am here to enquire about the boy's fate. And upon my honour, I'll see to it that the boy behaves in accordance with the blessed laws of Islam in the future.'

The man remained standing to hear the Prince's response.

'What was the exact nature of his crime, what kind of clothes did he wear?'

'May you live long, he wore his shirt immodestly. It was open in the front and exposed parts of his body it shouldn't have and he was wearing gold objects around his neck.'

'Is he a good looking boy?'

'He's not bad looking, sir.'

'Then you'll never see him again.'

The laughter was loud and long; the petitioner, still standing, joined in to protect himself. The Prince, visibly enjoying himself, spoke again.

'You need not bother about your employee. Sooner or later they'll find him and send him home to his mother. There is no question of his returning to work. We cannot permit loose men like him to infect our country with their ways.'

The manager thanked the Prince and left. To this day, he has no idea what happened to the boy. When not in Saudi Arabia, the Prince wears Western clothes, frequents nightclubs to chase blondes and drinks like a fish. In Saudi Arabia he drinks in private and marries often.

Two years later, in Riyadh, in the middle of the country, a Lebanese journalist who is in the pay of the House of Saud attended a majlis of Prince Salman, the Emir of Riyadh and head of the House of Saud's family council. Initially the journalist occupied the seat of honour, to the right of the Prince, but continued to make way for important people as they arrived and was soon at the other end of the diwan. Behind Prince Salman stood a tall black guard with a sword and a gun. Following is the report of the journalist:

'Everything big and small is handled in a majlis. Believe me, there was a blind man who was there to petition the Prince to allow him to have a driver's licence. He was questioned in an amusing way then dismissed. Some Bedouins spoke to the Prince and they addressed him by his first name, the way Bedouins have called rulers since the Prophet Muhammad. The House of Saud claim the majlis is their way of staying in direct touch with the people, and in a way an open house serves this purpose. But damn it, though Salman is probably the best among them, the whole thing is arbitrary and some aspects of it are most unattractive. Let me give you some examples.

'There was a seventy-year-old man, a Saudi from Riyadh. He had married a 15-year-old-girl in Cairo and, because marrying a foreigner needs special permission, he wanted to bring his Egyptian bride home. The old so-and-so turned out to be a regular at the majlis and it led to an amusing exchange between him and the Prince.

'The Prince: "But, old man, are you able to support your young bride?"

'The old man: "No, no, but I told her we have a generous Prince and she'll never need as long as he's alive."

'The Prince laughed. "How many times have you been married?"

'"A mere eleven, may you live long, but I promise this will be the last time."

'"But you have made this promise before?"

'"I do remember, Allah bless you, but I do not think I can go beyond this beautiful thing."

'Everybody laughed. The Prince issued an order approving the marriage and granted the old man funds to bring his bride home.

'But it isn't funny most of the time. Later, in the same majlis, there was a delegation of Korean and Filipino workers. They came to petition the Prince because their Saudi employer hadn't paid their salaries for two months and they didn't have money to eat. The Prince had heard about the case and he wasn't amused. He asked the spokesmen for the delegation whether it was true that they had demonstrated against their employer. When they admitted that they had, he ordered them deported from the country. He saw their action as a disturbance of the local peace which superseded the gravity of their grievance.

'Even later that day, an American banker appeared in front of the Prince and his case showed how uneven the majlis's ways can be. He had had an automobile accident with a Saudi in which the latter died.

'Unaccustomed to the way a majlis works, the banker proceeded to explain the accident; he blamed the Saudi driver and claimed that he had no driver's licence. The Prince moved his hand in a motion which asked the American to stop and ordered him to pay a sum of money to the victim's family. In the final analysis, the rights and wrongs of the case as we understand them and as they would have been judged by an insurance company didn't matter – what counted was the death of the Saudi driver.

'What is wrong with a majlis is beyond the obvious and by that I mean the lack of pattern, precedence and the competence of a prince. What is wrong with it is the freedom of the person who renders judgement, that he is not bound by a recognizable law. Take big cases where both sides of an argument are heard. If you analyze them, you'll find that their friends always come out ahead. And if their friends are ahead, then think of the fact that you can't lodge a complaint against any of them, or indeed about their officials. The closer you get to them the less effective the law becomes. So: who do you go to and how do you go about it? No way, they're immune.

'Yes, injustice is inherent in the system. It is completely out of date and certainly cannot cope with the complex problems of one of the wealthiest countries in the world. Do you remember the joke about the Saudi who snatched the purse of a woman with his right hand and when a policeman caught up with him the man kicked him with his left foot and they amputated his right arm and left leg. That's it, the majlis has no vision. What you need is something flexible to deal with a country racked by the pace of change.'

Another observer of the majlis and the pace of change racking the country was the writer Peter Theroux, whose book *Sandstorm* is one of the better existing records of the unreality of Saudi Arabia. Theroux's judgement on the majlis supports and intellectualizes the opinions of my Lebanese journalist friend: 'They [the petitioners] gave the Prince all their rights. It was medieval sight, a tableau of cynical patronage.'

The new slave state started in the late 1950s. Egyptian teachers, Syrian and Lebanese doctors, Palestinian businessmen and Yemeni shop owners began arriving in Saudi Arabia in pursuit of the petro-dollar. Their numbers were small and most of the time they left their families behind because there was no accommodation for them and whatever existed was expensive. In addition, living in a country that lagged considerably behind their place of origin carried with it the prospect of sociological dislocation and shock. Those who made the move used to resurface from Saudi Arabia every year or so on long leaves, telling stories about the horror of it all. They spoke of the merciless heat: 'the sun is only a few yards away'; the summary executions carried out by bin Jalawi; rare diseases including a rampant non-fatal syphilis and general orthopaedic weaknesses (bone problems because of lack of calcium); the lack of sanitation and amenities, which did not bother the native Saudi; the strange ways of the majlis; and the loneliness of living in 'a desert camp'. Those among them who used alcoholic beverages came back behaving as if they were out to quench a desert thirst; they drank beer because alcohol was available through local stills. The Americans who worked for ARAMCO developed a local hooch called *sidiki*, or 'friend', and their attempts to make it drinkable went as far as flavouring it with mint and fruit tastes.

Overall, the expatriates looked down on the Saudis and their Bedouin ways, while their hosts accused them of greed, haughtiness and of being effete city slickers who 'ate with their mouths closed, just like goats'. Despite all the difficulties – and they were bad enough to warrant an unhappy report by the British diplomatic mission in 1955 – it was a clear-cut supply-and-demand relationship and both sides were joined by a common language and, for the most part, a common religion. Both sides had an interest in limiting the damage.

In the 1960s Saudi Arabia's need for human resources expanded and accountants, clerks, mechanics and artisans began arriving. This group was a mixture of Arabs and Muslims from Pakistan, India and Iran. Unlike teachers and doctors, these professional groups were employed by individuals and new Saudi companies and their activities were often subject to the whims of employers, which meant unreasonable demands as to the amount of time they spent working, less attractive job benefits and shorter holidays.

'He couldn't understand why I wouldn't spend 16 hours a day working on the books,' says an accountant about his former Saudi employer, and adds: 'to him, I was there to work and not to live.' A Kurdish Lebanese mechanic who managed to survive five years of lucrative hardship had a different problem: 'The higher up they were, the more unreasonable they were. They wanted their cars back in the shortest possible time, regardless of what was wrong with them or how badly they had bashed them. To them, if you're a mechanic then you should be able to fix any car problem in a few minutes.' Even a sympathetic Saudi offers his own lament and says: 'Most of us treated them like robots; it wasn't a healthy situation.'

This group of new expatriates numbered about 300,000 and did not receive the respect accorded their predecessors. Also, because they reacted negatively to the demands of the work, social pressures and loneliness, their relationship with their hosts was openly unfriendly. There was no middle ground, and the worse one side behaved the worse was the reaction of the other. In the end the expats settled for calling the Saudis *wohoush* (beasts) or *klab* (dogs) and the Saudis responded by refusing to use the polite 'brother', 'mister' or their professional appellations when addressing them. They lived in small rooms offering little comfort and no television set. In a way, the old slavery which was abolished in 1962 was replaced by this new version, almost simultaneously.

From the late 1960s, except for the suave Lebanese and Palestinian deal-makers and wheeler-dealers (see Big Deals and Dangerous Games), most of the arrivals were Yemenis or non-Arabs. The Yemenis, a proud, hardworking people, provided street sweepers, coffee and errand boys, servants and more shopkeepers. A high proportion of the rest were Thai nannies, Filipino bellboys and waiters, Korean construction workers and Somali and Ethiopian, Indian and Sri Lankan servants and menial workers. The numbers of this group multiplied in proportion to the growing wealth of the country and by the time of the 1973 oil shock, there were over a million of them.

The tensions which began with the first arrivals and were heightened with the second wave of expatriates grew much worse. Often there were language and cultural problems. The Saudis could not understand the discipline of the Korean construction workers who lined up every morning to salute their flag; they saw the natural subservience of the Filipinos as licence to abuse them and did not understand the requests of Thai nannies to have time off, leave the house or visit other lonely compatriots. But it went further, for as usual having money led to xenophobia and arrogance, and people who had lived in a tent until recently did not know how to treat their helpers. To them they were real slaves. Now the total number of foreign workers in Saudi Arabia, the people commonly described as expatriates, is over three million people, over one third of the indigenous population of the country.

It was not merely a case of abuse by individual Saudis which created the new slavery. The inherent unkindness of the Saudi *nouveaux riches* was compounded by the laws enacted to govern this situation and by the emergence of a new class of labour suppliers who traded mercilessly in human commodities. A number of laws were introduced which purported to protect imported labour. The Saudi Government also went as far as to sign unilateral agreements with some countries, but essentially what superseded all the humane articles of the imported-labour laws were the articles which were aimed at protecting the rights of the Saudi employers. This overriding consideration made the laws exacerbate rather than ease the results of the master-and-slave relationship which had developed. The story of foreign workers is

one of the saddest and cruellest episodes in the history of a country
which has produced more than its share of sadness and cruelty.

There are two major elements of official Saudi policy which
contribute to foreign workers' wretchedness. Saudi law allows
the employer total control of his imported labour and definition
of their job function and how it is to be performed. Some workers
are brought in by Saudi employers in the thousands and then
'retailed' in smaller numbers to others. Workers cannot change
employment without a 'release' from the employer who imports
them, which means that they can be retailed a second and a third
time after a certain job is finished and they revert to their importer.
Sometimes the retailer's margin goes up with every transaction and
a labourer gets less after spending five and six years in Saudi Arabia
than when he or she first arrived. If we add the fact that imported
labourers come from countries which, because of dependence on
Saudi financial help or other considerations, cannot afford them
the barest protection, and the fact that they receive considerably
lower wages than their Saudi counterparts, then we end up with
officially sanctioned slavery.

Individual horror stories, unhappily, are in ample supply, but it is
more revealing to recall examples of abuse which occur frequently.
Many women are enticed to work in Saudi Arabia by lucrative
salaries and job descriptions of work which does not exist. Women
from Pakistan have been hired as seamstresses at twice what they
make at home plus accommodation and food. But in Saudi Arabia
they discover that they are expected to work as maids for one third
of what they had been promised and their lodgings and food are not
fit for animals. Their embassies cannot help; most workers lack the
wherewithal to make an official complaint and those able to lodge
a complaint are either branded foreign troublemakers or seduced
by the police officer. They cannot go home because they cannot
get an exit visa without their employers' consent, nor can they seek
other employment. At the end of their 18-hour day the scraps of
food they are given to eat cannot sustain them to do the work of
another day.

Some maids are beaten; others are sexually assaulted and some,
because they speak no Arabic and are not allowed to get out to see
their compatriots, spend months without exchanging a word with
anybody. As a result of all this, the suicide rate among Oriental
maids working in Saudi Arabia is high and Saudi newspapers
are full of advertisements enquiring as to the whereabouts of
missing maids who have escaped their servitude. (Even the royals

abuse their help as in the already mentioned cases and Amnesty International recorded a case of Prince Saad Al Saud forcing his maid to work 18 hours a day and beating her up when she would not and indeed could not.)

Male labourers do not fare much better. Much of the time their retailers charge them a substantial part of their salary, up to 50 per cent, just for getting them visas – and this before they subtract their margin from what a labourer eventually realizes. Many are promised lodgings and made to sleep in discarded shipping containers. Even those who import labourers to work for them are not above forcing them to renegotiate contracts after threatening to send them back home to poverty or to report them for practising Christianity or whatever alien religion they profess. It goes beyond labourers, for even foreign shopkeepers and owners of other businesses must have Saudi guarantors to start their businesses. The latter charge exorbitant sums of money for providing guarantees.

In 1979 I was in Dhahran when Korean workers rioted against the local working conditions. The following day an Army unit lined them up, picked out three of them at random and executed them, 'to teach the rest a lesson'. I broached the subject of the summary executions with a prince, a pilot in the Saudi Air Force. 'But they were Korean workers. Why are you concerned about them?' was his answer. When I stated that they could have been innocent of any wrongdoing, he shrugged his shoulders and told me that there had not been any riots since and 'that's what matters'.

In December 1984 there was a similar incident involving Pakistani workers. Saudi Army officers shot a number of them and Pakistan, which receives some Saudi aid, made no protest. The Turkish workers around the Tubuk airbase were sent home for complaining about living conditions; Sudanese workers have been flogged publicly; Ethiopian workers have been deported for worshipping at home on Sundays and so have Muslim labourers who were suspected of being Shias.

More recently, during the Gulf crisis, on 2 February 1991 hundreds of foreign workers were arrested and tortured when a group fired on a bus full of American servicemen and slightly wounded two of them. As it turned out, the shots had been fired by dissident Saudis to protest about their government's pro-American policy. During the Gulf War the workers in the country's eastern province, the area nearest to Saddam Hussein's army, could not consider moving out of harm's way because their employers left them behind so that they could continue to work but took their passports with them.

The protests of international human rights organizations have been ignored, along with their repeated requests to conduct on-the-spot investigations. Not only has Saudi Arabia refused to adhere to international labour standards, but officially the Government has been taking serious steps backwards. In 1987 it rescinded the law which afforded foreign workers some social security coverage. Now a sick expatriate worker is at the mercy of his employer.

The problem is not one of laws and treaties, however. Deep down the Saudis would like to do without outsiders in their country and resent their dependence on them. This feeling, and the fact that theirs is a society whose oil-rich members derive satisfaction and status from enslaving others, are what shape the attitudes of the Saudi people and Government. As the following two incidents demonstrate, this climate matters more than the letter of the law. When a Yemeni shop owner quarrelled with a taxi driver over the fare, the driver told the police that the Yemeni was an ingrate who had criticized Saudi Arabia. The police accepted the story and deported the Yemeni. In an equally absurd incident, a Saudi involved in a car accident with a foreigner told the police: 'It is his mistake. The accident wouldn't have taken place had he not come to this country to work.' The police took this into consideration.

Ridiculous as these incidents may be, they do considerably less damage than Saudi Government actions against the citizens of a country which is opposed to Saudi policies. Not only are governments unable to protest over abuse of individual citizens, but, every once in a while, a country acts without total appreciation of the Saudi response to its people and the results can be disastrous. To the Saudi Government, citizens can be held responsible for the political behaviour of their country.

In one incident, this retaliatory Saudi policy was used against people who are not workers: the Iranian pilgrims performing the Hajj. The thousands of Iranians in Saudi Arabia in 1988 were subjected to considerable harassment by members of CAVES who acted in a manner which expresssed the Saudi Government's anti-Shia, anti-Iranian attitude. The Saudi security officials behaved so intolerably that the Iranians finally rioted. The police opened fire on a large Iranian crowd and when they were done 400 Iranians lay dead and 600 were wounded. There was no serious investigation of the matter; King Fahd settled for expressing his government's regrets. The following year, in a totally apolitical incident, Saudi carelessness during the Hajj led to a tunnel incident and stampede in which 4026 people were killed, mostly Iranians. Again there was no serious investigation of the incident.

During the Gulf War, Palestinians, Jordanians and Yemenis were deported when the PLO and the two governments concerned supported Saddam Hussein. The Palestinians and Jordanians, many of whom had spent over ten years in Saudi Arabia, were a sad enough case, but the story of the Yemenis was truly tragic. The Saudi Government, acting indiscriminately, deported 800,000 Yemeni workers, many of whom had been in the country for decades and some who were born there, at the rate of over 40,000 a week. Most had to leave without their belongings, scores were beaten and, according to Middle East Watch, 32 died for lack of medical attention. It was not simply a case of innocents paying the price of their own government's foolishness; Saudi Arabia itself came near to a standstill because the Yemenis owned all the groceries and retail outlets. In numbers and scale of cruelty, it was an act which surpasses what happened to the Neisei, the Japanese–Americans who were interned during the Second World War, and it is a foul example of ethnic cleansing. Yet what matters most is the total lack of official remorse and the prospect of a repeat performance.

There is a strong racial content to how the Saudis and their government view and treat foreign workers. This is because certain national groups are associated with certain functions and the amount of protection foreign governments are capable of providing their nationals varies. But while differences in treating outsiders exist and, in the past, Western governments were more likely to react to abuse of their nationals, Saudi xenophobia still affects the 60,000 American, British and other Western civilians who live there.

To begin with, the conditions under which Western diplomats in Saudi Arabia operate amount to an inhospitable atmosphere. They are confined to major cities, may not worship openly and accommodate local customs by operating according to Saudi *ma'lesh* time (even Saudi officials are always late and justify this by saying *ma'lesh*, or 'never mind'). More importantly, as documented by bulletins issued by the American, British, French and other embassies, Western diplomats are more likely to blame their own citizens for not knowing how to behave and do not come forward to protect them except under extreme conditions.

That this occurs is demonstrated by the case of Helen Smith, a Jeddah-resident English nurse who, along with a Dutchman by the name of Johannes Otten, met a violent death while attending a party of Western expatriates. The investigation of her death by the Saudi authorities produced a verdict of accidental death from a 70-foot fall from the balcony of a fifth-floor apartment. Initially the British Embassy accepted the verdict and acted in an embarrassed way. After all, the Embassy was in the business of warning British citizens against attending parties where alcoholic beverages were served, let alone where the sexes mixed freely. The Embassy's posture amounted to a subdued she-shouldn't-have-been-there attitude.

What the British Embassy, and indeed the British Government, did not count on was the attitude of Helen's father. A former police detective in Leeds, Ron Smith rushed to Jeddah to claim the body of his daughter only to discover considerable evidence which cast doubt on the 'accident' verdict and convinced him that she had been raped and probably battered to death before 'falling'. In fact, the injuries did not suggest a fall.

Ron Smith refused to receive his daughter's body and began his own investigation. Many people at the Baksh Hospital, where Helen had worked, openly suggested that she had been murdered, but everyone at the party, though contradicting each other on important details, insisted it was an accident. Forgetting that the punishment for adultery is death by stoning, the hostess went as far as admitting that she was having sex with one of the guests during a critical time when, if she had been up and about, she could have shed some light on the circumstances of the couple's death.

Confronted with such nonsense, Smith, aggrieved and angry, returned to Britain and proceeded to badger the Foreign Office and the press with questions about the case. The Foreign Office held to the official Saudi and British Embassy line and hoped Smith would disappear, but the press rose to the occasion and began running stories which supported Smith's suspicions. In Britain, the case began to assume the shape of a national scandal, a lone father against a government determined to place its Saudi interests above justice.

Smith returned to Jeddah, but his second trip was less fruitful. Fearful members of the expatriate community, the British Embassy and the Saudi authorities would not cooperate with him and placed hurdles in his way. Meanwhile, given the circumstances of drinking and other violations of Saudi law, including adultery, the other expatriates at the party received exceptionally light sentences from a Saudi court, a maximum of a one-year prison sentence for the host and public floggings for the others.

This strengthened Smith's resolve and the press accommodated him by conducting their own investigations. With time, two vital pieces of evidence surfaced. The first was the fact that an attempt had been made to tamper with Johannes Otten's clothing and belongings to cover up his murder and suggest burglary as the motive. The second was the presence of a mysterious Saudi at the scene of the crime a few hours after it was discovered, when the Saudi police finally arrived to conduct their preliminary investigation.

The valiant efforts of Ron Smith met with relative success: he agreed to bring his daughter's body back to Britain after Leeds City Council agreed to hold an inquest to investigate the cause of death. Sadly, however, this too proved unproductive and there was an open verdict. Nevertheless, the open airing of the case did establish that Smith and the press had good reason to question the Saudi investigation of the case and to suspect British connivance in a cover-up. In my view, the mysterious Saudi is the key to the whole affair. The Saudis do not shy from extracting confessions from people and they got none from the expatriates involved in the case, and let them go with uncharacteristic lack of fuss. Beyond that, they did everything to create a cover-up, and they normally would not do that except to protect one of their own.

Lesser examples of how other Western expatriates are left to the whims of Saudi law occur every day. The British engineer Neville Norton was imprisoned for a period of three years over a contract dispute and was released only in 1991. It was the type of dispute which is normally handled by a commercial court and there was no reason to imprison him except for the fact that he had a money claim against a royal. In this case, the British Embassy pretended ignorance of the whole affair until the poor man was released. There have been many cases when British and American citizens working in Saudi Arabia were flogged publicly for selling alcohol or for lesser crimes and in all cases the concerned diplomatic missions had very little to say for themselves.

This relatively recent reluctance by Western governments to protect their citizens, which coincided with Saudi Arabia's rising importance as an oil supplier, has emboldened the Saudis and this has reflected itself in the activities of CAVES members. In November 1987 AT&T Saudi Arabia issued a letter to its American employees in the country which contained an admission that they could do very little to protect them against increasing harassment by CAVES. Simultaneously, another letter was sent to the US Ambassador to Saudi Arabia, Charles Freeman, citing examples of this harassment. This was followed by complaints by James Baroody, the President of the Association of American Workers in Saudi Arabia. This too produced no response.

In fact, besides international and regional human rights organizations, the only political entity to complain about the Saudi treatment of foreign workers was the European Community, which settled for a diplomatic expression of concern. The situation of workers in the country continues to deteriorate and what is happening now deserves close scrutiny if incidents similar to those which affected the Yemeni workers and led to the death of Helen Smith are to be avoided in the future.

Conduct of state affairs aside, even the emergence of a new slave state and the visible contradictions of everyday Saudi Arabian life, of comparing camels with cadillacs, do not tell enough of what is happening in the country. The social divisions racking the place touch and twist every aspect of ordinary life. Fahd has been king since 1982, and, as has been shown, more than anybody else he has proved that the only constant, unalterable Saudi facts of life are the way the royal family views itself and the way this vision is expressed. In fact, the background against which the royals conduct themselves has changed dramatically, but the commitment to family absolutism is so intact that it is difficult to imagine any curbs on their power taking place. In the words of a Lebanese journalist well acquainted with the country: 'They've had 90 years to change and they haven't done it; their attitude is part of them, even the most educated and enlightened among them believe their ways to be right and that they're beyond criticism. Crazy as it may sound, things are getting worse.'

But, while the family and the armed and paramilitary forces have always had priority claims on the finances of the country, the hugeness of the oil income has transformed the place, more in the way the people live than in the way they think, but measurably in both. This transformation began in the early 1960s, when the oil income exceeded first the family's and then the Army's needs and enough money filtered through to the people to create one of the longest-lasting and broadest economic booms in history, an economic explosion sustained by the needs which go with catapulting a seventeenth-century country into the twentieth century. To appreciate what this means, it is enough to consider that only 1 per cent of homes had bathrooms and now over 50 per cent of them do – and the most expensive and decorative types at that. (A character in Hilary Mantel's remarkable novel about Saudi Arabian life, *Eight Months on Gaza Street*, delivers the memorable and in all likelihood real-life line: 'I have witnessed the largest transportation of ready-mixed concrete in the history of the human race.')

As with all booms, this one created a rich merchant class, in this case an impressive *Forbes* and *Fortune* magazines list of billionaires made up of old trading families and new ones (the royals are ignored). The Olayans, Mahfouzes, bin Ladens, Kamels, Ali Rezas, Zamils, Ghoseibis and Jamils imported food, cars and construction equipment and built highways, housing for workers and whole towns, dozens of schools, hospitals and, naturally, palaces and chichi army barracks. Now they provide services which keep the country going, huge cleaning and maintenance contracts which employ thousands of people and run into billions of dollars, and they use their surplus funds to trade worldwide. They have substantial shareholdings in Chase Manhattan Bank, Citicorp, Hyatt Hotels, Whittaker, Mobil Oil and many other corporations; join major oil companies to prospect for 'black gold' in other countries; and own huge chunks of real estate in five continents. Naturally, nobody is ever big enough to forget what matters and, in order to continue, they all need the blessing if not the active support of the House of Saud.

The second way oil wealth produced results was through the creation of an educated class. Estimates vary, but in the late 1980s somewhere between 15,000 and 20,000 Saudis graduated from universities every year. Yet this is a recent happening and, unlike in other Arab countries, the royal family acted only when their surpluses became huge and for years the educational benefits were limited to the upper crust of society who could afford it or had enough influence to get Government grants for their children. Furthermore, not all Saudis have participated in the universal Middle Eastern rush to become educated. As a result, literacy is still somewhere around 55 per cent, slightly lower than destitute India and considerably behind poor Jordan. Nevertheless, the composition of the educated class in Saudi Arabia differs little from those in other countries and there are electronic and oil engineers, doctors, sanitation specialists, city planners and even interior decorators. Of course, masses of people have graduated in the arts and humanities, though, understandably in view of the attitude of the House of Saud, the law still lags far behind.

Until the late 1980s, mostly because of a tenfold increase in the number of civil servants between 1965 and 1985, almost all college graduates have been able to secure lucrative jobs; in the words of a knowledgeable American who lived there for years, the Government has been able to 'absorb or bribe them – take your pick'. But the expansion in commerce and this bureaucratic build-up have reached saturation point: the ability of the Government to hire more people and to continue to pay civil servants over the odds is no longer a reality and the expansion of the trading houses is experiencing a slow-down. For the first time this century, educated Saudis are taking jobs below their level of competence and their unhappiness about this promises serious problems in this area, particularly in view of an emerging financial crisis brought about by serious mismanagement of the country's formerly huge surpluses and the cost of the Gulf War.

Naturally for a country which is a royal dictatorship, the third visible human component of change is the numbers and status of members of the armed forces and the paramilitary National Guard, the pampered but historically unreliable guardians of the throne. Together they officially total over 100,000, and in 1982 the yearly cost per Saudi soldier was $470,000, compared with $103,000 in America and less than half of that in Britain, Germany and France. More tellingly, in 1982 the defence cost per Saudi citizen was $3014, compared with $782 in America and $471 in Germany. The natural historical importance of the armed forces is exaggerated by local anomalies not subject to sound planning or financial controls. Officers are promoted and their already impressive houses upgraded. The salaries of all members of the forces are increased and they are given bonuses every time the country faces a crisis. Also, the West responds to these crises by supplying Saudi Arabia with more sophisticated and expensive weapons. The Gulf War saw the royal family hand out huge special financial rewards to officers, something other countries would never consider doing, and in amounts they could not afford. And even internal problems such as the suppression in 1979 of street demonstrations in some Shia towns produced a massive exercise in royal largesse and, ominously, a reaction by Saudi opposition groups who saw fit to publish a list of the recipients.

The colossally rich merchants, along with those who are extremely wealthy by normal standards, the bureaucrats, teachers and doctors and members of the armed forces, constitute the new Saudi class. (A Harvard University study calls them 'Middle Class' and claims that their numbers have increased from 2 per cent of the population to 11 per cent in the late 1980s.) They are the beneficiaries of the oil boom and the building of a modern army.

This new class and how it appears to outsiders, along with what is known about the royal family, merge to create the total image of today's Saudi Arabia. Despite lack of participation by large segments of the population, it is what some writers describe as the petro-personality. And the needs of this society and its excesses have transformed the country into a figurative Mecca for international salesmen and contractors and made it the home of over three million foreign workers.

This state of financial well-being is used to promote a picture of Saudi Arabia where all is well. With their advocates, the members of the House of Saud equate the obvious economic advances with something more substantial which reflects favourably on the social and political situation within the country. But though the image of wealth, albeit often exaggerated, is a fact, the results are the opposite of what is assumed. The impact of wealth and the rush to modernity, whether skin-deep or real, have destroyed the social values of this Muslim society much faster than they could conceivably be replaced and have led to stresses which have produced a considerable loss of social cohesion. For example, the number of reported crimes rose from 1775 in 1966 to 21,826 in 1985 – many times more than in neighbouring countries and one of the highest increases in the world.

Furthermore, despite the economic benefits which were enjoyed by the merchant class, bureaucrats and army officers, any judgement of what they are all about must take into consideration the number of anti-Government conspiracies in which they have participated. This reveals ample signs of resentment against the absolutism of the royal household. Indeed, this is where a chasm between the Government – the royal family – and the people manifests itself. There is a conflict between how members of the new class live and their refusal to accept the House of Saud's attempt to stifle their wish for greater personal and political freedom. Whether the new class's political thinking is a reflection of rising expectations, their education, an inherent human wish to be free or, as generally suspected, a combination of all these things, matters less than the fact that it exists.

When the boxer Cassius Clay espoused Islam and became

Muhammad Ali, he made a trip to Saudi Arabia to perform the pilgrimage and promote himself. He was received by all important members of the royal family, including the King. While with Prince Salman, the Governor of Riyadh and head of the important family council, Ali lapsed into his usual way of talking. 'Hey, Your Highness,' he is supposed to have cracked, 'doesn't anybody in this place smile?' Salman is reported to have stared at him without saying a word. Whether anybody told Ali that the Saudis keep their more bitter than sweet smiles to themselves is not known. Again the country and its inherent oddness are exposed in the words of another Hilary Mantel character: 'It's a stimulating place if you're in the construction business.'

But smiling openly is not the only thing which looks odd in the strange, contradictory atmosphere which envelops Saudi Arabia and which accounts for the continued unhappiness of all its people. Saudi Arabia is a country where old men pray five times a day while their sons listen to the Rolling Stones. It is a country where old people eat lamb and the young import 20,000lb of American-made Oreo cookies a year. It is a country where the punishment of serious crimes is publicized as a deterrent, but the crimes themselves are not mentioned, so nobody knows what they should avoid doing. True, dictatorships do not point out the flaws in their system, but in Saudi Arabia this maxim has been carried to extremes and rapists are beheaded in a town's 'Chop Square'. The press carries the gruesome pictures of the sordid affair along with the name, age and place of birth of the man without a word as to why the ultimate punishment is being meted out.

Contact between unrelated men and women is illegal and violating this rule can lead to severe punishment, but telephone sex is rampant. Among others, Peter Theroux, the American writer who spent three years teaching in the country while observing its ways, recorded instances of women telephoning him because he was a foreigner and hence more likely to indulge in the forbidden sport. And it goes further and women shop carrying little pieces of paper with their telephone numbers on them − just in case they run into deserving handsome men. According to the Saudi writer Anwar Abdallah, these petro-flirtations often lead to serious affairs which are consummated when the participants give content to their frustrations by meeting outside the country. But when they go to see the doctor, the same frustrated women who participate in telephone sex and its extensions have been known to bare everything but keep their faces covered. Most women who live in cities spend hours making themselves up to look pretty and wear expensive Chanel and Yves St Laurent dresses but hide their looks and dresses under full-length *abas* when they go out in the street. Many of these women are so smitten by the glamour of Princess Diana that they have named their daughters after her. They write anonymous letters to magazines complaining about their social status and the denial of their rights – but they still cannot leave home except in the company of males.

American-educated Saudi males greet each with, 'How you doin', man?' while wearing Arab robes and head-dresses and sacrilegiously shorten the name Muhammad to Mo. They indulge in other aspects of imported hipness, including the use of drugs, and they negotiate multi-million-dollar business deals while massaging their toes in an unattractive Bedouin way. Those who can afford it drink whisky secretly, at $100 a bottle, within a short distance of the Muslim muezzin calling for prayers.

During Ramadan, the Muslim month of fasting, activity in the whole country comes to a screeching halt, but any Saudi worth his barrel of oil takes off for London, Spain or the South of France to continue 'living', and effects a similar escape to join in the fun of Christmas and New Year. (A deputy director of Petromin, the country's oil marketing arm, chartered a plane from Dhahran to Paris so that he and his friends could spend New Year there. When Selim Louzi, the late brave Lebanese journalist, confronted King Fahd with this, the latter described the episode as 'regrettable'.)

Unsurprisingly, these escapes from Muslim constraints were pioneered by members of the royal family. And the Americans and other well-to-do expatriates in Saudi Arabia participate in the madnesses, confirming the living absurdity of the place. For example, an American woman had an art exhibition which contained nothing but the presents given her by princes of the realm who appreciated her beauty: Persian carpets, diamond necklaces, emerald rings, diamond earrings and an antique four-poster bed. None of the trophies exhibited was for sale.

Such absurd aspects of Saudi modernity often have weird consequences and I have experienced two telling instances at first hand. My over 20 trips to Saudi Arabia have instilled in me a morbid fascination with the number of road accidents and how they take place. I discovered that the total had gone up from 4047 in 1971 to 24,594 in 1983 but I could never look at the resulting wrecks and fathom how they happened – something the mind usually figures out automatically. I finally asked an old Saudi schoolmate of mine to decipher the accidents for me. 'The accidents are impossible to understand because people here drive like maniacs, don't observe any traffic rules and do nothing to clear the way before they leave the scene of the accident,' was the answer I got.

In the other incident I was stranded in Dhahran desperately trying to return to London. The clerk manning the flight desk was black with an Afro hairdo and spoke like an American from the Deep South. I tried to befriend him in the hope that he would get me a flight connection. In the course of our conversation, I asked him what part of the States he came from and was startled to be told: 'I'm Saudi, man, and I've never been to America. I learned my English listening to the radio station of ARAMCO.' (The American compound in Dhahran houses over 30,000 US citizens and they are entertained by radio and television stations which carry regular American programmes.)

Yet Saudi Arabia is very much the home of the holy shrines of Mecca and Medina and is ruled by members of the strict Wahhabi sect. Judged by the existence of 30,000 mosques, or one for about every 300 people, it remains the most Muslim country of them all. Like oil, Islam, the basis of family rule, is a commodity which is promoted by the Saudi Government, which contributes to the building of mosques, and it is a source of influence and power for the country among the Arabs and Muslims. But the part of this same ultra-Muslim country which has been affected by oil wealth has leapt into the twentieth century unprepared. The practices resulting from the oil wealth and exposure to Western ways are in direct conflict with the pseudo-legal and cultural Muslim foundations of the place. No prince, not even those whose ugly behaviour has been mentioned earlier, professes anything except a strict adherence to Islam and its ways. Moreover, the Government expects everyone to do the same. The irony of the most Muslim state of them all in some ways becoming the most Western-looking country is there for all to see. To bridge the gap between the two, to create a centre where none exists, hypocrisy, official and personal, has been elevated to a science. Not only are we confused by Saudi Arabia's contradictory stance on the subject of a resurgent Islam, but nothing is called by its right name. Thus to accommodate Islamic tenets condemning usury even bank interest payments are called service charges but greedy bank managers who make a lot of exorbitant service charges have to close shop and observe the call to prayer.

The social contradictions of everyday life are real, substantial and dislocating and their results are the wounds and scars of change, a massive sociological free fall which, among other things, has created a generation gap of several centuries. And to repeat, this dichotomy in social behaviour is matched by a political one or by actions which have a bearing on the political future of the country. For example, to please the Arabs, Saudi Arabia condemns the foreign policy of the USA and calls for a Muslim Jerusalem in a week which sees it ordering more American missiles to protect itself against the same Arabs it is trying to please. At the same time the Government continues in its absolute ways, which are totally intolerant of dissent, while sending young Saudis to foreign schools which teach them about democracy, freedom and equality. In Saudi Arabia, being anti-West and pro-West and pro-Arab and anti-Arab at the same time and the confrontation between a Western-educated young man weaned on Rousseau, Hobbes and the federalist papers and a prince arbitrarily demanding a share of his company's profits is part of the country's make-up. Moreover, the result of the confrontation between the commoner and the prince who demands a share of his wealth is as contradictory as the situation: the Saudi lets his prince have his way while secretly cursing him.

These contradictory elements in the social and governmental sphere go forward with their own momentum. Moreover, because of lack of understanding of their consequences by the people who run the country, no policies have been adopted to deal with them and the damage they produce is getting worse. The divisions between being pro-Arab and anti-West and the opposite, between the old and the new and between the Government's ways and the desire of the people for greater freedom, are getting wider by the day. The country's Arab and external policies will be analyzed later, but in the internal sphere the Government believes its own propaganda and accepts the acquisition of wealth by some of its citizens and their rising levels of education as enough to keep the people happy. It does not feel threatened by what surrounds it and, as a result, even the behaviour of members of the royal family is getting worse – and more unacceptably colourful.

In fact, the dichotomies run so deep within the country that even the misbehaviour of the royals is exclusive. Though cocktail parties and hashish parties are everyday occurrences among them and among some members of the new class, nobody who belongs to the latter group dares emulate the licentiousness of the royals without risking offending them and suffering the application of the letter of the law. I know of an important merchant who was scolded by the King for giving his daughter a lavish wedding. King Khalid was angry because the man had 'gone too far'. The man explained the episode thus: 'They don't want anybody to compete with them.' Outside the country, the royals act as a model for other Saudis who, while careful not to offend them, ape them in building houses in Marbella, gambling in London casinos, chasing starlets in Hollywood and the South of France. But, regardless of the degree of real and imitative social change shown by the activities of the new class and indeed despite its corrupt ways, the House of Saud has not been able to neutralize its demands for political adjustment. In other words, regardless of wealth and the indulgences afforded them by the oil boom, members of the new class still resent the royal family's monopoly on power and their own reduction to political vegetables. This situation is particularly evident when the House of Saud's suffocating separateness is revealed through new methods which infringe on the new class's comforts: rich merchants have to run ads wishing the King happy holidays, telephone tapping is universal and members of CAVES continue to treat them the way they treated people 50 years ago.

But, as under Ibn Saud, the only safety-valve the family has to offer is the antiquated and ill-used majlis. But the majlis has not worked and this is why the country has continued to experience many rebellions and assassination attempts. From the 1950s to the 1980s the increase in the level of education, wealth and awareness changed the source of the opposition, from the tribes and religious fanatics to nationalist movements made up of the new class, including the Army, and more recently non-traditional Islamic fundamentalism.

Since the inception of the Eisenhower Doctrine of the late 1950s, the Americans have openly guaranteed the security of the country in an inclusive way; the guarantees are aimed against both external threats and internal upheavals. These guarantees, the sheer numbers of the House of Saud and their relations and the geography of the country have led to the failure of all the attempts to change the government of the House of Saud.

The boldest expression of the American commitment and involvement to defend Saudi Arabia was the Gulf War, which will be addressed separately later, but this was preceded by several unpublicized alerts, particularly in 1969, 1972 and 1979. On these occasions the Americans were ready to respond to 'trouble' within Saudi Arabia, army conspiracies, but the Saudis managed to control

things and eliminate the conspirators without outside interference
– and without trial. (The elimination can take hideous forms,
and there is evidence that King Faisal ordered 29 suspect Air
Force officers to be ejected from planes without parachutes.)
What the Eisenhower Doctrine's guarantee of the safety of the
country against destabilization started has been reaffirmed by every
American president who followed him and this US commitment
acts as a check on the advocates of change, who have to take it
into consideration.

In addition, the numbers of the House of Saud are another
major barrier to internal attempts to change the Government.
Not only are there too many of them, but they are scattered all
over the country, holding key positions and controlling the local
government apparatus. Their numbers allow them to control all
the key posts in the Air Force and the Ministries of the Interior
and Defence have never been out of their hands. Also, the Wahhabi
and Bedouin National Guard, a paramilitary organization which
was created for the sole purpose of protecting the family and which
now has tanks, helicopters and other sophisticated weaponry, is
under the Crown Prince. Naturally, the dreaded internal security
apparatus is headed by a prince, Fahd bin Faisal, a nephew of
King Fahd.

The best way to judge the importance of the number of royals
is to realize that in Saudi Arabia killing the King and 50 or 100
relatives would only lead to other members of the family assuming
power and it is physically impossible to gather all the thousands of
princes who form the House of Saud in one place and do the job.
America would anyway always find someone to make king.

But it is not solely a question of the policies of the USA and family
numbers; geography is a third protective factor. The country is not
only huge; it is multi-centred, with Jeddah, Mecca and Medina in
the west, Riyadh in the centre and Dhahran in the east. Organizing
a simultaneous move against all of these centres at the same time
would undo any conspiracy because too many people would have
to know about it.

With all these protective elements in place, one would think the
Saudi people who want change would not even try. But this is not
the case and, despite the odds stacked against them, attempts to
change the regime continue to take place. It is a simple case of
the injustices of the House of Saud producing a totally human
response. Saudi Arabia has never been a sea of tranquillity
and the Saudi people have never been the punching-bag the

House of Saud and its supporters and advocates make them out to be.

Because of the great number of uprisings against the House of Saud since the death of its founding father, it is beyond the scope of this book to deal with them individually. I will settle for identifying their source and presenting examples of how they were dealt with.

Understandably, because they were exposed to outside influences, among the first political movements in Saudi Arabia were the labour unions formed in the oil city of Dhahran. On several occasions in the 1950s and 1960s workers there struck and demonstrated. They demanded reasonable working hours, higher wages, the elimination of discriminatory policies (ARAMCO provided them with housing inferior to what their American counterparts got), and political rights. Initially, under King Saud, this movement achieved some success, until he acted against it and it was crushed by the authorities. In 1962, when Faisal ran the country, 12 leaders of the movement disappeared, most of them never to be seen again.

From 1958 to 1964 several members of the family, with Prince Tallal (the father of the Citicorp agent) in the lead, left the country, formed the Free Princes and advocated change through joining forces with Nasser's Arab nationalist movement. The movement of the Free Princes, although a serious one which undermined the foundations of family unity, failed but met with a gentler end. Prince Tallal has never been completely rehabilitated, but he and three brothers have been allowed back into Saudi Arabia and were reintegrated into the system on condition of silence. This, and the fact that rebel princes succumbed to the lure of money and became wealthy, put an end to the hopes that the family might correct its ways. The only inter-family differences which now remain concern branches of the family vying for power, or competing for defence and other contracts.

In 1955 there was a pro-Nasser local army rebellion in the city of Taif and in 1969 a serious Air Force mutiny occurred at the Dhahran airbase. Again in 1969, several leading citizens and Air Force officers made a valiant attempt to topple the Government. In 1975 the Chief of Staff, General Muhammad Shamimairi, was arrested and later executed for conspiring against the monarchy. The earliest reported Army uprising took place at the Dhahran airbase, and it is the one incident where a royal, Prince Faisal bin Saud bin Muhammad Abdel Aziz, was killed.

The Army officers involved in the Taif rebellion were executed summarily. The 1969 Air Force rebellion produced a number of executions which included Colonels Daoud Roumi and Said Al Omari. In addition, serious change in the process of selecting Air Force officers took place and now they may only be members of the House of Saud or from a few 'reliable' families. Little is known about the fate of those involved in the Dhahran rebellion.

Another serious Army–civilian rebellion in 1969 was led by Yusuf Al Tawil, the son of Muhammad Al Tawil, a man who conspired against Ibn Saud in the 1930s. Tawil, who was a classmate of mine at Beirut's International College, was spared and so were many of his co-conspirators. Their numbers and background meant that their execution would have backfired, but Colonel Saud Ibrahim Al Muammer, another IC classmate and a close friend of mine, died under torture and 23 lesser conspirators disappeared.

One of the most serious uprisings against the Government took place in 1979 when a group of religious fanatics occupied the Grand Mosque in Mecca for two weeks. In November of that year, a religious fanatic by the name of Juhayman Muhammad Otteibi led 300 armed men to occupy the Grand Mosque until most of them were killed by French paratroops who flooded the place with water and applied electricity to it, having been given special dispensation to enter the Islamic city. The Grand Mosque rebellion was costly: 227 people were killed and over 400 wounded. Juhayman was killed but 63 of his followers were distributed to cities all over the country and beheaded publicly, without trial. Saudi television broadcast the executions live to teach the people a lesson. On the two days following the Mecca rebellion an open Shia insurrection took place in the country's oil-rich eastern region which was put down violently. No figures are available but estimates place the number of Shias killed at over 200.

Nowadays, in the wake of the Gulf War, dozens of students, teachers, journalists and religious leaders have been imprisoned for posing 'a threat to the regime'. The nature of this threat has never been disclosed, but many are still in detention and are tortured methodically. Among the best known of those imprisoned recently are Gulf War opponent and Sophist leader Muhammad Al Fassi and human rights activist Muhammad Al Misaari. Despite the repeated efforts of international human rights organizations, their families have not been allowed to visit them and their whereabouts are unknown.

Clearly, the numbers of the House of Saud and their geographical spread, while instrumental in foiling anti-Government moves, have not acted as a deterrent and people have continued to try. The fact that the past decade has seen no major attempts to topple the House of Saud is undoubtedly the result of an increasing awareness of the blatant American protection given to the royal family. Yet this should not be overstated to imply that the people or the Army have submitted, and there is a perceptible increase in street-level opposition to the Government. The periodic dismissals of Army officers – and there have been two since the Gulf War, in April 1990 and May 1991 – indicate continued unhappiness in its ranks and the regular increases in the salaries paid to officers and soldiers are no more than a crude unsuccessful attempt by the House of Saud to buy their loyalty. But in the main, the major resistance to the House of Saud has undergone another shift. The failure of previous revolutionary attempts and the increase of Western support have led to the adoption of new ways. Now there is an attempt to subvert one of the major sources of support of the House of Saud: Islam. The opposition accepts that the country must continue within an Islamic framework and makes noises about cooperating with the West but does not accept the royal family's interpretation of Islam and accuses them of perverting it. It wants an Islamic representative government.

Whether this new way, with its broader appeal to the masses, will succeed where narrow-based nationalist movements failed is difficult to assess but what is clear is that it has become a danger to a fundamentally shaky façade. In the words of the writer David Howarth: 'The kingdom is clearly one of the richest and ripest prizes in the world for a revolution.' Understandably, the exiled Saudi writer Muhammad Sadeeq offers a more emotional assessment. 'The lights are out in my country, FOR NOW.'

One way to judge how dissatisfaction within the country works is to listen to Saudis and hear how preoccupied they are with the lack of political reform. To them, the constant violation of human rights forms an unhappy part of everyday conversation and, immediately after the Gulf War, this unhappiness expressed itself in a petition to the King asking for greater freedom. It was signed by 50 of the country's leading notables, scholars, business leaders and former Government officials, including former Minister of Information Muhammad Abdou Yamani (no kin to his famous namesake, the former Oil Minister). The petition went unanswered, and in the West these serious developments appear as nothing more than small news stories – they are denied the space they deserve. Nor do other serious developments reflecting on conditions within the country get the coverage they merit. On 16 October 1988 the *New York Times*, *Washington Post* and *Wall Street Journal* reported that the Saudi Council of Ulemas, a House of Saud-appointed Wahhabi religious body, issued a fatwa (encyclical) sanctioning the execution of members of opposition political parties. That same month, despite pleas by many international human rights organizations and the Kuwaiti Government, the Saudis executed 16 Kuwaitis accused of causing trouble during the Hajj.

More recently, according to the human rights organization Article 19 and the Minnesota Lawyers' International Human Rights Committee, the Saudis killed and wounded a number of Iraqis who had taken refuge in their country from Saddam Hussein. Over 20,000 of them are held in the Rafha desert camp under inhuman conditions, suffering from summer heat of 120° F in the shade. When they rioted, demanding better accommodation and more food, the Saudi security forces opened fire at random. The Saudis have refused all requests by human rights organizations to visit the camp. Western governments responded to the atrocity by granting some of the refugees emigration visas (3000 to the USA and 700 to Sweden, among others), but no government condemned the behaviour of the House of Saud. All these acts are talked about and resented by most Saudis, many of whom are bitter about the attitude of Western governments and about the apparent indifference of the Western media (see The Last Line of Defence).

Since the Islamic fundamentalist revolution in Shia Iran, the massive discrimination against the Saudi Shias has gone beyond the periodic issue of religious fatwas denouncing them as heretics and the denial of jobs and economic opportunity. In September 1991 Saudi newspapers carried a statement by a senior Wahhabi cleric, one Abdallah bin Jibreen, an appointee of the House of Saud and one who does not move without their approval, in which he described the Shias as 'idolators who deserve to be killed'. The following year this inflammatory opinion was confirmed by an official fatwa. As if to bolster these unbelievable incitements to murder, the Government detained 26 Shia religious leaders, many of the Shia citizens of the village of Umm Al Kura disappeared and an outspoken citizen, Muhammad Al Farrash, was publicly executed. The security forces have razed four Shia mosques and, unlike in other places, the number of Shia mosques is small. The Government refuses to license the construction of new ones, and measures stricter than ever were introduced to stop the Shias celebrating most of their religious holidays. In 1988, 340 Shia employees of the Jubeil refinery, in the eastern part of the country, were dismissed, 'because Shias are unreliable', and the Shias seldom hold Government jobs and cannot join the armed forces. People continue to be arrested without being charged, tortured without being allowed to see their lawyers and in September 1992, in an act which defies the imagination and which reflects panic in the House of Saud, two Shia divinity students, Turki Al Turki and Abdel Khaliq Jannaabi, were awaiting execution because they read the Bible as part of their syllabus. They have since been released in response to an international outcry by human rights organizations.

Naturally there are laws, directed at the population as a whole, which stifle dissent indiscriminately. A person can be arrested for acting suspiciously with no clarification of what that entails, Government employees are forbidden to write letters to the press and everyone is discouraged from talking to foreign reporters. But it goes beyond that: suspect doctors cannot practise and suspect professors cannot teach, and 52 non-Shia clerics who objected to these measures were imprisoned in 1992. Torture of Saudi political prisoners is universal and has been documented by Amnesty International, Middle East Watch and the Committee for Human Rights in the Arabian Peninsula, the Minnesota Lawyers' International Human Rights Committee and others. The methods used are among the most brutal in the world. Many prisoners are kept in dark, humid cells measuring three feet by four feet for months at a time; the fingernails and toenails of some are extracted to get confessions; difficult male prisoners have their penises tied up and are filled with water until they burst; and occasionally prisoners have been thrown into swimming pools while guards with sticks stood around to stop them climbing out. Inevitably, they drowned and the security forces were able to claim that they died of natural causes.

Even women are imprisoned, and one of them, Alia Makki, wrote a haunting book about her experiences in solitary confinement and how she lived with a huge population of ants, cockroaches and bugs and eventually lost track of day and night. When she was finally released to her father after six months of unexplained detention and torture, the security officer in charge demanded that her father confirm that she was in good physical condition despite the wounds, bruises and other visible signs of torture. Her father obeyed, then wept uncontrollably.

Years ago, before I was banned from visiting Saudi Arabia, I was amazed at the number of educated and religious people who had served time for political crimes. But not only was it impossible most of the time to determine what their crimes were; I also became aware that nobody was immune and that the only thing standing between me and revealing the names of higher-ups, including Army officers, who suffered imprisonment was fear of reprisal against them. However, a good example of this is found in Linda Blandford's *The Oil Sheikhs*. She recorded a disturbing interview with Abdel Aziz Muammer, former Saudi Ambassador to Switzerland, brother of the executed Colonel Saud Al Muammer and an acquaintance of mine. Blandford described how confinement to a dark cell led to loss of his eyesight and even now he is not totally in control of his faculties. When she asked him why he was kept in solitary confinement for 12 years, his simple answer was that he had no idea. I remember this Muammer as an extremely intelligent, civilized man and know that his family did not know whether he was dead or alive for seven years. His wife had to go through the indignity of kissing King Faisal's feet and begging for mercy to find out where they were holding the descendant of one of Saudi Arabia's leading families, a tribe who were the equals of the Al Sauds and who once ruled Nejed. This is not a strange or isolated example, but because of strict Saudi censorship and fear, there is no way of knowing the number of political prisoners in the country, or their fate.

Perhaps it is enough to say that even now the laws governing political arrest are considered a state secret and have never been published, while the number of CAVES offices has grown to 200 and there are 150 detention centres. Meanwhile, all published and spoken promises of reform are deflected or never applied, above all the ones that require legal representation and protect people against arbitrary arrest and torture. Predictably, no outside group has ever been allowed to investigate reports of torture on the spot and second-hand reports, including some thoroughly documented ones by officers of the US State Department, are dismissed by the Saudi authorities as propaganda.

Perhaps it is because in the end money does not make people happy, but there is certainly little to smile about in the place, as Muhammad Ali observed. Bearing in mind the recorded number of attempts to overthrow the Government by members of the new class and others, empirical judgement can only conclude that money is indeed not enough. Now, after 40 years of oil wealth, the new class have come to take their financial comforts for granted and fewer of them view their position as a gift from the House of Saud. This means that their loyalty to the royal family is weaker than ever before and suggests a consequent increase in the prospects for turmoil. This is particularly evident when we consider the growth in the numbers of this class, their ability to organize things better than in the past and the increased pressures on them in the wake of the Gulf War. For example, despite all Government attempts to destroy them, political parties expressing the unhappiness of the new class are growing stronger. The Free Nejed, Labour Socialist Party, Arab Nationalist Party, Democratic Saudi Party and many smaller organizations are flourishing and their calls for an end to oppression are growing more strident by the day.

As pointed out above, the religious leaders representing most of the people are being assailed and are unhappy, and though with some exceptions they have so far been excluded from harsh retribution, this has come to include the Wahhabi-run and lavishly sponsored Council of Ulemas. Fanatics like Sheikh bin Jibreen aside, the recent rift between the Wahhabi religious leaders and the Government represents one of the major contradictions of the country, because the Government purports to depend on them for support, rules in the name of Islam and insists on using the Koran as a constitution. Essentially, this contradiction is created by another one: the way the royal family have used Islam as a cover without adhering to its tenets – a posture more convincing to ignorant people outside Saudi Arabia who mistakenly blame Islam for much of what takes place there.

No religious leader, however removed from worldly affairs, is isolated enough not to know that the House of Saud indulges in the forbidden activities of drinking, gambling and womanizing. These activities are condemned by all Muslim sects, who further-more reject the concept of monarchy and the principle of royal succession. The Prophet was quite outspoken against both and so were the caliphs who followed him. According to Islam, the governor is elected by the people through a *bay'a* (the nearest English word to describe this democratic concept is fealty) and he is elected to administer justice, to institute laws in accordance with religion, to dispense knowledge and to rule to the best of his ability. Above all, Islam is very clear about the unacceptability of the use of force against people and torture is forbidden by very specific laws.

Until recently the Wahhabi-run Council of Ulemas overlooked the misdeeds of the members of the House of Saud because they were their co-religionists and sponsors and criticizing them could have led to the Wahhabis' overthrow and the end of their dominance. But in recent times, this barrier to criticism by the highest official religious authorities of the land has disappeared. Now young Wahhabi clerics are so adamant in their opposition to the personal ways of the House of Saud and the lavish display of wealth by the very rich and powerful that they have forced their conservative elders into a turnaround. This new position, which on one recent occasion expressed itself in a refusal by the Council of Ulemas to condemn a petition critical of King Fahd, has led to the royal dismissal of seven members of the Council, an unprecedented and extremely dangerous step. In addition, the young ulemas, like the Ikhwan of the 1920s, question the Government's close relationship with the heretic West and have forced a degree of change over this matter. The elders' response cum acceptance of the attitudes of the young religious rebels was made possible because the Wahhabi old guard fear a split in their ranks and the growing strength of the new class. They also fear the adoption of Western ways which would go with their assumption of a posture which made them a counterweight to the royal family.

The Wahhabi ulemas are also very worried that the ways of the House of Saud are forcing practising Muslims to cluster around other religious groups, and in December 1991 this fear took the form of an attack on new, popular Islamic fundamentalist groups. Furthermore, in an overall response to the pressures on them to either act or lose credibility in 1991 Sheikh Abdel Aziz bin Baz, the Wahhabi head of the highest religious council of the land, issued an appeal for reform addressed to the King. This, carrying the signature of 500 religious sheikhs, deplored the state of corruption in the country and lack of freedom, and demanded political reforms which included an independent, elected Consultative Council empowered to help legislate against and remedy the present excesses. Coming as it did from a body which has so far supported the House of Saud, the appeal was a stunning blow to King Fahd, particularly the part which explicitly compared his ways with those of his deposed brother, King Saud.

But if the moderate Wahhabi-controlled Council of Ulemas goes this far, and its appeal's words are harsh but do not go beyond advocating reform from within, then non-Wahhabi religious leaders and their followers go much further. The Shias' opposition to the regime is total – and, judged by the treatment they receive, unsurprising. There are also the banned but growing and effective religious parties of Hezbollah, the new Ikhwan, the Islamic Revolutionary Party, the Muslim Brotherhood and others, who all demand a reversion to Islam which precludes the continuance of the House of Saud. Though these groups operate mostly in secret, they are growing more vocal by the day and their protests are coming close to becoming a popular outcry.

The people's unhappiness is expressing itself in many small daily acts. One of the anti-Saud audio cassettes distributed by members of one of these groups is so popular that the Government offered a reward of $500,000 for any information about its author and another equally popular cassette is called SUPERGUN, a reference to the gigantic weapon Saddam Hussein threatened to use against the country. On this effective resurgence of religious opposition, the Syrian journalist and one-time adviser to King Faisal, Nihad Al Ghadiri, provides an astute comment: 'Islamic fundamentalism differs from Christian or Jewish fundamentalism; it is not the case of a sect taking a different approach, it is a case of all the Muslim sects wanting to revert to the word of the Koran.' This is why the House of Saud is finding it impossible to completely suppress these parties.

The distribution of audio cassettes, pamphlets, books, copies of anti-royal petitions and other articles promoting a cleansing Islamic revolution has become an everyday occurrence; they compete for top position on the bestseller list and the audiences for these revolutionary tools are growing in numbers. Also, courageous open dissent has occurred in some mosques where calls for a change of government have been made during Friday prayers despite the certain arrest of the speakers, and on 30 January 1992 the Government acted to stop a planned Muslim fundamentalist demonstration. These serious acts signalling the emergence of an overt challenge to the regime have led King Fahd and some of his nephews to use their press conferences to attack the fundamentalists.

A convergence of dissidence, though it was unthinkable until a few months ago, now appears likely. A July 1992 petition to King Fahd by 108 clerics, professors, merchants and others – an angry petition long enough and detailed enough to ask him to stop

115

building palaces – has just surfaced and others are likely to follow. The severe social tensions are exacerbated by questions as to how the country's 1982 $140-billion surplus has disappeared and why the House of Saud persists in befriending a West which is against the Muslims in Bosnia and Palestine. Above all, the Government's unwillingness or inability to deal with the problems of what the Lebanese writer Georges Corm describes as 'a society sick with oil' is driving more and more people into opposition.

Former US Ambassador to Saudi Arabia James Akins uses many of these elements to create a convincing scenario which resembles what existed in Iran on the eve of the overthrow of the Shah, when the religious people and merchants joined forces to topple him through open, street-based rebellion. The ability of the Saudi people to join in a popular, unstoppable rebellion is debatable, but other experts question the family's ability to continue to defeat the challenges facing them, and speak of their questionable plans to build an army and their cynical support of religion as tantamount to sponsoring their eventual downfall. But not so Western leaders, and the American administration has welcomed the recent announcement about a toothless Consultative Council under the total control of the King as 'a considerable step forward'. The question neither Bill Clinton, John Major, François Mitterand nor any Western leader who has extended guarantees to the House of Saud has ever answered is what he would do in the case of a serious internal rebellion. What would the Western nations do if the streets of Saudi Arabia echoed with the shouts of people wanting democracy? What would they do if an anti-House of Saud Islamic republic was declared in Mecca? Would they bomb Mecca and thus declare war on over a billion Muslims? The time to intercept the House of Saud's march towards disaster is now and massive changes must be imposed on King Fahd and his family.

5

Brotherhood is Selective

Saudi Arabia has two identities, an Arab identity and a Muslim one. Except for Lebanon, Islam is the dominant religion of all Arab countries, and this dual identity claims all of them. Until the recent radicalization of Islam and the electoral and other successes of Muslim fundamentalists which enabled them to influence state affairs, the rest of the Arab countries, unlike Saudi Arabia, wore their Muslim identity lightly and had no problem placing their national identity above their religion. Saudi Arabia has never been able to do that, and for practical reasons has never tried to. As the birthplace of the Prophet Muhammad and the home of Islam's two holiest cities, Mecca and Medina, where all able Muslims are commanded to go to perform the Hajj, it has forced upon it a greater Muslim role. Furthermore, Saudi Arabia made religion the foundation of the state.

In Islam there is no clear division between religion and politics – God and Caesar overlap – so the country's religious position is also a political one. Thus Saudi Arabia's commitment to the propagation of Muslim ways means involvement in Muslim politics. In addition, the various kings of the House of Saud have never tried to limit Islam's external claims on them; they welcomed them with relish in order to offset their inherent weaknesses among the Arabs. So, while other Arab countries faced no problems in reconciling their two identities, the House of Saud sought to create a division between the two and always manipulated its bonds with the Muslim world to balance the historic, linguistic and geographical Arab claim.

The dual identity is a reality and a convenience which manifests itself in many ways, including the constant reference to 'Islamic brotherhood' in the texts of all the treaties Saudi Arabia has with Muslim and Arab countries and in King Fahd's adoption of the title of Guardian of Islam's Holy Shrines, which was originally coined for Sultan Selim of Turkey. This exceptional ethno-religious position and power have been enhanced by Saudi Arabia's control of 25 per cent of the world's known oil reserves (by this is meant oil recoverable at a reasonable price). The oil wealth and the relative weakness of the Arabs and Muslims could have led to the country's assumption of a position of true leadership in both worlds. But, much to the chagrin of Saudi Arabia's friends in the West, it has not. The generally accepted Saudi position of Arab and Muslim leadership is superficial. Saudi Arabia feigns it, and it is not accepted by most Arabs and Muslims, and by others only for brief periods of time and because of specific financial needs.

There are obvious traditional reasons for Saudi Arabia's inability to lead and they include its small population, the Bedouin backwardness of the country and the House of Saud's adherence to Wahhabism. But there are other reasons which are of the House of Saud's own making: its divisive role, a total failure to develop constructive long-range policies, the royal family's corruption and continued commitment to absolute rule, and the weakness and lack of skill of most of its kings. Whether the House of Saud could have done anything about the built-in traditional reasons is arguable, but the family-made reasons began with the conquest of most of the Arabian Peninsula and the proclamation of the Saudi state. Oil, which came later and should have facilitated the assumption of sensible Arab and Muslim positions, did the opposite. It created a distance between the Saudis and the rest. More recently oil has been used to turn the Arabs and Muslims against each other.

But even without much interest in Arabism or the Muslim world, Ibn Saud still could not denounce either. He was unwillingly Arab and Muslim while trying his utmost to keep both from upsetting his personal gains and ways. During the 1920s, soon after the completion of Ibn Saud's conquests, Saudi Arabia, a new state, immediately developed border disputes with all its neighbours (Iraq, Jordan, Qatar, Kuwait, Oman, the Yemen and the Trucial States – the latter are now the United Arab Emirates). Ibn Saud accepted British-sponsored solutions for these problems and went further and signed meaningless friendship treaties with some of his neighbours. He did little beyond that and most of the Arab countries were weak colonies fighting for their own independence, hardly in a position to force on him a greater Arab commitment or to sponsor his people against him. But the Muslim context differed substantially. His occupation in 1925 of the holy cities of Mecca and Medina precluded ignoring Islam. In this case infidel Britain stood aloof; Islam and Islamic unity did not threaten it and control of the holy cities might prove useful. The Muslims thought Mecca and Medina belonged to all of them and demanded a say in the way they were governed. They issued specific calls for the institution of a democratic all-Muslim government for Mecca and Medina with Ibn Saud as 'guardian'.

Aware of the non-acceptance of his Wahhabism, Ibn Saud initially attempted to assuage Muslim unease by announcing that his occupation of Mecca and Medina was temporary, to be replaced by a more acceptable religious body to be defined later, but still with him in control. This was not enough to appease the doubters. Protests against Wahhabi acts of terror were vehement and, because the non-Wahhabi people of the Hijaz were in sympathy with the outsiders, dangerous enough to force Ibn Saud in 1926 to call a Muslim conference 'to have fellow Muslims know us as we are, and not as we have been described by our enemies'.

The Islamic conference was attended by kings, presidents and representatives from over 40 countries, but in the absence of a universally accepted Islamic church hierarchy to decide religious issues, it proved to be a non-event. The issues were heatedly debated and calls for religious tolerance and the banning of granting 'any commercial concessions to foreigners' were added to opposition to any change in the nature of the holy cities and Ibn Saud's assumption of the non-Islamic title of king. But, after many threats and counter-threats, the conference produced no results – just the creation of a committee to deal with these things headed by Prince Faisal. Though they were unhappy, there was not a single Muslim country in a position to alter the situation.

Ibn Saud dismissed the Islamic conference after he expanded his promises regarding the sanctity of the holy cities and emphasized that the pilgrimage, which he promoted because it was his only indigenous source of income, was safer under him than ever before. His deportation of the Indian delegation revealed a great deal about how secure he felt. Though Ibn Saud did not renege on all his promises, including the important one of granting foreign concessions, until much later, the pan-Islamic importance of Mecca and Medina was reduced, but they remained under Saudi control.

The border disputes and doctrinal questions made for an inauspicious Arab and Muslim start. Except for promoting the Hajj to safeguard the income it generated, Ibn Saud concentrated on consolidating his internal position. The Muslims of the world stopped looking to the Governor of Mecca and Medina for

religious guidance and they and the Arabs had no interest in
Ibn Saud's internal policies. Until 1932, except for minor Iraqi
attempts at cooperation with Ibn Saud, which Britain's committed
stand against Arab cooperation blocked, the only people who paid
serious attention to Saudi Arabia were star-struck Orientalists and
British agents. But control of most of the Arabian Peninsula
and Islam's holiest shrines precluded long-term uninvolvement
in Arab and Muslim affairs. Soon three major problems surfaced.
A religious dispute with Egyptian pilgrims, a serious territorial
dispute with the Yemen and the budding conflict in Palestine
represented major issues which forced Ibn Saud to reveal his true
position on the Arabs and the Muslims.

The Saudi refusal in 1929 to allow the Egyptians to conduct
their colourful ceremony of Mahmal resulted in the death of over
30 Egyptian pilgrims and led to a rupture in diplomatic relations.
It sent a signal to all Muslims, particularly to the Shias of Iran,
whose ways were more colourful and more offensive to Wahhabi
strictures and sensibilities than those of the Egyptians. For the
first time in centuries, Muslims performing the Hajj did so under
censorship. It widened the schism between the ruler of Mecca and
Medina and the rest of Islam.

The territorial dispute with the Yemen in the 1930s was the
culmination of a long-simmering enmity between the only two
independent countries in the Arabian Peninsula. The Yemen had
become independent in 1918 and its borders were determined
by the Turkish-sponsored Violet Line Agreement of 1914. But
the nature of the Yemen was a challenge to the Saudis: it was
a populous country with more than half the population of the
whole Arabian Peninsula, had a solid urban history and was more
advanced than its new neighbour. It also represented a thorn in
the side of British colonialism, a possible springboard for action
against their control of Saudi Arabia and all the makeshift tributary
sheikhdoms and emirates of the Gulf. In particular, the Yemen
represented a threat to the British colonization of Aden, a territory
which considered itself part of a greater Yemen which had been
dismembered by colonialism.

As usual when Saudi Arabia and Britain had similar interests,
Ibn Saud expressed British policies and began making trouble for
the Yemen and its rulers. The problems had begun four years
before he gained control of the Muslim holy cities, in 1921, when
3000 Yemeni pilgrims who were passing through Saudi-controlled
territory on their way to Mecca were slaughtered in cold blood. The

extent of this butchery and the feeble Saudi excuse of mistaking the pilgrims for an invading army augured poorly for the future but the Yemen was trying its best to avoid a confrontation with Saudi Arabia and its British backers and it accepted compensation.

In 1932, the year that Ibn Saud gave the territory he ruled his name, both countries competed over the control of Assir, now the south-western part of Saudi Arabia, always a neglected territory governed by the most brutal of the House of Saud emirs. The Assiris were Zeidi Shias, the co-religionists of the Yemenis and historically their wards, but the Saudis, even when the disputed territory represented no strategic imperative for them and despite their insistence that the Shias were heretics, wanted to weaken the Yemen and claimed the territory as theirs. The initial military confrontation over this attractive mountainous part of the Arabian Peninsula was settled without any alterations in the territory's status and the two sides signed a friendship treaty.

But neither Ibn Saud nor the British were satisfied with a treaty which left the Yemen relatively strong. Ibn Saud ignored the treaty and sponsored anti-Yemeni cross-border raids until it led to open warfare between the two countries. With British financial support and military equipment, his forces gained the upper hand and the Yemen was forced to sign the 1934 Taif Peace Agreement, which 'leased' Assir to Ibn Saud for a period of 20 years, to be renegotiated on its expiry. The Yemenis knew that they would never get the territory back and it was a humiliation they have never forgotten or forgiven.

The war with the Yemen exposed two articles of Saudi foreign policy which are still in existence. First, Saudi Arabia was intolerant of the presence of any other powerful force in the Arabian Peninsula. Secondly, particularly in view of unsuccessful Arab attempts to stop the war from breaking out, Saudi Arabia continued to prove itself willing to place its relationship with an outside power above its supposedly brotherly relationship with an Arab country.

The third problem, one which eventually became more important than the Yemen, was that of Palestine. To restate, the British wish to have a free hand in deciding the future of Palestine was among the reasons they sponsored Ibn Saud, who accommodated them by implicitly accepting the idea of a Jewish state. Internal and regional pressures to speak on behalf of Arab rights in Palestine and Muslim rights in Jerusalem on occasion forced him to make pronouncements which appeared to contradict his original stance, yet he continued to take his lead from Britain.

From the late 1920s and for a decade or so, Ibn Saud's inter-Arab policies on the subject of Palestine consisted of playing the two Arab sides vying for its leadership against each other, while simultaneously trying to bargain away Arab rights in return for British support to expand his domain. He opposed the claim to Palestine of the Hashemite King Abdallah of Jordan and pretended to support his enemy, the militant Mufti of Jerusalem, Haj Amin Al Husseini, by giving him limited financial help. Abdallah was a Hashemite rival to be kept from getting strong, but Ibn Saud's support for the Mufti was never wholehearted. He consistently advised the Mufti to negotiate with the various British commissions which were sent to study the Palestine problem. More seriously, in 1936, Ibn Saud tricked the Mufti into ending a 183-day Palestinian national strike which was successful in putting pressure on the British Mandate Government. Ibn Saud promised the Mufti to intercede with the British on his behalf and was explicit in his belief in 'our British friends' intentions'. There is no record of this intercession in the British Foreign Office documents of the time. In fact, Ibn Saud sought to weaken the Mufti as well by establishing contact with leading Palestinian families opposed to him, the Nashashibis and Shawas.

Ibn Saud went beyond using Philby as an emissary to the British Foreign Office and Churchill to negotiate his willingness to accept openly the Jewish claim to Palestine in return for Britain withholding support from his Hashemite rivals, who were now kings in Jordan and Iraq. On 17 September 1939 Philby met with Chaim Weizmann, later the first president of Israel, to negotiate Ibn Saud's overt acceptance of a Jewish state in return for £20 million. Ibn Saud was broke and, as usual, set money above brotherhood and principle.

Ibn Saud's support of the Mufti against King Abdallah of Jordan while sponsoring the Mufti's enemies was one of the earliest examples of a divide-and-rule policy on the Arabs. His acceptance of British policy was a signal that his old subservience to them would continue. His attempt to extract money from Weizmann was very much in character; the reason he was always successful in buying Bedouin loyalty was because he was one of them. But ignoring the Arabs and Muslims was easier in the 1920s and 1930s than it was in the 1940s – among other things the time when the Palestinian problem as an Arab and Muslim issue occupied centre stage.

In 1945 Saudi Arabia unavoidably joined the Arab League, an organization committed to fostering political and economic cooperation between the Arab countries. Joining the League satisfied his people and the rest of the Arabs but he had every intention of keeping it and its cooperation plans at arm's length. By 1947 and 1948, most Arabs looked to this new organization to save Palestine. Ostensibly the League decided on the level and nature of the Arabs' Palestinian involvement. Saudi Arabia, a member of an Arab organization for the first time, had no option but to participate in defending the Arab position in the United Nations and other international forums and to vote for sending Arab armies to help the people of Palestine.

During Ibn Saud's life, Saudi involvement in the most important Arab problem of the century never went further than providing verbal support. In the mid-1930s he had ignored the calls of King Ghazi of Iraq to form a common Arab front to defend Palestine. Then, in 1948, he sat on the sidelines and refused to contribute forces to liberate Palestine (even Philby admits this) and placed hurdles, such as the denial of transport, in the way of Saudi citizens who volunteered to join Arab forces fighting there. He continued to pay the Arab position lip-service to the extent of publicly instructing his son and Foreign Minister, Prince Faisal, to attack US support of Israel while conducting secret negotiations with the Americans for the building of the huge US airbase in Dhahran. His previous commitment to British policies had been replaced by a new American one and America was solidly pro-Israeli.

The 1948 Arab–Israeli War ended in the defeat of the Arabs and Ibn Saud's ensuing behaviour revealed no remorse – only a genuine fear that the popular feeling surrounding the Palestinian problem might infect his kingdom and undermine his position. Ibn Saud withheld financial support from the Egyptian and Jordanian forces still occupying parts of Palestine, but spent money supporting several military regimes in Syria to keep it from uniting with Iraq to create a military counterweight to Israel. According to Glubb Pasha, Ibn Saud was always apprehensive of such a union and how it might engender feelings for Arab unity among his people. The Saudi volunteers who managed to join the Arab forces in Palestine returned home to be harassed and imprisoned by the security forces. Saudi Arabia refused to admit qualified Palestinians who sought employment there because of fear of political agitation. Laws forbidding Saudis to marry Arabs without prior governmental permission, which was seldom given, were introduced for the first time. The Saudi press was ordered to tone down its pro-Palestinian rhetoric and reduce its reporting of the misery which had befallen the Palestinians. Ibn Saud refused to contemplate the possible use of oil to pressure America into a more even-handed Palestinian policy and, according to the Palestinian leader Jamal Toukan, a member of a delegation who visited him to ask for assistance, he was preoccupied with burning what food remained after the feast he gave them, lest it fall in the hands of poor people who might get accustomed to eating meat.

The acts aimed at distancing Saudi Arabia from the aftermath of the Arab defeat, even the smallest of them, amounted to an adherence to a Saudi Arabia-first policy. The Saudi people felt differently, however, and even then Saudi writers and poets wrote about the problem constantly and tearfully. Such a policy in reality meant the House of Saud came first. And a House of Saud-first policy meant financial and political reliance on America, the oil concessionaire who held the purse strings.

Briefly the policy worked. Saudi Arabia's level of political development, Ibn Saud's repression and the rising oil income allowed it to escape the consequent upheavals which beset other Arab regimes. To many observers, this completed the picture. The Saudi attempts to undermine the Yemen, Ibn Saud's aloofness from Muslim independence movements and Arab calls for cooperation, and his intolerance of non-Wahhabi Muslims, were capped by his attitude towards Palestine. This left his country's Arab and Muslim positions both tarnished and weak, and opened the door for America.

In 1953, it was left to the inept Saud to face the consequences of his father's policies. The inevitable internal pressures which Ibn Saud had failed to neutralize were ignited and compounded by Gamal Abdel Nasser, the Egyptian leader who assumed power in 1952 and later espoused Arab nationalism and became its leading twentieth-century exponent.

Nasser, a former Egyptian Army colonel who saw heroic combat in Palestine, rose to power as a result of the 1948 Arab defeat. His Army group seized power in Egypt from the corrupt King Farouk and was committed to eliminating the causes of the defeat in Palestine and to punishing the ruling social establishment responsible for it. Nasser's initial target, the Egyptian royal family and the land-owning Pashas, was expanded in 1954 when Nasser claimed leadership of Egypt's three circles of power: the Arab, Muslim and African worlds. The African role was uniquely Egyptian, but Nasser's claim in the Arab and Muslim arenas, though Nasser was loath to admit it, was an extension of the Hashemite claim of leadership of all the Arabs against which the House of Saud rose to power. And Nasser did not stop there; using as a base Al Azhar, Islam's oldest university and the leading recognized source of Muslim learning, he also presented a Muslim challenge. Because the House of Saud had not permitted anything to flourish in Mecca and Medina except Wahhabi teachings, Al Azhar was an attractive pan-Islamic alternative and its ulemas enhanced their position by adopting the issue of Jerusalem.

Nasser's Arab and Muslim appeals struck a chord with the Saudi people. Their Saudism was new and, despite four decades of attempts by the House of Saud to promote it, an unsatisfactory replacement for their Arab and Muslim identities. Saudi people needed and wanted to express their Arab and Muslim selves. Nasser's threat was not to invade Saudi Arabia, but his ability to subvert its people by appealing to their frozen identities and to their dissatisfaction with the House of Saud. It was a simple case of the external idea depending on internal support and Saudi political groups such as the Arabian Peninsula Peoples' Union supported Nasser and established offices in Cairo. Nasser's attempt to undermine the House of Saud utilized new technology, and the confrontation took the form of a battle between the old and the new. A new Egyptian radio station, the Voice of the Arabs, specialized in telling the Arab people of the misdeeds of their leaders. There was no shortage of material on Saudi Arabia, and the numbers of the King's wives and palaces and the gambling and womanizing of his brothers were recited in the manner of a scandal magazine of the airwaves. Of course, the promise of what Arab unity and Islamic solidarity would bring were exaggerated. The denunciations and exaggerations were combined in the slogan: 'Arab oil for the Arab people.'

King Saud faced a greater threat than had ever confronted his father. The previous Saudi position of safety had depended on the lack of responsiveness by the country's people to outside stimuli and the weakness of its enemies, and Nasser represented a reversal of both elements. The Arab threat was from within and Saudi Arabia's diminished Islamic credentials left it little room to manoeuvre. To avoid being left adrift politically, religiously and culturally, the Saudi Government decided to reclaim its two identities. William Quandt of the Brookings Institution in Washington, in his remarkable *Saudi Arabia in the 1980s*, suggests, 'It isn't sentiment which draws Saudi Arabia into Arab politics' to make a point about Saudi Arabia's response to the Arab threats to its safety. Quandt's observation holds true for the Saudi involvement in Muslim affairs. The Nasser challenge brought an end to its Arab and Muslim isolation. The Saudis had either to confront Nasser or to appease him.

King Saud was surrounded by foreign advisers in the manner of his father but the Americans had not replaced Philby with an influential court personality to keep him in line and his weakness and the mixed advice of his Syrian and Palestinian courtiers led to confused policies. In 1955 Saud quarrelled with Nasser over the latter's espousal of socialism, but in 1956 he went as far as to enter a tripartite alliance with Egypt and Syria which, however, he soon allowed to wither away. The resulting deterioration in the Saudi position enhanced the popularity of Nasser within Saudi Arabia and made other Arab leaders opposed to Nasser reluctant to befriend its government.

Suddenly there was Suez. When Nasser failed to secure total American support for his policies, his ambitions to control the Middle East and to eliminate what remained of British and French political influence and economic interests culminated in his 1956 nationalization of the Suez Canal and the consequent British, French and Israeli invasion of his country. This time, unlike in 1948, the weakness of Saud and Nasser's popularity and the resulting threat of internal upheaval forced the Saudis to respond to the multinational attack on Egypt. Saud offered Egyptian military aircraft safe haven in his country and, unlike his father in 1948, ordered the cessation of oil shipments to Britain and France. ARAMCO, the American oil-producing consortium, encouraged by official American disapproval of the Suez invasion, obeyed the Saudi decision meekly and established a precedent which came back to haunt the company in the early 1970s, when the USA itself became the target of an oil embargo.

The selective oil embargo and courageous safe-haven offer were followed by generous financial aid to Egypt. Privately furious over Nasser's policies of confrontation, Saud acted to avoid being toppled. But, contrary to Saudi and other expectations that Suez was the end of Nasser, the Suez defeat strengthened rather than diminished Nasser's popularity and his threat to his Arab neighbours. Eventually the shakiness of the Saudi regime registered with the Eisenhower administration and forced it to act to protect its oil interests.

Rather than use diplomats to develop a Saudi–American plan to contain Nasser, America played on Saud's simple Bedouin instincts and in January 1957 invited him to the USA, where he was met on the tarmac by none other than Eisenhower himself. The negotiations which ensued and were followed up in Saudi Arabia produced a declaration of the Eisenhower Doctrine. This policy articulated the so-far secret American guarantees to Saudi Arabia (see The Brutal Friendship) and extended them to cover the safety of other countries friendly to the USA against the expansionist designs of Nasser or communism or both. At long last Saud's mind was made up for him.

As we will see in the following chapter, the Eisenhower Doctrine also formalized the replacement of the Anglo–French hegemony over pro-West Middle Eastern countries with an American one. But, like Britain before it, America had no long-term policy for Saudi Arabia and beyond the threat of military intervention it did nothing to define Saudi Arabia's role in the Arab and Muslim worlds.

In 1957 King Hussein of Jordan, encouraged and aided by the CIA, overthrew his own popularly elected pro-Nasser cabinet. (Contrary to popular history, which alleges that the cabinet tried to overthrow Hussein, the plot was concocted in Beirut and the CIA had a team of agents directing the operation from the King's palace.) This palace coup represented a confrontation between the pro- and anti-Nasser forces throughout the Middle East. America prevailed on King Saud to cast aside the historical Saudi–Hashemite enmity and to support King Hussein. This time Saudi Arabia used money against Nasser and it went further and stationed Saudi troops in Jordan to help stabilize it. It was the first use of Saudi troops in an Arab dispute beyond its borders.

Nasser's threat to the whole Middle East was deeply entrenched, however, and was anchored in the desire of the Arab people for unity. In 1958 Syria, a shaky republic lacking in permanent leadership and prone to *coups d'état*, gave expression to this desire and decided to join Nasser and become the junior partner in the union with Egypt which created the United Arab Republic. To counter this threat to their security, Jordan and Iraq decided to merge and form a union of their own. What Saudi Arabia had always dreaded most, the emergence of strong Arab neighbours who could act as a magnet for its people and bring an end to the

House of Saud's rule, became a reality. The American guarantee of its national integrity was deemed insufficient protection and Saudi Arabia felt obliged to try to stop both unions from being realized.

Saudi Arabia's attempt to intercept the march towards Arab unity took the form of a sophomoric plot in March 1958 to assassinate Nasser by shooting down his plane as it was about to land in Damascus. This was to be followed by other assassinations of pro-Nasser Syrian leaders, including the Syrian President, Shukri Kuwatly. The scheme was conceived by Yusuf Yassin, a Syrian adviser to Saud, and approved personally by the King. Nasser was nothing if not a publicist, and he got considerable mileage out of exposing the plot and giving journalists copies of the £2-million cheque the Saudis paid his Syrian chief of intelligence to do the job. Instead of eliminating Nasser, the plot played right into his hands and he convinced the Arab people, including many unhappy Saudis, that Saud was a Western lackey and that the West was the plot's real instigator. (Egyptian Foreign Minister Mahmoud Riad and a former Palestinian adviser to King Saud insist that it was a CIA plot but provide no evidence to back their allegation. Others have hinted at CIA–ARAMCO involvement, again without adequate proof.)

Saud's fate was sealed. His brother Faisal, too shrewd to personally lead a move to force Saud to step down, allowed other members of the family to do it. There was no way for Saud to outlive creating an atmosphere which alienated the Saudi people to the extent of endangering the rule of the family. In 1958 he initially agreed to cede power to Faisal to run the country while remaining a figurehead.

One of the first problems to confront Faisal after his initial assumption of power was what to do about the ostensibly pro-Nasser *coup d'état* which overthrew the Hashemite Iraqi monarchy and put an end to unity plans between Iraq and Jordan on 14 July 1958. Eliminating the Iraqi monarchy, always a more substantial establishment than its poor Jordanian cousin, had been a goal of the House of Saud, but replacing it with a revolutionary regime posed a bigger threat. It took Faisal several days to recognize the new regime, since he was reluctant to accept the demise of his more predictable conservative enemies.

As it was, the new Iraqi regime became opposed to Nasser. Later, in 1961, Syria seceded from the union with Egypt and this time Faisal's anti-Arab-unity policies led him to immediately recognize the new regime and provide it with financial help. The regional balance of power was back to square one and Saudi Arabia moved to reclaim its old position, keeping the Arab world divided.

Meanwhile Faisal was uneasy with his *de facto* position and this encouraged a number of House of Saud moves which culminated in Saud's abdication in 1964. Nasser was faced with a united House of Saud and a worthy adversary who was totally free to follow his own policies and, fortunately for King Faisal, the battleground where the latest Egyptian–Saudi confrontation was taking place favoured him.

In 1962 another pro-Nasser revolution overthrew the monarchy in the Yemen. Whether Nasser personally was behind it remains a subject for debate, but his followers were and his pan-Arab leadership position precluded disowning an anti-royalist *coup d'état*. Throughout the Arab world, the nationalist followers of Nasser recovered from the Syrian secession and were euphoric; they and their leader expected Saudi Arabia to follow the Yemen. But Faisal, initially as prime minister and regent and later as king, knew the people and terrain of the Arabian Peninsula much better than Nasser did and responded to the challenge in his backyard with firmness and cool. In this he was supported by President Kennedy, who used the Eisenhower Doctrine by holding joint military manoeuvres with the Saudi Army and provided Saudi Arabia with unlimited material support.

With America guaranteeing his safety, Faisal adopted the Yemeni royalists who had escaped the coup and supplied them with money and arms to start a civil war against the pro-Nasser republican regime. Faisal knew the Yemen's new leaders could not stand alone – not when he was buying the loyalty of its fickle Bedouins with salaries bigger than they had ever dreamed of. And he knew that Nasser could not afford to fail in the Yemen and survive. Nasser would have to divert forces to the Yemen which he desperately needed for his on-going confrontation with Israel. Like his father when he attacked the Hashemites in the Hijaz in 1925, Faisal was happy fighting a war he could not lose. America was ready to intervene against any Nasser-inspired move into Saudi Arabia to deny the Yemeni rebels safe haven. In fairness, Kennedy was not enamoured of the Yemeni royalists and knew that the republicans were a more advanced and wholesome lot, but he had no choice. It was war by proxy, an extension of the cold war; Kennedy acted because the USSR supported Nasser.

Emboldened by his early Yemeni success, Faisal expanded his

challenge, but in this case initially without the support of the Nasser-admiring Kennedy. Fully aware that Nasser's popularity with the Arab masses precluded winning in the Arab arena, he visited Iran and some North African countries and decided to play his country's Muslim card by convening an International Islamic Conference in Mecca. The main outcome of the conference was the emergence of the Saudi-financed World Muslim League. The league's conservative membership included the anti-Nasser Egyptian Muslim Brotherhood and its first proclamation left no doubt as to its purpose: 'Those who distort Islam's call under the guise of nationalism are the most bitter enemies of the Arabs whose glories are entwined with the glories of Islam.' At long last the riches of Saudi Arabia allowed it to drive a wedge between Arabism and Islam.

With Nasser behaving unpredictably, this open subordination of Arabism to Islam gained the wholehearted support of America. An open campaign which accused Nasser of being anti-Islamic followed and so did attacks on Nasser's backer, the USSR, for its treatment of its Muslims. This coincided with a generous Saudi aid programme to Jordan and a move by Faisal to create a special relationship with the only Muslim country capable of providing him with military help, Pakistan. The USA was reluctant to commit its troops on holy Muslim soil and instead encouraged the secret agreements between Saudi Arabia and Pakistan. On the popular level, Faisal went beyond funding anti-Nasser Muslim groups and sought to counter the substantial and effective Nasser propaganda machine by sponsoring anti-Nasser newspapers and magazines in the emerging communications centre of Beirut. Beirut's pamphleteers emphasized the un-Islamic nature of Nasser's socialism and friendship with the USSR (see The Last Line of Defence).

Internally, Faisal, with considerable help from the CIA in the form of operatives attached to ARAMCO, encouraged the formation of anti-socialist Muslim groups, particularly around the oil centre of Dhahran. (There is reason to believe that some of the anti-Saudi and anti-American Islamic groups in existence today are the radicalized successors of these groups.) Faisal's moves represented an entire programme which advanced his country's and the Middle East's Islamic character at the expense of its Arab one and which used the CIA to run internal security in an open way which included direct dealings between the King and the CIA's Arabic-speaking local station chief. The then leader of the Egyptian Muslim Brotherhood, Sayed Kuttub, a man Faisal sponsored to undermine Nasser, openly admitted that during this period 'America made Islam'.

Meanwhile the war in the Yemen dragged on, and Nasser's troops were hampered by their inability to pursue their enemies into Saudi territory, proving unequal to the task of conquering a mountainous country. After the loss of Syria and the blunting of Nasser's revolutionary momentum in Iraq, where the West, in this case with Britain in the lead, saw fit to support the ultra-radical but local Iraqi regime to halt the pan-Arab Nasser avalanche, the situation became intolerable. (Sir Michael Wright, the then British Ambassador to Baghdad, went as far as to advise his government to overlook the Iraqi regime's unjustified arrest and detention of some British citizens.) Nasser's camp began to show strains and vulnerability. Tellingly, one of the leaders of the new anti-Nasser Syria was Colonel Abdel Hamid Sarraj, the very officer King Saud had bribed to kill his one-time idol Nasser.

Nasser grew weaker and Faisal grew stronger. Nasser was supported by the USSR and the Arab masses while Faisal depended on the West, oil wealth and the rulers of the conservative Arab and Muslim countries. Faisal concentrated everything on the Yemen and limited support to Muslim countries while Nasser was overextended battling in the Yemen, against Iraq, in Jordan and the Sudan and helping anti-French Arab rebellions in North Africa. Nasser was reeling under the financial strains created by his adventures and the USSR, worried by the prospects of a confrontation with the USA, would not provide him with the financial support he needed. But there seemed to be no end to Faisal's financial resources. The Arab people, never steadfast in the best circumstances, began abandoning Nasser's revolutionary bandwagon.

The USSR's failure to match the combined Saudi–Western assault on his Arab nationalism, and accusations of pro-Western Arab governments that he was no more than a paper tiger, prompted Nasser to call on what *Time* correspondent Wilton Wynn called his 'Samson Complex'. He played his Arab card to its limits and opted for a confrontation with Israel. Either he won the confrontation and with it the Arab world or he brought the house down on himself and everybody else.

Nasser was ill-prepared for war because 100,000 Egyptian soldiers were bogged down in the Yemen and he secretly told the UN that he was not desirous of open conflict, but he stole a march on his enemies. Arabs everywhere began calling for an end to war in the Yemen to free Nasser's hand against Israel. Aware that time was running against it and that Nasser's military commitment in the Yemen afforded it a special opportunity which might soon disappear, Israel, in June 1967, launched a surprise attack on Egypt and Syria and then Jordan. The Arab armies were defeated in six days. Sinai, the Golan Heights and the West Bank and Gaza Strip were occupied and Arab dreams were shattered. Israel's victory was total; and so was Faisal's.

Bowing to Arab pressure, Nasser and Faisal met at a conference of Arab heads of state in Khartoum. There was no doubt as to whose day it was. Nasser agreed to leave the Yemen and asked Saudi opposition groups and former King Saud to leave Cairo. The latter, in an attempt to regain his throne, had gone to Nasser's side and had visited the Egyptian-occupied Yemen to rally the republican faithful against his country. In return, Faisal offered Nasser some economic support. It amounted to total surrender.

Unlike in 1956, America, the only country capable of pressuring Israel into withdrawing from the occupied Arab territories, was in no mood to do it. After all, Nasser had advocated the nationalization of oil and had threatened its strategic position in the Middle East. This time Nasser could not claim victory; there was no humiliated colonial Britain or France to talk about. For Nasser, it was the beginning of the end. For the House of Saud, it heralded a deeper involvement in Arab and Muslim affairs. Their recent experience made them accept the obvious, that they could not remain aloof and safe. Instead, they would try to extend their new position to advantage, to use their oil wealth to neutralize all other threatening political movements.

Fortune smiled on Faisal in the person of Denis Michael Rohan, a crazed Australian Christian fundamentalist who in July 1969 set fire to the Aqsa Mosque in Jerusalem. Arab and Muslim feelings were likewise inflamed, and theories of conspiracy and Israeli collusion abounded. The question of whether the response to the incident should be Arab or Muslim assumed a critical importance. In a bold pre-emptive move, Faisal called for the convening of the first Muslim heads of state conference in Rabat, Morocco. The response was overwhelming and, except for secular-socialist Syria and Iraq, the conference was attended by all the Arab heads of state. It produced a number of decisions in favour of political and economic cooperation and a declaration of commitment to Muslim rights in Jerusalem. That simple act expressed Faisal's new policy and confirmed the ascendancy of his country's Islamic policies. Faisal followed this by making statement after statement about his desire to pray in Jerusalem; he publicized Muslim rights to the city but said little about Arab rights. Of course, to wrongfoot his pro-Soviet Arab competitors and to please his Western backers, he kept equating Zionism with communism.

If the God-sent problem of the Jerusalem fire provided Faisal with a chance to give the Muslim world priority over the Arab one, then what followed in Jordan gave him a chance to strike a blow against the leading Arab revolutionary movement, the PLO. In September 1970 civil war erupted in Jordan between the then radical but totally secular PLO and the forces of King Hussein. Faisal, according to documents made available to me by one of his former assistants, again with the blessing of the USA, ordered the commander of the Saudi forces still stationed in Jordan to provide King Hussein with all the assistance he needed, and sponsored Pakistan to send units of its air force to attack the Palestinian forces and their Syrian backers. Hussein triumphed, the PLO was driven into Lebanon and Saudi Arabia eliminated another revolutionary threat. Subduing Nasser and the PLO reduced the pull of the Palestine problem as a rallying point for Arab nationalist forces and placed Saudi Arabia in a position of Arab and Muslim supremacy. Instead of acting negatively to frustrate the designs of others, Saudi Arabia was in a strong political and financial position to tell some of them what to do.

The untimely death of Nasser in 1972 expanded the Middle Eastern power vacuum which the West wanted and the rest of the world expected Saudi Arabia to fill. But Saudi Arabia would not move. The Western desire overlooked the very basic fact that Saudi Arabia, though responsible for creating the leadership vacuum, wanted nothing from either the Arab or Muslim worlds except to be left alone. To Faisal, a true position of Arab or Muslim leadership would force Saudi Arabia to respond to the relatively sophisticated demands of the Arabs and Muslims and enhance pan-Arab or pan-Islamic cooperation. Because he was opposed to these things and because Saudi Arabia was not administratively or developmentally ready to assume leadership, Faisal rejected what he considered counterproductive, and expensive. Saudi Arabia decided to limit its act of leadership of both worlds to pretending to lead and to use this pretence to stop others assuming the position. After the selective use of money, it settled for selective leadership without overall responsibility.

With modifications, the decision to pretend to lead governs the Saudi Arab and Muslim policies to this day. It has been applied to the Arab problems of Palestine and Lebanon, the wars between Algeria and Morocco, the various Syrian–Iraqi feuds and, in a more complicated way, to Egypt's decision to sign the Camp David peace agreement of October 1978 with Israel. In the Muslim arena, the same principle was applied to Afghanistan, and to a lesser degree in Uganda, the Philippines, the Sudan, the Horn of Africa, Biafra and in Saudi Arabia's worldwide approach to Muslim problems. In all cases, it did not seek hegemony and its sole purpose was to keep others from achieving it.

Saudi Arabia backed the mainstream PLO headed by Yasser Arafat by affording it financial support of $100 million a year to stop it turning to others. But its fear of a strong PLO was enough to prompt it to bankroll the terrorist Abu Nidal to unbalance Arafat. Abu Nidal's bloody credentials proved no barrier to this expression of Saudi self-interest. In Lebanon, Saudi Arabia pretended that it was playing the impartial peace broker while providing financial help to the conservative pro-West Christian Phalange against the pan-Arabist Mourabitoun and the militant Shias of Amal and Hezbollah. Saudi Arabia mediated in the Algerian–Moroccan war to protect the conservative King Hassan of Morocco against his populist neighbour and it pretended to mediate between Syria and Iraq while providing financial support to Syria to help it resist Iraq's unity calls. Even relatively remote Libya did not escape Saudi attempts to unbalance it. Saudi Arabia saw in Qaddafi a greater threat than was justified and supported his more militant Islamic opponents. These Saudi efforts to maintain an imbalance were continued even when that imbalance, as in the case of Lebanon, called for them to ignore the rights of their co-religionists, the Muslim majority, which had undoubtedly suffered from an insensitive Christian control of power.

Saudi actions in the Muslim world followed the same line. Pakistan was supported so long as it followed a Saudi line and did not try to act independently and lead. Pakistani President Ali Bhutto's refusal to follow this formula saw Saudi Arabia provide his army with financial help and promises of more to overthrow him. Uganda's Idi Amin was provided with financial support because Uganda did not matter and backing the despot afforded Saudi Arabia a chance to manifest phoney Muslim concern at the expense of the country's Christians in a remote, insignificant place. Muslim rebels in the Philippines were supported for the same reason without Saudi Arabia knowing what their rebellion was all about. The Mujahadeen in Afghanistan were funded to a much greater degree because their situation afforded Saudi Arabia a chance to be anti-Soviet and pro-West and because Saudi propaganda, in an attempt to pre-empt militant Iran, depicted the civil war in the country as a Muslim life-and-death issue. In the Horn of Africa, the despotic Muslim regime of Siad Barre in Somalia was supported against Christian Ethiopia despite worldwide recognition that the conflict would lead to tribal chaos, the breakdown of both countries and famine.

Saudi Arabia backed its pretensions of leadership with the only thing it has, money. But because the money it paid was to per-petuate problems and to intercept the emergence of an alternative power fell short of providing lasting solutions, what this policy in reality meant was that Saudi Arabia was in the business of renting solutions, in some places on behalf of itself, in others as a front for the West and in most because it suited both. Neither they nor the West knew what would result from eliminating Arafat but they wanted to keep him in check and, unlike the West, the Saudis could hire a terrorist to do the job. The Saudis knew they could not maintain Christian supremacy in Lebanon for ever, but not knowing how to replace it without creating a regime not beholden to them, they paid to keep it going. Financing Syria against Iraq was a short-term lease-solution which they had to keep renewing, but they could not think of a way to keep the countries permanently apart without destabilization threatening to them and to Israel and the West. Above all, Afghanistan was the classic case of Saudi money serving the aims of America's policy of containing the USSR, and, of course, it was given a Muslim label.

The natural limits on renting solutions were the length of the lease, the fact that rental costs kept going up and the willingness of the party to accept a Saudi offer. The volatile nature of the Middle East meant rental solutions lasted a short time; most of the people who were being paid by Saudi Arabia, in particular the Lebanese Christians, kept demanding more money. But these obstacles do not compare with the three major problems which did not lend themselves to short-term leases and hence either fell outside Saudi reach or forced it into expensive, long-term rentals. These are: the Egyptian decision to negotiate a peace agreement with Israel, the Muslim fundamentalist revolution in Iran and the Iran–Iraq War. In addition, there emerged the problem of many Muslim groups accepting money then turning against their Saudi sponsors.

Before he journeyed to Jerusalem to seek peace, Sadat's relations with Saudi Arabia had been good. Unlike Nasser and Farouk, he had been happy to concede a leading role to Saudi Arabia and align his policies with its rulers. He even coordinated the October 1973 War with King Faisal and convinced Saudi Arabia temporarily to embargo the sale of oil to the West (see The Brutal Friendship). Both Egypt and Saudi Arabia felt compelled to respond to the Arab reaction to the 1967 defeat, the explosive popular wish to avenge it, and both saw and planned the October War as a relief valve and a way to prod the West to solve the still-simmering Arab–Israeli problem. The cooperation between the two sides worked. The ensuing oil embargo and shortages of petrol and other fuels, though they accidentally almost got out of hand, sent a chill through the West's body politic and prompted a search for a permanent solution to the Palestinian problem.

But Sadat was determined to go forward to finalize his plan while Saudi Arabia, as usual, moved slowly. It wanted to start a peace process without suffering the consequences. Faced with the prospect of rupture with Saudi Arabia but unable to delay, Sadat acted alone, but only after using Saudi intelligence chief Kamal Adham to relay his decision to Crown Prince Fahd. The Arab people and most Arab governments reacted to the Sadat trip to Jerusalem with anger and called for the punishment of traitorous Egypt. The Saudis were caught in the middle. Supporting Sadat would please America but it meant the possible emergence of a new radical regional leadership and the prospect of internal turmoil.

The House of Saud, after heated debates which saw the pro-Sadat Crown Prince Fahd go to Spain to an angry self-imposed exile, decided to oppose Sadat. Simultaneously, the Saudis assured the Carter administration of their true intentions and moved to contain Arab attempts to punish Egypt and its leader. (They went as far as trying to bribe my journalist father to write a story about their commitment to the West.) The Arab censure of Egypt was comparatively mild, but the Saudi decision to support it was a tacit admission that, unlike in the past, there were internal and external pressures which precluded following the West blindly.

This example of helplessness exposed the limits of the policy of rental solutions. This major problem was followed by a more serious one which found the House of Saud unable to pretend. Iran – Shia, independent, strong and pro-West under the Shah – was the Middle East country where Saudi Arabia had the least influence. In 1979, when disturbances broke out against the Shah,

Saudi Arabia rallied to his support and described them as 'minor'. Later, alarmed at the apparent strength of Khomeini's movement, they resorted to calling his movement un-Islamic. Even for some time after the Shah was overthrown and replaced by Khomeini's Islamic fundamentalist regime, the Saudis continued to speak of 'the legitimate government of the country' to describe the exiled Shah and sponsored some feeble attempts to overthrow Khomeini, including a repeat performance of the Nasser assassination debacle, and in 1981 a publicized $10-million bribe to Iranian Air Force Colonel Raed Rukmi to stage a coup. But Iran's new revolutionary government proved permanent and it was against monarchies, alliances with the infidel West and the Saudi policy of maintaining low oil prices. In addition, the new Iranian leadership showed special concern for the Shia minority in Saudi Arabia.

The various manifestations of Iran's Islamic stance amounted to a single policy: the West and its friends were the enemies of Islam and their hegemony over the Middle East and the Muslim world should be brought to an end. This revolutionary call was the exact opposite of King Faisal's use of Islam as a conservative pro-West counterweight to secular revolutionary ideas. The foundations of the Saudi Islamic policy began to crumble, but Saudi Arabia could not go back on its Islamic posture. Instead, it began to compete within a Muslim framework; now it was revolutionary Islam versus traditional Islam.

As with Nasser, Iran was trying to use Saudi Arabia's own people against it. Even non-Shia Muslims, many of them groups hitherto supported by Saudi Arabia, sympathized with happenings in Iran and the 1979 uprising in Mecca was stimulated by the success in Iran of the ayatollahs. The Saudis were caught in their own Islamic folly. But, militarily weak and restricted by its supposed leadership of the Muslim world from waging war against another Muslim country, Saudi Arabia eventually changed direction and hid, albeit temporarily, behind an Arab identity.

Iran and Iraq have been enemies since time immemorial. In modern times this enmity was encouraged by a West which desired to control the Middle East and which saw in the continued bickering between the two countries a way to weaken them and to keep them from acting against Western strategic interests, particularly the West's oil-producing satellite states. When Ayatollah Khomeini rose to power there were a number of border and navigation disputes between the two sides which were exacerbated by his emphasis of religion at the expense of national identity. Iraq, run by the socialist and pan-Arabist Ba'ath Party, championed nationalism and, however misguided both sides were, the confrontation and eventual war between a theocracy and a secular nation-state was one of the few wars of principle this century.

But the Iraqi march to war was aided and abetted by Saudi Arabia, with the United States behind it. Unable to deal with Iran militarily, Saudi Arabia, with considerable American encouragement, sponsored Saddam Hussein to do it. The negotiations between the Saudis and Saddam to find ways to face the common Iranian threat lasted a long time and in August 1980 they concluded a secret agreement whereby Saudi Arabia guaranteed to provide Iraq with 'all the financial aid required to undertake all the necessary moves to protect its national honour'. States ABC Chief of Correspondents and Middle East expert Pierre Salinger: 'There is no doubt about it, both countries [Saudi Arabia and America] wanted Saddam to attack Iran.' In fact, before opting for 'the Iraqi solution' in 1980, President Carter's National Security Adviser, Zbigniew Brzezinski, made a public threat to use force against Iran. Later the United States had satellite pictures which showed that Iraq was preparing to attack Iran but did nothing to intercept the outbreak of hostilities. The assertion that 'the Iraqi solution' had US backing is confirmed unattributably by a former US Ambassador to Saudi Arabia and a former US Undersecretary of State and openly by Saddam Hussein's adviser Sa'ad Al Bazzaz, the author of *The Gulf War and the One After*. Says Bazzaz: 'We told them we're going to attack Iran; they knew.'

The following month, foolishly thinking that an attack on Iran would lead to its disintegration rather than to a gathering of support behind Khomeini, Iraqi armour thrust into Iran. Saudi Arabia made an initial payment to Iraq of $4 billion. It was another war by proxy; certainly an example of a grand-scale rentals policy and of fronting for the West against militant Islam.

The outbreak of hostilities between the second and third largest exporters of oil led to mutual aerial attacks on their production facilities and a serious decline in their output which, under normal circumstances, should have led to an increase in the price of oil and consequent American attempts to settle the conflict to restore prices to their pre-war level. But nothing of the sort happened. Saudi Arabia was prepared and it pre-empted the anticipated sequence of events by doubling its oil output and keeping the prices down. There was no urgency to end the war and Henry

Kissinger bluntly encapsulated the Saudi–American attitude by stating: 'Too bad both sides can't lose.'

In 1984 there was a real threat that the Iraqi military lines might break under the numerical weight of their Iranian enemies. Saddam Hussein panicked and pleaded with Saudi Arabia to reduce its oil production as a way of prodding outsiders to try to bring the war to an end. The Saudis refused to do it. Says Bazzaz: 'We knew they wanted the war to continue, but we were too dependent on them for financial support to complain out loud. They were following an American policy which called for weakening both countries.'

Yet playing Arab against Muslim through sponsoring a savage war was not a permanent solution to a threat posed by either and the longer the Iran–Iraq War lasted the greater was the threat of exposure of Saudi and American plague-on-both-your-houses intentions. To guard against the unpredictable outcome of the war, Saudi Arabia in 1981 capitalized on both sides' preoccupation with it to strengthen its immediate surroundings against both. It created the Gulf Cooperation Council, with Kuwait, Oman, Qatar, Bahrain and the United Arab Emirates as its other members. Ostensibly the GCC was a loose economic grouping of rich countries but in reality it dealt mostly with the areas of defence and security and its creation undermined the already weak Arab League. From the very beginning there were GCC voices which expressed Saudi fears and warned that the eventual victor in the Iran–Iraq conflict was likely to turn their attention to them and their wealth. Because subversion was considered a greater threat than an outright military invasion, the security apparatuses of this grouping employed a staggering 100,000 people, compared with a total of 137,000 in their uncoordinated armed forces.

Saudi Arabia created the GCC while trying to justify the Iraqi war effort in Islamic and Arab terms. King Fahd advertised his constant contacts with Saddam Hussein and described him as 'the sword of Islam' and wired him to say: 'We're with you every step of the way.' Saudi Minister of the Interior Prince Nayef stated: 'Iraq is protecting the Arab nation.' But the evaporation of the initial Iraqi successes and the possibility in 1982–4 of an Iranian victory prompted Saudi Arabia to seek a precautionary accommodation with Iran. Fahd eventually toned down his anti-Iranian rhetoric and exchanged emissaries with the country's leadership, but he continued to help Iraq.

Saudi Arabia not only paid the Iraqis huge sums of money; it allowed them commercial passage to circumvent the threat to their narrow Gulf coast by the Iranian army, helped them to pump oil through a pipeline which ran through their territory and allocated 200,000–400,000 barrels a day from the Neutral Zone to support the Iraqi war effort (the oil production moves also helped keep the price down.) Eventually it prevailed on the West to assist Iraq militarily and to waive its strictures on the use of arms it sold to Saudi Arabia and permit the Saudis to transfer military planes and other hardware to Iraq. (In 1984 *Newsweek* reported the Iranian capture of a considerable amount of Western-made and Saudi-supplied equipment.) It was Saudi envoys, including the Ambassador to Washington Prince Bandar, Crown Prince Abdallah and Defence Minister Prince Sultan, who met with Margaret Thatcher and members of the Reagan administration, including Vice President George Bush, to convince them to look the other way while embargoed arms and electronic gear reached Iraq. And it was King Fahd and Saudi Foreign Minister Prince Faisal who identified Iran as the greater danger to the stability of the region.

Britain and America obliged. The former supplied Iraq with a sophisticated electronic command centre made by Plessey and followed this by permitting the sale of NBC (nuclear, biological and chemical warfare) suits, guidance systems for their radar and many other military items that were embargoed. America provided Iraq with interest-free credit to buy wheat, sold them parts for their chemical weapons plants and, through Jordan, supplied them with sophisticated electronics. (See The Brutal Friendship for the author's personal involvement in this effort.) According to veteran ABC correspondent John Cooley, America went as far as to order units of its Gulf fleet to jam Iranian radar to help Iraqi aerial attacks on Iranian oil terminals (Cooley was not able to file the story at the time). Meanwhile, because fears of the consequences of the victory of either side were growing – the prospect of a victorious Iraq becoming Arab leader or Iran claiming Muslim leadership – several meetings between Saudi Arabia and Iran took place, including a visit to Iran in 1985 by Foreign Minister Prince Saud Al Faisal. The Saudi assessment of the situation was correct: trouble was on the way.

The eight-year Iran–Iraq War ended in 1989 in a stalemate. Iran's numerical superiority was balanced by Iraq's possession of more modern equipment. But because outside help to Iraq forced Iran to sue for peace, Iraq claimed a psychological victory. The perceived way the conflict ended created a shift in emphasis by

Saudi Arabia. Suddenly the Iraqi danger loomed larger than the Iranian one and talk about Saddam's ambitions and one-million-strong army assumed more importance than everything else. (See The Brutal Friendship.)

The end of the war and the danger which followed coincided with a belated Saudi awareness of the rising cost and short life of their rentals strategy and its inadequacy, and forced the evolution of a hybrid new Saudi policy. What emerged was a combination of the old one of non-involvement and an amended pre-emptive rentals approach. Saudi Arabia decided its minor involvements were creating some problems, opted to remain aloof from them whenever possible and to limit itself to actively dealing with the broad problems rather than their manifestations. This meant sponsoring some countries to stop impending unfriendly developments, rather than actual events, in others.

Beyond the Iran–Iraq War and the GCC, in the general Arab arena, with the desire for political unity long gone the Saudis were faced with the choice of supporting a loose federation, various forms of cooperation which fell short of that or of opting for policies which perpetuated the existing divisions. This time the Saudi decision against federation or cooperation was an active, deliberate one. Saudi Arabia followed policies which would not interfere with its relationship with the West and its ability to act independently even in the smallest matters.

Politically, the Saudi response to the 1982 Israeli invasion of Lebanon was hardly audible. Fahd coordinated his moves with Ronald Reagan more than he did with the beleaguered Yasser Arafat, even when Israeli armour threatened to destroy Beirut and eliminate the PLO. The era of encumbering Saudi–American friendship with internal and pan-Arab considerations came to an end during the Israeli siege of Beirut.

There were other, less dramatic, signs which underscored the Saudi refusal to commit itself to an Arab stance. By refusing to channel aid money through established Arab organizations such as the Arab League, Saudi Arabia, by omission, produced a divisive policy. In the past the sum total of their mostly ad hoc case-by-case acts amounted to the same divisive policy. Now creating, maintaining and even encouraging divisions was deliberate and it touched even the most innocent acts of inter-Arab cooperation.

For example, Saudi Arabia undermined the AACO (Arab Air Carriers Organization) by refusing to pool their spare-parts purchases or maintenance operations with other Arab airlines. The acceptance of this scheme would have saved the participating Arab airlines, including their flag carrier, Saudia, a great deal of money. It was a political vote against pan-Arab economic involvement helped by the desire of members of the royal household to realize commissions from monopolizing the Saudia maintenance and spare-parts business. Saudi Arabia was a founding member of Arabsat (Arab Satellite Project) and owned 26 per cent of its outstanding shares, but it held back funds earmarked for this project when it became apparent that it could not dictate the type of programming to be telecast. To the House of Saud even scientific and literary programmes were to follow the restrictive local diktats rather than a pan-Arab approach and it was a vote against Arab cultural integration. Saudi Arabia refused to entertain an Arab League suggestion to create an Arab High Court to deal with legal problems in accordance with the Sharia laws of Islam. It would not allow a broad Arab interpretation of the Sharia to replace its narrow, Wahhabi-based one. And even the rebuilding of the Hijaz railway linking Saudi Arabia with Jordan, something which existed during the time of Lawrence of Arabia, was not approved lest it lead to economic interdependence between the two countries. There are many more examples.

Naturally enough, this active negativism aimed at perpetuating Arab divisions extended to the already mentioned attempts to stifle progress in the political sphere: the moves towards democracy by neighbouring Arab states. Several Kuwaiti decisions to hold parliamentary elections were rescinded after Saudi Arabia expressed its displeasure with them by thwarting Kuwaiti moves towards closer security cooperation within the GCC. Kuwait needed Saudi Arabia more than before because it was beginning to worry about Iraq. On occasion Saudi Arabia refused to participate in any GCC discussions until Kuwait made appeasing pronouncements which amounted to delaying elections. On one occasion when no 'appropriate' Kuwaiti response materialized, the Saudis postponed their decision to participate in the creation of a GCC customs union.

Bahrain was more vulnerable than Kuwait, and Saudi threats to close the lifeline causeway linking the two countries and stop hundreds of thousands of Saudis from visiting Bahrain were made to stop it proceeding with the idea of holding parliamentary elections. Notice was served on Jordan that the Saudis viewed its plans to hold parliamentary elections with unease and that Saudi Arabia would 'respond' to any results which it did not like by, for example, cutting off economic aid. Rumours persist that the Saudis, having failed to stop the elections, went further and sponsored some 'safe' candidates for the Jordanian parliament. If this is true then they have nothing to show for it because most members of the Jordanian parliament are anti-Saudi Islamic fundamentalists.

In the Sudan, the gateway to Africa for the Saudis, the new stable government of the country is suffering the results of their attempt to strangulate it economically and destabilize it politically because the Sudanese Government refuses to accept the role of a satellite country and preaches a militant rather than an opium-of-the-people Islam. Not only have the Saudis withheld much-needed economic aid, but they have supplied Sudanese anti-Government rebels with 400 Tow missiles and other arms. Beyond supporting the Karnak and Inkath Watani Sudanese separatist movements, as with Iran and Egypt before, the Saudis got themselves involved in several assassination attempts, including one against Hassan Turabi, the country's religious leader. The Saudi policy has prolonged Sudan's destructive civil war and there is a danger that it might turn the country into another famine-stricken Somalia.

The government of populous and populist Yemen, in the mind of the House of Saud still the one country capable of denying it hegemony over the Arabian Peninsula, has been subjected to a clear attempt to destabilize it. The Saudis initially resorted to the old successful formula and tried to bribe the tribes of the Yemen to rise up to stop parliamentary elections and the union of North and South Yemen. Though they paid out huge sums of money and there were several bombings which killed many innocent people and caused some minor disturbances, the union took place and so did parliamentary elections.

Now Saudi Arabia is trying to impede the Yemen's progress by supporting the Hadramout separatist movement through a more sophisticated terror campaign which includes the use of letter bombs. It has gone further and resurrected an old border dispute, claiming that oil discoveries in the Yemen are in territory which belongs to it. It has openly threatened the 40-odd oil companies operating in the Yemen with economic reprisals including acts against their interests in Saudi Arabia and in 1987 went as far as to mount a military raid against the country which left 500 Yemenis and Saudis dead. The Yemen has complained about all Saudi acts against it, especially its resort to state-sponsored terrorism, but without success. The countries which campaign against international terrorism, including the USA and Britain, do not want to hear about Saudi-sponsored terror. Says a bitter

Yemeni President Abdallah Ali Saleh of the vicious, unchecked attacks on his country: 'The royals are behind it all.'

This Saudi policy has gone further than intercepting Arab cooperation and destabilizing countries committed to democracy and Saudi Arabia has seen fit to increase its support for pro-Saudi despotic regimes. Before the rise of the present regime in the Sudan, it supported the safe President Ja'afar Numeiri, a man accused by the present government of being corrupt and a drug addict. Saudi Arabia has backed Syria's divisive intervention in Lebanon to guard against the emergence of an independent Lebanon not to its liking. It has mended its fences with an Egypt at peace with Israel to create an Arab counterweight to Iraq. The key word is 'anti': anti-democracy, anti-popular government and anti the emergence of a strong regional power. In reality, in the Arab arena, the new Saudi policy is not new at all, but simply a more active, broader approach to the old anti-union, anti-cooperation, anti-democratic and anti-progress policies of Ibn Saud. In fact, the House of Saud seems unable to pursue positive ideas, and King Fahd's 1981 peace plan for the Palestinian problem, although it had received considerable Western and Arab support, was abandoned for no reason.

However, in the Muslim sphere this active negativism represented a total reversal of an old policy. Fahd's leadership shortcomings coincided with the emergence of a militant Islamic Iran and the growing threat of the Muslim fundamentalist movements in Lebanon, Egypt, Algeria, the Sudan, Afghanistan and Pakistan. This has meant that the previous policy which supported Islam at the expense of Arabism was no longer viable. Fahd's personal behaviour and his open commitment to America make him unacceptable as a Muslim leader. For the first time in centuries an inflamed Islam is on the march to confront the conservative Muslim regimes and the West.

At present the only Islamic movements which receive Saudi support are those in far-away places which pose no threat to its security, even if they become radicalized, and a few nearby ones which they use to undermine more immediate threats. This is why the Islamic Palestinian movement Hamas, which represents a clear danger to Palestinian Christians, is financed to challenge the PLO and Yasser Arafat. It is why Islamic movements in Turkey are supported to keep that country from growing strong enough to assume a leadership role in the Middle East and with the new Muslim republics of the former Soviet Union. Simultaneously, Muslim Bosnia and Kazakhstan can be supported because they are preoccupied with problems which do not affect Saudi Arabia and represent no danger to it.

It is true that Iran acts as a new magnet for militant Islam, but other fundamentalist movements, many of which owe their rise to Saudi support, have turned and now follow Saudi-threatening militant policies. These movements represent another failure of the short-term rentals policy. The Algerian Islamic Front, known by its French acronym, FIS, was provided with Saudi financial support to undermine the moderately socialist government of the country. It grew strong and militant and more threatening to Saudi Arabia than the government it was supposed to keep in check. Algerian fundamentalists have become openly opposed to their previous sponsors; they find their views incompatible and Saudi corruption unacceptable. The Muslim Brotherhood in Egypt, an old fundamentalist group which goes back to the late 1920s, received Saudi support to keep the Egyptian Government from outgrowing its Saudi-chosen role. The movement has produced some militant offshoots which, as witnessed by recent attacks on tourists, threaten the overall stability of Egypt and call for the violent overthrow of the Saudi monarchy. It was the puppet regime of Sudanese President Numeiri which began the shift towards Islam in that country, and now the country has become radically Islamic fundamentalist and out of Saudi control. Islamic movements in Pakistan such as Jama'at Islamiah were supported to keep the country from following secular policies that were not to the liking of Saudi Arabia, but now their opposition to the Saudi regime is open and uncompromising. The Pakistani Muslim cat is so far out of the bag that the Islamic movements there are actively supporting anti-House of Saud Muslim fundamentalist groups in Saudi Arabia such as Hezbollah of the Hijaz. Even the anti-Arafat Hamas is beginning to create problems for Saudi policy makers because it opposes the Middle East peace process which Saudi Arabia supports and it has begun to accept assistance from Iran.

There is very little conservative Islam left to support, and one of the reasons for that is the Saudi, and Fahd's, claim to its leadership. Most of Islam, including groups created by Saudi Arabia, has turned militant and the rest are heading in that direction. Contrary to superficial analysis, the Arab masses who supported Nasser, Qaddafi, Saddam Hussein and other movements have not disappeared and they still oppose the House of Saud through the adoption of radical Muslim politics to achieve their old aims. The Muslim identity Faisal developed to undermine the Arab nationalist movement of Nasser has backfired. In fact, the new Islamic threat is larger and more radical than the old threat of Arab nationalism. Certainly Islam has captured the imagination of the people inside and outside Saudi Arabia in a more serious, harder-to-oppose way. Among other things, it was easier to discredit Nasser and his followers by underscoring their un-Islamic socialism or referring to their close ties with the USSR than it is to undermine people who claim all they are doing is following The Book.

Even now, with the Muslim threat staring them in the eye, there is no way for the guardians of Islam's holiest shrines to shed their Muslim identity and the responsibility which goes with it, nor is today's Arab identity strong enough to replace it. So Saudi Arabia, once the pretender to the leadership of all of Islam, has become its captive. It continues to pretend it leads the Muslims through small, innocent acts which have little effect on Muslim politics: in addition to those already mentioned, the causes of Filipino, Kashmiri and Somali Muslims. It sponsors Russian and Chinese Muslims to visit Mecca, gives aid money to new Muslim republics, builds mosques for Muslim communities in far-away places, donates money to restore the Dome of the Rock in Jerusalem and joins fundamentalist Muslims in condemning the writer Salman Rushdie. But it does not lead; leading the Muslims means leading Egypt, Pakistan, Indonesia, North Africa and places nearer home and this would mean subscribing to a new Islam and undermining Saudi relations with the West. The House of Saud certainly cannot lead the Muslim world when even its Wahhabi co-religionists, the people who openly criticized the policies of King Fahd in a 1992 petition, accuse it of being too pro-West, too corrupt and too un-Islamic.

In late 1993, Saudi Arabia's Arab and Muslim policies look like a failure. Libya, Algeria, Iraq, the Sudan, the Yemen and Jordan oppose them. Egypt, Syria and Tunisia are always unhappy with their policies because they want Saudi Arabia to give them more money or to employ their citizens and the Saudis cannot do the first and have decided against the second (see The Brutal Friendship). Kuwait and Bahrain object to Saudi interference in their internal affairs and relations between them are cool. Qatar is upset over Saudi attempts to annex some of its territory (the Saudis have gone so far as to attack the Qatari border post of Khufus). The Arab masses think the House of Saud's rule is obscene and resent it. The only good Arab relations they have are with far-away, despotic and unpopular King Hassan of Morocco and, though they are already complaining about Saudi attempts to dictate to them, perhaps Oman and the United Arab Emirates. In the words of former American Ambassador to Saudi Arabia James Akins: 'None of their Arab neighbours like them.'

The Saudi Muslims' position is no better. Saudi Arabia is opposed by Iran, looked down on by secular, democratic Turkey, kept at a distance by Pakistan and, because of an oil policy which calls for accommodating the consumers at the expense of the producers, resented by Indonesia. Even the Afghanistan Mujahadeen, now that they are in power, scoff at Saudi attempts to continue to buy them and have turned against Saudi Arabia to the extent that there was an armed attack on the Saudi Embassy in Kabul in October 1992.

As we have seen, King Fahd is too unintelligent to think of long-term plans and, even if capable, too lazy to develop any. The Saudi failure of the rentals policy was followed by another failure of its extension: the policy of active negativism. These failures to contain the threats from the Arab and Muslim worlds and the bad conditions within Saudi Arabia itself underscore the new total dependence on the West. Ibn Saud's ceding of his country's foreign policy to the British early in the century took place when the country was incapable of conducting its foreign affairs. Its present total dependence on American support and protection suggests that Fahd has followed in his father's footsteps. This calls into question the generally accepted assertion that Saudi Arabia has never been a colony.

6

The Brutal Friendship

Without the West there would be no House of Saud. The Saudi people or their neighbours or a combination of both would bring about its end. But the West has always had reasons to support the Saudi monarchy and to guarantee its existence and the West's, particularly America's, continued need for oil will keep this support intact for the foreseeable future.

Nevertheless, America's failure to save the Shah of Iran and the consequences of using its military power on holy Muslim soil undermine its ability to ensure the survival of the House of Saud against the internal threats which confront it. America has not been able to devise a substitute for its present better-the-devil-you-know policy, something that would guarantee the continued flow of oil and reflect its commitment to a more democratic Saudi Arabia. Meanwhile all the threats grow stronger, mainly because the House of Saud abuses America's support to continue to ignore the valid demands of its people and its neighbouring countries. This dismissiveness by the House of Sand has turned its internal and external enemies against America and this, in turn, underscores American fears and inability to change direction and perpetuates the explosive stalemate.

The unhealthy political reality of America's inability to disown a dangerous alliance with a backward and unpopular regime governs the way the House of Saud and America behave towards each other. The latter's paralysis, often mistaken for a policy, determines its attitude towards internal conditions in Saudi Arabia and the Arab and Muslim worlds. The *de facto* alliance with the House of Saud extends itself on momentum and now includes an implicit acceptance of the House of Saud's and its lackeys' personal activities outside Saudi Arabia and the use of Saudi money in illegal sponsorship of unauthorized American covert operations. The uncharted, deepening American commitment is sustained by successful efforts by the House of Saud to maintain it through the adoption of a generous pro-American oil policy and attempts to buy Arab and Muslim support for both sides.

Britain created Ibn Saud to protect its Middle East imperial interests and to eliminate those who threatened them. America came on the scene as a replacement in the 1940s and its concern was to protect oil-rich Saudi Arabia itself. This too meant eliminating the external threats to Saudi Arabia and its rulers. The result was the same: protecting the House of Saud was the primary consideration.

Britain had it easier. From early in the century until it was replaced by America, it operated according to an old colonial principle of manipulating Saudi Arabia and other Middle East countries through their chiefs. Britain designated Saudi Arabia, Iran and Iraq as the three axes of power in the Arabian Peninsula and the Gulf, made their monarchs dependent on its support, kept them apart and weak and, on occasion and mostly in Iran and Iraq, prevailed on them to follow sensible internal policies to guard against upheavals which might undo its work.

America's late arrival on the Middle East scene coincided with the emergence of new problems. Oil and the anticipated growing dependence on it meant that America was in the Middle East to stay, but its strictly commercial approach precluded deeper neo-colonial interference in the running of the region. America's oil-based involvement did not allow for having to deal with people who had begun to question the ways of their leaders, nor did it foresee the cold war and its threats or the Palestinian problem and its consequences. These elements interacted and produced major subsidiary problems which grew to destabilize the region in ways beyond America's ability or wish to cope with them. For example, Nasser rose to power with America's blessing, if not outright support, but soon afterwards he tried to export his revolution and threatened America's oil interests. It was America's refusal to reconcile his pan-Arab ambitions with its oil interests and support for Israel which ended his brief pro-American revolutionary phase and drove him towards the USSR. Even inside Saudi Arabia, a higher level of education is one of the major results of oil wealth and it has led to greater non-acceptance of House of Saud absolutism and, inevitably, of America as its primary supporter.

America's final answer to Nasser's oil challenge, what eventually turned into a Nasser–House of Saud confrontation, was typical. Its anti-colonial history, inclinations and lack of preparedness ruled out direct attempts to solve the complex problems of the area. Among other things, America viewed advising the House of Saud to behave rationally as an unacceptable interference in its internal affairs; and this despite its willingness to do so elsewhere, as it still does to this day. So protecting its oil interests and refusing to play the puppeteer made America provide the House of Saud with its initial uncritical support, which was eventually extended against internal threats. The refusal to 'manage' the affairs of its wards led to an exclusive reliance by America on the people in power, the House of Saud. With time, and because all attempts to find a workable substitute entailed danger, this delegation of duties became what is now seen as policy.

The American fear of involvement was heightened by the increasing complexity of the problems of the Middle East and produced a policy of running the area through deputies. Naturally the deputies were chosen to deal with specific problems or geographical areas or both. On occasion, Israel, democratic and militarily strong, was the deputy chosen to balance the power of pro-Soviet Arab countries. At other times, Iran under the Shah deputized for America to fill a regional power vacuum, particularly after the British withdrawal from the Gulf left its small sheikhdoms in need of protection. Now, particularly after the Gulf War, it is the House of Saud which deputizes for America on a much broader Arab and Muslim scale.

As with Israel and Iran in the past, the people of the Middle East find Saudi Arabia an unacceptable regional leader and, judged by its military strength, it is inadequate. To maintain its deputy-sheriff position, the House of Saud has used its oil income to pretend it is performing a leadership role and this has kept others from assuming it. It has relied on short-term solutions to perpetuate its pretence while converting its ineffective American-sponsored deputy-sheriff role into a permanent instrument of family survival. The American wish to protect the oil and the House of Saud's wish to perpetuate its rule became one and the same.

America is caught. Israel as a deputy was only acceptable against the Soviet threat and it is unacceptable now for fear of alienating the Arabs and aborting any solution to the Palestinian problem. Former President Nixon described Iran and Saudi Arabia as 'the twin pillars of Gulf stability', but Iran is now Islamic fundamentalist and anti-American. Iraq is neurotic and dangerous. Egypt, another potential deputy, is impoverished and unable to lead. So the House of Saud has become America's sole deputy by default,

The founder and first king of Saudi Arabia, Abdel Aziz Abdel Rahman Al Saud, better known as Ibn Saud.

King Faisal and Crown Prince Khalid.

King Faisal and Ahmad Zaki Yamani ran Saudi Arabia's oil policy together during OPEC's heyday in the late 1960s and early 1970s.

King Fahd and President Reagan in Washington. Saudi Arabia financed American policy in Afghanistan, the Horn of Africa and Central America.

George Bush visited King Fahd two months before the start of the Gulf War.

King Fahd bowed to
Islamic pressure and
adopted the title Guardian
of Islam's Holy Shrines.

Prince Abdel Aziz, King Fahd's favourite son. The King transferred $300 million into his
personal bank account.

Anti–House of Saud demonstrators in the east of Saudi Arabia photographed secretly in 1979.

Anti–House of Saud pickets in London. The placards demand the release of political prisoners.

Saud Al Ahmad, a Shia dissident who was executed in 1981 for smuggling banned books.

What remains of a Shia mosque torn down by the Saudi Arabian police.

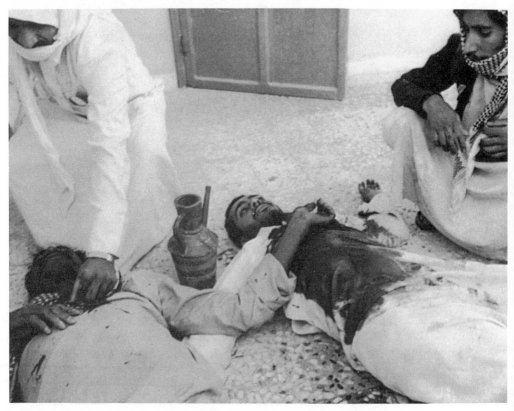

Two Shias who were wounded during anti–House of Saud riots in 1981.

though in the 1970s and 1980s America briefly considered relying on Saddam Hussein. All America's misgivings about the House of Saud's backwardness and inadequacy notwithstanding, this has extended and broadened the American support for Saudi Arabia, and for the lazy Fahd and his family. The monster of a child Britain adopted has become an embarrassing relationship for America.

To repeat, the House of Saud pays for America's support directly and indirectly. Keeping the price of oil low is essentially an outright cash payment, and conditional aid to Arab and Muslim countries to keep them from turning too anti-American is an indirect one. Under the Reagan and Bush administrations, paying for America's support was expanded in a way which dangerously affected the conduct of US foreign policy. Saudi Arabia's sponsorship of many covert or unauthorized policies of the executive branch of the American Government went beyond aid to the Contras in Central America and the Unita rebel movement in Angola and included indirect military assistance to Siad Barre of Somalia and the supply of oil to South Africa. These situations have no bearing on the Saudi national interest and are nothing but bribes. The deputy has corrupted the sheriff.

The brutal friendship between the House of Saud and America proceeds without constraints because there are no serious challenges to it by accepted Saudi groups, the US Congress or outside powers and the rest of the Western countries, particularly Britain, support it. The resulting blanket support shows itself in other ways. The unattractive, and often ignored or protected, unwholesome behaviour of members of the House of Saud and many of the country's businessmen and other citizens (the Lockheed and BCCI scandals are major examples) has affected the image of the Arabs in the West. The pervasive atmosphere of friendship which has produced a Western willingness to ignore official Saudi corruption, has encouraged the spread of Saudi abuse at the expense of the reputation of the rest of the Arabs.

The original British and American wish to safeguard their interests continues unamended and as such ignores the enormous social changes and political sophistication which have occurred in Saudi Arabia and the Middle East. This situation suits the purposes of the House of Saud; and for the foreseeable future means the following:

- The House of Saud will not participate in asserting Saudi, Arab or Muslim rights against the interests of the West. This would undermine the West's present unnatural dependence on and support of it.

- As a result, the House of Saud's position with its own people and the Arabs and Muslims will continue to deteriorate.
- The deterioration in the standing of the House of Saud internally, and with the Arabs and Muslims, will lead it to resort to greater repression and more divisive Arab and Muslim policies.
- To guarantee continued Western support for its policies of repression and division, the House of Saud will continue to offer its services to the executive branch and the secret services of America.
- The elements which brought an end to the Shah of Iran, the abuse of Western support to create a blind, haughty obliviousness by a hated ruling class, are all in place.

A few years before the British adopted him, in 1901, Ibn Saud, wanting an outside sponsor, wrote to the Sultan of Turkey offering 'to accept any terms you impose on me'. The Turks' rejection of his offer produced another Ibn Saud expression of subservience to their British enemies: 'May the eyes of the British Government be fixed upon us and may we be considered as your protégés.' This plea to C. A. Kemball, the British Resident in the Gulf from 1900 to 1904, was one of many such expressions of submissiveness addressed to British officials and emissaries during that period.

We know what followed. According to the great authority on the early phases of Saudi–British cooperation, Jacob Goldberg, the British placed Ibn Saud above 'people who were religiously, politically and strategically more important'. The cooperation which followed is best exemplified by the photograph of Ibn Saud and Sir Percy Cox at the signing of the 1915 Darea Treaty, the one which fundamentally reduced Ibn Saud's realm to a British protectorate. In the picture the two men are standing in front of a tent in the middle of the desert. Sir Percy Cox is wearing a top hat, dressed for a formal occasion. Both men are sitting on chairs and Ibn Saud looks obviously uncomfortable. In fact, the British caused him discomfort in more substantial ways, in the restraints they placed on him to curb his *ghazzu*, or raiding, instinct, their desire to have him abolish slavery and the pressures they applied on him to change his rule from a religious Wahhabi one to a Saudi state one. Overall the British knew that he needed their small subsidies and support more than they needed him; they had alternatives and he did not.

The first pictures of Ibn Saud with Americans showed him with oilmen. Taken sometime during the 1930s, well before the United States established a permanent diplomatic mission in 1942, they dramatically demonstrate the difference between the British and American attitudes. The oilmen are in full Arab dress, Hollywood style, glamorized versions of the real thing, and they are smiling in the manner of actors on the MGM lot. They are acting out a role, playing a trick on the local sheikh, or perhaps he was playing one on them, for he was the one who decreed that American oilmen were to wear Arab dress in his presence.

But those photographs from the 1930s tell another, more subtle, story, for the men in them represent the American presence in the country. The businessman-philanthropist Charles Crane, prospector Karl Twitchell and oilman Lloyd Hamilton arrived with the 1933 'American invasion of Arabia', well before the diplomats did, and for a decade America 'handled' Saudi Arabia through its diplomatic mission to Cairo. British business followed British colonialism, but with the Americans it was the oil companies which pressured the State Department into its *de jure* recognition of Saudi Arabia in 1942 and the first American diplomatic mission was headed by a chargé d'affaires by the name of James Moose. (Interestingly the USSR recognized Saudi Arabia in 1926, but it was a short-lived affair; Ibn Saud kicked them out after discovering their inability to sponsor him.)

In dealing with Saudi Arabia, American statesmen and diplomats adopted the attitude of their pioneers, the oilmen who sought to accommodate local leaders to make money. That is why Roosevelt did not smoke during his 1945 meeting with Ibn Saud, when the imperious Churchill refused to bend. The Americans had no experience of dealing with the likes of Ibn Saud and commercial considerations and their coming dependence on his oil determined their behaviour. They were so insecure in their ways, even in the 1950s, that they worried about the intentions of the more experienced colonialists and were afraid that Saudi Arabia might turn to the British or French and award them oil concessions.

Although their reasons for pursuing oil were different, the relationship between the oil companies and the US Government during the 1940s was close. Diplomats became oilmen and vice versa, and a President of ARAMCO, Terry Duce, had been a US Government official and was given his new job by the

Government. Even US Minister to Saudi Arabia William Eddy resigned his post and became an adviser to ARAMCO. It was the time when Secretary of War Henry Stimson and Secretary of State Cordell Hull became convinced that oil was too important to leave in the hands of a 'purely' private sector. Reflecting official American Government opinions, *Time* editorialized: 'the future and disposition of this great reservoir of oil is a matter of incalculable national importance.'

In the 1940s the growth of the cold war and the emergence of the Palestinian problem enhanced the importance of Saudi Arabia. The American Government, prodded by the oil companies, who were not yet producing enough oil to do it themselves and who were worried about the poverty and instability of the country, stretched the law and included Ibn Saud in the lend-lease programme. They gave him grants when Britain could not; paid a $10-million fee to build the then useless Dhahran airbase and declared null and void the Red Line Agreement which governed the sharing of concessions between international oil companies and which would have left things exclusively at the mercy of commercial interests. The Americans were 'buying' Saudi Arabia, but even all this official American financial assistance was not enough to satisfy Ibn Saud's profligate ways; in 1942 $190 million of the $292 million America gave him was used by the family. In the words of Philby, 'the till was empty', and Ibn Saud hocked his country's future and invariably borrowed money from the oil companies against future royalties.

The British were no match for the wealthy, accommodating Americans. By British standards the American subsidy, for that is what it was, was colossal and even an attempt to match it would have been cancelled by the American willingness to deal with Ibn Saud on his own corrupt terms. The British continued to protest about the American refusal to prod Ibn Saud to change and reform – to spend less – and the great Arabist Glubb Pasha blamed America's hands-off policy for Ibn Saud's corrupt behaviour. The British Minister in Jeddah, S. R. Jordan, vociferously made the same complaint on the spot, but the Americans dismissed these protests as a ploy or an act of jealousy, and vilified Jordan. Their willingness to take Ibn Saud's orders is something the British would have never accepted: the borrowing of huge sums of money, the doubling of ARAMCO employees' salaries, the building of an unneeded railway and the transmission of a message from Ibn Saud to President Truman to use the A-bomb against the USSR.

The profit motive, Saudi oil as a US national interest, the cold war and the necessity of oil for the recovery of post-war Europe and the need for a voice of moderation within the Arab camp superseded all else.

To Ibn Saud, the American reaction to the cold war was a windfall. He welcomed the increased American dependence on his country with enthusiasm. But the Palestinian problem was a much more difficult matter. Some American officials, citing payments to Ibn Saud, naively expected him to openly support America's pro-Israeli policies, while others, notably Secretary of the Navy James Forrestall, feared angering Ibn Saud and argued for ditching Israel to guarantee his loyalty and his oil. President Truman, desperate to win the 1948 presidential election, opted to offer Israel instantaneous recognition and wholehearted support without listening to his advisers. The Truman move was instinctive, the work of a man who openly spoke of needing the Jewish vote, but Ibn Saud's failure to respond to an anti-Arab move, his continued 'cordial exchanges with President Truman', was a much more complex one. As with Britain before, Ibn Saud placed his relationship with his new sponsor above his Arabism. (General Taha Al Hashimi, who headed an Arab League delegation which asked Ibn Saud to make an empty threat to cut off supplies, reported that Ibn Saud told him: 'Oil has nothing to do with politics.')

Ibn Saud's acceptance of America's friendship was understandable for many reasons, unlike reliance on a Britain which manipulated things itself. It meant an enhanced regional position, a free hand in dealing with his own people and, above all, wealth. What the American officials, fearing Ibn Saud's reaction over the Palestinian problem, had overlooked was that American diplomatic and financial support and the oil income had created the ideal of what Ibn Saud desired, a *rentier* state.

Because oil was an unearned income, the result of a stroke of luck rather than economic development, Ibn Saud was able to exercise total control over it and use it for his own purposes. The only party capable of altering this situation was the payer, but in this case the payer was not interested. So, Ibn Saud's loyalty to the payer-sponsor was what mattered and this is what a *rentier* state is all about.

How Ibn Saud undermined Arab efforts regarding the Palestinian problem and his superficial support of the Arab and Muslim positions has already been detailed in the previous chapter. But because his *rentier*-state status was unacceptable to his people and the Arabs and Muslims, he treated it as secret Saudi–American covenant and appeased his critics through repeated public condemnation of America. However, this means of assuaging the Saudi people and his Arab critics was easier for the executive branch of the American Government to understand than it was for Congress, journalists and members of the Jewish lobby. How to stop these groups from acting on open Saudi policy and undoing the whole Saudi–American relationship became a problem for both sides. The executive branch of the American Government responded to congressional and other disapprovals of statements by Saudi Foreign Minister Prince Faisal the same way that Ibn Saud responded to Arab pressure over Palestine: by public condemnation. Both sides were following contradictory open and covert policies.

But the Americans went further. President Truman seconded the guarantee of the security of the Saudi state originally given by President Roosevelt. Then, in an incredible move aimed at circumventing Congress, the Jewish lobby and the press, the Government ceded the conduct of its relations with Saudi Arabia to the oil companies. The presidential security guarantee was in essence a treaty which did not have to suffer congressional approval, supervision and control. Says the *Washington Post*'s Walter Pincas, the maker of the television documentary *The Secret File*: 'There was a pattern of secret agreements [between the US and Saudi Arabia] beginning in 1947. It was done with Franco's Spain later.' Strangely, Congress has never looked into this aspect of the two countries' relationship and, on the day-to-day level, Congress and the Jewish lobby condemned the oil companies without effect, for the companies were not directly beholden to them and they could indulge Ibn Saud without suffering for it.

To help the oil companies manage Saudi relations sensibly, during 1947–8 the American Government prevailed on ARAMCO to expand its Government Relations Department and transferred a number of diplomats and CIA agents to staff it – Ellender, Elliot and Barracks – in addition to the highly placed Duce, Davis and Thornburgh. The major result of this attempt to support Ibn Saud in a way which circumvented Congress was a tax break which was called 'The Golden Gimmick'. In the autumn of 1950 the diplomat-oilmen resurrected a 1918 tax law and used it to exempt the payments made to Ibn Saud from US tax. This increased the oil companies' income, and the royalty share of it they payed to Ibn Saud. The price of his pro-American loyalty was raised to meet his ever-increasing financial demands, without having to go through Congress to give him direct aid. As usual, money prompted him to ignore all other considerations. He died in a state of pro-American bliss.

The idea of America's Minister to Saudi Arabia, William Eddy, of pleasing his hosts consisted of two things: making strong anti-Israel statements and collecting the stories of Juha, the mythical Arab joker. Ridiculous as it sounds, this represented the overt American policy on Saudi Arabia when Saud became king in 1953. Washington's contradictory Middle East interests consisted of guaranteeing the flow of Saudi oil while maintaining its support of Israel. To reconcile the two, the State Department allowed its field officers considerable leeway to criticize Israel while Washington assured Israel of its full support.

The American presence in Saudi Arabia in the early 1950s grew with the increase in the production of oil, the expansion of its Dhahran airbase and the building of an oil pipeline to the Lebanese port of Sidon, TAPLINE, or the Trans Arabian Pipeline. This ran through Jordan, Syria and Lebanon and represented the increasing economic influence of Saudi Arabia on its neighbours. The Saudis were now realizing enough money to use it regionally. The substantial American military presence in Dhahran was matched by an increase in CIA activity through such organizations as the inter-Arab TAPLINE Government Relations Department and AFME, the American Friends of the Middle East. Washington-based senior CIA agents such as Kim Roosevelt and Harry Kern visited the kingdom and the King and advised on everything from the use of fly killers to hiring the public relations firm Hill & Knowlton. On occasion, to appease the King's desire for big-name emissaries, they used people like former Secretary of Treasury Robert Anderson, a close friend of President Eisenhower. Interestingly, this was also the time when the Americans started sponsoring Saudis to go to college in the USA, to them a way of making the Saudi people pro-American, though inevitably a danger to their interests because educated people tend to act independently. (Saudi Arabia's first Oil Minister, the anti-American Abdallah Tariki, was a product of this policy and so were most of the Saudis who conspired to overthrow their government in the 1960s and early 1970s.)

What the Americans did not take into consideration during the critical 1953–7 period was the changing nature of Middle East politics and the character of King Saud. The presence in

Washington of the two Dulles brothers, Secretary of State John Foster Dulles and CIA Chief Allen Dulles, facilitated and extended the use of oilmen and CIA agents as crypto-diplomats. The oilmen and CIA agents were committed to two wrong precepts: that Saudi Arabia was immune to popular regional movements and that King Saud was as dedicated to and capable of maintaining Saudi Arab separateness as had been his father. In fact, Juha was no substitute for Nasser and Saud was instinctively more Arab than his father. Saud accepted the Arab claim on Saudi Arabia.

Saud saw Nasser as a new Saladin, and naively thought that he could march under his banner without threatening the House of Saud's supremacy in his country or its source of income. Saud was a raw Bedouin without wile and saw the formation in 1954 of British-sponsored CENTO, the military alliance of Turkey, Iran, Pakistan and (Hashemite) Iraq, as threatening because it included the House of Saud's traditional enemies. Above all, Saud thought that he could join the Nasser camp without undermining the oil-based special Saudi–American relationship.

In 1955 Saud contracted to have a 200-man Egyptian military mission train the Saudi army. The following year he responded to CENTO by joining Egypt and Syria in an alliance. Egyptian teachers and engineers arrived in his country in their thousands and Egyptian newspapers and magazines became extremely popular. The country's official and popular love affair with Nasser was so strong that Nasser's 1956 visit to Riyadh produced the largest demonstration of support in its history.

Saud was not alarmed, but Washington was. In fact, it was America's friends in the Middle East who rang the alarm bells. Prime Minister Nuri Said of Iraq and President Camille Chamoun of Lebanon led the way in calling attention to the danger of the merger of Saudi money and Nasser's popularity, and they were supported by anti-Nasser Syrian and Egyptian elements and Britain's Foreign Office. President Chamoun was so incensed at America's lack of response to the Nasser problem that he attributed the Americans' inaction to the local embassy and began dealing with CIA agents.

The gap between the anti-Nasser British attitude and the reaction of regional leaders and the Americans was the product of divisions within the crypto-diplomatic CIA. Having helped Nasser attain power in Egypt, major CIA operatives, including Miles Copeland, Kim Roosevelt and Jim Eichelberger, continued to believe that he was essentially pro-American and that his revolutionary rhetoric and flirtations with Russia could be contained. Following American tradition, they avoided playing the puppeteer and were distrustful of traditional leaders. They believed that only a popular Arab leader could make peace with Israel, and hence there was no alternative to Nasser. On the other hand, another CIA group, headed by William Crane Eveland, believed that American support should go to those who were openly pro-American, and Eveland strongly supported his friends Said of Iraq, Chamoun of Lebanon and Hussein of Jordan. These two CIA camps competed so openly that they divided the American press corps in the Middle East along similar lines; *Time* correspondent John Mecklin led a pro-Roosevelt group while *New York Times* correspondent Sam Pope Brewer took his lead from Eveland. More importantly, both CIA sides operated against a background of Secretary of State John Foster Dulles's Bible-based anti-communist policy (he always read the Bible before meeting the USSR's Foreign Minister Andrei Gromyko).

Why Dulles and his brother Allen, however briefly, accepted the argument of the Nasser advocates remains a mystery. Certainly Kim Roosevelt, who had helped restore the Shah to his throne in 1952, Copeland, who 'knew' Nasser well before the latter overthrew King Farouk, and Eichelberger the supreme espionage intellectual, were more accomplished strategists, power-game players than Eveland. They managed to convince the Dulles brothers that supporting unpopular traditional rulers would require greater anti-Israeli concessions to make it possible for them to make peace with Israel, and that, in any case, opposing Nasser would lead him closer to Russia and make him a bigger threat.

By early 1956 the reasons for supporting Nasser were exhausted. All the promises he had made during the CIA's covert contacts with him, and they were frequent and with many agents, produced no results and the popular momentum of his movement was clearly anti-American. The undoing of the pro-Nasser CIA group had the support of the ARAMCO and TAPLINE CIA, which had gone anti-Saud and anti-Nasser in 1954 when the King sanctioned the creation of a tanker fleet in partnership with Greek shipping magnate Aristotle Onassis to break the ARAMCO monopoly of transporting oil. (See Oil, OPEC and the Overseers.) America changed direction overnight and decided to face Nasser directly, in the place which mattered most, Saudi Arabia. It withdrew its offer to finance the huge Aswan Dam, Nasser's pet project, and instructed its emissaries, including Robert Anderson, to tell King Saud to distance himself from Nasser.

One of the consequences of the withdrawal of the offer to build the Aswan Dam with American money was the nationalization of the Suez Canal, which resulted in the 1956 Anglo–Franco–Israeli attack on Egypt. The Americans and Saud were caught unprepared. Saud responded by overtly extending his honeymoon with Nasser and helped him, and America, still adamantly against colonial solutions, condemned the tripartite attack while organizing to totally replace Britain and France and to contain the Nasser movement through the Eisenhower Doctrine. This approach called for protecting friendly countries against the communist threat, in this case personified by the USSR's ally Nasser.

In 1957 Saud went to America to see Eisenhower and accept the Eisenhower Doctrine. The machinations which preceded his trips revealed a split between America and its allies, confirmed that oil came before supporting a popular leader and exposed the inadequacy of secret diplomacy as a substitute for long-term policy. The trip itself demonstrated the division between an in-the-know executive branch and the popular and congressional attitude towards Saudi Arabia. In response to the open known policies of Saudi Arabia, Mayor Robert Wagner of New York City refused to greet Saud and accused him of being anti-Catholic and anti-Jewish and, among others, Senator Wayne Morris of Oregon objected to US financial support for Saudi Arabia, the King's backward ways and the nature of his rule.

Despite these irritants, the trip, on the surface, was a success. Saud renewed the lease of the Dhahran airbase, accepted the Eisenhower Doctrine, settled the oil-tanker issue and enjoyed the attention afforded him and his infirm seven-year-old son Ma'shur. But beneath the surface, the bankruptcy of America's Middle East policy was exposed. Eisenhower found Saud lacking and unfit for leadership, the decision not to support the traditional regimes was still in place and America gave up its policy of using Nasser to make peace with Israel. Once again, America's concern with protecting its oil interests decided its approach and trapped it into supporting an unfit king.

The temptation to enmesh itself in Saudi internal politics, something America had sought to avoid, presented itself when the House of Saud wanted to replace Saud. Faisal was available and interested in the position. Faisal transmitted a letter to Eisenhower and Dulles which could not have been more explicit, in which he said: 'I know Americans think Saud is friendlier to America, this is not true.' In fact, Faisal and America had the same objective, the use of Saudi Arabia and its increasing wealth to unbalance Nasser's Arab nationalist movement and to establish regional hegemony, but neither side had a plan to do it.

It is true that it was members of the House of Saud who forced the unprecedented and dangerously unbalanced steps which produced the change from Saud to Faisal, but the background to them reveals a remarkable oneness of purpose between Faisal's and the US's approach. It was during the 1958–60 period that the US State Department began to exaggerate the communist threat to the Middle East, and the ARAMCO CIA, and indeed the Beirut and Cairo CIAs, began supporting Islamic fundamentalist groups as a counterweight to Nasser. In part, this was an extension of Kim Roosevelt's earlier successful use of Muslim elements (Fadayeen Islam) against leftists in Iran. The anti-Nasser Muslim Brotherhood was funded, religious leaders were prodded to attack the USSR and its anti-Muslim ways and the Egyptian magazine *Al Musawar* wrote an exposé of ARAMCO's support for small religious cells in eastern Saudi Arabia. (One of the men named in the article, CIA agent James Russell Barracks, confirmed this to me in 1961 and described it as 'an extensive programme', but he refused to elaborate.)

This is when Faisal began to promote his country's Muslim identity at the expense of its Arab one, to confront Nasser. The secular Arabs who opposed Nasser, as shown by the anti-monarchy Iraqi coup of 1958, were unpopular and could not hold the line against him. To historians, promoting Islam was a dangerous long-term solution, but in American terms it was a broader, sounder approach than the previous efforts of the CIA's crypto-diplomats.

'I urge my descendants to maintain the friendship of our American brothers and to renew this agreement.' This advice, written in the margin of the original Dhahran airbase agreement signed between Ibn Saud and Roosevelt in 1945, governed the Saudi attitude towards America. The sons of Ibn Saud never strayed far from it except to mould it to fit their survival strategies; in a way it was left to America to define the relationship between the two countries and give it content.

The accession of Faisal, undoubtedly a more capable man than his brother, afforded America a chance to transform the relationship and elevated America's dependence on Saudi oil to a policy. Faisal's personal behaviour, his domestic policies and his regional and international strategy, misguided but clever, made it easier for America to depend on Saudi Arabia to deputize for it. America approved of his austere ways, helped him balance his 1964 budget, intermittently used him against threatening Arab nationalism and joined him in trying to create an anti-communist Islamic front.

The Americans were not blind to Faisal's brutal internal suppression, his land give-away schemes and his refusal to curb the misdeeds of his family and encouraging them to enter commerce. Yet his ways were clever and his overall policies meant that the oil and Israel were safer. Nobody in the American Government foresaw the consequences of adopting Islam; nobody, that is, except President John F. Kennedy, who, totally in character, tried to superimpose true American ideology on Middle East politics.

Kennedy instinctively liked Nasser. They were the same age, represented a break with the past and Kennedy appreciated Nasser's hold on the Arab masses. Very early in his administration, Kennedy conducted a secret correspondence with Nasser in which the US President warned against border incidents with Israel 'pending a final solution of the Palestinian problem' and remarkably there were very few. This strengthened Kennedy's pro-Nasser attitude and produced a rare American attempt at balancing its oil interests with a sensible policy which accommodated the popular movements in the Middle East.

There were a number of occasions during the Yemen civil war, the major confrontation between the traditional and progressive forces, when Kennedy took Nasser's side. In 1962 he not only recognized the republican pro-Nasser Yemeni regime, while making it clear that Saudi Arabia would be protected, but followed it by accepting the 1963 plan to settle the problem developed by his emissary, Ambassador Ellsworth Bunker. All this was masterfully balanced by keeping Nasser in check, for it was the same Kennedy who, also in 1963, dispatched American fighters to Saudi Arabia to stop Nasser from going too far.

But the Yemen was not Faisal's only confrontation with American ideology. Kennedy, though totally opposed to a Nasserite penetration or destabilization of Saudi Arabia to the extent of overlooking the imprisonment of many educated pro-Nasser Saudis, was deeply concerned with conditions within Saudi Arabia. He refused to accept the advice of the advocates of a continued hands-off policy and pressured Faisal to make internal changes as a way of protecting America's long-term interests. Kennedy used Faisal's visit to Washington on 5 October 1962 to question America's policy in the Yemen to make three points of his own. He wanted the slaves freed, called for the inclusion of non-royal Saudis in the conduct of their country's affairs and went as far as to demand the lifting of restrictions against American Jews working in Saudi Arabia. His letter of 20 October to Faisal, following the trip, is explicit: America would support Faisal on the basis of 'a new chapter in American Saudi relations based on people's right to self-determination, progress and freedom'.

Faisal, confronted with conditional American support, acted to please Kennedy, for he could not turn to others for help and was unwilling to adopt Nasser's Arab nationalism. In November 1962 he formed a new government which adopted a ten-point programme that abolished slavery and called for the creation of a consultative council of religious people and commoners. Sadly, the Saudi–American relationship of productive friendly tension came to an end with Kennedy's death and the emergence of the Vietnam problem. President Johnson, who was wont to make fun of the Arabs, their dress and their ways, had to deal with more pressing international concerns. Faisal had a free hand.

The Johnson years were the golden years of the Saudi pan-Islamic policy. The Secretary General of the World Muslim League, Muhammad Sabbah, was elevated to the post of minister; Saudi Arabia invited Pakistani troops to protect the oilfields and Johnson's open-ended support led to the equipping and training of the Saudi National Guard to protect the family and, more importantly, the short-lived 1968 attempt to form a pro-American Muslim alliance between Saudi Arabia, Turkey, Iran and Pakistan (it was the brainchild of presidential adviser Walt Rostow).

Because the Kennedy approach was a brief, personal one, it was as if it had never been. Faisal could not re-enslave the 4000 people he had freed, but he did nothing about creating a consultative council. There was nobody to stop his Yemeni policy, which contributed to the 1967 War, nor was there anyone to question his Muslim schemes and the consequent divisions in the Arab camp. Internally, Faisal went beyond the intelligent theft of land and greater involvement in commerce. He allowed his brother-in-law and security adviser, Kamal Adham, to realize a whole 2 per cent of the income of the oil concession Faisal gave the Japanese in the Neutral Zone. However, the increase in oil income made this gift of hundreds of millions of dollars possible without causing the internal problems that had beset Saud.

The defeat of Nasser by the Israelis in 1967 completed the picture; it brought to an end Nasser's propaganda war against Faisal – sadly, indirect and marginal as it was, the only outside instrument available to attack his abuse of power. It was left to the Saudi people alone to try to curb Faisal's ways and this, from 1967 to 1973, produced the greatest number of attempts to overthrow the Government in the history of the country. The attempts failed because America had helped in the creation of the sophisticated Saudi internal security apparatus by selling the country equipment and lending it personnel. But these manifestations of internal unrest, ignored, dismissed and hushed up by the Americans, were taken seriously by Faisal. This determined Saudi policy on the war of October 1973.

The question Western governments, and indeed individuals, ask about the 1973 oil embargo, 'How could a friend of ours do this to us?' is the wrong one for the circumstances. It totally ignores Faisal's sound decision that doing nothing would lead to serious internal and regional turmoil. The more appropriate question is whether or not the oil embargo was the least damaging consequence of the inevitable march to war which exploded in October 1973. The answer is yes, but the reasons deserve close analysis.

By 1973 Sadat had reduced his links with the USSR and was following a pro-Saudi, pro-American policy. Wrongly, he assumed this would lead to American pressure on Israel to end the occupation of Egyptian territory it had conquered in 1967. But America did nothing and Israel showed no signs of planning to leave the Sinai Peninsula and had allowed the building of some settlements there. Faisal, determined to keep Egypt from reverting to a radical stance, time and again made statements to the press and pleaded with the United States to apply pressure on Israel. In the summer of 1973 Faisal transmitted a personal message to ARAMCO president Frank Jungers pointing out the danger to the flow of oil of the continuing Egyptian–Israeli stalemate. All this got nowhere. America was preoccupied with Vietnam and Watergate.

To Faisal, refusing to help Sadat meant reigniting regional radicalism and endangering his Muslim position and re-creating the atmosphere of conspiracy which led to so many attempts against him within his country. When his attempts to get America to act failed, he accepted Sadat's decision to go to war and promised the use of oil to support him.

What followed came close to strangling the West economically, but it was the result of a series of mishaps rather than of a clear Saudi policy aimed at that end. A total oil embargo was the last thing on Faisal's mind. The war started on 6 October and Faisal immediately offered Egypt $200 million worth of aid. On 12 October, hoping to prevent America helping Israel, Faisal and fellow Arab oil producers announced a 5 per cent reduction in their output. On 16 October the reduction was increased to 10 per cent and a promise of a further 5 per cent cut every month. Until this point, Saudi Arabia was the primary mover behind the cuts in production and there is no doubt that the promise of incremental reductions was more of a threat than a foregone conclusion.

Meanwhile, on 18 October, President Nixon received Faisal's special envoy, Ambassador Omar Saqqaf, who asked Nixon to make an Arab-pleasing announcement that would diffuse the confrontation. Nixon, beset by Watergate, the threat to his presidency and the forced resignation for corruption of Vice President Agnew, was in desperate need of domestic support and did not respond to the Saudi request. He opted instead to supply Israel with $2.2 billion worth of arms to woo Jewish voters. Faisal's response was forced on him. Sheikh Zayyed of Abu Dhabi's answer to the Nixon move to resupply Israel with arms was to announce a total oil embargo. Faisal's attempts to modify his demands daily came to an end; he had no option but to follow the Zayyed lead.

After the embargo was in place, Saudi Arabia went to work to lift it as soon as practicable. The records of the Faisal–Kissinger meetings during the following three months reveal an unmistakable Saudi desire for a face-saving measure to end the impasse. In February 1974 America tried to bribe Saudi Arabia by agreeing to sell it more tanks, aircraft and naval vessels than it had ever done, but it made it clear it could not go further. Meanwhile, during the same month, Faisal journeyed to Pakistan to attend an Islamic conference and was received as a hero. Feeling that the embargo had served his Islamic leadership purposes and that nothing more could be gained from maintaining it, on 19 March 1974 he gave orders for it to be lifted.

Faisal got no American concessions for the Egyptians or the Palestinians. What Faisal got was a quadrupling of the oil price – basically the increase in the price of oil due to shortages was maintained – an enhancement of his position in the Arab and Muslim world which was unearned and American arms to protect his country. The people who ask how a friend could 'do this to them' should wonder, if Faisal was an enemy indeed, why the Americans agreed to arm him? The suffering of the Western consumer and the signal of how things might be under a truly anti-Western Saudi leader, were more the doing of Richard Nixon than they were the child of Faisal bin Abdel Aziz. Even Henry Kissinger accepts this and speaks of the situation being mishandled, without elaboration. Certainly the Nixon administration knew enough of what had happened to continue its relations with Saudi Arabia without any alterations to the basic relationship an embargo by an enemy would have created, and Nixon visited Saudi Arabia in 1974 and was received as a friend by none other than Faisal himself.

When Faisal was assassinated in March 1975, the Saudi propaganda machine had made so much out of his announcements regarding praying in a Muslim Jerusalem, and his courage in imposing an oil embargo, that the House of Saud found it easy to label him a martyr. The Arab masses took this a step further and decided Zionism and America were behind his murder. In fact, it was America which lost a reliable ally and had most to fear, though the income from high oil prices guaranteed the smooth succession of Khalid and Saudi stability.

Though Saudi Arabia has no bars, the 1975–9 period was undoubtedly its 'happy hour'. King Khalid ruled a country where the oil-propelled GDP increased by 85 per cent and the country's income grew faster than its ability to use it to show annual surpluses of between $6 billion and $32 billion. All Saudi college graduates were absorbed in highly paid jobs; the private sector flourished and the number of expatriate workers more than doubled; there was a shortage of Chevrolet pick-up trucks, hotel rooms to accommodate visiting salesmen and cement for building. The ports of Jeddah and Dhahran were so congested that bribes equalling the value of some goods were paid to obtain priority customs clearance.

In the field of foreign policy, renting solutions and leaders became an affordable Saudi habit, and axiomatically most rentals were aimed at keeping the lid on problems common to Saudi Arabia and America, a form of fronting for America. Yasser Arafat visited frequently, got more money each time and was told to 'cool it' and not get too radical; Assad of Syria was kept happy with money and Saudi Arabia had America pressure Israel into accepting his dominance in Lebanon to stop its radicalization; Siad Barre of Somalia received a check for $200 million to eject the Soviets from Barbera seaport in his country and always got another check for himself; Mobutu of Zaïre was given $50 million to fight pro-Soviet Angolan rebels; and Filipino Muslim rebel leaders were kept in Jeddah hotel suites and afforded a lifestyle which made them forget the reason for their being there. Riyal rentals became the essence of Saudi diplomacy. (This was the beginning of the Saudi invasion of the world, the time when manifestations of Saudi wealth became a topic of everyday conversation.)

It was also the period which saw the smallest number of internal attempts against the Saudi monarchy. Jimmy Carter's commitment to human rights was still applicable, but only in an absolute sense. The number of Saudis involved in political activity or agitation was small indeed; they operated against a background of a proven old maxim that people with full bellies do not start revolutions. Says former National Security adviser Robert Komer, 'Doing something would have disturbed a scene which wasn't so bad.'

In reality, even the Egyptian–Israeli Camp David agreement of 1978 failed to disturb the Saudi state of internal and external bliss. It is true that a family split resulted and that the then Crown Prince Fahd wanted to support Sadat and America, but the Saudi decision to boycott Egypt should have been predictable. Supporting Camp David entailed some danger of internal upheavals, making the rest of the Arabs and Muslims unhappy and provoking external threats. Opposing Camp David had few costs. According to Jimmy Carter's memoirs, both King Khalid and Crown Prince Fahd assured him of 'their unequivocal support for Sadat', but they would go no further, not openly. What Carter wanted meant assuming a leadership posture and fronting dangerously for America. The history of Saudi Arabia reveals an unwillingness to do either. As has been shown, they have never really led and fronting occurred only when it could be done without endangering the House of Saud or when it could be presented as a Muslim or Arab effort. The wise Saudi decision was to stop others from radically opposing Sadat and to proceed as if nothing had happened. They bribed all of Sadat's needy opponents.

This honeymoon came to an abrupt end in 1979. In January of that year, Khomeini took over in Iran; in November there was the Mecca Mosque rebellion and in December the USSR invaded Afghanistan to support the puppet government of Barbak Kemal. The shock to the House of Saud was immeasurable. Suddenly King

Khalid and Crown Prince Fahd were confronted with external and internal dangers which money could not eliminate. They could not understand America's inability to save the Shah, and coupled with America's lack of response to the invasion of Afghanistan and its helplessness regarding the Mosque rebellion, it underscored the limits of America's power and threatened to make America an unreliable ally. The Mosque rebellion signalled the transfer of the internal opposition to the House of Saud from an Arab to a Muslim mould. The House of Saud, loath to admit that years of prosperity had not eliminated all opposition to its ways, de-emphasized the political nature of the rebellion and described it as the work of a fanatical Muslim monk intent on emulating outsiders. Without meaning it, this, with what was happening in Iran and Afghanistan, was an admission that the Muslim policies begun by Faisal had come to naught. To make things worse, a group of Faisal's sons presented King Khalid with a 33-page document calling for across-the-board political reforms covering the country's internal policies and external relations. In addition, an Islamic group, the Islamic Revolution in Arabia, was allowed by Sadat, who was angry over lack of Saudi support, to use Radio Cairo to beam anti-House of Saud broadcasts.

America tried to allay Saudi fears through the transmission of reassuring private messages to the King and Crown Prince, but that was not enough. Finally, on 13 September 1980, a State Department spokesman announced that the United States was committed to protecting Saudi Arabia against 'all internal and external attempts to destabilize it'. This was followed by extensive military manoeuvres by American Air Force units stationed at Dhahran and American threats again Iran. Saddam Hussein's attack of September 1980 on Iran took place against a background of a Saudi Arabia in panic and an open articulation of America's commitment to protect it. Since relations with Egypt were still suspended because of Camp David, Saddam Hussein was the only viable Arab card the House of Saud could play against a resurgent Islam, and America, unprepared to face the new dangers, accepted the premise and supported it.

Beyond adopting Iraq as the first line of defence of Saudi Arabia, there is no evidence whatsoever that a Saudi, American or Saudi–American strategy was ever developed to cope with the consequences of the Iran–Iraq War. There were some small moves: the negative one of creating the Gulf Cooperation Council, providing Jordan with $200 million to create a military contingency

168

capability to help Saudi Arabia in case of internal need and the beginning of the mending of the fences with Egypt. But how to live with a victorious Iraq or Iran was beyond Fahd's thinking and, more dangerously, Reagan's.

In 1980 America became the world's biggest importer of Saudi oil (it was tenth in 1970). Reagan understood this simple fact and little else. The ensuing Fahd–Reagan partnership (Fahd had been the strongman even before Khalid's death in 1982) was one of the most destructive alliances of this century and its consequences will haunt us for years to come. Their combined and complementary policies amounted to support for the Saudi policy of active negativism. For its part, America depended on Saudi Arabia to provide financial backing for executive branch adventures, and welcomed a Saudi decision to place most of their $100-billion-plus surplus funds in US banks and certificates of deposit. In return, the Americans indicated a willingness to interfere in regional and Muslim disputes beyond Saudi Arabia's reach and capability.

With Muslim Iran and Arab Iraq at each other's throat, this was the heyday of illegal activity in Nicaragua and Angola, the sponsoring of divisions among the Palestinians, the creation of the GCC, the building of bridges with Sadat, the perpetuation of war in Afghanistan, the support for despots like Siad Barre and the shipping of oil to South Africa. In return the United States unsuccessfully tried to stop the 1982 Israeli invasion of Lebanon, contained Libya's Qaddafi, supplied Iraq with arms and kept the Egyptian and Israeli positions in balance and refused to allow either to replace its Saudi deputy.

Meanwhile Saudi money was kept in America, Saudi Arabia was buying more arms and a Saudi alliance with American business was developing. There was so much Saudi money in American banks, according to Anthony Sampson and others, that it led to a rush to lend money to Third World countries and eventually to the debt crisis. Some American banks, such as Irving Trust Company and Morgan Guarantee Trust Company, turned down excessive Saudi deposit money and refused to indulge, but the rest did.

Saudi Arabia bought F-15s, Stinger Missiles, C-130 transport planes, M-60 tanks, leased AWACS and extended and expanded the contract of the US Army Corp of Engineers and the US Military Training Mission. But the Saudi involvement with American business went further and AT&T borrowed $650 million and IBM, Proctor and Gamble, TWA, FMC Corporation and United Airlines felt so dependent on Saudi business that they lobbied the

US Government to approve the sale of arms to the country. And the Americans' love of Saudi money went so far that the door was opened for promoters of Saudi interests to try to affect American public life, directly or through individuals. The Saudis contributed money to Reagan's second presidential campaign and to some senators and congressmen. Former Secretary of Defense Clark Clifford worked with them and so did former Vice President Spiro Agnew, former CIA Chief Richard Helms, former superspy Miles Copeland and a slew of former US Ambassadors to Saudi Arabia and other Arab countries.

In fact the House of Saud and Americans were having fun while the Iranians and Iraqis were killing each other, and they paid no attention to the Saudi people. Meanwhile a few voices sounded a note of warning. Former Ambassador James Akins kept up his attack on Saudi corruption, former Assistant Secretary of State William Quandt studiously pointed out the eventual Iraqi danger to Kuwait and former President Carter advocated wealth sharing with the country's poor neighbours, but nothing could stop the avalanche created by the Fahd–Reagan amity of ignorance. In the UK, there continued a strong business connection with Saudi Arabia, if not in the arms trade. This was evidenced by the activities of Mark Thatcher and the current Minister of State for Defence, Jonathan Aitken, the latter with King Fahd's son Muhammad.

Between 1981 and 1987 there were no reports about internal conditions in Saudi Arabia – not even by human rights organizations – but the Saudi Ambassador to the USA Prince Bandar's $500,000 party received full media coverage, Boeing bragged about King Fahd's flying palace, Saudi businessman Ghaith Pharoan made news when he put champagne in the fountain of a Paris nightclub and 52 journalists attended the multi-million-dollar coronation of arms dealer Adnan Khashoggi as King Adnan I. Saudi money, even when used in this stupid fashion, gave the impression that all was well in the Middle East.

But it was not: political conditions within Saudi Arabia and the Arab and Muslim worlds either had not changed or had worsened. Certainly the behaviour of the Saudi royal family had got out of control. The one major thing which had changed went unnoticed: as in refusing to support the Palestinians in Lebanon, Fahd was no longer willing to appease his people or the rest of the Arabs by periodically going anti-West. The Fahd–Reagan alliance, given the simplicity of the two men, foolishly ignored Saudi Arabia's other circles of power and left the country totally, and extremely dangerously, dependent on America.

Trouble lurked beneath the apparently calm surface bequeathed by Ronald Reagan. It was left to George Bush to deal with the impending trouble in the Middle East created by the Fahd–Reagan short-term policies of active negativism. The end of the Iran–Iraq War left the Middle East with a militarily strong but economically wobbly Iraq and an angry Iran forced by military failure into a reassessment of its expansionist militant Islamic policies. Saudi Arabia's policy of active negativism had failed and come to an end; the House of Saud prayer 'Allah vanquish Khomeini without making Saddam victorious' had not been answered.

All this coincided with a continued weakness in the oil prices which had begun in 1982 and which was beginning to interfere with Saudi schemes for supremacy through money. Between 1982 and 1988 Saudi Arabia suffered seven years of budget deficits and the Saudi treasury was empty enough for the country to float internal debt bonds. This undoubtedly affected its ability to try to help Iraq on the scale required. On the sidelines, Egypt, which had been readmitted to the Arab fold, was desperate to reclaim a leadership position within it; Syria feared Saddam's growing popularity with the Arab masses and Israel eyed the impressive Iraqi army uneasily.

With Iran looking inwards, the threat to the Gulf was Iraq and its new regional ambitions. Unlike Britain after the Second World War, Iraq was not a cohesive enough society to accept the idea of being victorious and broke (it came out of the war owing $40 billion) and Saddam trapped himself by claiming victory to a people who wanted its benefits. Beyond that, there was an ominous sign of trouble which America and Saudi Arabia ignored. Unlike Iran, Saddam would not demobilize his massive army.

To the average outsider, Saddam Hussein of Iraq was an unknown quantity. But to official America, Britain, Saudi Arabia and others, he was a man who had been a serious part of the Middle East equation for some time. A brief review of American–Iraqi relations, with Saudi–American relations as background, is in order.

The American encouragement of Iraq to attack Iran had occurred after secret flirtations in the 1970s and was followed by more secret contacts between the two countries between 1981 and 1984. Both phases had the blessing of Saudi Arabia.

The first phase of secret diplomacy was aimed at prising Iraq loose from the USSR's grip in return for allowing Iraq to acquire American and other Western technology. The second opened the door wide for direct American support against Iran which included sharing intelligence data gathered by AWACS planes supplied to Saudi Arabia. (I was personally involved in both phases of this rapprochement. Acting on behalf of Iraq, I held negotiations to get a major American bank to open an office in Baghdad and, in the middle of the war with Iran, I carried an American message telling the Iraqis that the USSR was providing Iran with satellite pictures and later an American offer to maintain Iraq's technological edge by supplying them with the ultra-sophisticated Harpoon missile.)

In 1986 US–Iraqi relations were strained by the Irangate scandal, the supply of arms to Iran in which Saudi Arabia participated. And in 1987 an Iraqi warplane accidentally attacked the American destroyer *Stark*, killing 37 sailors. But these major developments produced no long-term repercussions because both sides avoided them. By the end of 1987 economic and technical agreements were reached, including the extension of billions of dollars worth of American credit for the purchase of grain. In 1988, in a protest over Iraqi use of chemical weapons against the Kurds and renewed accusations of Iraq's sponsorship of terrorism, the USA embargoed the sale of agricultural products to Iraq but Secretary of State George Schultz still had a friendly meeting with his Iraqi counterpart, Tariq Aziz. The diplomatic visits between the two countries in 1989, aimed at stopping a budding deterioration, were followed in 1990 by the visit of a congressional delegation led by Senator Robert Dole.

A month after Dole's visit, while on a visit to Amman, Jordan, Saddam Hussein attacked US policy in the Middle East and demanded the withdrawal of the American fleet from the Gulf. The fleet was and is there to protect the oil supplies, above all from Saudi Arabia. Saddam Hussein was making his first move; to the Saudis, he was challenging their special relationship with the United States.

These manifestations of an uneven American–Iraqi relationship over a period of two decades took place within a framework of regional strategic considerations. These considerations did distance Saddam from the USSR and managed to stop the march of Khomeini's Islamic fundamentalism, but they left Saddam in possession of unconventional weapons and able to threaten the Gulf and Israel. (The blueprint for the first Iraqi chemical warfare plant came from Pfaulder Corporation in Rochester, New York.)

The end of the Gulf war would have forced a disclosure of enormous Saudi-approved Western complicity in arming Saddam Hussein and making him a regional threat. But this natural course of events was intercepted by Kuwait. A few days after the Iran–Iraq War ended, Kuwait, in violation of OPEC agreements, decided to increase its oil production by pumping oil from the disputed Rumailla oilfield, which is partly in Kuwait but mostly in Iraq. Coming on top of cheating by other OPEC members, this sent the price of oil tumbling from $22 per barrel to $16, and for brief periods even lower. So Iraq, which depended on oil for 90 per cent of its income and desperately needed to rebuild and please its people, found Kuwait infringing on its sovereignty and reducing its income by over $4 billion a year, a development which threatened the country with financial collapse and undermined Saddam's position with his people.

Was the Kuwaiti decision and its timing as much of a mystery as it has been made out to be? Did Saudi Arabia refrain from objecting to Kuwaiti moves because the Saudis wanted to divert attention from their past role and to cripple Saddam? One thing is clear: Kuwait did not need the money it was realizing from increasing its oil production. A nation of one million people including expatriate workers, it had reserves of over $90 billion and producing oil in accordance with its OPEC share was more than enough to meet its needs. Followed as it was by a Kuwaiti denial of air rights to Iraqi civilian aircraft, a Kuwaiti hesitation to congratulate Iraq on its 'victory', the deterioration in relations with America and a Saudi refusal to lend Iraq more money, it led Saddam to conclude that a conspiracy to topple him was in the making.

Kuwait did not stop there. It demanded the immediate repayment of the $8 billion it had lent Iraq during its conflict with Iran. And it secretly invited Iranian Foreign Minister Velyatti to visit Kuwait and began a strange unexplainable series of contacts with the CIA. (During the first five months of 1990 CIA Chief William Webster secretly visited the Emir of Kuwait three times and the reason for these visits is still unknown.) When, after dismissing the initial demands for debt repayment as pro forma, the Iraqis responded to a strongly worded repeat demand by truthfully stating that they had no money, Kuwait initiated contacts with Lloyds Bank in London to sell the Iraqi debt notes at a huge discount. Had it happened, this would have added to more defaulting in the payments of debts by Iraq and destroyed its ability to borrow desperately needed money on the international market.

For sixteen months the Iraqi–Kuwaiti confrontation, despite its serious implications for the stability of the whole Middle East, was viewed as a minor local problem. One month after the cessation of Iraqi–Iranian hostilities, in Casablanca, then later during the visit of Iraqi Foreign Minister Saadoun Hammadi to Kuwait and finally during the May 1990 conference of Arab heads of state in Baghdad, the Iraqis tried to discuss their border problems with Kuwait without success. The Kuwaitis, despite long-standing international recognition that the Rumailla oilfield and the area around it were in dispute, simply would not budge. In June 1990, in an attempt to overcome Kuwait's intransigence, the Iraqis unsuccessfully tried to convene a heads of state conference of Iraq, Kuwait, Qatar, the UAE and Saudi Arabia, but Kuwait saw fit to receive the Iranian Foreign Minister instead. The culmination of the Iraqi efforts was a regional agreement to reduce oil production and raise prices which was reached on 17 July 1990 in Jeddah, Saudi Arabia. An hour after this 'settlement', the Kuwaiti delegate unexpectedly announced that Kuwait would abide by it for a mere three months. This produced a run on the Iraqi dinar which saw it lose 50 per cent of its value. It amounted to a Kuwaiti declaration of economic warfare.

There is little doubt that part of the reason for Iraq's keeping the Kuwaiti–Iraqi problem an Arab one was its distrust of America. But why the latter, which was meeting with the Iraqis regularly to discuss many outstanding problems between the two countries, accepted this exclusion despite some open Iraqi threats to Kuwait's sovereignty, is impossible to understand. America's mysterious inactivity was exacerbated by an equally unexplainable Saudi wish not to be involved.

Some analysts state that Saudi Arabia had shied away from involvement in the territorial dispute between the two countries because it was based on a historical Iraqi claim and to accept that principle would render questionable Saudi Arabia's very being. Also Saudi Arabia was committed to low oil prices to help America. Even if true, these two factors are less important than the Saudi belief that Saddam should suffer and his power be reduced. Certainly, even if we take into consideration the straitened circumstances of the country, the Saudi failure to bribe Iraq into silence went against tradition. So, Iraq, unable to turn anywhere, began threatening Kuwait openly and the Iraqi threats created an atmosphere of crisis which, under ordinary circumstances, the Americans would not have ignored.

The record of the meeting on 25 July 1990 between Saddam Hussein and US Ambassador to Iraq April Glaspie is now available. Saddam initiated the meeting, at which Glaspie thought she was going to see Iraqi Foreign Minister Tariq Aziz. Still Glaspie gave Saddam something he had not expected. She told him, in clear terms, that America did not object to raising the dollar price of oil to a figure in the mid-twenties and described the Kuwaiti–Iraqi border dispute as an inter-Arab affair in which America did not wish to interfere.

The Saddam–Glaspie meeting was followed by considerable inter-Arab activity which culminated in a meeting in Riyadh between Kuwait, Iraq and Saudi Arabia on 31 July 1990. Iraq, emboldened by Glaspie's green light and a friendly letter of 27 July 1990 from George Bush to Saddam, made much of the fact that it was being bled to death economically. America's explicit friendly intentions preceded Iraq's interception of a message from British Prime Minister Thatcher to the Emir of Kuwait in which she promised him 'reject Iraqi demands and we will back you'.

Saddam's conspiratorial instincts betrayed him and he interpreted Kuwaiti actions in the light of the Thatcher message. To him it was colonial Britain which was trying to undermine Iraq and not America, and America was what mattered. This emboldened him to act.

The meeting which took place on 31 July in Riyadh, the last hope to stop an invasion, had had four things going against it: the Glaspie–Bush green light, Iraqi belligerence, Kuwaiti stubbornness and King Fahd's lack of interest. The Iraqis demanded billions of dollars worth of compensation for the oil from the Rumailla field proceeds and a permanent border adjustment. The Kuwaitis would not give on either point and Fahd, behaving oddly, spent half an hour with the delegations and left his brother, the gentle but incompetent Prince Abdallah, to mediate. When news reached Fahd that the Kuwaiti and Iraqi positions appeared irreconcilable, all he did to settle the issue was to make a gesture the Iraqis were sure to refuse: he offered Iraq $1 billion in aid. The Iraqis, now angrier with Kuwait and smarting over Fahd's unattentiveness and the deliberately insulting offer, left without accepting it. War was 36 hours away.

A few hours after Iraqi armour thrust into Kuwait on 2 August 1990, King Hussein of Jordan received a telephone call from King Fahd. The Guardian of Islam's Holy Shrines was agitated. He kept repeating the same question: why had Saddam Hussein done this without waiting for the results of Arab mediation? Amazingly, however, Fahd had nothing concrete to suggest; even the traditional Saudi bribe was withheld. To King Hussein and Yasser Arafat, the two Arab leaders who had repeatedly tried to mediate the dispute with very little at their disposal, the wrong person was asking the wrong question. Nobody had expected anything from the perverse Kuwaitis, but Saudi Arabia was the only country which could have forced Kuwait to change direction and which was capable of doing something about oil prices, and Fahd had had a year and a half to do something about both. The Arab house was bitterly divided: Saudi Arabia and the rich oil sheikhdoms came out against Saddam; Arafat and Hussein did not accept the occupation of Kuwait but saw Saddam's action as justifiable in the circumstances; the Yemen supported Saddam out of enmity for Saudi Arabia; and the other Arab countries, including Egypt, occupied the middle ground. But, because of its geographical position, oil wealth and special relationship with America, it was Saudi Arabia which mattered most and the decision as to what would happen next rested with Fahd as much as it did with Saddam and George Bush.

Between the invasion date of 2 August and the conference of Arab heads of state on 10 August, King Hussein of Jordan, Yasser Arafat of the PLO and President Mubarrak of Egypt met each other and Fahd and Saddam. As a sign of his willingness to effect a total withdrawal from Kuwait, Saddam accepted a pledge from King Hussein that an Arab solution was in the offing and on 6 August ordered the withdrawal of 10,000 Iraqi troops from Kuwait, and another 10,000 were pulled back to the Iraqi border the day after. Arafat got an initial agreement by both Saddam and Fahd to meet somewhere along the Iraqi–Saudi border and another for a five-way meeting in Jeddah with Iraq, Kuwait, Saudi Arabia, Egypt and the PLO participating. Fahd initially agreed to both suggestions then turned them down without explanation. Meanwhile, Mubarrak insisted that an Iraqi acceptance of the principle of withdrawal must precede all else and worked for an Arab solution based on this principle.

What nobody had counted on were the results of the 6 August meeting between US Secretary of Defense Dick Cheney and King Fahd. Cheney went to Saudi Arabia accompanied by General Norman Schwarzkopf, two intelligence personnel and one Middle East expert, and the Saudi Ambassador to the United States Prince Bandar, the son of the Saudi Minister of Defence and a favourite of his uncle, Fahd. The American Ambassador to Saudi Arabia Charles Freeman joined the American group. The King met Cheney and his group accompanied by Crown Prince Abdallah, Defence Minister Sultan (the father of Bandar) and several members of the royal family.

There was no discussion of any initiative to solve the problem short of war, nor were the Americans, or Fahd, interested in the results of the efforts of Arab intermediaries. Using satellite maps, Dick Cheney showed King Fahd that 200,000 Iraqi troops were poised to attack Saudi Arabia. Cheney said nothing about the extremely important facts of the small withdrawal of Iraqi troops and the pull-back of other Iraqi units from the Saudi border. Cheney asked Fahd to invite US troops to Saudi Arabia, 'to protect our friends', and the King nodded agreement, but Crown Prince Abdallah wanted to hear more about the disposition of Iraqi troops, the intended use of the American troops after they arrived and the conditions under which they would leave the country.

Cheney's answer to the points raised by Prince Abdallah was vague. Instead of answering them directly, he is reported to have addressed himself to Fahd and told him that there was a strong possibility that the Iraqi invasion of Kuwait was part of an Iraqi–Yemeni–PLO plot to destabilize the Arabian Peninsula and divide it among themselves. He added that, at that moment, there was nothing to stop the Iraqi army from marching on Riyadh. Cheney added that it was difficult to determine whether King Hussein was part of this sinister partition plan.

This unbelievable story was told to me by two former American Ambassadors to Saudi Arabia, a former member of the National Security Council and a disaffected member of the House of Saud. At this point, there are no documents to confirm it and it is impossible to establish whether the official US record of the meeting alludes to it, but there is little doubt that Cheney's total presentation reflected America's intentions to destroy Saddam. Even if the satellite pictures had not shown the Iraqi withdrawal and the fact that Iraq had no more than 80,000 soldiers left inside Kuwait, this information had been transmitted to Washington by King Hussein, who had personally given it to President Bush to allay his fears over an Iraqi thrust into Saudi Arabia. Judged against the background of the Glaspie meeting and Bush's letter of 27 July, the American attitude amounted to capitalizing on a situation they had created and forces the question of whether or not Saddam had been set up and the whole war was nothing more than a plan to eliminate the only Middle East power capable of challenging America's hegemony over the Arab world. Certainly Saddam's demand for the withdrawal of the American fleet from the Gulf should have produced something different from Bush's friendly letter and Fahd's billion-dollar offer – a response in proportion to the threat.

Fahd took the decision to invite American troops to his country without the concurrence of Crown Prince Abdallah and other important members of his family, and before consulting the religious ulemas or others. The constructive contacts he had kept with King Hussein and Yasser Arafat became erratic and he was no longer in the mood to listen to them; hence the failure of more attempts to convene a meeting including Fahd and Saddam.

When the Arab heads of state met in Cairo on 10 August, King Fahd had very little to say and refused to meet Taha Yassin Ramadan, the head of the Iraqi delegation, who was there in Saddam's place. The surprise Arab League decision against mediation and for the use of force against Iraq was sponsored by President Mubarrak of Egypt and, unusually for an occasion which required a unanimous decision, it was carried by a simple majority. When King Hussein protested to Mubarrak and claimed that this violated a telephone agreement they had reached regarding a peaceful Iraqi withdrawal, Mubarrak, without ever explaining his statement, revealed that someone had 'held a gun to his head'. Whatever gun had been held to Mubarrak's head, and undoubtedly it was a threat to cut off Saudi or American aid, or both, had led him to behave strangely. He had housed the Iraqi delegation to the meeting in the Andalus Guest House, a small hotel with an unreliable telephone switchboard from which they could not contact other delegations, and he cut off the microphone of the Iraqi chief delegate as the latter was trying to make a statement guaranteeing the safety of Saudi Arabia and the acceptance of the stationing of Arab troops on its soil. But Mubarrak would not have done any of these things without Fahd's approval and before, during and after the meeting with Cheney Fahd had behaved as if he had known what was coming.

What followed outside the Middle East consisted of a number of UN resolutions and attempts at mediation. The original UN demand for Iraq to withdraw from Kuwait kept getting expanded. There were cries about the stupid Iraqi act of holding Western hostages and an embargo on Iraq was deemed insufficient and not given enough time to work. King Hussein, the USSR, France and

UN Secretary-General Pérez de Cuellar indulged in official mediation efforts and dozens of others such as former British Prime Minister Edward Heath, former Governor of Texas John Connally and Jesse Jackson were self-appointed mediators. But the die was cast. Iraq, convinced that it was the subject of an American–Saudi–Mubarrak conspiracy, refused to move, and the USA and its allies, faced with Iraqi stupidity, kept enacting ever more punitive UN resolutions which left Saddam little room to manoeuvre. Fahd did absolutely nothing; a shooting war was a foregone conclusion.

The prelude to the Gulf War produced a propaganda war the like of which had not been seen since the First World War. The man who took the lead in creating the atmosphere of a sick carnival was George Bush, one of the architects of America's friendship with Iraq even under Reagan and a man who never learned to say Sud-am but insisted on calling him Sa-dam. But the man whose behaviour made war inevitable was Fahd bin Abdel Aziz.

The Saudis' acceptance of foreign troops saw hundreds of thousands of them descend on the country. The Council of Ulemas had approved the measure without knowing its extent and under considerable pressure and with considerable reluctance, and King Fahd issued a large number of debt notes to Turkey, Syria, Egypt, Pakistan, Bangladesh, Britain, France, America and others to join the holy war against Saddam. It cost him between $55 billion and $62 billion, but, in this case, he accepted the cost of his fronting act with no apparent reluctance.

The very few voices which saw the coming war and the exaggeration of Saddam's military capability as unjustified made no dent in the atmosphere of war hysteria which enveloped most of the world. (I stopped appearing on television after some friends told me it was a bad idea which jeopardized my presence in Britain.) On 16 January 1991 aerial attacks of unprecedented intensity were unleashed against the Iraqi army and civilian targets by a joint allied command which made its decisions without consulting King Fahd or his commanders. For over a month, Iraq was pulverized while its air force and aerial defence system were unable to defend it. Saddam managed to hit Israel and Saudi Arabia with some Scud missiles, but their effect was minor – more psychological than real.

Besides some makeshift military bunkers, the only Saudi with an underground bunker was King Fahd, and like Saddam's in Baghdad, it had all the comforts money can buy. King Fahd resurfaced on 27 February 1991, the day the Iraqis signed a truce agreement tantamount to surrender. In less than a year, the Middle East and his country had changed beyond recognition.

The Gulf War achieved its real purpose: it protected the oil and eliminated Iraq as a regional power capable of threatening it and the security of the producer countries. But by destroying the strongest secular power in the region, it created an ideological vacuum in the area which only Islamic fundamentalism can fill. Because the Saudi brand of sponsored, conservative fundamentalism is no longer acceptable, radical fundamentalism is sweeping the area and it has already won elections in Algeria, Jordan, Kuwait and the Sudan, and is threatening Egypt, Tunisia, Morocco and other countries. Naturally Islamic Iran looms large as a regional power and magnet for the disaffected. The prospect of a dramatic switch to another short-sighted policy aimed at re-creating Saddam Hussein to confront the new Islamic challenege is a real one.

The Saudi purchase of the support of countries like Egypt, Syria and Turkey has come to an end because the Gulf War left it broke and unable to renew the rent. Saudi Arabia is incurring a budget deficit for the twelfth year running (see Oil, OPEC and the Overseers and Too Late?) and the total disappearance of its reserves and its $60-billion-plus debt burden means that it cannot reactivate this policy even as a stopgap measure. Saudi Arabia too was eliminated as a regional leader.

The American and other armies, true to the promises made during the crisis, have left Saudi Arabia, but their brief stay created problems which refuse to disappear. Beyond frowning on their government's decision to allow female GIs clad in shorts in their country, all Saudis are questioning the expenditure of more money on procuring more useless military hardware, the ulemas have served notice on the King 'never again to invite foreign troops on Muslim holy soil', and, above all, Muslim fundamentalists within the country, people who saw and see Iraq as a Muslim country deserving of their loyalty and affection, have grown stronger and are demanding wide-ranging reforms.

All this leaves King Fahd clinging to America for protection. Of necessity, he feels closer to America than ever before and he still has oil to offer and at a reasonable price. Because nobody has tried to change his ways, America, sooner rather than later, will have to defend Fahd and his family – or leave it to Saddam Hussein to do it. Another costly military exercise, or war, which is likely to leave the Middle East in even worse condition, is on the way, and this time the oil may not be safe.

7

Big Deals and Dangerous Games

Despite the various promises to control the flow of arms to the Middle East made by President Bush, Prime Minister Major and other Western leaders during the crisis and subsequent Gulf War, one of the results of this war has been an acceleration in the already massive Saudi armaments programme. Superficially it looks as if Saudi Arabia is building a strong army to protect itself against future contingencies, but this is not the case and recent Saudi arms purchases are nothing more than an extension of an old policy which was exposed as ineffective when the country proved itself unable to face the Iraqi threat alone.

Even before August 1990 Saudi Arabia had more arms than its small armed forces could use, or master. This fact, known to both Saudi Arabia and its arms suppliers – America had a military training mission in the country – was disguised to fool the Saudi people and the country's neighbours and potential enemies. The House of Saud pretended it could use the arms to conceal its dependence on the West for protection. The Saudi people, particularly the strong Muslim fundamentalist movement, would have objected to too close a relationship with the infidel West and the Arabs and Muslims would have seen the dependence as neo-colonialism and would have tried to foment trouble regionally and within the country.

The country's Western protectors, particularly the Americans, shared the concern of the House of Saud over their people's as well as Arab and Muslim reaction to any disclosure of the truth. In addition the West had an interest in selling Saudi Arabia military hardware, even when it knew that arms purchases alone could not produce an effective military force. These two considerations made the West an implicit co-conspirator in the game of pretence. The maintenance of this pretence and its elevation to the status of a defence policy were aided by the existence of a powerful inter-mediary establishment, an influential group of princes and arms dealers who realized billions of dollars worth of commissions from the country's huge military procurement programme. For the most part the intermediaries were the very same Saudi decision-makers who formulated their country's phoney defence policy.

Now, with the Gulf War as background, the House of Saud uses all the original reasons for pretending to build a strong army and finds it easier to justify them. Instead of producing a more coherent defence policy, the increasing internal pressures on the Saudi Government to distance itself from the West have made the House of Saud perpetuate the pretence. Simultaneously, in the West, the reductions in defence budgets and their consequent effect on the defence industry have made the Saudi arms business more important than before; instead of stopping or reducing the flow of arms governments are openly trying to sell more. So Saudi Arabia is buying more arms than ever, and, in addition to the West's reneging on promises to control arms sales to Middle Eastern countries, the traditional constraints over selling the House of Saud ultra-modern equipment have all but disappeared. The game goes on despite what the Gulf War revealed and the bitter lesson of Iran, under the Shah the one country which diverted funds needed for development purposes to buy more arms than it needed.

Saudi Arabia has 4400 miles of exposed border and – except for a number of sheikhdoms and emirates with small populations and insignificant armies – no friendly neighbours. For different reasons, Iran, Iraq, the Yemen, Jordan and the Sudan are anti-Saudi and have a combined population of 100 million people and standing armies which number two million soldiers. Their quarrels with Saudi Arabia translate into a wish to change its governmental system, share in its oil wealth and cancel the political effects of its alliance with the West on the Middle East. This is not to forget Israel, which continues to overstate the Saudi military potential and resents Saudi Arabia's 'special relationship' with the West. (Various Israeli studies available to me, including some by the reputable Dyan Centre, depict Saudi Arabia as posing a serious military threat to Israel and argue in favour of exclusive Western reliance on Israeli military might to keep the Middle East under control.)

This is why, even after the disappearance of the communist threat, Saudi Arabia continues to feel vulnerable and insecure. And it is why the ostensible policy of Saudi Arabia calls for the building of a strong army, air force and navy and why it spends so much money on armaments. And, of course, it is this 'commitment' to building a strong army and equipping it with the most modern weapons which has made the country the world's biggest arms importer and has provided the background which produced most of the world's best known intermediaries cum arms dealers. The world knows more about these two subsidiary situations – Saudi Arabia's role as the top arms importer and the home of unprecedented intermediary activity – than it does about the more basic issue of the country's military capability. Happenings in these areas grab the headlines and overshadow their source, the ostensible wish of the Saudis to be able to defend themselves against the encroachment and pressure of their covetous and unfriendly neighbours. In fact, though some reporters were aware of Saudi shortcomings and wrote about them, until the Gulf War none of them knew how bad things were and most believed all or part of the game of pretence.

Forced by circumstances to deal with the basic issue of the military capability of the country, reporters are now happy to use the Gulf War, exclusively, to provide answers. But, as with reporting on so many Middle Eastern situations, the answers are superficial and unsatisfactory. First of all, Saudi Arabia was not invaded and there is a big question as to whether Saddam ever intended to invade it. (I am in possession of Iraqi documents which show that invading Saudi Arabia was the last thing on Saddam's mind and Pierre Salinger's masterful *The Gulf War Documents* and other reliable reports support this contention.) Ejecting or helping to eject an invading army from a neighbouring country is not the same as defending one's own, particularly when the neighbouring country is as unpopular with one's people as Kuwait is with the average Saudi, who, like the rest of the Arabs, has always seen the Kuwaitis as libertine, arrogant money-grabbers and troublemakers. Also, the reasons behind the Gulf War have never been as clear-cut to the typical Saudi as the Western press has made out. Many Saudis, particularly devout Muslims, had serious misgivings about joining forces with outsiders to fight fellow Arabs while others found it difficult to believe that the billions of dollars spent on defence had failed to produce an army capable of defending their country without considerable outside help. On the other hand, Saudi Arabia cried wolf or, prompted by high-level US officials, was told to do so. In either case and in a move which should have brought an end to the policy of pretence, it made an important admission that it could not cope with Iraq alone or even with Arab and Muslim help.

Another element calls into question the use of the Gulf War to provide a full answer. Militarily Iraq was Saudi Arabia's strongest neighbour, a country which had spent billions acquiring and mastering modern weapons including unconventional ones, and it had a standing army of a million battle-hardened soldiers who had acquitted themselves relatively well during the country's eight-year war with Iran, albeit with direct and covert Western help. Iraq was a special case.

Any sensible assessment of Saudi military competence must result from a thorough analysis of Saudi defence aims, the nature of the country's armaments programme and what the two have produced. Luckily there is enough information available to deliver judgement. But, before delving into the facts and figures which make this judgement possible, a cautionary note is in order. The Saudi armaments programme may or may not be the result of Saudi aims, though they are undoubtedly closely related. In other words, it may reflect considerations which are not contained in or at variance with the stated defence policy of the country.

The overt Saudi response to the dangers surrounding them consists of plans to arm the country and guard its wealth against greedy poachers. With Saudi Arabia and the House of Saud still one and the same, this has meant that the survival aims of the country as expressed by all its kings are tantamount to maintaining the House of Saud as the absolute rulers of a personal fiefdom. Disenfranchised as they are, the Saudi people have no quarrel with their neighbours and believe that a moderate amount of wealth-sharing is necessary. But, as we have seen, the Saudi Army and Air Force have not been reliable and their commitment to the House of Saud remains in doubt. So an interim question arises: in view of the fact that a strong army would be better positioned to topple the House of Saud, is Saudi Arabia really trying to build one to defend itself against its neighbours – and thus endanger itself? It is the answer to this question which drives experts such as the Royal United Services Institute's Rosie Hollis to state: 'What they do has little to do with a rational defence policy.' I take her condemnation to mean a simple no. Saudi Arabia is pretending it is building a strong army. The House of Saud wants to maintain itself but it does not want a strong army capable of overthrowing it.

That the Saudi Army has never been trusted is attested to by the presence of the National Guard and its growing importance. The Army, whose official if exaggerated numbers have fluctuated between 40,000 and 60,000, is made up of townsmen, with whom the tribal House of Saud has never been in sympathy. On the other hand, the National Guard, now 32,000 strong, is made up of Bedouins and Wahhabi co-religionists, a more dependable lot whose loyalty can be bought the way it was at the time of Ibn Saud. The Bedouins and Wahhabis are less susceptible to nationalistic ideas and outside ideology; in fact, their loyalty to the House of Saud is a personal and tribal one which excludes the idea of a country or the complex notion of a nation-state.

Further proof of the House of Saud's attitude towards the Army and the National Guard comes from their disposition within the country. The Army is stationed in camps far away from the cities, where it cannot attempt a *coup d'état* by trying to control the centres of government, but the National Guard is based in the cities, including Riyadh, Jeddah and Dhahran, and is entrusted with protecting the royal family. The policy which calls for using the loyal National Guard as a foil to the suspect regular Army is a consistent one and has involved increasing the former's numbers and upgrading its equipment to match new arms purchases by the latter. Now the National Guard has armoured personnel carriers and helicopters and is planning to buy heavy tanks. The numbers of the National Guard have increased from 22,000 in 1975 to their present size while the Army has not grown at all. So the National Guard is moving ahead quantitatively and qualitatively. (Several experts, including Rosie Hollis, support the contention of Saudi opposition groups that the size of the Army is overstated, but, unlike the opposition, they shy away from claiming that the real number is no more than 25,000 and admitting that the official figures are overstated.)

But perhaps it is the Air Force's lack of dependability which has spread the greatest fears among the members of the House of Saud. As mentioned before, repeated rebellions in the ranks have led to a decision to keep the Air Force's planes unarmed and now nearly 70 per cent of the pilots come from the House of Saud, relations and 'reliable families'. Beyond that, because of its history, the Air Force has been a special target for the security apparatus of the country: a high proportion of the non-royal recruits are security service spies. Amazingly, all this has not put an end to problems in this service, as witnessed by the (hushed-up) defection of six non-royal pilots during the Gulf War, four to Jordan and two to the Sudan.

But the solidest confirmation of the House of Saud's decision not to build up strong armed forces comes from the make-up of these forces. There is no conscription in Saudi Arabia and the so-called reserves are somewhat of a joke because Bedouin sheikhs are encouraged to declare some of their followers as reserves when they are never trained and some of them are too young, too old or non-existent. For example, the Sheikh of Wablah's tribe in Asir is supposed to control 4000 reservists, many of whom are long dead. During the critical years between 1975 and 1982, a period of turmoil and challenges such as the Iran–Iraq War and the Mecca Mosque rebellion, events which should have produced the opposite results, even the official figures showed a decline in the Army's numbers. More recently, soon after the Gulf War, family disputes over the size and nature of the armed forces developed when Prince General Khalid bin Sultan announced, without consulting King Fahd, that the Army's strength would be doubled and that it would be merged with the National Guard. Rumours persist that this is what led to Khalid's resignation/dismissal (the announcement was ambiguous). King Fahd stuck to family policy, which called for keeping the armed forces small, separate and weak, against the wishes of the war's best-known Arab commander, a military man who recognized that a country with a long, exposed border and many enemies needed a large, integrated army. (The official figures reveal that the armed forces of Saudi Arabia represent a mere 0.7 per cent of the population compared with 5 per cent in Iraq, 6.5 per cent in Syria and 7.5 per cent in Israel.)

So once again, and on a vital issue affecting the country's survival, there is a contradiction between the Saudis' claim that they are building a large, strong army and the facts of the situation. Yet in this case the pretence exceeds most others in its seriousness and cost, and the armaments procurement programme continues in full swing. In fact, it is this activity, the seemingly incessant buying of modern arms, which creates the illusion of a militarily strong Saudi Arabia and which deserves analysis.

On 18 May 1987 the *Washington Star* claimed that the Saudis could only operate one out of five of the AWACS planes they leased from the USA. The senators and congressmen who had heatedly debated this lease in Congress did not take this prospect into consideration as much as they should have. On 12 July 1988 the *Financial Times* stated that the Saudis lacked the personnel for the arms they were purchasing, but Saudi plans to purchase more arms went ahead unabated. Then, on 18 July 1988, the *Economist* reported that Saudi Arabia was incapable of manning the 1000 Osario tanks it intended to buy from Brazil. Almost simultaneously, David Wood of the *International Herald Tribune* compared the Saudi army to a gold watch which has faulty moving parts. In 1989 the prestigious Institute for International Strategic Studies provided a conclusive judgement: 'The Saudi Arab army is not growing in proportion with the hardware at its disposal.' But these reports have not altered the mistaken general perception of the situation created by a mostly pro-House of Saud Western press which ignores the obvious and continues to speak of 'the country's legitimate defence needs'.

Furthermore, in the wake of the Gulf War, the hardware being purchased for the Saudi armed forces will continue to outstrip their ability to use it. Saudi Arabia has embarked on an armaments shopping spree which includes contracts to buy American Patriot Missiles; F-15s; laser bombs; a Hughes Aircraft aerial-defence system; Canadian Halifax frigates; French Helec torpedo boats and British aircraft; and helicopters and boats from British Aerospace, Westland Helicopters and Vospers Thorneycroft. In the first six months of 1992 alone, Saudi Arabia signed $17 billion worth of military hardware contracts. The $6 billion contract for 72 F-15s followed in August 1992, and this time conditions within the defence industry dictated approval; unlike in 1985, there was no congressional opposition and the deal went through virtually unopposed. This is not to speak of plans to build whole military cities, including a $12 billion, 600-square-kilometre development south of Riyadh, in the middle of the Empty Quarter.

This particular economic problem, the offspring of Saudi pretence, has been going on for a long time. Over the past 15 years Saudi Arabia's armaments procurement budget has averaged between $12 billion and $18 billion a year, and is growing. Meanwhile, even if assuming the Government is telling the truth, the number of people in the country's armed and paramilitary forces has remained at around 110,000 (50,000 in the Army, 32,000 in the National Guard, 15,000 in the Air Force, 4500 in the Navy and 6500 in the Frontier Guard). This means an annual *published* hardware expenditure of $113,000–150,000 per soldier, airman and seaman. However, these exorbitant figures are put into perspective by *unpublished* ones: the value of the oil Saudi Arabia uses to barter for arms. As shown by the AWACS, Lightning and British Aerospace Yamama 1 deals, massive amounts of oil were used in barter deals for this purpose and the price of this oil is not included in the published defence budget figures. This method of payment is a major part of the colossal Yamama 2 contract with the UK, which is discussed later. So while the figure for 1982 is unusually high, these 'normal' figures are still considerably above those of other countries and the Saudi defence budget is between the eighth and sixth highest in the world. Adding the hidden value of the oil which is used in payment produces a minimum of $1.5 million worth of hardware per member of the armed forces over the years 1982 to 1990. It is safely assumed that an air force is the most expensive branch of a country's armed forces and if we took the 543,000 personnel in the US Air Force and applied these figures to them we would get a hardware procurement budget of $65–86 billion. The real US Air Force figure fluctuates but it has always been less than half of that.

But the story is worse than what a simple financial analysis of arms purchases reveals. The number of armoured vehicles the Saudi Army has, excluding what is on order, is 2600 (consisting of French AMX, German Leopard, American M60 and M60AI, British Scorpion and Brazilian Osario tanks and armoured personnel carriers from different countries). It also has 800 pieces of artillery, mortars and Howitzers.

This simply does not work. The Saudi armed forces do not have enough people for the equipment – nor indeed for the installations. In 1984 the Air Academy was built to accommodate 50,000 cadets, instructors and other staff and it has never had more than 6000 occupants; the Hafr Al Batin Army Base, built to house 14,000 people, has a mere 2000; the 15 airbases in Qutaif are so undermanned that one of them has a total of three people; and the $8-billion King Khalid Military City built to house 80,000 people and three armoured brigades is less than 20 per cent occupied. Between 1982 and 1985 the Korean construction companies Kean Nam Enterprises and Sambo and contractors from other countries built more than 7000 National Guard villas and furnished them with everything, including VCRs, yet most of them are unoccupied.

To use a topical example, extrapolating the Saudi hardware figures and applying them to the pre-Gulf War Iraqi army would produce an Iraq which had 61,000 tanks and armoured vehicles and 16,000 pieces of artillery. And we thought Saddam's 3700 tanks were bad enough.

The story of the Royal Saudi Air Force is the same. It has 400 combat planes, 320 helicopters, 260 other aircraft and 15,000 people, certainly the highest aircraft-to-personnel ratio in the whole world. Of course, Saudi Arabia has already signed an agreement to buy an additional 72 American F-15s and is negotiating to buy more British Tornados, even before those they already have on order have been delivered.

The situation of the Royal Saudi Navy is even more absurd. It has 190 naval vessels, including four frigates, four corvettes and nine Peterson patrol boats. This gives us 21.6 people per vessel: a truly incredible statistic regardless of the size of the vessels.

Sometimes the quantities of equipment bought by the Saudis are patently senseless. An example of this is the purchase of one million nuclear, biological and chemical (NBC) warfare suits. This is nearly ten suits per soldier, airman and seaman and the cost of a total NBC outfit, including boots and a helmet, is somewhere around $450, so $450 million was mostly wasted or pocketed or both.

In most of the preceding cases the analysis of the ratio of equipment to personnel neglects the type of equipment involved. But this does not matter, for the figures tell the same story regardless of whether the pieces of equipment involved are sophisticated or simple, big or small. In fact, when we assume that the inherent inefficiency of the Saudi armed forces results in a need for more people per item of equipment than the US, UK or Germany, then the figures become worse. Laments former US Ambassador to Saudi Arabia James Akins, 'They shouldn't get except what they can use – this is unacceptable.'

Indeed there were instances during the Gulf War which revealed how equipment is wasted. According to Robert Fisk of the *Independent*, a dump of hundreds of trucks which the Saudis had forgotten all about was discovered in the middle of nowhere. An Arab journalist with the BBC laughingly confirms: 'I have no doubt that they had more trucks than drivers – I saw it for myself', and a CBS reporter who also spoke anonymously, goes further: 'Judged by equipment they have an army; judged by men they don't.'

The shortage of defence personnel is compounded by the already mentioned efficiency factor. The Saudis suffer from a lack of training in the use of sophisticated weapons, something which the presence in the country of a US military mission since 1951 has failed to cure. The ability of members of a society which is only 55 per cent literate to handle long-range ground-to-ground missiles such as the 1200-mile Deng Fo (Eastern Wind) weapons bought from China is in doubt, as is their ability to learn how to handle the advanced electronic gear in F-15 fighter aircraft or the friend-foe identification radar system made by E-Systems of Texas. The latter weakness was exposed tragically when the Saudis shot down two friendly Bahraini planes during the Gulf War, because they could not tell them from unfriendly Soviet-built Iraqi planes. (The pilots, who were decorated, kept their medals. The mistake was discovered but hushed up.)

The problem goes further, however, than a native inability to handle sophisticated weapons, for the Saudis are completely unable to integrate the diverse equipment they have purchased from several countries. Among other difficulties, their complex mix of American, French and British armour creates an unmanageable and ineffective armoured corps. According to the American expert on Middle East armaments Anthony Cordesman, the Western powers have resigned themselves to the Saudis' inability to field an effective military force and follow their commercial interests without making any attempt at coordinating their sales to Saudi Arabia or between Saudi Arabia and its small Gulf allies. In fact, it is the impossibility of integrating all the equipment the Saudis possess which totally cancels the widely accepted theory that the equipment is there to be used by American forces in cases of emergency.

But there is another factor: the even more basic fact that the Saudis in the armed forces are people who cannot make it in civilian life even in an oil-rich country. They tend to be underachievers who are lured by the prospect of lavish villas, servants and free telephones. But even if they were willing and able, we have to consider what is done to their morale after they enlist. The simple fact that the officer class more and more consists of members of the royal family and their relations and friends cannot but call into question the *esprit de corps* of the armed forces. That the command structure is subordinated to nepotism is attested to dramatically by the fact that all the operations and intelligence directorates are always headed by a prince who bypasses his superiors by having a direct line to the Minister of Defence. In fact, the combination of lack of technical competence and nepotism is seen as being so damaging that it prompted a member of a Washington DC think-tank to tell me: 'It's all a game. They won't be up to any of their big neighbours for 50 years to come.'

So, we have more hardware than people to use it and more housing than people to occupy it and the people available lack the competence to handle what they have. And on top of all this, there is nepotism. This results in a Saudi army even weaker than its small numbers suggest and totally incapable of defending its country against countries which can field huge, more professional armies – Iran and Iraq, for example. Yet the game continues and King Fahd speaks of 'building and strengthening the armed forces' while objecting to expanding their numbers and Minister of Defence Prince Sultan speaks of future wars requiring superior technology and supposes that transfer of technology involves the simple act of buying modern arms. He shows no signs of stopping the shopping spree, which is reported to include eight submarines. Says Rosie Hollis in words with which other experts agree: 'They always provide a rationale for what has been acquired or is about to be acquired.' As usual, members of the Saudi opposition in exile go further and one of them speaks of the King and his brother, Prince Sultan, in the following terms: 'rationalizing the mad expenditure of $100 billion worth of arms since the Gulf War ended'.

This bizarre situation conceals further deception. The reality of the situation is that Saudi Arabia cannot protect itself and must look to the outside for protection. Friendly Arab countries such as Syria and Egypt cannot provide the needed protection, because the quality of their armed forces is suspect and neither of them is ever friendly enough long enough. Saudi Arabia wasted no time in asking the suspect Syrian and Egyptian troops to leave its territory after the Gulf War. Muslim countries, despite Pakistan's previous dispatch of troops to protect the Saudi oilfields, are also unreliable. The rise of radical Islamic fundamentalism stands in the way of further dependence on them. In fact, it was fear of religious turmoil which prompted Saudi Arabia to ask Pakistan to recall the Shia soldiers among its Saudi-based army contingents and which led Pakistan to withdraw all of them. This is why Saudi Arabia must depend on the West, particularly the United States, and why, with the internal and external dangers facing the country on the increase, this dependence is likely to deepen.

But Saudi Arabia, though more capable of doing so than in the past, cannot openly admit this dependence without increasing the danger to itself from its own Muslim fundamentalists and its Arab and Muslim neighbours. But even if the internal and external objections and the danger they carry are overcome, the United States is unable to enter into an open military alliance with Saudi Arabia. Says former US National Security adviser Robert Komer: 'Part of the problem is that the Israeli lobby would never stand for a military pact between the two countries [the USA and Saudi Arabia]. This forces the Saudis into their present posture.'

It is easy to extend the above speculation and theorize about the existence of a conspiracy between the House of Saud and their defenders, the West. Both sides have a vested interest in disguising the dependence and in order to do that Saudi Arabia buys more and more arms to pretend it does not exist. Recently the increasing importance to the US economy of Saudi arms purchases has become another extremely important factor. Not only does the United States, and the rest of the West, pretend to be helping the Saudis defend themselves, but the high level of unemployment in the defence business in the US, UK, France and Brazil has made these countries seek hardware orders like never before. This reliance on Saudi purchases is so great that the French arms maker Metra developed the Shahine missile to meet Saudi Arabia's specific needs, Brazil signed a five-year joint manufacturing agreement with them and, according to Britain's Minister of State for Defence Jonathan Aitken, the United Kingdom is looking to them to fund the manufacture of the European Fighter Aircraft. This advanced fighter is supposed to meet European defence needs well into the next century.

The US is not far behind. In 1978 the sale of F-15s to Saudi Arabia took a year and a half to complete. Now, not to be outdone, US defence contractors and senators and congressmen representing states where the former are located are rumoured to be petitioning the US Government to allow them to offer the Saudis their most modern wares. Because of the cost and sophistication of the equipment involved, a Saudi commitment to buy something more advanced than the McDonnell Douglas F-15 aircraft they already have means that huge sums of money will continue to be wasted and pocketed. And when, as we have seen, all this is taking place in a country where the policy-makers and the intermediaries are one and the same then what is happening suits their policies and their pockets.

The most mysterious aspect of this convergence of interest which produces a wasteful armaments procurement policy is the role of the intermediary. The image of the Arab 'fixer' popularized by the Western press is a vague and incomplete one of a blonde-chasing, casino-haunting, jet-setting international smoothie with endless supplies of money to support these activities. But despite assiduous reporting of this kind, the picture of the vital role of intermediaries in places like Saudi Arabia remains incomplete.

Fundamentally he – or on extremely rare occasions she – is someone who can help a foreign corporation obtain business in this oil-rich country. Even when the business is there and the company is qualified to do it, a fixer is needed. To most Western corporations, a piece of business, in this case winning a contract, is an organized, legal transaction which is expected to yield benefits to those participating in it. In Saudi Arabia, it is not a business transaction but a deal, and it is a highly private affair which is often extra-legal. Therefore how much profit is realized and how, is subject more to personal whims and greed than to standard business practices. For example, even a recognized need, be it for medical equipment or army Jeeps, is not addressed until the mechanism is established to guarantee the intermediary his share. The fixer is the man who bridges this gap in perception by translating the ways of one side to the other side to effect a modus vivendi acceptable to both.

But what is a fixer? Above all, the confusion surrounding his function is compounded by the number of names used to describe him. I am talking about the terms 'intermediary', 'middleman', 'go-between', 'wheeler-dealer' and 'promoter'. In fact, 'deal organizer' or 'deal fixer' are closer to the truth than the rest, but they are cumbersome expressions and the commonly used 'intermediary' is the most appropriate substitute.

In addition to reconciling the business ways of East and West, the intermediary's job is to provide a company wishing to do business in Saudi Arabia with an advantage over its competitors and to turn this advantage into the largest profit possible. He does this through getting a prince of the House of Saud to favour the company's interests over those of others in return for a commission/bribe which is shared by the intermediary and his sponsor. Intermediaries have become identified with the arms trade because that is where commissions are larger. Saudi defence expenditure has exceeded 30 per cent of the country's total budget for years and individual defence contracts tend to be larger than others. At present there are 22 defence contracts of over $500 million each. Furthermore, the uniqueness of some defence products and consequent absence of competitive pressure allows the intermediary to charge a very high percentage. But again, this is only part of the background to Saudi arms purchases, though it is the aspect which has excited the world because it has produced commissions and scandals worth talking and writing about.

The way in which the intermediary performs his duties begins with his assumption of his role. To become an intermediary, a person must ally himself with a Saudi prince who knows where contracts are and who can influence their awarding. After he becomes an extension of the prince the intermediary goes out to match companies with the business his mentor can 'deliver': the right company for the right contract, at the greatest possible benefit acceptable to the corporation for himself and his boss. While intermediaries mostly get competent defence contractors to supply hardware and provide services, they have been known to err against policy and get such services from the wrong country or choose contractors with less than the required competence. Construction companies with little experience in the field have been awarded contracts to build armaments depots (Fotenhauer Enterprises of Florida, for example) and Ford and Chevrolet trucks which cannot meet the brutal demands of the desert have been bought. (In other fields the wrong suppliers of laboratories to schools have been used and the Saudis have bought equipment using different measures than are standard in their country.)

This matching game reveals the intermediary's sophistication or lack of it, but the demands on his ability go further. First there is his ability to entice a corporation into cooperating with him, something which very often depends on his track record and the influence of his princely sponsor. For example, Adnan Khashoggi is a super-intermediary because he is a close friend of King Fahd and Minister of Defence Prince Sultan. He is also a worldly man who is at ease using Western corporate language and his track record includes obtaining business for major Western corporations such as Lockheed, Rolls-Royce, Grueman and others. It is difficult to imagine someone with credentials to match his. (I have yet to discover any corporation which refuses to deal with him because of his flamboyant lifestyle, involvement in several scandals or the fact that he served a prison term. (See Servants of the Crown.)

Of course, with the great majority of the 7000 princes available to indulge in influence peddling, cases develop when the sponsor is not influential enough for the particular project under consideration. A prince in the Eastern region, a nephew of the King and a colonel in the Saudi Air Force, got his intermediary to engage a company capable of building a huge army munitions depot only to discover that a better-placed prince, a deputy minister and likewise a nephew of the King, was after the same project. Clearly, the colonel was in no position to 'deliver' the contract. Ostensibly two princes vying for the same contract creates competition, but influence peddling in the country is the exclusive domain of the royal family, an extension of absolute power, so the competition is strictly between big and small princes.

Beyond the intermediary, there is a little-known but much more important person involved in Saudi business deals. He is the intermedler, or 'skimmer'. The intermedler may be the intermediary's immediate boss or someone higher up. He is the powerful prince whose demands must be met, the prince who is in a position to decide who gets the deal, a royal member of the Cabinet, a province emir, the head of a branch of the armed forces or the head of a royal commission entrusted with overseeing a specific development scheme (the building of the oil-terminal cities of Jubeil and Yanbu was supervised by a royal commission). Some skimmers use their own intermediaries while others deal with other members of the family who use intermediaries. In the first case the commission is divided two ways and in the second the intermediary and his boss share their commission with the intermedler. Because the intermedler cannot lose, all the intermediaries and their bosses are in the business of keeping in with him.

Prince Sultan bin Abdel Aziz, Saudi Arabia's Minister of Defence and officially number two in line to the throne, is probably the world's leading example of an intermedler and is certainly one of the wealthiest men alive. Merging the functions of policy-maker and intermedler, he decides what the country needs, and has to be satisfied regardless of who wins a defence contract. Given the value of business transacted through his ministry, the rest follows as a matter of course, except in cases when what the contract yields is beneath his dignity. The competition between the USA and the UK to supply Saudi Arabia with F-15s or Tornados – it was decided in favour of the USA – was under Sultan's control every step of the way. As will be explained below, this did not mean that the makers of these planes offered to make direct payments, and Sultan is able to realize his money in ways which satisfy the constraints placed on the company by the laws of its country. In big contracts like those for the supply of aircraft, because hundreds of millions of dollars of commission are involved, the skimmer realizes most of the money while the intermediary and his boss settle for a 'normal' share. (It is axiomatic that the intermediary on the British-made Tornado aircraft deal (known as Yamama 2) accepted a small percentage but the supplier of American-made uniforms received a much higher share.)

Royal skimming represents the House of Saud's share of all business done in Saudi Arabia. But to judge it simply as an abusive, corrupt act solely in terms of the amount of money it yields is to overlook the additional disastrous effect it has on the merchant class of the country. When the skimmer arrives late, when he belatedly decides a contract is big enough to deserve his attention, he can disrupt the whole process of awarding the contract. An example of this is the Swedish contractors who won a $900-million contract to build the harbour at Jeddah. The contractors' Saudi agent had accepted a 2 per cent commission and taken all the known influence peddlers into consideration. The prince-governor of the province heard about this after the fact and demanded a 3 per cent payment, or else. Because the company was unwilling to increase its payment, their Saudi agent had the choice of paying much of the required money out of his own pocket or incurring the prince's wrath. He paid. In the defence area, the contract to supply a million nuclear, biological and chemical warfare suits went ahead without a skimmer because the original request was for a mere 20,000. The skimmer appeared when the order was increased to a million. Because the product was unique and carried a high commission, the intermediary was able to cover the skimmer's commission and still make a lot of money.

But who the Saudi intermediaries and intermedlers are and what they do are not the only things which are elusive and misunderstood. The level of commission paid and how it is paid is another grey area. In fact, it is the level of commissions paid which reveals why policy-makers and intermedlers are one and the same.

While the budgets of Saudi Arabia have fluctuated widely to reflect the price of oil and how much of it the country has exported, it is safe to assume that at least 70 per cent of the business transacted in the country is subject to commissions (some put the figure at 90 per cent). So, in a year when the budget is $50 billion, the commissionable business amounts to $34 billion. Assuming a conservative level of commission of 10 per cent, the commissions paid would amount to $3.4 billion. But the waste of money, or the reduction of its real value through recycling, does not stop there. Instead it continues vertically, with commissions piled on top of each other at every step on the ladder.

To explain this, I will take two examples. The building of a palace for the King, a lavish $2 billion affair for which the Government pays, is subject to the commission system. The contractor agrees to pay a 15 per cent commission, or $300 million. But subcontractors handling work worth $1.2 billion pay the contractor a 15 per cent commission: $180 million. Before that, suppliers of equipment and material pay the subcontractors 15 per cent on $500 million, or $75 million. So, without compounding the figures, the total commission paid is $555 million, though in all likelihood even more, a rate of over 25 per cent. On another occasion the supplier of a electronic defence system was a British company which had an agent who had no sponsor in high places, but the product was unique and needed. In this case, the intermediary took over from the agent after covering him. The people who had to be satisfied were the agent, intermediary, intermediary's boss and skimmer. Naturally the uniqueness of the product sanctioned the necessary increase in commissions. Here, again, we may be talking about a commission of 25 per cent. If we assume this is applicable to the commissionable budget as a whole, then the total figure is about $9 billion a year, considerably more than the budgets of most developing countries, including the needy Arab ones of Jordan and the Yemen, and equal to the entire foreign-aid budget of the USA. This is why there are so many House of Saud billionaires.

But a straight commission payment, when it takes place, no longer represents all the money realized from contracts. Straight payments can be traced and result in scandals such as the one which involved Lockheed. The USA in particular has enacted anti-corruption laws against them. And, as evidenced by the amount of reporting surrounding the British Tornado and American F-15 deals, the press in the West is certainly on the lookout for them. To circumvent anti-corruption laws and avoid scandals, more elaborate and elusive commission schemes which escape the eyes of trained accountants and government auditors have been developed. In fact, if both supplier and purchaser are interested in concealing payments, then they will find a legal way to do it.

Essentially four basic ways to realize commissions indirectly, in effect to hide them, are used regularly. The first is to provide the services of an intermediary under a different name. For example, in America most Saudi contracts with US corporations contain payments to 'consultants' and the consultancy fees, though regulated, can be substantial, and, on the surface, totally justified. Some companies claim their Saudi 'consultants' have offices in Saudi Arabia which employ dozens of people to assist them in their endeavours when no such entities exist except on paper. The intermedler, when needed, uses his influence with the Saudi Government to provide the 'paperwork'. Naturally this doubling or trebling of the real costs is done with the full knowledge of the contractor. Also there is room to use other local services which are not needed – for example, lawyers and translation agencies, remunerated at an exorbitant level.

Some of the favourite in-laws of King Fahd, the Ibrahims, used this method when they decided to assume the role of skimmers on an already existing deal with an American military-electronics firm. The Texas-based corporation had supplied Saudi Arabia with military radar for years and had transacted $50 million worth of skimmerless business annually through a Riyadh agent.

Fahd's in-laws approached the company and demanded that they be paid a commission on their on-going business. The company protested that it was already paying its agent the limit allowed by US laws, and that paying more would threaten its profitability. The skimmers were unimpressed, and in the words of a vice president of the company, who spoke on condition of remaining anonymous: 'It was like talking to the wall.' Thinking of ways to get through to them, the company rightly claimed that it was one of two companies in the world who make the type of radar needed, something which is vital to the security of the country. The threat to Saudi defences implied by cancellation of the contract was met by an open threat to make the company's presence and the agent's life miserable. After lengthy 'negotiations', the company succumbed and appointed them on-the-ground consultants who charge millions of dollars for a fully staffed office which does not exist. Lamented my informant: 'There was nobody in Saudi Arabia or the United States to protect us; we were at the mercy of people who do not shy from threatening the security of their country and using crude methods.' Referring to the source of power of the Ibrahims would have been gratuitous.

A second way of realizing indirect commissions occurs when oil is used in a barter deal, as was the case with the purchase of the British-made Lightning aircraft in the 1960s, the Boeing 747s in the 1980s and the lease of the AWACS during the same decade.

Oil was used to pay for the aircraft, but in an indirect way and the companies involved are probably innocent, or at least they did not benefit. In these cases, realizing the commission was an internal accounting procedure. On the books in Saudi Arabia, the value of each aircraft was exaggerated – for example, instead of a plane being worth ten barrels of oil it was entered on Saudi books as being worth eleven. After that the oil was shipped to Rotterdam and sold on the open market, with the proceeds from ten barrels being paid to the company and those from the extra barrel to the intermediary group. The Lightning deal went through without difficulty, but, to his credit, Saudi Oil Minister Yamani, afraid of undermining OPEC's production and pricing policies, unsuccessfully tried to stop the Boeing 747 deal (see Servants of the Crown).

There is no way for the supplier country to control situations like these. Not only is it impossible to get the Saudi books and examine them without infringing on the sovereignty of the country, but the books open to inspection tell an innocent story backed by an official cover-up. The document used by Fahd's in-laws listed the names of 40 full-time employees and the Ibrahims and Fahd are quite capable of producing 40 phoney Saudis.

A third totally local and legal way of disguising commission payments is through the awarding of subcontracts. The intermediary group locates a subcontractor to do the 30 per cent of the work of a project which, according to a Saudi policy developed by the decision-making head of this intermediary group, must go to local contractors. The policy-making intermediary group prevails on the company to pay the subcontractor inflated fees amounting to 40 per cent, including an extra 10 per cent to cover their commissions. All the main contractor has to do is to accept the price of the subcontractor and look the other way. This is why, compared with prices in the West, the costs of certain Saudi projects such as the building of army barracks and palaces make no sense. Certainly the huge sports cities built in Jeddah, Riyadh and Dhahran by Prince Faisal bin Fahd qualify as examples of this kind of exaggeration, most of them accommodating more people than ever attend sports events in Saudi Arabia, and so is the $3.4-billion Bechtel-built King Khalid International Airport in Riyadh. ('I can build five airports for the price of this one,' lamented an American contractor.) More recently, the costs of the catering contracts to feed US troops during the Gulf War differed dramatically. One figure was $133 per American soldier per day while another was $70 – both considerably higher than the $30 per day it cost to feed French soldiers.

A fourth, relatively new elaboration of the subcontracts are the offset deals, when the Saudi Government insists that a contractor place a proportion of the value of a contract with Saudi companies, ostensibly a move to encourage them to acquire new disciplines. In contracts with a high technical input which fall under the Ministry of Defence and which are covered by this policy, the intermediary group creates a new company to take care of this business because existing companies do not qualify.

The American sale to Saudi Arabia in 1986 of an air defence system produced an example of the use of this new policy to make money. A Saudi company, Al Salem, was created to handle the maintenance part of the contract, 35 per cent of $1.2 billion. Boeing, ITT and Westinghouse, the contractors, who refuse to comment on the deal, lived up to their part of the contract. They contributed $4.5 million towards the creation of Al Salem while the Saudi partners provided an equal amount and the Saudi Government, through the Saudi Industrial Development Fund, provided $21.5 million and commercial banks $10.75 million. In other words, the control of the company fell into the hands of the Saudi partners, who paid a mere $4.5 million of the required $43-million capitalization.

The select group which contributed the $4.5 million are close to the royal family and among them are four members of the royal household and the bin Laden contracting company, known in Saudi Arabia as 'the King's private contractors'. There was no competition for Al Salem because there were no local companies with the necessary competence and even the company's American acting president, Larry Warfield, admits that its level of profitability is not possible in the United States. Naturally the Gulf War increased the need for the company's maintenance services, and again the competitive environment which keeps a lid on the level of profitability in other countries did not exist. This particular contract was one of many awarded under the Desert Shield programme, a complex, and obviously unsuccessful, multi-billion-dollar plan to provide Saudi Arabia with the capability to defend itself against aerial attacks.

The use of these various ways to realize a commission should not be seen as mutually exclusive and very often a deal involves a number of them. A big deal may involve direct commission payments (from companies from countries which allow them), barter, subcontracts, offset deals, consultancy fees and subsidiary payments in the form of sending people's children to university and making charitable donations in their names.

What we have is a House of Saud which makes the procurement policies of the country and allows its members to execute them in a way which vitiates the effectiveness of the purchases by the commission percentage they realize. Members of the House of Saud award themselves the same contracts their policy creates because winning contracts involves wielding power and all power is in their hands, in all fields. Thus there is no check on the level of commissions, and companies and governments, even when they are loath to pay them, cannot avoid them. Says the vice president of the already mentioned Texas-based electronics defence contractor: 'I can see the whole thing as having nothing to do with us, after all it's their money – even when they increase the price by 100 per cent. They aren't cheating Uncle Sam, or our company – they're cheating their own treasury.' This is the glib amorality which now determines the attitude of Western companies and governments.

The announcement of a big arms deals with Saudi Arabia produces the same reaction: the press and public begin to speculate on who is getting how much and how. Sadly much more is written about the pay-offs, commissions or bribes than about what the deal contributes to Saudi defences – not to speak of the immorality of it all. The governments and contractors behind deals do not even concern themselves with the obvious; to them, an arms deal with Saudi Arabia is cash in the bank and greater employment.

This is particularly true of the Yamama 2 arms deal between Saudi Arabia and Britain. In this case the estimates of the size of the deal and the potential commissions have dwarfed all else and have generated considerable reporting and gossip. 'Anything new on Yamama 2?' and 'Is the money going to himself?' are oft-heard questions. But even the final size of the deal is unknown and newspapers have placed it at somewhere between $60 and 150 billion. So far $34–40 billion has been committed (the figures are not exact and the fluctations in the exchange rate and use of oil to barter affect them).

In reality, the confusion over the size of Yamama 2 is not difficult to understand. It is not an arms deal in the conventional sense, rather a whole armaments programme which calls for the UK to meet the needs of Saudi Arabia in the areas of creating a modern air force and building an aerial defence system. But how Saudi defence needs are assessed is not clear, and with the Saudis' inherent inability to use modern arms in mind it sounds more like a supplier selling a purchaser a Rolls-Royce when a Chevrolet would do nicely. Unlike the US, the UK has had no effective pro-Israeli lobby to stand in the way of concluding a deal involving the most advanced equipment, and UK laws governing the payment of commissions are comparatively lax. So the UK entered into a modular arms deal with Saudi Arabia, a situation which resembles a corporation providing the most modern state-of-the-art data-processing technology to someone who needs a home computer. Whether America's newly acquired permissive attitude will lead US defence contractors to try to redirect this deal remains to be seen.

The original Yamama deal was signed in September 1985 and included the purchase of 72 Tornado aircraft of various types, Hawk trainer jets, improvements in Saudi airbases and the supply of spare parts and provision of maintenance personnel. The total value of the deal was around $10 billion and there was an oil-for-arms aspect to it, in that some payments to lead contractor British Aerospace were to be made in oil or through the sale of oil allocated especially to pay for this purpose.

The huge Yamama 2, to author of *The Arms Bazaar* Anthony Sampson 'the arms deal of the century', did not go the UK's way without an Anglo–French fight. British Secretary of Defence Michael Heseltine and his successor George Younger and Air Field Marshal Sir Peter Huntington trekked to Saudi Arabia to plead their case with Saudi Minister of Defence Prince Sultan, who accepted an invitation to visit Britain. French Defence Minister Charles Hernu met King Fahd in the South of France to sing the praises of the French Mirage 200 aircraft. Influential arms dealers were invited to parties given by Prime Minister Thatcher and the French gave Akram Oje, an arms dealer friend of Prince Sultan, the Légion d'Honneur. The British and French press went as far as to hint at official pimping.

Yamama 2 made the first, $10-billion, Yamama resemble a sample order. It was concluded in July 1988 and the initial part of the deal involved 50 Tornado combat aircraft, 60 Hawk trainers, 50 Westland Black Hawk helicopters made under licence from the USA's United Technologies Corporation, four minesweepers and the building of at least one airbase. This order was part of a 20-year programme; what would follow depended on the updating of Saudi defence 'needs' and the availability of new hardware to meet them, something like the $50-million European Fighter Aircraft. Like the first Yamama, there were oil-for-arms provisions.

The ability of Saudi Arabia to absorb the hardware of either Yamama deal was never considered; to repeat, how what was and is being purchased was arrived at is vague, though in all likelihood it was by a committee representing the sellers and policy-makers/intermedlers. A few commentators and think-tank analysts wondered about the Saudis' problem of hardware indigestion, but their opinions made little if any impact. The British Government, from Margaret Thatcher down, described both agreements as a triumph for British industry and talked about the number of defence jobs dependent on them. Even the simple questions of what would happen to the old equipment rendered obsolete by these deals and identifying the potential enemy were neglected.

As it now stands, this extendable deal contains all the elements which facilitate the payment of commissions – if the programme fulfils its potential, perhaps the largest commission in history. British Aerospace, the lead contractor and manager of the whole deal, has no problem using agents to pay commissions. As explained before, the barter of oil facilitates commission payments; and huge subcontracts will be awarded to Saudi companies adept at padding their costs and the Saudi Government has included a number of suspect offset deals.

That British Aerospace uses agents and pays commissions is a fact which the company has never denied. I am in possession of copies of contracts which confirm its willingness to pay huge commissions in connection with the selling of Jaguar fighter-bomber aircraft and the building of airbases. In connection with Yamama 2, the *Observer* newspaper has alleged that the early stages of this programme have already produced $300 million worth of direct commissions. British Aerospace has neither denied nor confirmed this report. That aside, indirect commissions are likely to be larger.

Initially, Saudi Arabia allocated 400,000 barrels of oil a day to pay for part of this deal, but this figure was increased by 100,000 barrels a day two years ago. Depending on the price of oil this amounts to between $2.7 billion and $3.5 billion a year. The details of how the Saudis are disposing of this oil are not known. British Aerospace has a trading subsidiary which is capable of selling it or helping to sell it. British Aerospace refuses to comment on either possibility.

According to the terms of Yamama 2, the subcontracts to house and feed the British Aerospace personnel stationed in Saudi Arabia, somewhere between 3500 and 5000 engineers and technicians, who implement the on-the-ground segment of the programme, must go to Saudi companies. The value of these contracts is unknown but ranges between $175,000 and US$500,000 a day. The ability of the local Saudi contractor to manipulate these contracts is wide open and, as we have seen, there is no business reason for British Aerospace not to accept an inflated figure. This is another opportunity for commission realization.

A further indirect way of realizing commission is through the offset programmes. Yamama 2 has provisions calling for the placement of several maintenance and personnel contracts with Saudi companies. Among them is a joint venture for maintaining the air-to-air missile plant. This joint venture is funded by the Saudi Arab Offset Investment Committee headed by Prince Fahd bin Abdallah. If, as British Aerospace Chairman John Cahill states, the whole programme could reach $150 billion over 20 years, then conservative estimates place the value of subcontracts, offset deals and oil at between $55 billion and $75 billion. Though it is difficult to deal with the huge figures involved, we are talking about a commission of $12–20 billion dollars.

Not only is Yamama 2 of exceptional size, but it involves most of the UK's defence contractors: British Aerospace, Westland Helicopters, GEC, Vospers, Plessey, Rolls-Royce and many others. The deal continues against a background of growing awareness of Saudi inability to use the hardware they have already purchased and serious questions about the country's human rights record. Once again, the British press has raised new questions about the appropriateness of Yamama 2, but the British Government appears totally impervious to all criticism.

The investigations carried out by British newspapers have gone beyond judging the merits of the deal to address the size of commissions and who is involved. In particular, questions have been raised about British participation, namely whether Government officials have joined the intermediary group. The purpose of their involvement would be to guarantee the suppliers', the companies' and the Government's facilitation of the commission arrangements. (Belatedly the House of Commons has ordered an investigation to determine Mark Thatcher's involvement in Middle East business deals.) With some newspapers claiming that the rake-off amounts to 30 per cent of the value of the deal, potentially $45 billion, the press pressure on the British Government to come clean on the whole deal became so great that it led to an investigation by the National Audit Office. However, though the report compiled by this Government watchdog has never been published, the Government insists that it uncovered nothing illegal. In an amazing violation of procedure and a highly suspect move, the Government has also refused to submit copies of the supposedly innocent report to the Parliamentary Public Accounts Committee, the House of Commons overseer of these matters.

The argument between the press and the Government continues.

The press stubbornly argues in favour of the right of the public to know, while the Government persists in claiming that Yamama 2 is a government-to-government deal which precludes pay-offs. Statements by Secretaries of Defence Michael Heseltine and George Younger betray a haughty exasperation with a press which pursues moral issues at the expense of British jobs.

Suddenly, as often happens, an insider began to level serious accusations at the British Government and the supplier companies. It came from an unexpected source. A legal case which began in the District Court of the District of Columbia in October 1991 has focused on the question of the commission payments of Yamama 2. The strange suit was brought by one Lieutenant Colonel Thomas Dooley (Rt) against United Technologies Corporation. Dooley is demanding $130 million in compensation.

Dooley alleges wrongful dismissal, denial of opportunity, invasion of privacy, denial of the right to exercise stock options, defamation and suffering distress and loss of peace of mind. Put in more pertinent terms, Dooley alleges that United Technologies Corporation demoted him for blowing the whistle on a bribery scheme involving Westland Helicopters. Westland, which is 15 per cent owned by UTC, is licensed to manufacture and sell the Black Hawk helicopter and through Yamama 2 it had contracted to sell 78 of them to Saudi Arabia.

He claims that Westland, with the knowledge of UTC, agreed to create two Saudi companies to handle the maintenance and the personnel needed for this deal. The Saudi companies are jointly owned by the Sikorsky Aircraft Division of UTC and Saudis close to the royal family, 45 and 55 per cent respectively. According to Dooley, the Saudi companies, Thimar Aviation and Thimar Al Jazzira Group, headed by one Ibrahim Al Namla, were 'handling' a contract, acting as a front while, in reality, others were doing the work. In other words, they are no more than shell companies who use the personnel of other companies and pocket the difference between the real cost and the inflated cost which they charge and which this scheme allows them.

Dooley maintains that it was his objection to this phoney scheme whose sole purpose was to overcharge for services provided by Sikorsky to the benefit of the royal family which landed him in trouble. It is supposed to have led to his demotion, punishment and the issuance of threats against him.

The Dooley v. UTC case gained importance and momentum

after the plaintiff began filing his evidence. The Dooley papers filed with the Washington District Court allege the existence of Mafialike international groups who manipulate the underground world of the arms trade. The group handling the non-US aspect of the deal are called the Global Enterprise Group while the ones dealing with the whole world including the USA are called the Enterprise Group. The groups include several members of the House of Saud, corporate officers in the USA and Britain and Government officials. Beyond the existence of these sinister groups, the Dooley papers allege the following:

- Westland knowingly agreed to and helped in the establishment of phoney Saudi companies without competence to handle the work assigned to them.
- Five members of the Saudi royal family, including Prince Bandar, the Saudi Ambassador to Washington and a close personal friend of former President Bush, and General Prince Khalid, his brother and the former commander of the Saudi Air Force and the Arab forces during the Gulf War, were involved in organizing the deal.
- It is alleged that the deal is in violation of US laws, including the Arms Export Control Act, which prohibits the payment of commissions on arms deals.
- The deal is also alleged to violate RICO, the Racketeering Influence Corruption Act.
- According to Dooley's allegations, even the equipping of the Black Hawk helicopters with missiles was subject to discussions which centred more on which suppliers were willing to pay the highest commissions than on the most suitable missile.

Broad as they are, Dooley's allegations leave two vital points unclear. Did UTC, a company which on a previous occasion sent 20,000 telegrams to lobby for passage of the AWACS lease deal to Saudi Arabia, acquire part of Westland and license it to make and sell the Black Hawk helicopter to circumvent US laws prohibiting the payments of bribes by US corporations? One of Dooley's documents (Trip Report Kingdom of Saudi Arabia 18–27 April 1989) filed with the court mentions 'M. Thatcher's son' in connection with the deal, and though this a clear reference to Mark Thatcher, Dooley has refused to elaborate on what this means.

So far, the UTC response to this legal suit represents nothing more than an example of unimaginative corporate thinking. The corporation asked that the suit be dismissed because of 'act of state doctrine', claiming that the law which places limits on the ability of US law courts to deal with corporations under the jurisdiction of another state applied to Westland. It also asked that the case be transferred to Connecticut, the state where it is headquartered. Both motions were rejected and the case is pending.

Once again, Dooley alleges that there is a larger picture. His law suit has confirmed that UK companies stop at nothing to accommodate their Saudi clients. It strongly suggests that the whole of the Yamama 2 programme is being handled with that in mind. It implies that US corporations have found ways of circumventing their country's laws in order to pay bribes to members of the Saudi royal family and their appointees.

Above all, when set against the background of Mrs Thatcher inviting known arms dealers to 10 Downing Street and George Bush's close friendship with Prince Bandar, the Dooley allegation that both governments are party to the commission conspiracy comes as no surprise.* It is the attitude of the governments of the USA and Britain, as well as France and others in other cases, which amounts to a sordid conspiracy of silence to use Saudi Arabia to keep their defence industries going. It is another reason why the West's support for the House of Saud appears stronger than ever.

This symbiotic Saudi–Western relationship, which starts at the highest policy level of pretending to create a strong Saudi Arabia and descends to embracing payment of commission and keeping the West's defence industry busy, is gathering momentum. Now the realities of the defence industry in the West make the situation resemble what always existed in Saudi Arabia: the sellers and policy-makers are one and the same.

There are other complications in all this. The Saudi purchase of 72 F-15 aircraft during the American presidential election was a hurried affair aimed at helping George Bush's election chances. Beyond involving a number of subsidiary offset deals which might lead to a congressional investigation to determine if commissions are going to be paid, the deal is a landmark attempt by the Saudis to influence US politics. The Saudis have found another use for pretending to need arms.

---

*Dooley won a substantial out-of-court settlement in 1994.

The dangers are many in this sequence of errors which multiply as they perpetuate themselves. The acceleration in Saudi arms purchases to guarantee Western political support has not escaped the attention of the Saudi opposition, both the liberal new class and the Islamic fundamentalists. The most recent petition to King Fahd, signed by 124 ulemas, demanded the immediate enactment of a considerable number of reforms including the immediate curtailment of arms purchases and the reallocation of the money to the areas of health care and education. On this, the religious opposition has the support of the new class. In the words of a wealthy Saudi car distributor: 'Somebody better tell the West to stop this. Even taxi drivers in my country know that we're being taken for a ride.' The more arms the West sells to the House of Saud, the fewer friends it has in Saudi Arabia.

8

The Last Line of Defence

Ibn Saud employed the Lebanese writer Amin Rihani to write articles for him. King Saud was analphabetic. King Faisal introduced strict local press censorship and forbade the ownership of newspapers and magazines by individuals, families or groups. King Khalid could not deliver speeches which were prepared for him. King Fahd reads nothing, but spends tens of millions of dollars to buy non-Saudi Arab newspapers or to bribe or pressure Arab governments into silencing their press and curtailing its freedom.

Even after 90 years of rule, the House of Saud is naturally inclined against the written word – except those of flatterers. It is firmly opposed to granting the press in Saudi Arabia any freedom, tries to limit the scope of its activity in the rest of the Arab world and, recently and foolishly, used its power to interfere with the traditional functions of the press in other countries, even the United States and the United Kingdom.

Once again, the general impression which exists in the West of such illiberality being an Arab tendency is incorrect. In fact this attempt at controlling or perverting the press is new and does not represent an inherited Arab or Saudi attitude. Independent newspapers which assumed the role of informers and protectors of the public good existed in Saudi Arabia as far back as 1908. *Al Hijaz* was published in Mecca, and it was followed in 1909 by *Al Raked* and *Al Kibla*. The press in the rest of the Arab world began earlier, when Napoleon brought a printing press to Egypt in 1785 and in the nineteenth century healthy journalism flourished in Egypt, Iraq and Syria.

In the early 1960s, when Saudi attempts to 'buy' or control Arab journalists and journalistic establishments began in earnest, an enterprising press which took its responsibilities seriously existed in Beirut, and in other Arab countries it was moving towards greater freedom. The efforts at perversion which occurred under King Faisal represented an attempt to counter Nasser's successful propaganda machine and his hold on the Arab masses. Now, in the absence of an Arab ideological counterweight to Saudi Arabia, the House of Saud has moved beyond total control of its local press and manipulating the press in other Arab countries through money. It is trying to gain complete control of the pan-Arab media and to pressure Arab governments into imposing strict press censorship similar to that which exists in Saudi Arabia. The Saudis' efforts have met with considerable success. This is an extremely serious step backwards; in the absence of parliaments or other channels for popular expression, the media had tried to assume the roles of a natural centre for debate and the protector of the people's right to know. The last line of defence against tyranny has been breached; we are in the middle of a House of Saud-sponsored Arab dark age.

Al Hijaz, Al Kibla, Al Raked and other turn-of-the-century publications in Arabia followed enlightened policies, encouraged healthy discourse and carried articles by writers from throughout the Arab world. They were forced to close down soon after Ibn Saud conquered the Hijaz in 1925. Initially Ibn Saud ordered their editors to promote his regressive policies and their refusal to succumb prompted him to order members of CAVES to arrest the people who read them in public. When this produced unsatisfactory results, he confiscated their printing presses. From early 1925 to late 1927, Saudi Arabia was without a single newspaper or magazine and, because the Wahhabis frowned on reading anything except the Koran and pro-Wahhabi religious tracts, and because Ibn Saud ordered writers to obtain governmental permission before starting a poem, article or a book, there was nothing to read in the new kingdom, not even the mainstream Muslim books which had been around for centuries.

Amazingly, one of Ibn Saud's instinctive responses to the non-acceptance of his Wahhabism was to establish an official newspaper in 1927, *Umm Al Khura* (The Mother of Villages). This publication was a poor monthly substitute for what had existed before, as it was edited mostly by non-Saudis who did not represent a local point of view and had little interest in the welfare of the people. It took it upon itself to answer all criticism of the Wahhabis and to present a totally new version of Arab history which emphasized the glories of the new monarchy. Beyond trying to get Wahhabism accepted by the majority of the Muslims, it was *Umm Al Khura* which initiated the reference to the territories which had been controlled by Ibn Saud's ancestors as kingdoms, instead of the more appropriate territories or regions, and naturally it represented Ibn Saud as the great liberator and unifier of the Arabs.

Despite his committed opposition to writing and writers, Ibn Saud had an obsession with his image, something which concerns all members of the House of Saud to this day. In addition to controlling the overall content of *Umm Al Khura*, Ibn Saud had articles of self-praise published under his own name. They were written by the mercenary Lebanese Christian writer Amin Rihani, and though some of them dealt with Islamic doctrine and attitudes, in effect they told the world what a wonderful ruler Ibn Saud was. Ibn Saud's use of Rihani as a ghostwriter is in line with his dependence on non-Saudi advisers, though surrendering Islamic issues to a non-Muslim is unique and reflects the ruler's fear that a Muslim writer would have had difficulty with what he had to say. Indeed most would have refused to attack the Shias or to promote Wahhabi strictures at the expense of mainline Sunnism.

Other non-Saudis, non-Muslims and Muslims for hire followed Rihani, and among them was George Antonius, the famous author of *The Arab Awakening*, and Yusuf Yassin, an adviser-writer who wrote an appalling book called *Ibn Saud, Unifier of the Arabs*. But while all three served Ibn Saud in return for money it is interesting to note how representative they were of what developed in the 1960s, by which time the Saudis' attempt to control the Arab press had begun to assume an organized form. Rihani and Yassin sold out completely; they wrote what Ibn Saud ordered them to write without hesitation or moral constraint; but Antonius took money under the pretence of doing Ibn Saud's bidding and then felt free to criticize his benefactor's history, behaviour and policies.

Ibn Saud, for valid reasons as well as through short-sightedness, did not see the Arab press in other countries as a threat. There were logistical problems which precluded the sale of outside Arab publications in Saudi Arabia and Ibn Saud did not believe in their ability to influence his people and had little interest in what they had to say within their own countries. Also, their preoccupation with their own internal affairs left them with little room for attention to what was happening in Saudi Arabia. Even the effects of the start of Arab radio in Egypt, Iraq and Palestine in the 1930s were limited. The transmission signals were weak and when they worked very few people in Saudi Arabia had radio sets and most of them were monied people who did not represent any threat because their wealth meant they were close to the throne.

The importance of the Arab press and its possible influence on

Saudi affairs assumed importance during the 1950s, when Nasser used Voice of the Arabs radio and the Egyptian and pro-Nasser Lebanese press to attack the House of Saud and its ways. The attacks, like Saud's relations with Nasser, were an on-and-off affair, but Nasser's popularity and the bad House of Saud image they created proved beyond doubt that the Saudi people were susceptible to propaganda and that the power of the press posed a threat with which the House of Saud had to contend.

King Saud's legendary simplicity and openness extended to the way he tried to ignore his local press and allow them some freedom and to bribe Arab journalists. For the most part, he allowed the Saudi press to exercise self-censorship and this led to some healthy developments which included discussion of foreign policy and some criticism of government departments and officials. When Arab journalists visited him, he gave them money without expecting anything in return and during an official visit to Beirut in 1953 he left cash-stuffed envelopes for all the journalists who covered the event.

King Faisal did not give presents, but he expected something just the same. He used the Arab press outside his country to advance his policies and the image of the House of Saud. In the early 1960s, because of Nasser's dictatorial ways, Beirut had replaced Cairo as the centre of the free Arab press. There were hundreds of newspapers and magazines and many Lebanese journalists followed Nasser ideologically or in return for little money. Faisal used Saudi money to prise them loose from Nasser's hold and they proved vulnerable to the lure of substantial Saudi payments. The late editor of the leading Lebanese weekly *Al Hawadess*, Selim Louzi, divided the Lebanese journalists who took money from the Saudis – then and now – into 'pirates and beggars; the first group threatened the Saudis until they paid them bounty, and the second just begged for money to do their dirty work.' (Louzi was a pirate who took the Saudis for millions of dollars and so was columnist Alexander Riyashi, who wrote to Faisal, 'Pay or I'll tell the truth.') In either case, there were enough Lebanese journalists for hire to work for Faisal. Non-exclusively, some, including a few Christian Maronite journalists, supported Faisal's Islamic stand against Arab nationalism; others attacked Nasser's closeness to the USSR and a third group advanced the image of the Saudi monarch by exaggerating stories of his and his family's good deeds.

Simultaneously, Faisal addressed himself to organizing the press within his country. In 1963 Faisal decreed laws which systematized governmental control of the Saudi press, in order to stunt its growth and its natural bent towards assuming the traditional role of a guardian of the public good. Afraid that a free press meant power, something he was not willing to share or even countenance, he cancelled the right of individuals and families to own publications. Instead all newspapers and magazines were turned into limited-liability public companies the licensing of which was renewed periodically and subject to Faisal's personal approval. He also introduced laws which dealt with who could become a journalist, restricted the contents of publications and stipulated heavy fines and imprisonment for transgressors.

Faisal's attempt in the 1960s to control the press in the Arab world was a direct response to Nasser's and other Arab nationalist challenges to the traditional regimes. He rented the loyalty of Lebanese journalists not only to counter the propaganda threat to the House of Saud, but to advance his Islamic position and to get Arab public opinion behind it. But Faisal knew better than to try for total control; at that time Lebanese journalists, the object of most of his efforts, could turn to other sponsors and their support of the House of Saud stopped short of being totally illogical or sounding ridiculous. They accepted Saudi guidelines, but blind subservience and tolerating day-to-day editorial interference was against their nature.

In fact, beyond being compared to pirates and beggars, they divided into those who opposed Nasser, the Ba'ath Party and other advocates of pan-Arabism and thus were Faisal's ideological bedfellows and a strictly mercenary group whose only interest was Saudi money. The most important Beirut journalist-editor of the time, Kamel Mroeh of *Al Hay'at*, cooperated with Faisal because he opposed Nasser ideologically, and money was a vehicle which allowed him to present his well-thought-out, elegantly presented point of view. When Nasser's attempts to intimidate the brave Mroeh failed, he had him assassinated, but, by silencing a voice of moderation and reason, Nasser's move backfired and threw the door wide open for less able and less intelligent people.

Mroeh could not be duplicated; there was no one left who could match his honesty or reasoned attacks on Nasser. There were some pirates left, and Selim Louzi was one of them; but attractive as the word 'pirate' is, most were nothing but blackmailers. Someone who stoops that low will do anything in return for money, and they did. You could always tell how happy a pirate was with the amount of money Saudi Arabia was paying him by the strength of his attacks on his enemies. For example, when he got all he wanted Nasser was nothing but a Soviet stooge who was leading the Arab world to ruin, but if the Saudis were not paying enough, he simply represented a different point of view.

The beggars never withheld their support or moderated it. Their way of responding to inadequate financial support was to try to endear themselves to their Saudi masters by attacking their enemies more viciously. One of them wrote critically of Nasser's wife accompanying him to a meeting with President Tito of Yugoslavia and claimed that her presence was un-Islamic despite the well-known fact that Mrs Nasser was a housewife and a loving mother who never ventured far afield. Another underlined the fact that the Ba'ath Party leadership had some Christians among them and hence they were suspect.

In the 1960s the Saudis' efforts to control the Arab press concentrated on Beirut because it housed most of the pan-Arab newspapers, those which sold beyond the boundaries of their small country. But the campaign was not limited to Lebanon, for there were successful attempts to bribe the editors of strictly local newspapers in Syria, Jordan and Morocco, with the aim of converting the ordinary people of these countries. While Lebanon had a free press which tolerated all shades of opinion, the Saudi effort in other countries needed the acquiescence of the local dictatorship. Except for an occasional Syrian Government which had friendly relations with Egypt or its own objections to Saudi policy, the governments concerned proved forthcoming, for Jordan and Morocco feared pan-Arabism as much as Saudi Arabia did. One of the results of Nasser's defeat in 1967 was a reduction in his hold on the Arab press outside Egypt. Those who had followed him ideologically were also defeated and subsidies to his mercenary advocates had to be reduced. Many Beirut newspapers switched sides and joined the Saudi camp. By the time Nasser died in 1970, Saudi Arabia had replaced Egypt as the country which sponsored most of the privately owned Arab newspapers and magazines in Lebanon, Morocco, Jordan and Syria.

After Faisal, during the heyday of OPEC and oil at $40 a barrel, Saudi Arabia paid across the board, and it became difficult to find an Arab journalist who did not receive a 'present'. There was a brief period when Iraq sponsored newspapers and magazines which advocated a pan-Arab rather than a Saudi line. But though the pro-Iraqi press proved relatively effective and promoted some constructive exchanges between the progressive secular regional forces and the Saudi-controlled press, it suffered both from an inability to match the Saudis dollar for dollar and the absence of a promotable individual at the helm (Saddam Hussein was never the charismatic figure Nasser had been). In the final analysis the battle between Iraq and Saudi Arabia for control of the Arab press was an argument between two absolute dictatorships with little popular following – at the expense of the truth.

By 1979 the Saudis' ability to buy all the talent available for sale was complete. But they were still unhappy with whatever opposition to their ways still existed and resented having to rely on outsiders. This is when they tried to extend their control of the Arab press through direct ownership, by having their restrictive internal policies adopted by other countries and by attempts to eliminate their enemies. This restrictive move was expanded beyond the indirect control they had exercised on countries such as Lebanon. The rest of the GCC member countries, some of whom had liberal press laws, were pressured into adopting the Saudi model.

Saudi ownership of the pan-Arab press started in 1979 with the newspaper *Sharq Al Awsat*, which they edited in London and transmitted via facsimile to printing presses throughout the Arab world. This was followed by the purchase of an old Lebanese newspaper, *Al Hayat*, which they also edited in London. Women's, sports, business and political weekly magazines in London, Paris and Beirut followed. The financial backing given by the House of Saud to its own publications gave them an edge over the competition, which could not afford news bureaux or modern printing presses, and made it easy for Saudis to pressure the others into joining them in return for financial aid. It was a choice between following a Saudi line or perishing, and by this time the Saudi line meant total Saudization of the editorial content.

Saudi Arabia's decision to have its own pan-Arab publications was coupled with an attempt to influence the press in non-Arab countries, through financial and other pressures. Refusal to grant visas to foreign correspondents and not inviting them to GCC or other meetings, threatening to cancel subscription to wire services, and newspapers' and magazines' syndicated offerings or the outright purchase of the loyalty of some British and American journalists who covered the Middle East are the most obvious methods used by the Saudis. (While I am not suggesting that it ever happened, I find it difficult to believe that the Reuters

News Agency, Agence France Presse or the Associated Press would jeopardize their substantial Saudi business and run an anti-House of Saud story.) The sinister, mostly secret activity of trying to influence Western publications has been relatively successful and part of the reason the ugly deeds of the Saudi regime have not received the press coverage they deserve is that major news organizations do not want to alienate the Saudi Government and because some Western correspondents covering the Middle East take bribes.

In the wake of the Gulf War and the total disappearance of Iraq from active participation in Arab affairs, Saudi Arabia has a free hand to dictate its terms to the Arab press, both privately owned publications in Lebanon, London and Paris and the government-run ones in countries which depend on Saudi Arabia for financial support: Egypt, Syria, Morocco and others. At present, the Arab press is divided into a Saudi-owned press, a Saudi-controlled press, a press controlled by the GCC and other countries friendly to Saudi Arabia who are loath to offend it and a small number of publications which oppose them and are fighting against huge odds. And the Saudis are still buying the loyalty of an increasing number of Western journalists.

But they have not stopped at the purchase or direct or indirect control of Arabic-language newspapers and magazines and pressuring foreign publications or bribing foreign correspondents. They have broadened their approach to ownership to accommodate technological developments which affect their overall purpose. They own Middle East Broadcasting Corporation, MBC, an Arabic-language television station in London which serves the expatriate Arab community and transmits to the Middle East via satellite; ANA, the Arab radio station in Washington DC; and Radio Orient, the Arabic-language radio station in France. In 1981 some of their friends bought 14.9 per cent of London's TV-AM through a highly circuitous financial route and businessmen beholden to the House of Saud have bought into mainline London newspapers and are eager to buy more. Recently they acquired United Press International for $4 million.

Nor is having control of the press and placing inexperienced, incompetent Saudi editors in charge enough for the House of Saud, for it has shown signs of wanting to control book publishing (at least two London publishers of books about the Middle East depend on them for their livelihood). Some of my books failed to find Arabic publishers because of fear of Saudi reprisal and one of them was bought by a publisher who, unbeknownst to me, acted for them; he paid a lot of money for outright Arabic-language rights and then did not publish it. More seriously, in 1982 the Saudis objected to a book about the Mecca Mosque rebellion by the Egyptian writer Ahmad Al Sayyed and to another about the Gulf War by Dr Safra Al Hamadi, and went as far as threatening to cut off aid to Egypt in order to have both books confiscated by the Egyptian authorities.

The Saudis punish publishers of anti-Saudi books by banning all their products from their country and get members of the GCC to do the same. No publisher can afford the accusation of being anti-House of Saud and Quartet books suffered for publishing *God Cried*, a book about the Israeli invasion of Beirut, because, according to the Saudis, God does not cry.

Among others, the well-known Egyptian writer Muhammad Haikal, Lebanese editor Ghassan Tweini and the Palestinian publisher Abdel Barri Attwan have spoken out against Saudi control of the Arab press and warned of its consequences. But, famous and influential as they are, they are no match for what Saudi money can buy, and the Saudis have been known to hire Arab journalists for ten times their previous salaries. Says Lebanese journalist and media historian Jean Diah: 'The Arab press is in the worst shape since Hidikat Al Akhbar in 1858.' As if to prove him right, recently, in an editorial which exposed the low level to which the Arab press has descended, the editor of the Saudi-owned *Al Hayat*, Jihad Al Khazen, wrote an editorial in which he accused some of the people who object to the Saudi control of the Arab press of being frustrated Mossad and CIA agents.

The Saudis' hold over the Arab press is one of the most dangerous developments to face the Arab world in the past 50 years. Having retarded the progress of democratic institutions, succeeded in destroying Nasser's pan-Arabism and eliminated Iraq as a base for evil but necessary secularism, their control of the press is aimed at destroying the Arabs' ability to learn, change and advance. But they have not done it alone; they have been aided every step of the way by Arab journalists, Lebanese and Palestinians in particular, whose commitment to money outweighs their attachment to principle and the welfare of the Arab people. Nothing could demonstrate the Saudis' idea of what the press should be allowed to report more than this news item carried by six Saudi newspapers in 1991: *'The Council of Ministers met today and discussed several issues and took appropriate decisions.'*

*   *   *

It was Turki Al Sudeiri, a relative of King Fahd, a prince of the realm and editor-in-chief of the daily newspaper *Al Riyadh*, who in 1981 dubbed the Saudi Ministry of Information the 'Ministry of Denials'. He did so in a front-page editorial which attacked the ministry's role in disowning all news that had not been approved by the Government before publication. Sudeiri got off lightly: the Government dismissed him from his job and then reinstated him.

But Sudeiri's ability to survive his burst of anger had more to do with his name and less with a lenient government policy towards criticism. Hamid Ghuyarfi, the editor of the daily *Al Youm*, was dismissed that same year and never reinstated; in 1982 an *Al Youm* reporter, Muhammad Al Ali, was arrested and detained for two years; Zuheir Issa Safrawey of the magazine *Al Majallah*, which is actually owned by the House of Saud, was arrested; and *Al Youm*'s literary supplement was ordered to suspend publication. A month after Al Ali's arrest a Saudi daily reported a speech by King Fahd in these words: 'What impressed the audience more than his linguistic elegance, frankness and knowledge was his wit and humility.'

The press laws of Saudi Arabia represent a blatant attempt to suppress the truth, deny or distort it until a semi-literate, secretive, ignorant, humourless and arrogant man is turned into the exact opposite. But the censorship and distortion practised by the Ministry of Denials do not stop at re-creating the person of the King and members of his family but cover the reporting of ministers, generals, ambassadors and other government officials. At the same time the laws and regulations of the ministry are stretched seemingly endlessly and in all directions. Religion cannot be discussed except to promote the point of view of the Wahhabi Council of Ulemas – and recently even this has become a problem. The armed forces cannot be written about because everything about them is a state secret. Friendly heads of state may not be criticized lest it undermine the foreign policy of the country. Defamation is strictly forbidden and information about some of the King's friends making too much money out of questionable business deals falls under this heading. Reporting an increase in thefts is tantamount to encouraging it and is forbidden, while reporting the success of movements of which the House of Saud does not approve, like the Muslim fundamentalists in Algeria, is the equivalent of promoting destructive ideology. Promoting women's rights violates the ministry's Teach-Them-Home-Making-And-Stop-Them maxim. Relaying citizens' complaints about the water and telephone companies is an incitement against public order.

This stranglehold on the press explains why the Gulf War was not reported for two days – until official governmental statements were issued, and until King Fahd assumed personal control of the press and added censor to his other titles. This latter development further explains why control of the press in Saudi Arabia is stricter and worse than in Iran, China and even Iraq (the Iraqi press promotes women's rights and certainly reports complaints about government departments).

There are 13 daily newspapers and seven weekly magazines in Saudi Arabia. Their licensing and what they are permitted to print are controlled by the Press Information Council, which is headed by the Minister of the Interior, Prince Nayef, with the Minister of Foreign Affairs, Prince Saud Al Faisal, and the Minister of Information, Ali Al Shaer, as the council's two other members. The composition of the council reveals a great deal about its importance and how the House of Saud views its function. In particular, appointing the man who oversees CAVES and the regular police to head it is tantamount to equating the dangers of the press with those of criminality and sedition. Of course, Nayef is a full brother of King Fahd and that is why he, rather than the Minister of Information, is better qualified to assume the important function of protecting the image of the House of Saud.

The control of the Supreme Information Council on publications begins with their licensing. A special licence to publish has to be obtained from the Ministry of Information, which examines the background of the applicants and ascertains their loyalty to the Saudi throne. In fact prospective publishers are hand-picked for their loyalty to the House of Saud, and I know several people who failed to qualify because they were deemed 'disinclined to take orders'. (Their names are withheld to protect them.) This stage does not stop at approval of the publisher, for the editors' names have to be submitted to the ministry and individually approved. A licence to publish can be approved after that, but every reporter has to be vetted at a later stage, even when he has been around for a while and the publication has been in existence for a long time. But it does not stop there: newspaper and magazine retailers must have a special licence and must be Saudi citizens; selling the written word is too important to be left to foreigners.

Controlling the personnel of a newspaper or magazine goes beyond determining the safety of their inclinations; constant supervision has to be maintained. Editors of all publications are required to meet with Prince Nayef once a month to receive the latest instructions on what is 'permissible' and 'desirable'. Nayef's authority is so extensive that he is empowered to set the price of publications and adjudicate on how much advertising they may carry. After the Iraqi invasion of Kuwait, he had to approve the exact words and phrases to be used to describe Saddam Hussein and his allies, Yasser Arafat and King Hussein of Jordan. But his powers go beyond the important affairs of state to the selection of which pictures of the King and other members of the royal family to print and how to describe such facts as heavy rain, the arrival of official guests, the Miss World contest in Atlantic City and even how to characterize those who blow their noses in public. The weekly *Al Yamama*'s Muhammad Alawi, in another editorial outburst – they are becoming more frequent among Saudi editors – bitterly asked that journalists 'be given a permanent list of forbidden words and phrases to live with'.

What this situation produces is what the American writer and authority on the Arab press William Rugh described as a loyalist press which does not criticize the King or the regime and presents a totally optimistic picture of the affairs of the country. And in this case the loyalist press is also a state monopoly by proxy. Any attempt by a publication to go beyond the constraints placed on it by the Government is met by fines, the imprisonment of the reporter and/or editor or, in cases where the loyalty of the whole establishment is deemed suspect, the revocation of the licence to publish. Of course, laws and their application do not tell the whole story and the Government uses its control of direct subsidies, subscriptions and advertising to exert pressure and to intercept things before the law has to be applied.

The 1979 Mecca Mosque rebellion, a serious, extremely violent uprising against the House of Saud, is a good case-study of how the Ministry of Information controls the dissemination of information. Because it was an unexpected happening, the press waited for the Ministry of Information to tell them what to say and did not report it for 24 hours. But the ministry, having no idea who the rebels were, could only fall back on guesswork. Initially it accused Khomeini of being behind the insurgents, then it switched direction and accused Sadat of Egypt, with whom the Saudis were quarrelling over Camp David. Later the finger was pointed towards Libya and the PLO and immediately after that the whole thing became a Zionist conspiracy.

Nothing was said about the arrival of Jordanian, British and finally French troops to quell the rebellion after the Saudi armed forces had failed to do it. Nothing was said about the very important fact that the non-Muslim French troops were given special dispensation to enter holy Mecca. And even after the rebels were identified, their nationality was changed and they were described as 'misguided foreign elements', when, except for five of them, they were all Saudi citizens. Needless to say, the official number of the dead and wounded was understated.

The sympathetic Shia rebellion which broke out two days after the start of the Mosque rebellion was not reported, despite the death of over 200 people; nor was the state of high alert ordered for the armed forces throughout Saudi Arabia and the arrival of an unusally large number of American military aircraft at the Dhahran airbase. But there was no hiding the response to the Mosque rebellion, for important members of the House of Saud cancelled their majlises and took to wearing bulletproof vests and using dozens of bodyguards.

After the Mosque rebellion was put down, the House of Saud decided to present this most serious episode as the work of demented religious fanatics. No mention was made of the fact that its leader was a Wahhabi, a former student at Medina's Islamic University, where one of his teachers had been none other than Abdel Aziz bin Baz, the head of the Council of Ulemas; nor was there any mention of the political reforms he and his followers demanded.

The whereabouts and number of the rebels who surrendered were never revealed and the decision to execute them summarily was announced only on the day of the beheadings. After the executions the press ceased to say anything about one of the most important episodes in the modern history of the country. To the House of Saud the whole thing, including the Shia rebellion, had not happened. The cover-up was so stupid and flagrant that the *Wall Street Journal* and *Washington Post* rightly saw fit to question the Saudis' version of events and to point out its contradictions.

Nobody in Saudi Arabia accepted the official, press version of the Mosque rebellion and everybody knew about the Shia uprising. All the denials and attempts at suppression did was to undermine in a serious way what little credibility the Saudi Government still had with its people and to open the door for rumour-mongering. The real story got around through word of mouth and was exaggerated every whisper of the way. Newspaper and magazine editors knew that telling the truth would have done less damage than gossip but kept their own counsel and held on to their jobs.

Unsurprisingly, the handling of the *Death of a Princess* episode, the killing of the Iranian pilgrims, the deportation of hundreds of thousands of Yemeni workers and the presence in Saudi Arabia of hundreds of female GIs were handled in contradictory, stupid ways. An odd situation exists where the line between news reporting and editorializing is non-existent. The pro-House of Saud stories, full of adjectives as they are, are editorials in disguise; and there is no investigative reporting or research – the press never even mentions how a thief entered a house or what effect oil wealth is having on society. In fact, one way to see the Saudi press is to view it as a collection of gossip sheets specializing in the happy news of the House of Saud. A recent issue of *Al Riyadh* carried 32 happy mentions of the royal household: marriages, births, arrivals, departures, the opening of buildings and attendances at public functions. Inevitably Himself and whatever he does or says consumes a lot of space and accounts for a wealth of glowing epithets.

Beyond the press and the special situation of ARAMCO radio and television in Dhahran, there are the Government-owned radio and television stations, started in 1949 and 1965 respectively. As we have seen from the incident when Fahd wanted the Indian film changed, radio and television programming is subject to the diktats of the House of Saud and most of it can best be described as advocacy programming, an incessant trumpeting of their achievements. Some 40 per cent of programmes are religious – a recital of the Koran and the sayings of the Prophet and Wahhabi interpretations of them – and the rest are cultural and news. There is very little local or Arab entertainment. There are films which, in accordance with the diktats of Prince Nayef, have no violence, sex or tight trousers; no crosses, nuns or priests; no mention of unfriendly countries or references to Israel, communism and venereal diseases. Of course, films cannot tell the stories of Jesus and Moses, though both are prophets to the Muslims, who are commanded to revere them.

Control of book publishing falls somewhere between press journalism and radio and television. Books by Saudi citizens still have to be approved before they are written, and a Saudi writer has to abide by this even when writing a book for a foreign publisher. This has forced into exile the most distinguished Saudi writers of our day, the novelist Abdel Rahman Munif, historian Osama Abdel Rahman and man of letters Abdallah Ghoseim. Meanwhile, the Government prints a considerable number of books and schoolbooks which contain the House of Saud version of history. In them the Shias are heretics, King Saud never existed, the Hashemites never ruled the Hijaz, Charles Darwin's theory of evolution is omitted, Karl Marx was a Jew-conspirator and Ayatollah Khomeini is not mentioned. Recently many books had to be re-edited to re-present Saddam Hussein; and the role of the Saudi army during the Gulf War is so exaggerated that you would think nobody else was there.

There is some private publishing, but it is small-scale and the exclusive domain of pro-House of Saud writers. For example, most poetry books are in praise of the King, novels deal with the heroics of the royal family or historical characters acceptable to them and some sponsored journalists provide their own interpretation of modern history to augment textbooks. A recent book about the 1960s Saudi–Yemen War did not once mention the Shia religion of the people of Assir and their affinity with their Yemeni co-religionists; in others, there is no reference to slavery, the existence of the American Dhahran airbase or the original agreements between Saudi Arabia and ARAMCO. Even past kings are de-emphasized, and now it is Fahd who did everything for Faisal and Khalid, who were nothing but frontmen.

This inclusive control of newspapers and magazines, radio and television, and book publishing is complemented by laws to control imports into the country. Saudi Arabia has strict rules on the importation of newspapers and magazines and audio and video cassettes; new books, because it takes longer to determine their content, are hardly ever allowed in; audio and video cassettes must have prior approval and not only does the regime jam the radio and television signals of unfriendly countries, but people have been jailed for listening to them. Most of the time this policing is carried out by local members of CAVES, some of whom have been known to accuse people of deriving pleasure from listening to anti-House of Saud foreign broadcasts and then arrested them or destroyed their radio or television set.

The Directorate of Publications, which controls press imports, empowers customs officers at all entry points to the kingdom to censor and confiscate foreign publications. Its remit covers publications sent to the country for distribution purposes and others carried by individuals. Often whole pages containing unacceptable or suspect stories and advertising are torn out, and the *Economist*, *Newsweek*, *Time* and others, including Arabic-language publications which appear in London and are beholden to the House of

Saud, have suffered this fate many times. If customs officials decide that it is too troublesome to tear out a story or a section, they ban the whole issue, and if the publication is accused of harbouring anti-House of Saud sentiments it is banned from entering the country. (At present the *Independent* and the *Washington Post* are among the publications which have been banned since the Gulf War.)

The issue of *Newsweek* which had a cover story on AIDS was banned; *Time* suffered the same fate for a story which mentioned the laziness of the king; *Libération* of Paris was banned for carrying an interview with Yasser Arafat; the *Economist* made the mistake of titling an article 'Arab Lost Glory'; the Saudi-owned *Al Hayat* offered an innocent coverage of the PLO; and Robert Fisk of the *Independent* committed the biggest crime of them all: he wrote a detailed account of the death of the Iranian pilgrims during the Hajj in which he referred to the incompetence of the Saudi authorities.

Books suffer a worse fate and the punishment for smuggling a book is greater than that for smuggling hashish or cocaine. English-language books are suspect, mostly because the customs officers cannot read English. The 'degenerate' French stand no chance and books in other languages which are not understood are automatically banned. The carrying or importation of the Bible or Christian prayer books is subject to punishment which can be as severe as five years in prison. Judges never read the books they ban; after all, they are profane and some of them are the work of the devil.

Some visitors or returnees to Saudi Arabia who want to smuggle books in put them under an acceptable cover. Others have two copies of a book and use one to bribe the customs official. Some people with connections with the royal family use the offices of a prince to import whatever they need. One wealthy Saudi merchant had my book *Payoff* transmitted to him via a fax machine, made several copies of it and distributed it to friends. A single issue of *Playboy*, which is subject to a permanent ban, can fetch up to $100, and *Playboy* and *Penthouse* parties are given by people who have several issues of the precious publications.

Audio and video cassettes are subject to the same strictures as are applied to newspapers, magazines and books. But it is much easier to re-label them and more difficult to examine their contents. This is one of the reasons a 'cassette war' has begun in Saudi Arabia; cassettes which are carried or smuggled in are duplicated and distributed because this is easier than printing books, though lately books also have been copied and distributed in huge numbers. Also there are considerably more locally taped anti-House of Saud cassettes because it is easier to import blank cassettes than to import paper to print books.

Time and technology are working against the Saudi Government's attempt to restrict the exposure of their citizens to anything except the official line of the House of Saud. Although they still resort to jamming unfriendly radio and television stations, it is becoming more difficult to stop them altogether. Satellite transmission of television signals has become a problem for the authorities and during the Gulf War the Saudi people tuned in to CNN to learn what was happening. As I write, the Saudi Government is studying a proposal by Prince Salman, the head of the family council and also of propaganda, which would require the licensing of satellite dishes. Already members of CAVES have destroyed some of these. There are over four million television sets and, as elsewhere, more people watch them than read.

But people still read and, as with everything else, the House of Saud's attempt to control what its citizens read and write has met with resistance on all levels and is being undermined in ever more sophisticated ways. Against all odds and the risk of the death penalty, an underground press is at work in the country. Some publications come and go, but *Rai Al Nas* (Opinion of the People) and *Rai Al Majid* (Opinion of the Mosque) have appeared for some time and tens of thousands of copies are distributed, causing the House of Saud a lot of trouble. The hand-picked editors and writers of the officially approved press are showing signs of resenting their lowly status and the increasing restrictions on them in the face of a growing, palpable wish by the people to know more. More alarmingly for a country with a high level of illiteracy, the radios of friendly countries, the BBC and the Voice of America are carrying more and more news not to the liking of the House of Saud. At the same time the viewing of satellite television is increasing and watching CNN is becoming a craze ('I heard it on CNN,' the Saudis whisper to each other). Saudi opposition groups have found ways to distribute leaflets, pamphlets and booklets containing the true record of many events soon after they occur. The many Saudis who travel overseas carry back information which they spread through word of mouth. The mosques are increasingly used to spread news and views developed by the Islamic fundamentalist opposition and even the House of Saud cannot close them down.

The House of Saud's response to the need of the people for more freedom and more information has been greater suppression. In addition to the journalists already mentioned, Ahmad Mahmoud of *Al Medina* was fired for complaining about censorship; another journalist on that newspaper, Muhammad Salluheddine, was fired for saying George Bush lost the presidential election because he did not respond to the wishes of his people; the editor of *Al Nadwa*, Yussuf Hussein Hamanhouri, was relieved of his duties for writing an article about Islamic fundamentalism; the literary editor of *Al Jazira* was also fired for writing about banned books and so was the social editor of *Al Riyadh*, Fawzia Bakr. Poet Fatmeh Kamal Ahmad Yussuf was arrested and tortured for writing unauthorized poetry. Writers-poets Abdallah Sarh, Badr Shehadeh, Abdallah Al Shaikh, Ali Al Darroura, Ali Ibrahim Hussein, and Ahmad Muhammad Mtawea have been subjected to harassment, arrest and occasionally torture. During the Gulf War, intellectuals Aid Karmi, Salam Mahdi, Ali Kamal Awa, Taher Shamimi, Hassan Makki, Ja'afar Mubarark, Jawad Jathr and Abdeil Karim Hubeil were arrested along with several sheikhs who used mosques to disseminate information (Safr Hawil, Muhammad Masamin and Mansour Turki). Whatever literary establishment exists in Saudi Arabia was against the Gulf War and inviting foreign troops into their country.

The repression has also affected very many ordinary people. Some have been arrested and tortured for owning banned cassettes, reading banned books, walking the streets during prayer hours, listening to foreign broadcasts, mentioning Saddam Hussein, talking to foreign journalists, taking the name of God in vain and, naturally, for not affixing respectful titles when mentioning the name of the King. Many, including 17-year-old Abdel Karim Nima, have been tortured to death for owning a banned book.

If propaganda and the suppression of information do not work, and the lies of dictatorships have a way of eventually catching up with them, then the lack of intelligence behind the House of Saud's efforts will always lead to early exposure of their fabrications. On 6 January 1993 King Fahd himself released the figures of the country's budget for that year. According to him, the budget deficit for 1993 would be $8.5 billion. But a cursory examination of the budget figures shows that the country's income is to be based on an oil price of $21 per barrel. However, the price of oil has not been this high for some time and the real price is closer to $17 a barrel. His Majesty was overstating his country's income by 20 per cent. Fahd was afraid that revealing the true deficit would lead to questions about why the country is spending so much money on military hardware and even more serious ones about how long the country can continue to run huge deficits. As it is, the lie is so elementary that it was exposed by the Saudi opposition hours after the figures' release. Fahd is not only a cheat and a liar, but his attempt at deception did nothing but make more credible the opposition's calls for curtailment of the royal purse and the defence budget.

Lebanese President Charles Hellou looked at the assembled group of Beirut journalists and could not help but smile and greet them: 'Welcome to your second country.' It was 1966 and the President was making a point about how their first loyalty belonged to their financial backers, who were, with minor exceptions, from Saudi Arabia.

In 1992 the *Guardian* carried a story about the increasing Saudi control of the overseas Arab press by an obviously shocked Kathy Evans, who wrote: 'The Saudis continue to pump money in, viewing financial losses with indifference compared with the political benefits such influence yields.' The correspondent was referring to continued Saudi sponsorship of money-losing pan-Arab publications in London, Paris and Beirut.

The editor of the London-based daily *Al Quds*, Abdel Barri Attwan, is making a rare, brave stand against total Saudi hegemony over the pan-Arab press. He offers an accurate summation of the state of the Arab press: 'The Saudis have bought or are trying to buy up every single journalist, author or independent thinker in the Arab world.' But what Attwan forgot to mention is that 42 of the 48 Arabic-language newspapers, magazines and bulletins published in London have a Saudi financial connection which they use to buy Arab journalists and writers.

Journalists Suleiman Al Firzli and Farid Al Khatib, honourable men with established reputations, are blacklisted by the pro-Saudi pan-Arab press. They are having difficulty getting employment appropriate to their level of competence because there are very few independent pan-Arab journals left. The distinguished Palestinian writer Edward Said has been asked to discontinue his column in the Saudi-owned magazine *Al Majallah*. Edward Said is unreliable because he thinks for himself.

The Saudi answer to cries against stifling debate by monopolizing the Arab press outside their country is as crude as the rest of their policies. Retorts editor Othman Al Omeir of the Saudi-owned newspaper *Sharq Al Awsat*: 'It's our turn, it's the Saudi trend.'

There is little doubt that Al Omeir is right, but whether or not giving the pan-Arab press in Beirut, London, Paris, Athens and other places an exclusively Saudi point of view is desirable is another matter. His statement ignores the obvious dangers of a most serious development which is revealed as even more so by an examination of its origins and development.

By the late 1960s the Saudis' use of money to promote their policies throughout the Middle East had gone beyond buying journalists and publications to include influencing the Arab press indirectly as well. Saudi aid to Jordan, Lebanon and other countries implied an acceptance by these countries' governments of some unwritten conditions attached to it and one of them was to limit criticism of Saudi Arabia. This placed involuntary restrictions on the freedom of the press in other Arab countries and came close to rendering the bribing of newspapers unnecessary. Beirut, being freer than other places, had more to lose and in the late 1960s and early 1970s there were a number of occasions when the Lebanese Ministry of Information and the Prime Minister interceded with newspaper editors to get them to tone down their attacks on Saudi Arabia and to stop them carrying anti-Saudi news.

In 1971 a test of the Lebanese Government's resolve to eliminate attacks on Saudi Arabia developed when Ali Ballout, the editor of the Beirut weekly *Al Distour*, refused to heed his government's warnings and criticized King Faisal. In this case suspicion lurks that the Lebanese Government was exercising more than self-censorship and that Saudi Arabia asked it to silence him. Casting aside Lebanese neutrality and the traditional freedom of the press, Lebanese Prime Minister Saeb Salam imprisoned Ballout for 17 days and released him only after the intercession of the Press Syndicate and the many Lebanese politicians who thought Salam had gone too far.

Because he was openly pro-Iraqi, Ballout's imprisonment was significant on another count: it also signalled that, officially to Arab countries, Saudi Arabia mattered more than the rest of the Arab world. Lebanese editors never forgot the incident and its results created a situation where praise of Saudi Arabia was possible but criticism of it was controlled. The Lebanese press was no longer free.

The death of Nasser and Faisal, along with the 1970s oil boom, made a bad situation much worse. The anti-Saudi press lost its magnet, while the pro-Saudi press lacked Faisal's deliberateness and clearness of direction and the sums of money available to bribe Arab journalists became extremely difficult to resist. Beirut's *Al Tadamun*, *Al Distour*, *Kul Al Arab* and *Al Wattan* tried to hold the line against the Saudi onslaught, but it was no use. Ghassan Zakkaria, the editor of the London-based weekly *Sourakia*, refers to this period as 'the time when Arab journalists started using oil instead of ink', and another Lebanese editor is more specifically damning when he states: 'Lebanese writers who work for the Wahhabi press descend to its level and do not elevate it, because it represents neither civilization, culture or free thought.'

The quality of writing in the Arab press declined and, coming on top of restrictions on content and the use of some talented journalists, meant that there was very little left of it that was worth reading. Those who could read foreign languages turned increasingly to English and French publications. The ridiculousness of the content of the pro-Saudi press is exemplified by the creation by a Lebanese weekly magazine's editor of a special column which reported nothing except the good deeds of the House of Saud. Others competed with him without formalizing their efforts. Writers spent too much time justifying themselves, talking about why they were pro-Saudi – a subconscious attempt to nullify their guilt.

But guilty they were and it showed in how they lived and the exaggerated way in which they continue to live. At present, I know of no fewer than 20 Arab journalists who receive money from the House of Saud and every one of them follows a lifestyle which normal journalism cannot provide. They wear expensive gold watches and diamond rings, own summer homes in the South of France and in Spain, run around in chauffeur-driven limousines, have maids and servants, and their wives are bedecked with jewellery and go shopping in designer dresses. They are mostly Lebanese and Palestinians who have become so preoccupied with money that they have not only lost all interest in Lebanon and Palestine, but also in their profession. A review of the film *Love Story* by a noted pro-Saudi Palestinian editor had the wrong names of the actor, actress and director and revealed that he had not seen the film; a supposedly original story about the American defence business was a literal lift from the *Los Angeles Times*; a writer rewrote five pages of my book *Payoff* without attribution; and some editors have hired writers and translators to do their work for them. Naturally, some of them write books about Fahd and his family which bear no relationship to the truth.

But the degeneracy of the pro-Saudi journalists does not stop at the quality of their professional output, for, to accommodate their masters, they have indulged in unquestionably shameful activities. Many journalists working for the House of Saud double as spies for Prince Turki bin Faisal, the head of Saudi intelligence, and spy on friends and colleagues. Others act as high-class procurers and the wives of some of them act as guides for the women of the House of Saud and, occasionally, teach them the flirtatious ways of the world.

In 1979 the creation of the Gulf Cooperation Council provided Saudi Arabia with another way to extend its influence over the Arab press. Suddenly, throughout the Gulf, there was a rash of newspaper and magazine closures and suspensions of publication. The *Arab Times* of the United Arab Republic was suspended several times because it carried stories not to the liking of the House of Saud. *Al Tahia* in Kuwait was forced out of business while *Al Qabas* and others suffered temporary suspensions. Kuwaiti writer Khaldoun Hassan Nakib was arrested for writing a magnificent book about Society in the Gulf. Naturally, Saudi pressure continued to be exerted in different ways in different places and the Paris-based *Al Distour* has now joined the Saudi camp while the Egyptian *Sawt Al Arab* was forced to close down.

The GCC countries, however, went beyond imposing internal controls and espoused the censorship policies of Saudi Arabia towards writers and publications from other Arab countries and the rest of the world. This meant that a newspaper or a writer banned in Saudi Arabia is – most of the time – banned in all the GCC countries, and the same holds for cassettes, films, television programmes, actors and actresses, and painters. This application of weight culminated in a scandal which rocked the Egyptian media establishment and exposed the limitless ambitions of the House of Saud.

A GCC secret document leaked to the press in London listed 48 Egyptian writers, artists and actors and actresses whose works were to be banned – at the instigation of Saudi Arabia. Besides known journalists such as Muhammad Heikal, the list included the famous actresses Nur Al Sherrif and Nadia Lutfi. A GCC ban on any Arab artist would reduce their market and could put many of them out of business since it would be uneconomic to publish the books of banned writers or make films with banned actors and actresses. Although this case has caused a big stir, it is unlikely to be the last Saudi attempt to cow Arab writers and artists into submission.

As if these pressures were not enough, the House of Saud has also resorted to violence. We have seen how it kidnapped the Saudi writer Nasser Al Said from Beirut, but six years later the Saudis sponsored the assassination in Athens of the critical publisher of *Al Nashua*, Muhammad Mirri. A year later a Syrian journalist, who does not wish to be named, was attacked by Saudi-paid thugs while on holiday in Marbella and both his arms were broken. In 1991 the Saudis pressured Jordan into deporting politician and writer Muhammad Al Fassi. More recently, because the use of violence backfires through prompting wide press coverage, they have resorted to elaborate techniques to frighten their enemies.

Sourakia magazine, which appears weekly in London, specializes in scandals of people in high places; in a way it is the equivalent of America's *Rampart* or Britain's *Private Eye*. While it has switched sides and changed policies a number of times since it started nine years ago, it has never departed from a belief in closer cooperation among the Arab countries and has always championed the rights of the Palestinians. In 1992, in a strange move, it ran seven consecutive cover stories on the House of Saud and their misdeeds and there is no doubt as to the originality of the information the articles contained and that they showed a House of Saud in greater trouble than the outside world realizes.

The Saudi response to the *Sourakia* attacks was to try to undermine it; as usual, through the use of money. Beginning on 1 August 1992, a strange, costly series of happenings began plaguing *Sourakia*. An Arabic-language sheet called *Al Maskhara* (The Teaser) began circulating in London. *Al Maskhara* attacked *Sourakia*'s editor Ghassan Zakkaria, his wife and his daughters, using the words 'liar', 'imposter', 'pimp', 'whore' and the like. Zakkaria contacted the police and his lawyer and it was determined that the magazine was printed in the United States and shipped to the UK through various means but that there was very little that could be done about it. In September 1992 there were two break-ins at the offices of *Sourakia* and the computer system and files were tampered with. Two months later advertisements began appearing in the *International Herald Tribune* asking people with information about the magazine to contact certain telephone and post-box numbers, and later it was discovered that the same advertisements had been turned down by several other newspapers. The material was traced to a security agency owned by Hambros Financial Services. Former and present employees of *Sourakia* were contacted and offered money by mysterious parties to provide financial information about the magazine and its editor. Counterfeit letters were written to the magazine's two banks, the Arab Bank and the Midland, asking for copies of statements and other information.

It is obvious that the anti-*Sourakia* effort had a great deal of money behind it and that its aim was to ruin the magazine financially, perhaps to intimidate its editor into stopping his attacks on the House of Saud or ceasing publication altogether. The finger points towards a Saudi businessman friend of the House of Saud. But, in the absence of written evidence linking the businessman with a specific activity, there is very little Zakkaria and *Sourakia* can do; and even if the evidence is there, they may not be in a position to afford a legal suit against an extremely wealthy man. Meanwhile the pressures on the magazine are so great and time-consuming that there is a good chance the Saudis will manage to put it out of business.

In a similar and so far smaller vein, the news that this book is being written (impossible to hide because of the number of people who were interviewed) has already provoked a campaign of vilification against me. Two Arab writers and a former columnist with a London weekly have been promoting two stories. The first is stupid enough to be discounted and it is an untrue accusation that I have been married seven times (in fact widowed once and divorced once). The second and more important accusation is that I am a Mossad agent determined to give the Arabs a bad name. And while the history of my family and our suffering and my own record stand solidly against it, some people who know neither have begun to repeat the story. But there is likely to be more trouble, and fairly solid inside information indicates that the Saudis are preparing a number of loyal journalists to attack the book when it is released, perhaps through writing reviews which pan it. While these attacks were taking place I was approached by a Lebanese journalist who told me that the Saudis might be interested in paying me to kill the book. If they ever make a real offer, I will take it, donate to charity and publish.

The creation of a favourable image in the West for the House of Saud began with Philby and his books and the process has never stopped. But Philby's reasons were complex ones of state and oriental romance, and though a liar who saw the Arab through colonial eyes, he was an educated man who wrote well. The Western writers who promote the House of Saud today have very few good attributes; their rottenness is due to financial motivation and they are a collection of semi-literate sycophants who take it upon themselves to distort and turn a blind eye to the truth. Through that they do the Saudi, Arab and Muslim peoples, and the West, a disservice, as well as contributing immeasurably to the disaster in the making.

In the 1950s American Minister to Saudi Arabia William Eddy wrote *The Oil People*, essentially a white man's view of simple, generous natives. CIA agent Kim Roosevelt wrote a book with the pompous title *Arabs, Oil and History*. Based on a two-month trip to the Middle East, it is full of superficial comment and reads like a book written about stupid people for stupid people. Again in the 1950s, Karl Twitchell, the first engineer sent by Charles Crane to look for oil, wrote a book and called it *Saudi Arabia*. The purpose was to tell people about a remote, romantic place but Twitchell's idea of what makes a just king fit to rule the Arabs consisted of a story about Ibn Saud visiting him while he had nothing on but a towel. H. C. Armstrong's *Lord of Arabia* followed in the late 1950s; it was nothing but a sophomoric presentation of the life of Ibn Saud, too saccharine for a five-year-old. In the 1960s Gerald de Gaury's *Faisal* was a study in hero worship; to him Faisal was the perfect Arab who never did wrong. In the early 1980s, Robert Lacey's *The Kingdom* and David Holden's and Richard Johns's *The House of Saud* alluded to some royal shortcomings but, deliberately or otherwise, both books understated some important things and exaggerated others (Lacey is quite dismissive of the *Death of a Princess* episode and Fahd's gambling). They stopped short of asking the fundamental question of whether the Saudis, Arabs and Muslims deserve better than their Bedouin kings. Despite that, both books were banned in Saudi Arabia, since the House of Saud refuses to settle for less than total support.

Other books critical of the House of Saud appeared mostly in the 1980s, notably *Arab Reach* and *The American House of Saud*, but interestingly they attributed the House of Saud's misery and lack of character to their Arabness. They criticized the Arabs as a whole and used the House of Saud as a vehicle to do the job. And, of course, there were Sandra Mackey's *The Saudis* and Linda Blandford's *The Oil Sheikhs*, both popular, headline-grabbing efforts which one could reduce to 'let me tell you about the crazy people who have so much oil and money, the A-rabs'.

With exceptions, and David Howarth's remarkable *The Desert King* is certainly one of them, the book treatment of Saudi Arabia can be reduced to two complex points. The House of Saud is the best thing for the Arabs because its members are good or it is bad because the Arabs are bad and deserve no better. So the Arabs suffer either way.

The original Western image of the House of Saud created by book authors was enhanced by press reporting in the late 1950s and 1960s. Beyond coverage of the Palestine problem, Western press interest in the Middle East coincided with Nasser's assumption of the popular leadership of the Arab world and his threat to Western interests. Oil, strategic considerations and Suez were what mattered and the House of Saud's enmity to Nasser guaranteed Saudi Arabia favourable press coverage. Again, I can find no substantial condemnation of the ways of the House of Saud; certainly little was said at that time about its governance, or about manifestations of backwardness such as the money its members squander. Public beheadings, floggings, the abuse of women and atrocious personal behaviour were presented as an Arab rather than a House of Saud activity. Even political executions were given an Arab label and I recall the *New York Herald Tribune* correspondent Joe Alex Morris, Jr. asking in 1959: 'Is it different from anywhere else in the Middle East?'

When the *Time* correspondent John Mecklin broke rank and wrote an article criticizing King Faisal (when he was Crown Prince and Prime Minister), his Chief of Correspondents cabled him back asking him whether he 'knew what the hell he was doing'. Overall, the Western press overlooked the atrocity of the House of Saud because they were 'on our side'.

In the 1970s the press busied itself with writing about Saudi wealth and how it was being used. In 1975 the stodgy *New York Times* ran 25 stories on Adnan Khashoggi, the man who epitomized Saudi wealth to the world. There were occasional mentions of what effect such wealth was having on the country's social cohesion, but most of the articles settled for considerably less. In fact, much more was written about Fahd's gambling and womanizing than about the social destructiveness enveloping the country and considerably more about how the Saudis squandered money chasing blondes overseas than about what was happening inside the country – even the various attempts to overthrow the Government.

In examining nearly 30,000 pages of 1970s Western reporting about Saudi Arabia and the Middle East, I found 20 times more mentions of the number of the King's wives than of the level of literacy in the country, and precious little was written about the killer diseases which could have been cured by diverting a small proportion of the House of Saud's income to fight them. Even the most serious development of them all, promoting Islam at the expense of Arabism, escaped press scrutiny and the danger of the Islamic movement, apparent to knowledgeable Arabs, who warned against it incessantly, was overlooked. (Because it only covers important international happenings, television is a better yardstick. In 1976 American television devoted nine minutes to Saudi Arabia, one third the time it gave Albania.)

Of course the oil embargo was extremely unpopular with the Western press; but instead of examining its basic purpose and what led to it, what the press objected to was Arab control of the precious commodity. This added to the picture of the Arabs being bad people who do not know how to behave; after 1973 they were bad people who were dangerous. In the ensuing reporting of OPEC, the membership of Indonesia, Iran, Nigeria and Venezuela and smaller non-Arab producers were all but forgotten and it was the Arabs who got the blame for price increases even on occasions when the instigators were outsiders.

By the 1980s the House of Saud, though it had escaped serious Western press criticism for decades, was no longer content to depend on the inherently friendly attitude towards it and decided to try to manipulate Western news coverage of Saudi Arabia and outside events with some bearing on it. Dictatorships do not take chances with how they are presented and are intolerant of criticism. However, the Saudi dictatorship is less tolerant than most and believes the use of money can cure all problems, including that of image.

Whether the attempt to manipulate the Western press was planned or simply the expression of a general attitude is impossible to know, but there is no doubt that it had a pattern to it. The efforts of individual princes to try to bribe Western journalists may not have been approved by the King personally, but they were undertaken to please him, and wealthy Saudi merchants prodded their Western business associates to influence Western media for the same reason.

The Saudis' effort to control Western press coverage of their country began simply. They rarely issued visas to foreign correspondents to visit the country and when they did it always took a long time during which they tried to discover whether the visiting correspondent was well disposed towards them. They favoured their 'friends', journalists who appreciated the advantage a Saudi visa gave them over suspect colleagues, and except on rare occasions, these 'friends' returned the favour by overlooking many small stories, thereby protecting their ability to visit Saudi Arabia again.

Interviews with the King and his brothers were arranged according to a stricter rule – the interview rather than its content was the event worth reporting. Those so favoured devoted most of their allotted space to writing about how the interview was arranged, the diwan and the King's sense of humour, and departed with presents of solid-gold incense burners studded with precious stones. Again correspondents sought to maintain their favoured positions; there were no hard questions about policies, and discussing personal things like gambling and womanizing was out of the question. Saudi Oil Minister Yamani was a master manipulator of this patronage system, knowing exactly whom to see and in what circumstances, and during the heyday of OPEC maintaining a good relationship with Yamani mattered to journalists more than writing stories about his unpopularity with fellow OPEC members or the occasional anti-House of Saud story.

The Saudi patronage system still differs from what normally exists in other countries. In this case it meant more than simple favouritism; it meant not being able to cover Saudi Arabia or OPEC from within. If we accept that covering the Middle East requires an ability to cover Saudi Arabia and OPEC, what we have is a situation where a journalist could not cover the Middle East unless he or she was on the good side of the House of Saud. To get a true picture, one has to imagine the President of the USA ordering unfriendly journalists not to attend his press conferences.

The combination of patronage and censorship satisfied the Saudis' ability to influence what was said about them; but, as with what happened to the Arab press, what they wanted was promoters of their ideas and their deputy-sheriff position. This is when the House of Saud began using the other powers at its disposal: the application of financial pressure on some journalistic establishments, the purchase of Western media and outright sponsorship or bribery of writers and journalists.

Applying financial pressure came easily to the House of Saud.

The Government had experience in using money to dictate to the country's press as well as the pan-Arab press in Beirut, London, Paris and other places. In the case of the Western press, the Saudis are in a position to have a publication banned from all the GCC member countries. Because these countries represent good markets, all the news agencies, picture agencies and syndicated services are vulnerable and must take the Saudi capability into consideration.

As I write, the syndication service of the *Observer* in London is not carried by a single Saudi-controlled publication. The *Observer* is loath to reveal the cost of this boycott, but it is substantial and it had to decide whether its various reports about the Yamama 2 arms programme were 'worth it'. Recently the *Washington Post*, without official notification from Saudi Arabia, began suffering the same fate because Pulitzer Prize-winning correspondent Caryle Murphey wrote a number of articles not to the liking of the Saudi royals. The *Post* too is sticking to its guns. But the great majority of news and syndication services are guilty by omission; they do not isssue directives against criticizing Saudi Arabia and the House of Saud to their correspondents, but the consequences of angering the House of Saud are taken into consideration by both management and the field reporters. This amounts to de facto self-censorship.

Perhaps the best way to assess this elusive area (people refuse to talk about it) is to examine the supplements about Saudi Arabia which appear in publications such as the *Financial Times*, the *International Herald Tribune* and *The Times*. Supplements are by definition special reports and contain a considerable amount of advertising by Saudi companies and outside companies which do business in Saudi Arabia. There is no way to get companies to advertise in a supplement which is severely critical of the country. So publications carry supplements knowing that they will carry news favourable to Saudi Arabia and of the eight supplements I have managed to examine none has reported the situation of the country accurately and, for the most part, they concentrate on noting the achievements of its government.

Even non-supplement regular advertising influences the editorial content of Western newspapers. Makers of expensive watches and jewellery are not likely to advertise in some editions of *Time*, *Newsweek*, the *Economist* and the *International Herald Tribune* if these publications are banned from the GCC countries because of their editorial content. The people of the oil-rich GCC countries buy a disproportionately greater number of these products per capita than any region in the world.

But neutralizing criticism is only a first step towards controlling positive reporting. To generate positive reporting, the Saudis began trying to buy Western newspapers, magazines and radio and TV stations. This new development began when Saudi interests unsuccessfully tried to buy into London's Channel 4 in the early 1980s. In 1986, the Saudi businessman Wafiq Al Said, a close friend of King Fahd and Prince Sultan and a man of considerable influence who, according to Middle East expert Anthony Cordesman, swung the massive Yamama 2 arms deal in favour of Britain, bought 35 per cent of London's *Sunday Correspondent*. The paper is now defunct and there is no evidence that Said issued direct orders against anything, but it would have been difficult for its journalists to cover the Yamama 2 deal adequately. Saudi businessman Sulayman Olayan is his own man and he owns 5 per cent of the shares of the *Independent* and the *Sunday Independent*. So far, the papers have shown no sign of being influenced by this, but what would happen if Olayan bought more shares in the financially unsteady company is anybody's guess.

The purchase in 1992 of the loss-making United Press International by Middle East Broadcasting of London, the television company run by King Fahd's in-law, the 31-year-old Walid Ibrahim, is the most blatant example of the Saudi attempt to buy into Western media for propaganda rather than sound business purposes. It was followed by an offer by Prince Khalid bin Sultan to buy the *Observer*, the newspaper which did most to expose the corrupt nature of the Yamama 2 deal, in which Khalid's father, the Saudi Minister of Defence, is involved.

Certainly the most serious development in the Saudis' attempt to pervert Western press reporting of the Middle East is their ability to bribe Western journalists and writers. In this regard, they have been most successful in London. I have ascertained that six well-known journalists who write about the Middle East for major London publications are either directly or indirectly in the pay of the Saudi Embassy. By this I mean people who receive checks and have direct involvement in Saudi business, rather than those who accept free trips to the country or expensive gold watches. Not only have I seen, though I was not permitted to copy it, an official list of the payments to some of them, but they show no sign of wishing to conceal their Saudi involvement. It is another case of Saudi corruption becoming an accepted facet of Western life.

Recently the *Sunday Times* correspondent Marie Calvin was invited to an official lunch with the Saudi Ambassador to the

UK. The invitation was issued by a well-known writer on Middle East affairs. When Marie was late responding because she was in Baghdad, a follow-up telephone call came from a regular contributor on Middle East affairs to a respectable national daily. Marie's reaction summed up the ugly situation: 'What the hell is going on here? I thought those guys were writers and journalists and they're acting like the Ambassador's office boys.'

The incident which demonstrates what is at stake more than any other was the reported $5-million offer to American journalist Charles Glass to write a biography of Prince Khalid bin Sultan, the commander of the Arab forces during the Gulf War. Glass thought the whole thing was a joke and turned down Prince Khalid's emissaries, but he made the mistake of talking about it to columnist Alexander Walker, who reported it. A week after Walker's report appeared, Glass received from a well-known British journalist an angry letter which objected to his indiscretion. It was a case of another Middle East expert having been hired to write the biography Glass had honourably turned down. But when a surprised Glass telephoned the writer of the letter and asked him about this, the man insisted that he was writing a book about the Arab commanders of the Gulf War. Glass, who had covered the war, had a difficult time remembering who they were.

Despite the Saudi purchase of United Press International, buying American media and journalists has proven more difficult than doing it in London. The American public would never stand for it and it goes more against the grain than in a colonial country with a long history of accepting the corruption of outsiders. But the Saudis may achieve their aim indirectly, for lately defence contractors who supply Saudi Arabia with hardware have objected to some stories about the waste of it all and, along with some oil companies, two are considering cancelling advertising in publications which criticize the Saudi defence policy. Another form of indirect influence, something resembling lobbying, is acceptable and in the United States the Saudis have followed this indirect route.

A brief list of people with business connections with Saudi Arabia reveals the names of former Directors of the CIA John McCone, William Colby and Richard Helms; former American Ambassadors to various Middle East countries Andrew Kilgore, Parker Hunt, Talcot Seelye and Harold Cutler; former Vice Presidents Spiro Agnew and Edmund Muskie; former senator James Abu Rizk; and dozens of lesser-known names. If not all of them, many of those people have spoken and written favourably about the House of Saud. Former CIA agent Miles Copeland devised a scheme which made Birmingham, Alabama and Jeddah sister cities, and in no time at all corporations located in Alabama were promised huge export orders and began singing the praises of the House of Saud.

In addition to hundreds of individuals and corporations who promote the Saudi image, universities and study centres have not proved immune to the influence of Saudi money. The University of Southern California, Duke University, Georgetown University and the Aspen Institute have accepted Saudi grants which implied non-criticism of the House of Saud. Many Middle East experts at American universities work in departments which are funded by the Saudis and during the Gulf War many of them were interviewed by the BBC, NBC, ABC and CBS and newspapers and magazines and proffered opinion favourable to the House of Saud or uncritical of it.

In summary, what we have is a situation where the Western press's ability to report on Saudi Arabia is hampered by the House of Saud's power to control journalists' entry into the country, and by the application of indirect financial pressure on journalistic establishments. On top of that, reporting which supports and approves the House of Saud is facilitated through the Saudis' ability to buy into Western media, bribe journalists and exploit their business and academic contacts.

The ability to influence the Western press comes on top of total control of Saudi internal media and the elimination of opposition within the pan-Arab media. The combined effect produces a false picture which everywhere overlooks, ignores or distorts the House of Saud's misdeeds. In prospect is a world waking up to a country in flames and wondering why things have gone so far without anybody knowing about them.

9

Servants of the Crown

Dictators do not act alone. They rely on others to impose their will and ways on their people and often to present them to the world in international forums. Though his books betray a desire to emulate Boswell, in reality Philby was to Ibn Saud what Goebbels was to Hitler and Tarik Aziz is to Saddam Hussein. The three are excellent examples of how the human instruments of dictators function.

Some members of a dictator's confederacy, the people who surround him and do his bidding, may accept their role out of a genuine belief in the dictator's ideology or because they see him as the individual who is capable of providing the best government for their country, or for both reasons. Others recognize the defects of the situation and try to behave constructively within it. Their work might be described as 'damage limitation'. A third group are there because of obvious motives of profit or power, or both. And a fourth group are yes-men who find themselves in key positions accidentally, without having had much time or desire to reflect on what they are doing or why. The reasons are not mutually exclusive and they overlap and produce endless variations, which makes judging a dictator's inner circle as a group difficult. That is why the world judged Hitler's henchmen differently: some of them were hanged while others were imprisoned or acquitted.

Whatever its members' motivation or aims, studying a dictator's inner circle tells us a great deal about his ways and inclinations and exposes the inherently corrupt workings of his government. A dictatorship, by definition, is more dependent on the whims of the dictator than a democracy is on the individual opinions of its leader. This is why judging the type of people used by a dictator, and how, usually tells us more than studying the laws and regulations he enacts, ignores or perverts. This is especially true when we take into consideration most dictators' tendency to operate behind closed doors, and to hide behind members of their confederacy and operate through them. Among others, neither Hitler nor Stalin left us a full record of their thoughts and what motivated them, and historians have had to depend on the diaries of their cohorts, the likes of Goebbels, Speer, Krushchev and Zhukov for insights into their minds and how they made their decisions.

With regard to Saudi Arabia, the books of Harry St John Philby and Hafez Wahbeh, suspect and misleading as they are, are indispensable sources for studying Ibn Saud's Bedouin dictatorship. Without intending it, both books tell us a great deal about his instinctive wile, criminal ways and preoccupation with sex. Both men were members of his court, both spoke for their leader and represented him in international forums. They wrote their books to present a pro-Ibn Saud version of history, but in the process they had to justify it, and examining the justifications and deliberate omissions, tell their master's story.

Most people who have served the Saudi kings (like Philby and Wahbeh, the great majority were mercenary foreigners) believed that their masters were eminently suitable for the situation at hand. To this group, the lack of social cohesion in Saudi Arabia and the pace of change racking it have produced more justification for a dictatorial system of government than exists in countries with an established social order. The Saudi kings have been seen as providing much-needed unity and continuity against undesirable alternatives. There is also the recently discovered reason of the need to protect the country against its greedy neighbours. In addition, the assumed backwardness of the Saudi people and the absence of a workable alternative have always been an implicit part of such arguments.

These socio-political reasons for supporting the House of Saud have been reinforced by a more cynical but rarely articulated reason. This is a belief by some of the servants of the Saudi monarchy that the House of Saud will survive as long as the West supports it, and that opposing it is tantamount to indulging in unproductive disruption which, if successful, would do nothing but produce something similar or worse. This is why servants of the Saudi crown take their instructions from 'His Majesty' and refer to 'the Government of Saudi Arabia' and 'our interests' without ever mentioning the people of their country and their interests. We are stuck where Edward Said left us: to the servants of the Saudi throne, the Arab is simple and naive and very much in need of a strong hand to guide him.

Amazingly, what distinguishes in a major way the Saudi servants of the crown from their counterparts in other countries is their possession of a higher level of sophistication than their masters. Unlike military juntas in South America and dictatorships in other places where the dictator depends on his equals or his likes, the Saudi kings, bereft of talent as they were and are, have always depended on people whose competence exceeds theirs. Philby fronted for Ibn Saud in dealing with Britain and the oil companies because he was the product of Westminster, Cambridge and the Foreign Office and Ibn Saud needed him to explain the mysterious West and to deal with it. Jamal Husseini, a Palestinian politician, advised King Saud when the latter got deeply involved in inter-Arab politics because Husseini knew the Arab world and appreciated its political dynamics infinitely better than Saud. Oil Minister Yamani knew more about the energy market than did King Faisal and put this knowledge at his disposal. Khashoggi knows more about realizing the greatest amount of money from an arms deal than does King Fahd – to the benefit of both. The Saudi kings used such men when it suited their survival purposes and image, but when they were no longer needed they were dropped and their talents totally neglected. This happened when a servant of the crown forgot that his purpose was the aggrandizement of the king; in the case of Saudi Arabia, that meant enriching him or bolstering his image, or both.

The fact that the lackeys of the House of Saud are more talented than their masters leads to another difference from other dictatorships. The House of Saud has never involved its confederacy in the business of governance; its members are competent specialists and at best their competence is kept in check through placing limitations on how it is expressed. This means that the nature of the relationship between the House of Saud and its changing confederacy produces a unique situation where there is a greater reliance on them as specialists, as isolated individuals who do not represent a cohesive group capable of rendering political judgement. The more competent they are, the greater the need to keep them at a distance from decision-making because involving them would expose the incompetence of their bosses. Fahd has to keep Khashoggi beholden to him to stop him from acting independently and manipulating the arms business, and Yamani's knowledge of the international oil market made him a perfect front for Faisal, who personally made all the important decisions.

Another area where the Saudi kings' operatives differ from those in other countries is in their relationship to each other.

Being specialists in different fields who have little say in the final decisions means that they seldom compete; they are not South American army colonels whose support is necessary or Sunni Muslims in Iraq who provide Saddam with a base to maintain his and their supremacy over Kurds and Shias. Members of the Saudi confederacy are outsiders who come from different backgrounds and they arrive at their positions differently. Their different backgrounds and preoccupation with specific functions keep them apart. So, the House of Saud confederacy is looser and weaker than most; they do not act in league and deserve the name only because of their common loyalty to the king. Yamani and Khashoggi were contemporaries, members of the same group which surrounded the Saudi throne in the 1960s and 1970s, but they had very little in common, except their belief in the supremacy of the king, and they acted separately. How they expressed their belief – so long as they did not undermine the whole group – was determined by their function and their personalities. For example, Khashoggi is still a behind-the-scenes operator motivated solely by money, while Yamani was an international spokesman who openly fronted for the crown.

The confederacy which currently serves King Fahd is no different. Even their individual efficiency is inevitably hampered by the incompetence of the King, who reduces rather than enhances what they have to offer. The following profiles of members of the confederacy of the House of Saud provide an indirect demonstration of one of the great shortcomings of a dictatorship: how an absolute dictator has no loyalty except to himself and the talented men who forget this maxim are often turned into worthless entities.

Ghaith Pharoan is short and somewhat overweight with a non-Saudi, slightly reddish colour. Balding, goateed and speaking Arabic with a distinct Syrian accent, he is a hardboiled, cigar-chomping wheeler-dealer representative of Saudi businessmen who operate on an international basis. He is currently wanted for questioning in the UK and the US, charged *in absentia* with embezzling hundreds of millions of dollars from the Bank of Credit and Commerce International (BCCI). Unlike other Saudis who have responded to similar accusations of embezzlement by paying back money, he has shown no inclination to clear his name. But he is beyond the reach of international law. Like the indigenous crooks of the Bamieh and other cases, he lives in Saudi Arabia and is protected by the House of Saud, whose members, amazingly, escape the Western criticism which is usually directed at those who harbour criminals. Perhaps he had acted on their behalf when he stole the BCCI money; certainly questioning him would expose some of the unattractive traits of his masters.

Pharoan was educated at Beirut's International College, the Colorado School of Mines, Stanford and Harvard's Graduate School of Business, and there is no doubt as to his intelligence. But his success, or notoriety, owes as much to his father's achievements as it does to his education and talents. His father was Dr Rashad Pharoan, formerly an adviser to Ibn Saud and chief of the council of advisers to Faisal, Khalid and Fahd. The elder Pharoan was a rare expression of the workings of the Saudi court; a foreigner who managed to meet the different personal requirements of four kings, the only yardstick of success in Saudi high office.

Rashad Pharoan rose to prominence through being one of the physicians of Ibn Saud. As we have seen, doctors were always prescribing potency potions and attending to the King's hypochondria, and, like so many leaders in developing societies, Ibn Saud had absolute faith in his doctors as people capable of doing almost anything. The elder Pharoan, a graduate of Damascus University, had gone to Saudi Arabia to seek his fortune in 1936. Rightly, he thought the odds were in favour of him making money through meeting and treating Ibn Saud and, like other doctors, he endeared himself to his master. He soon discarded medicine in favour of becoming a member of the King's original collection of trusted mercenaries.

It was the urbane Rashad Pharoan who pushed his four sons towards higher education and involvement in business. After they graduated from some of the world's leading universities, he cleverly advised the boys to create two separate business partnerships, one for Ghaith and Wabbel and another for Mazen and Hattan. This division understated the amount of business the partnerships realized; the royal family would have hesitated to give one Pharoan company too much business. He also advised them to deal with different princes of the realm, and not to take too much business from one department. Naturally, Rashad Pharoan worked to connect his children with the then king and the most important princes of the realm, the present King Fahd, Minister of Defence Prince Sultan, former Deputy Minister of Defence Prince Turki, Minister of the Interior Prince Nayef and many lesser figures. It was easy since Pharoan saw the Kings and their brothers regularly and his position meant that his children were discreet and reliable fronts.

Ghaith Pharoan grew up as a non-native privileged Saudi, an extension of a father who attained the highest office in the land available to a non-royal. When I knew him at Beirut's International College in the early 1950s, he was in the habit of describing himself as 'a Damascene with a Saudi passport'. But, because many of the Saudi students attending International College at the Saudi Government's expense were the sons of Ibn Saud's foreign cronies, many suffered from the same dual identity. The uneasy relationship this group had with contemporaneous native Saudi students, the Sudeiris, Ghoseibis, Muhtassibs and Bassams, made sense only in hindsight. Pharoan was never accepted as a Saudi, and the real Saudis viewed him with unease and detachment, especially when he mentioned his father's position, spoke of his identity and resorted to chichi non-Saudi expressions such as referring to his aunts as 'tantes'.

In fact, Ghaith Pharoan has never been a Saudi. Like his father before him, he did not have a real Saudi's handicap of suspect political leanings or a sensitivity to social conditions; he saw Saudi Arabia not as a country but as a place to make money. Retaining a non-Saudi accent when one is born and raised in the country is an indication of a broader attitude. He has never lived like a Saudi and, with the exception of members of the House of Saud, the people with whom he has worked, even within Saudi Arabia, share a separateness of lifestyle which includes using *au courant* French phrases, shopping in Europe and eating Levantine food. Most of the people who work for Pharoan's Saudi Research and Development Corporation (REDEC) in managerial positions are non-Saudis; the majority are Syrians, with whom he has greater personal and business sympathy and who, like him, think the Saudis are beneath their dignity and would never think of marrying them. They still marry girls from Syria, Lebanon and other Arab countries.

Pharoan's father capitalized on Ibn Saud's lack of personal sophistication and when he started in business in the early 1960s Ghaith himself focused on the same lack of sophistication, in his case in the family and the whole country. He did not start a local business, but adopted the role of a worldly, trilingual middleman between Saudi Arabia and the rest of the world. He was in the tradition of Gulbenkian of oil fame and the people who started the trading companies in India and Africa; someone who devoted his talents to amassing huge wealth at the expense of native ignorance. As with the people he emulated, the background to his ventures had to be right and his emergence on the Saudi business scene coincided with the oil boom of the 1960s and 70s and the needs and commercial opportunities which emerged with it.

Pharoan concentrated on businesses which were completely new and beyond local competence. He imported food, particularly meat and new delicacies, to meet the changing diet, opened hotels to accommodate the thousands of businessmen who began descending on the country, introduced insurance to meet the demands created by the changing business environment and formed joint ventures with Western companies to build the sewage systems for the cities of Jeddah and Riyadh. For the Western companies which appointed him agent or representative or who formed joint ventures with him, he was the ideal of what they needed, a man who spoke their modern business language and travelled the primitive corridors of power of the oil-rich country. His Harvard degree, languages and other aspects of worldliness helped in the West and his close familial relationship with the royal family facilitated operating in Saudi Arabia.

He dealt with members of the House of Saud, including King Fahd and Minister of Defence Prince Sultan, directly and easily in ways which satisfied them. He made money for them. He knew how to bribe them and his ability to do this directly meant that he could produce more money than others who had to go through a daisy-chain to do so. This pleased his royal sponsors. In the 1960s members of the House of Saud needed outside money more than they saw Pharoan as a problem-solver. This is when and why they became his partners. They not only granted him licences to import food, but also interceded with government departments and got them to buy it. They waived Islamic strictures which said everything is in the hand of Allah and approved his entry into the insurance business. They labelled the cement company in which he was a major partner, the Saudi Kuwaiti Cement Company, a strategic development and granted it huge subsidies, considerably more than what they gave to more-needed enterprises. In return, Pharoan educated them about the needs developing in their country and made them silent partners in his businesses, including his hotel business (several Hyatt Hotels).

In the 1970s Pharoan steered REDEC into the construction business, and the royals favoured him over others and gave him and his partners huge infrastructure contracts worth hundreds of millions of dollars. (He won a $500-million contract in partnership with the American company Parsons and was involved in the construction of Al Assard Military City, one of the largest military construction projects in history.) Pharoan made so much money that he accounted for a substantial part of the income of some of the princes. While an exact figure is difficult to arrive at, there were years when he handed back over $50 million in kickbacks.

In the mid-1970s, flush with funds, Pharoan became one of the first Saudi business leaders to go international. He bought control of the National Bank of Georgia and seven per cent of Hyatt Corporation. He paid over the odds for both investments, but there is little doubt that Pharoan and REDEC were making enough in Saudi Arabia to afford them and that doing business on an international basis elevated him in the eyes of his masters, some of whom followed him and invested in the same corporations. But what followed his initial investments is a classic case of somebody using and abusing his mysterious background and royal connections to expand his international business interests beyond his resources.

Pharoan retained former Texas Governor John Connally and former US national budget director Bert Lance as his American pathfinders and gained control of the Commonwealth Bank of Detroit in addition to the National Bank of Georgia and invested in other banks. He bought a substantial share holding in Occidental Petroleum. He formed a joint venture with Norway's Concordia Shipping Line. He ventured further and bought a chunk of France's Gervais Danone, formed a special company to insure oil going to Pakistan and invested in a palm-oil operation in Sabah, Malaysia.

Simultaneously, his business adventures began to affect his personal behaviour. He surrounded himself with expensive talent, put his trust in suspect American influence peddlers, gave parties which cost tens of thousands of dollars, bought a $15-million apartment in Cannes and Henry Ford's Georgia plantation and acquired a private jet. His dealings extended beyond Connolly and Lance: he ventured into other areas and contributed $150,000 to the campaign of Atlanta Mayor Andrew Young and spent time with President Carter and his family (the National Bank of Georgia was the largest lender to the Carter family business). He even visited President Mobutu of Zaïre to obtain concessions in his country and tried to convince him to use REDEC to front all investments in Zaïre. The Pharoan legend grew so large that the Italian Government sought to endear itself to him by awarding him a medal; he was made Commendatore of the Italian Republic.

What sustained Pharoan's forays into the international arena and provided him with money to meet the huge interest bill he was paying on the debts of his investment spree was the profit he was realizing from his Saudi businesses. But the 1982–4 decrease in oil prices reduced the level of business in Saudi Arabia and, under the added burden of high interest rates and an altercation with King Fahd, suddenly Pharoan's financial position deteriorated and he found himself unable to service some of his debt obligations. This is when he resorted to selling and buying companies and shares in them with incredible speed to avoid the scrutiny of the business community and the financial authorities of the USA. But it was no use, for some of his investments had declined in value and there were a number of published reports which claimed that he had a negative net worth.

BCCI loomed like an Allah-sent saviour. It was the only bank in the world willing to place a near-limitless value on his connection with the House of Saud, and it lent him $300 million against unsound holdings within Saudi Arabia. BCCI was forever trying to get closer to the House of Saud, and did this by endearing itself to members of the confederacy (along with Pharoan, Kamal Adham and Hamad bin Mahfouz either borrowed money against phoney assets or manipulated the shares of the bank). When the bank finally collapsed and exposed huge losses and the ineptness of the regulatory agencies in the United States, United Kingdom and other countries, Pharoan still owned it $285 million which he does not have.

Our concern, however, is not Pharoan the failed international businessman, but Pharoan as the creation of the House of Saud and a member of its confederacy. What was and is he to them? Was he an inherently corrupt man, or is his corruption an extension of theirs? How representative is he of the confederacy which represents the House of Saud in the business world? The answer to the first question determines the answers to the rest of them and I know of no better way to delineate Pharoan's relationship with the House of Saud than to tell a story involving him and the present King Fahd, a hitherto untold story which is considerably more revealing than the rest of what they did together and Pharoan's other forays in the international business arena.

King Fahd began summering in Marbella in the late 1970s when he was crown prince and the power behind the throne. The Spanish Government was more hospitable than others, the place had better weather than the rest of Europe and Fahd appreciated the privacy it afforded him. During his many visits in that period, Fahd appears to have developed a personal relationship with King Juan Carlos. The latter saw to it that the Prince was accorded the highest degree of comfort and protection, from special landing rights for his jets to lamb butchered according to Islamic rules. Juan Carlos visited Fahd whenever the opportunity arose.

In 1980, with the price of oil rocketing to $35–40 a barrel, the managing director of Hispanoil, the Spanish state-owned oil company, sought to use the developing relationship between the two royals. He approached King Juan Carlos through his Prime Minister, Suárez, and asked the latter whether the King would initiate negotiations with Prince Fahd towards the direct purchase of Saudi oil for Spain. Direct purchase meant bypassing the major oil companies and saving Spain $5–7 a barrel. Considering that Spain needed 180,000 barrels a day, this meant a minimum saving of $800,000 a day for the Spanish Government.

Juan Carlos, realizing the importance of the deal to the Spanish economy, obliged and discussions took place over a period of six months. Pharoan was in attendance on Fahd at three of the meetings with the King. In fact, his presence at the meeting was accidental, but the Spaniards could not have known this. Pharoan had arranged to be in Spain when Fahd was there because it was easier to discuss with Fahd some of the major projects in Saudi Arabia in which they were 'cooperating'.

Agreement was reached at the highest level and finalized by Hispanoil and Petromin of Saudi Arabia. Spain was able to buy oil at the price paid by Exxon, Shell and Mobil and Juan Carlos had good reason to be pleased, and so did Suárez and the managing director of Hispanoil. But this victory for Spanish diplomacy did not last long. A week after the deal was concluded, the managing director of Hispanoil was approached by Pharoan and asked for a commission of $2 a barrel of oil: $360,000 a day or $120,000,000 a year. The shocked Spanish executive reminded Pharoan of the history of the deal, appealed to him to withdraw his request and asserted, correctly, that Spain went directly to Fahd because they wanted no intermediary. Pharoan would not desist; he put his request in letters and telexes and even travelled to Spain to demand immediate payment.

The Spanish faced a real dilemma. They feared that Fahd had sent Pharoan to extort a commission and that telling him about the request would scuttle the whole deal. On the other hand, the commission was ridiculously high and meeting it, particularly after the fact, was impossible.

The managing director eventually told Prime Minister Suárez, who told the King. His royal dignity affronted, Juan Carlos telephoned Prince Fahd with the news. Fahd was reassuring and asked for copies of the correspondence and a record of Pharoan's visits to Spain to be sent to him in Jeddah. The file containing the record of the attempted extortion was with him in two days.

Fahd summoned Pharoan for an audience. He enquired about 'rumours' about a request for a commission from Hispanoil. When Pharoan denied the rumours, Fahd threw the file at him and asked him to read it. Pharoan was at a complete loss, and finally resorted to saying that he wanted the money to donate to a Saudi charity and not for personal gain. Fahd walked to where the cowed Pharoan was sitting, slapped him twice across the face, then spat on him, the gesture of deep insult reserved for the most profane of criminals. But he did not stop there; he ordered the Saudi Government agencies not to award any new contracts to REDEC and to delay all payments on projects already in progress. Naturally, no member of the royal family was willing to intercede on behalf of Pharoan, and they all behaved as if the incident was an offence against the House of Saud.

Pharoan and his companies suffered considerable financial damages at a time when he most needed money to pay interest on the debts he had incurred on his international acquisitions. He sat on the sidelines for over a year and used many influential friends to carry messages asking for Fahd's forgiveness. Sometime during 1982, Fahd decided to forgive him and Pharoan's first act was an audience with the King which saw him kneel and kiss the royal hand.

The error Pharoan made was clear. However powerful, he committed the ultimate sin of confusing his position with that of the most powerful member of the House of Saud. The people who front for the House of Saud in the international business arena are no more than slaves who are used to express their masters' wishes and greed, and must never offend them or infringe on their absolute rights. Fahd's anger had nothing to do with immorality of Pharoan's action, for he was among the creators of the conditions under which Pharoan operated. It had to do with how it reflected on his word and authority. Any member of the House of Saud would have done the same; their lackeys are not entitled to act on their own.

Fahd's willingness to protect Pharoan against the demands of the law enforcement authorities of the United States and the United Kingdom to interrogate him in connection with the BCCI scandal completes the picture. In this case Pharoan is accused of acting criminally. Even so, this was in Saudi character, against the rules and regulations of outside powers in the manner of, and as an extension of, the House of Saud. To Fahd, this is an excusable offence; those who front for the House of Saud in the world of international business reflect its members' attitude towards everything. All is permissible, as long as it does not affect the House of Saud's status.

Although he has been out of office since 1986, Ahmad Zaki Yamani, the former Saudi Minister of Oil and Mineral Resources, remains one of the best known people in the world. Everybody recognizes the neatly trimmed goatee and thick, curly hair, marvels at the beautifully cut suits, notices the ever-present prayer beads, and people speak about the piercing eyes and repeat the famous early 1970s joke 'Yamani or your house' on hearing his name.

In his heyday Yamani was the darling of the Western press and there is some evidence that his fame contributed to his downfall, that the egotistical King Fahd fired him because he resented his international reputation and his identification as a spokesman for Saudi Arabia as much as he disagreed with his oil policies. Clearly, Fahd is more comfortable with the present occupier of Yamani's old office, the colourless and less memorable Hisham Nazer.

To the Arabs, Yamani's name suggests that his family came from the Yemen and this is supported by his lack of a tribal linkage. His people were city dwellers and his father was a highly respected *qadi*, or Muslim judge, whose modest but admirable achievements meant a life in the shadows away from politics. The younger Yamani is a man of the limelight and the controversy which naturally goes with it but the lack of tribal connection and of political opinion suggests that he made it to the top because of talents which outweighed these deficiencies. The system, flawed as it is, apparently permitted the rise of a talented but politically insignificant person.

Yamani belongs to a small class of educated, non-activist technocrats and bureaucrats on whom the House of Saud increasingly depends to create an image that commoners are involved in the affairs of government. But rather than prevailing against the odds, it is this group's negative quality, their apparently built-in ability to ignore the conditions of their country and hopes of their people, which endears them to their masters. To a House of Saud committed to absolute family rule, this group appeals because they are unconnected, unconcerned and safe. In fact, the present Saudi Oil Minister, Hisham Nazer, belongs to this group and in his case his name suggests Turkish or Turkoman origins, again a lineage lacking in political weight, and he shows no signs of responding to anything except the demands of his job as defined by the King.

This was not always the case, and Saudi Arabia's first holder of this position, Abdallah Tariki, one of the architects of OPEC, was a forceful, imaginative man with solid Saudi credentials who objected to royal tampering in his domain. He rose to power under the unpredictable King Saud, but Faisal, loath to tolerate any questioning of his absolute power, dismissed Tariki and sent him into exile in 1962. Since then the only important ministry in the country held by a commoner goes to a technocrat who is willing to assume the title without the power which normally goes with it. This automatically nullifies the importance of the appointment. The influence a Saudi oil minister might be expected to have on Saudi, regional and international politics does not exist in practice and Yamani's and Nazer's careers support the contention that the kings are their own oil ministers and policy-makers. In fact, Yamani and Nazer are excellent examples of the bureaucratic confederacy of the House of Saud, the handful of ministers, ambassadors and departmental directors who give Saudi Arabia a semblance of modernity. They act as frontmen, but only to outsiders; the Saudi people know better.

Though classifying Yamani is not difficult, understanding him and others like him is not so easy. Whatever members of this subgroup do, they do it as humble, obedient servants of the crown, unquestioning robots. To this day, we do not know what Yamani thinks; he is reluctant to speak on matters of substance. Interviewers have discovered that why he was fired, like oil and regional politics, are closed subjects. His answers are full of technicalities and betray a resort to diversionary tactics. And he can be excruciatingly boring, because his responses to significant questions are no more than an attempt to emphasize their minor, safe aspects and a reiteration, with annoying regularity, of House of Saud-pleasing pronouncements. Hisham Nazer, the Ambassador to the UK and the former Minister of Health, Ghazi Al Ghoseibi, do the same; they are good interviewees until they have to answer substantive questions to which no House of Saud answer has been proferred.

But it is still important to analyze Yamani without the benefit of his honest thoughts. After all, he held for 25 years the highest office allowed a Saudi non-royal and even his acceptance of it without exercising its inherent powers may tell us a great deal about how real power in the country, including the formulation of oil policy, is exercised. And to understand Yamani, we have to understand his three aspects: the person, the businessman and the politician cum public figure.

Yamani is a glamorous figure, a dapper 62-year-old who is as comfortable facing flashlights as a movie star. I cannot find any picture of him with a single hair out of place, not even after gruelling day-long OPEC meetings. But unlike other public figures, for example the unnatural George Bush and the stiff John Major, his studied elegance works; it is in character and completes his natural good looks. When on holiday, his Savile Row suits are replaced by designer beachwear and he affects a slow walk which says hurrying is undignified, and even in that he is effective. He augments this picture of a worldly dandy in other ways; to my knowledge, every single reporter who has ever known or interviewed him speaks of how deferential Yamani is and how he always remembers to ask them questions which personalize their encounters and betray an interest in their welfare. He calls them by their first names, remembers something about the last time they met and says something about their employers or their families.

We do not know the background to Yamani's accomplished dandyism, but, generally speaking, the combination of being a *qadi's* son and a Harvard Law School graduate goes some way to explaining it. In Yamani, the gentility of the East merges with the best in the West, and the combination was polished by exposure to the finer things in life. His long service as Saudi Arabia's and OPEC's leading spokesman provided him with a chance to meet top oil company executives and oil ministers from other countries and to negotiate and befriend Richard Nixon, Henry Kissinger, Edward Heath, Giscard d'Estaing and other world leaders.

But it does not stop there and Yamani is more than a dandy with friends in high places; he is also a show-off. He owns houses in Beirut, Jeddah, Riyadh, Taif, London, Sardinia and Geneva, his yacht is over 200 feet long (the available figures differ) and he talks about his possessions in the manner of a believer in the if-you-have-it-flaunt-it approach. This irreverent display of wealth is coupled with a marked desire for haughty separateness. When he goes to a mosque, Yamani prays in a private room and some of his biographers claim that he used to gamble alone, again in a private room in London's Playboy Club. His public persona is a valid excuse for secret gambling, but praying in a private room is against the spirit of Islam, which favours group prayer. It demonstrates a lack of sensitivity to his own culture which, with his flagrant display of wealth, cannot but tarnish his image with a people who resent his totally Western demeanour.

In fact Yamani's lack of a solid Saudi background, resented as it is by an increasingly chauvinistic Saudi people, is made worse by the adoption of further non-Saudi attitudes. Unlike members of the royal family and other ministers who use the majlis to go through the motions of being members of a Bedouin society of equals, he is aloof towards a people who celebrate the common touch. When in office, he had nothing like a majlis and he was more available to foreigners than to Arabs. He was certainly more available to foreign journalists than to the Arab press contingent, and prominent Arab journalists Farid Al Khatib and Abdel Barri Attwan tell of how he ignored them in favour of unknown freelance writers from Western countries.

With foreigners, he always seemed to be selling something – not oil but Yamani the civilized man in Western terms. His wife and children were often present when he gave interviews and he introduced them to interviewers and spoke about them freely and with unconcealed pride. 'Have you met Tammam?' a Western journalist asked me, referring to Yamani's second wife. When I answered no, he told me that I had missed something and carried on about her and the children as if they were an integral part of the Yamani story. Others repeated the same refrain in their own way and some wrote of how Yamani flirted with his wife for their benefit. Yamani's promotion of his family is un-Saudi behaviour, and he says little about being still married to his first wife. He is a man who is distancing himself from his Muslim origins through creating a Western identity, perhaps someone whose exposure to worldliness overwhelmed the pull of his roots.

But Yamani knows that being a civilized man in the Western world does not stop at having a pretty, elegantly dressed, intelligent wife and well-brought-up multilingual kids, but that to complete the picture he needs other props which people can remember and talk about. To meet this requirement, Yamani found Islamically acceptable substitutes for a knowledge of wine. For years he has promoted himself as a gourmet, an authority on pistachio nuts and an opera-goer who is extremely fond of Wagner. He was and is fond of reciting the menus of famous restaurants, and, on occasion, criticizing those menus with rehearsed knowledge. On pistachios, he is almost unstoppable and, when Minister of Oil, he always had bags of them in his hotel suite and they would become part of the conversation. I find it remarkable that he always had one type of pistachio and that there were not varieties for purposes of comparison, but then no public figure has ever competed with him in this field. On music, he very often digressed from routine interviews about oil to ask interviewees whether they had seen the latest opera production, and on one occasion in Vienna in the mid-1970s he missed an OPEC meeting to attend a concert – a departure from schedule which naturally did not escape the notice of the press.

All of Yamani's image-building exercises are directed at a Western audience and most are excessive. During OPEC nego-tiations with the oil companies, he insisted on calling Exxon executive George Piercy by his first name in a totally non-Arab demonstration of chumminess. He endowed a Chair in Energy Studies at the University of Wales to the tune of £250,000 at a time when many Arab students and institutions of higher education could have used the money for a better reason. Also, according to his biographer Jeffrey Robinson, he used to go to Harrods after closing hours so that he and members of his family might have the place all to themselves. Somehow the press always found out about it.

Yamani the businessman does not contradict Yamani the person. He is a shrewd exponent of heroic materialism, a successful capital-ist with a bent for glamorous business behaviour. He opened the first organized law office in Jeddah and never allowed anybody to forget his legal credentials. His degrees from the University of Cairo, New York University and Harvard were there for everybody to see. His manner, deferential, meticulous and distant, certainly distinct from that of other Saudi lawyers, allowed him to choose his clients carefully and to treat them as if he were doing them a favour.

There were no Harvard lawyers in Jeddah in the late 1950s, when trading on an international scale which required different expertise had just begun, and Yamani soon became famous. Inevi-tably, he started doing work for the Government and eventually for the Ministry of Oil. That is when he caught the eye of the then Prime Minister and later King, Faisal. Soon he became a legal adviser to several ministries, was promoted to Minister of State and was made Minister of Oil and Mineral Resources in 1962. Faisal invited him to succeed Abdallah Tariki, the independent-thinking oil-nationalist co-founder of OPEC. Tariki advocated a policy of confrontation with ARAMCO and openly questioned the awarding of some oil concessions which did not make economic sense and which were granted to companies which bribed the royal family and their relations. Tariki's policies and popularity had become a problem for Faisal and in choosing his replacement the King wanted the opposite: someone who had no popular base, took orders without arguing and was acceptable to the oil companies. In fact when it came to Saudi relations with ARAMCO, Yamani was more than acceptable; he was a friend who ignored the company's attempts to undermine OPEC and to oppose the Saudi Government's wishes on many things, including appointing Saudi directors to ARAMCO's board.

This was the beginning of the Yamani we know, the elegant, wealthy public figure popular in the West and hated by his own people. It was Faisal who made the already comfortable Yamani very wealthy by giving him huge parcels of land around Jeddah which had been declared crown property. Given that Yamani was in the best position to judge the oil-based economic condition of the country, he sold the land when its value hit its peak. Estimates vary, but the land he received as a present fetched $300–500 million. By the time of the 1976 collapse in Saudi property prices, Yamani had disposed of all his landholdings while lesser mortals went bankrupt, and the people of Saudi Arabia well remember this whenever his name is mentioned. Yamani's Western ways did not present an obstacle to his indulging in what resembles insider trading.

The acquisition of this huge fortune coincided with the golden age of OPEC, the period when the supply-demand situation favoured the producers over the consumers. From the early 1970s until 1983 not a week passed without newspapers carrying a picture of Yamani opining on the oil crisis. The world got accustomed to the calm, correct delivery of the one man who became identified with the OPEC–West confrontation without knowing that he had no power and little influence. True, the major decisions to raise oil prices several-fold or to embargo the shipments of oil were made by fellow OPEC members and followed by Faisal, but the outside world did not know that and some commentators wondered why a man who sounded so reasonable would act in a contrary manner.

It was a time when what Yamani had to say got confused with the man. Undoubtedly, even when they disliked the decisions wrongly attributed to him, most saw him as an attractive spokesman for Saudi Arabia and OPEC. He reasoned and did not hector, and in a way diffused the danger implicit in the control by a handful of countries of a commodity the world cannot live without. Under the pressure of ceaseless interviews he deflected hard questions with an engaging smile and above all he came across as a moderate committed to cooperation between the producers and the consumers. Hindsight affords us a better view of what Yamani was doing and why.

The Yamani oil policy as enunciated by him – if it indeed existed – consisted of two elements: oil prices should not be raised to a level which would hurt the Western economies irreparably and they should not be raised to a level which would make feasible the use of alternative energy sources. In addition, he had a commitment to OPEC's long-term interest in remaining the primary oil supplier. He advocated this policy within the circles of power which influenced and controlled the situation, the Saudi Government, OPEC and the West.

In Saudi Arabia, Yamani dealt with his creator, Faisal, and Faisal alone. One of the reasons the present King Fahd resented him was because he behaved haughtily towards him when Fahd was appointed head of the Supreme Petroleum Council, nominally the royal personage in charge of oil policy. What had begun as a search for a politically safe man had developed into something more: if Faisal and Yamani acted like a team, perhaps it was an Arab father-and-son relationship in which the educated son put his talents at the disposal of a traditional, less sophisticated father who was nevertheless the decision-maker and who preferred to remain a shadowy background figure. From all the evidence available to me, it was definitely Faisal who made all the decisions and, capable though he perhaps was, Yamani consistently failed to take into consideration the vital factor of how his country's external oil policy affected the feelings of the people of Saudi Arabia. The following paragraphs explain how that worked.

Yamani always advocated an increase in Saudi oil production to keep the price down to minimize damage to the economies of the industrialized nations, particularly America. He was behind creating the image of Saudi Arabia as a 'swing producer', the country whose production policies determined the price of oil. Faisal, though solidly pro-Western, was much more wary of alienating the members of OPEC to please the consuming countries, and worried about the reaction of the Saudi people to keeping oil prices, and hence the national income, down. The policy which was adopted reflected Faisal's thinking: a balance between high prices and local and regional political considerations.

Yamani advocated spending his country's huge oil income in order to recycle it. He wanted to avoid the imbalance in the world's financial markets which the excess funds in the coffers of the oil producers would create. Faisal, for good and bad reasons, was extremely concerned over the social disruption which would be caused by spending too much too fast. The compromise decision was in Faisal's favour and this is when Saudi Arabia began to accumulate the huge $140-billion surplus which the House of Saud eventually frittered away.

Yamani was for separating oil from pure politics and resisting the Arabs' calls to use the oil as a political weapon against the West. Faisal, though wishing that he could do what Yamani was advocating, saw that oil and politics were closely related and addressed himself to minimizing the damage caused by the inevitable use of oil as a political instrument. The decision to follow other Arab countries in embargoing the shipments of oil to the West in the wake of the October 1972 War was made by Faisal without Yamani's consent, though he was asked to implement it. Faisal rescinded the decision as soon as that became politically feasible – when it became possible to do it without incurring the anger of the Saudi and Arab people, who were all for it, and not because of economic considerations.

Yamani appears to have been more interested in serving Faisal than in implementing policies in which he believed. Even when his policies and reputation were undermined (see Oil, OPEC and the Overseers) by members of the House of Saud, he still had no problem in speaking for Faisal on all these points.

Overall, Yamani's role during the heyday of OPEC betrays a commitment to glamour, an obliviousness to the sensibilities of the Saudi people, a disinclination to cooperate with Arab countries, and a disregard for the interests and opinions of fellow OPEC members. He was happy being a mere public relations man. The latter role produced the admiration he has earned in the West and drew him close to a Faisal who recognized its value. It also made him the most unpopular man in Saudi Arabia. I have had Saudi taxi drivers, businessmen, academics and others tell me how much they hated him. The reasons for this – and it was a surprising discovery at least in its extent – are simple: his haughtiness and a perception that he was willing to accommodate the interests of the West at the expense of the Saudi people. This does support Faisal's assessment of the existence of a Saudi public, and places Yamani alongside a long list of Arabs (Sadat of Egypt, Nuri Said of Iraq, Chamoun of Lebanon, among others) who thought pleasing the West was the only game worth playing.

The highly personal relationship between Faisal and Yamani could not be perpetuated after Faisal's assassination in 1976. The retiring King Khalid left things to Crown Prince Fahd, unlike Faisal a petty, arrogant man who craves the limelight for himself. Faisal, wily and secure, capitalized on Yamani's talents in a subtle way while Fahd, crude and unintelligent, felt the need to pay him back for his previous neglect and to humiliate him to remind him of his position as a dispensable servant of the throne.

Yamani remained in office for four years after Fahd became king, but things were never the same again. Fahd saw very little of him and made his life a pure hell. During this period the supply-demand situation had shifted to the advantage of the consumers and the price of oil was in a steady and precipitous decline. This situation was exacerbated by the Saudi royal family's inclination to undermine the price structure by bartering extra amounts of oil in excess of OPEC quotas to meet defence procurement needs and their personal aggrandizement plans. Fahd's disinclination to study any document or examine anything in depth cancelled Yamani's internal role; beyond being a public relations man, Yamani had thrived on providing his bosses with documents to enable them to make decisions. Eventually Fahd issued an impossible order to Yamani to remedy the decline in the country's income. The order called for the maximum level of oil output and the highest prices, more a magician's than a technocrat's field of endeavour. When Yamani could not carry it out, Fahd fired him in an unbelievably humiliating manner: the Oil Minister heard of his dismissal on television. The Saudi press carried the announcement without comment; it was treated as an insignificant event.

Though his love of the limelight made him accept serving Fahd, however ingloriously, Yamani had removed all his valuable papers from his office before his dismissal. The West mourned his departure and speculated about its causes, but to the Saudi people, the Arabs and OPEC it was a case of good riddance which, coming as it did before they got to know Fahd's stupid ways, temporarily made Fahd popular.

After he was fired, because of the inherent House of Saud concern about its image, Yamani was not allowed to leave the country for a long time and even the very few Saudi friends he had avoided him because doing otherwise was tantamount to affronting Fahd. The order keeping Yamani in Saudi Arabia was eventually rescinded and, instead of finding something constructive to do within his country, he now wanders the world in search of a role. He bought the Swiss watchmaker Vaucheron Constantin because he likes watches; he created Invescorp to handle his other investments; and he created the International Centre for Global Energy Studies as a way to remain involved in the oil business, giving places on the board of trustees to many of his famous friends with former high office, including Edward Heath and Valéry Giscard d'Estaing. Though he says very little about his country's oil policy, some claim that Yamani is waiting in the wings to make a comeback, that Crown Prince Abdallah is fond of him and is likely to recall him when he ascends the throne. This is doubtful; Abdallah is a simple man but he has a knack for doing things to please the people of his country.

In the final analysis Yamani is both a tragic figure and a ridiculous one. He rose to power under a man who did not listen to him and was fired by a man who resented his reputation and his manner. His talents never showed because neither king had any interest in a real Oil Minister. His appreciation of his essentially empty role remains a mystery and his absence has had little effect on his country's basic oil policy. When he was a minister, the only time he took a position contrary to what the royal family wanted was when he stood against the use of oil to barter and even this is now rendered questionable by the recent disclosure in the Arabic weekly *Sourakia* that his own son violated the rules governing total control by the Saudi Government of trading in oil (see Oil, OPEC and the Overseers).

As of now, unless one is enamoured of pistachio nuts, prayer beads, Vaucheron Constantin watches, or one is in the business of celebrating colonial subservience, there is very little to say for Yamani. He was a dispensable technocrat whose services were taken for granted, one of many who come and go according to the desires and transitory needs of the House of Saud. But, unlike the House of Saud's other fallen Oil Minister, Abdallah Tariki, Yamani is not missed. He is more the product of Madison Avenue than he is of Saudi Arabia and if he was a tragic figure then it was only in demonstrating the banality of glamour.

It would seem that the only thing people in the West do not know about Adnan Khashoggi is how to pronounce his name properly. A hard 'g' is followed by a soft 'g': Khashog-ji. In fact while the rest of him is supposed to be an open book and he has been the subject of several biographies, including Harold Robbins's 'faction' *The Pirate*, to which he contributed generously, his life remains as elusive as the correct pronunciation of his name. He deserves considerably more than the surface analysis he has so far received. Unlike others who have served the House of Saud and who are covered in this chapter, Adnan Khashoggi would have cooperated in anything to be written about him; but, to me, that would have been self-defeating. Seeing him from a distance as a thin, subsidiary line running parallel to the thick, unattractive one ploughed by the House of Saud is more to the point. Khashoggi, or 'K' as his jet-setting cronies refer to him, is a true reflection of his masters' fortunes and ways.

Khashoggi is a Turkoman, another non-Saudi son of one of Ibn Saud's doctors; the world's best-known arms dealer; a giver of multi-million-dollar parties full of blondes on the make; a man with a prison record in Switzerland and the United States; once the owner of one of the most lavishly decorated yachts in the world; a friend of former Presidents Richard Nixon and Ronald Reagan and a contributor to their presidential campaigns (reportedly $2 million to Nixon's 1972 effort) and the father of a liberated daughter (Nabilla) who openly lived with her boyfriend and who has very little in common with Saudi womanhood. Khashoggi is generous and loyal to his friends; and many of them, including many seemingly useless ones, became multi-millionaires clinging on to his wheeler-dealer's coat tails.

But the most intriguing thing about Khashoggi is how he has maintained his position in the inner circle of the House of Saud. It is true that he has never done anything to offend the members of the House. On the contrary, he is their loyal supporter and friend and the Saudi royal family and their involvement in his business interests are things about which he is silent. But everything else he does is in violation of what they pretend to stand for; his every act is contrary to the image they try to present to the world. When this pretence of the House of Saud is set aside, everything he does becomes a reflection of its members' hidden attitudes, of the true, private selves of the leading members of the royal family with whom he deals.

Khashoggi's partying and nightclubbing are un-Islamic and they should be offensive to the guardians of Islam's holiest shrines. But members of the House of Saud give parties secretly and many, including King Fahd, have frequented nightclubs, in his case in the company of Khashoggi. The latter acknowledges that he is an arms dealer who has made a lot of money out of the business, but they, particularly the Minister of Defence, Prince Sultan, have done the same without admitting it. Khashoggi has admitted that he was involved in supplying arms to Iran as part of the Iran-Contra scandal and that he dealt with Israeli politicians and intelligence agents in the process. He did this with the knowledge and approval of the House of Saud, who were fronting for America but who ostensibly espouse Arab policies which contradict this involvement. Khashoggi brags about his loyalty to friends and how they have made money working with him. And the House of Saud has helped its friends, including Khashoggi, beyond what is officially acceptable, to amass huge fortunes at the expense of the Saudi people. Female members of Khashoggi's family spend money as if it is going out of style and speak of their affairs openly while the female members of the House of Saud do the same quietly. The House of Saud's inability to openly behave in the Khashoggi manner is behind King Fahd's envious comments whenever he sees pictures of Khashoggi with pretty blondes (he is in the habit of escorting several of them at a time).

While Khashoggi's ability to live the life members of the House of Saud would like to lead goes a long way towards explaining why he is accepted and admired by them in personal terms, it does not explain how he became one of their most trusted business associates. We know why Philby was at Ibn Saud's side, how Faisal used Yamani, and of the relatively understandable connection between Ghaith Pharaon and the House of Saud, but in the case of Khashoggi the question of why him and not another may tell us more about what it takes to become a House of Saud lackey than the stories of the rest of the loyal confederacy.

Adnan Khashoggi's background differs substantially from those of Yamani and Pharaon.

He attended Chico State College, in California, hardly an institution which provides people with superior educational crendentials. Nor was his father anything but a doctor; Muhammad Khashoggi was one of the few men of medicine who attended Ibn Saud who failed to elevate themselves to the position of an adviser. It goes further and whatever acquaintanceship Adnan had as a young man with members of the royal family did not deserve the name friendship.

In describing Khashoggi's beginnings, all one can say is that his non-Saudi background and its inherent appeal to the House of Saud was his only recognizable asset. But there were a lot of people who had this qualification, and many of them had access to members of the House of Saud and tried to endear themselves to them without success. The process of elimination I have followed leaves me with the conclusion that Khashoggi did indeed have something unique to offer the Saudi royals.

Khashoggi's original success had no royal patronage behind it. He began wheeling and dealing in the mid-1950s, while a student at Chico State College, and at that time there were fewer than 3000 college graduates in all of Saudi Arabia and very few people within or outside the country realized its business potential. It is true that he was hardly an average Saudi, but his purchase in America and resale to the bin Laden Group in Saudi Arabia of 50 Kenworth heavy-duty trucks betrays an uncanny knack for what his country needed.

This relatively small deal was followed by others involving the importation of trucks and gypsum, and he was so enamoured of dealing that he left college early and started Al Naser Trading Co, which he later renamed Triad Holdings. There was nothing new in the import business Al Naser did – nothing, that is, except its proprietor's wandering eye, which was on the lookout for new, more lucrative business opportunities. The war in the Yemen in the early 1960s and Faisal's commitment to defeat Nasser provided Khashoggi with his first big opportunity; he saw the Saudi need for arms faster and more clearly than anybody around him.

The American defence contractors Lockheed, Raytheon, Grueman and others either had no representatives in Saudi Arabia or depended on people who represented them throughout the Middle East. It was a perfect situation for a matchmaker and Khashoggi filled the breach to become a power broker between King Faisal and the companies manufacturing defence equipment. With his amazing ability to grasp the usefulness of a weapon, Khashoggi emerged as a problem-solver for both sides. He endeared himself to Faisal by waxing eloquent about how the arms and equipment in question could tilt the scales in Saudi Arabia's favour. At the same time he educated the companies about the size and importance of the Saudi market and convinced them that he had mastered its intricacies. (Because of their colonial history, the British and

French are less inclined to use agents for local situations than are the Americans.) Even when they had agents, the companies prevailed on them to cooperate with Khashoggi and, remarkably and intelligently, he never tried to cut them out.

The war in the Yemen was bigger than people realized; Saudi Arabia needed a lot of arms and Khashoggi's business flourished. But, unlike other successful businessman, he was not happy with what he had and spread his net in a way which eluded most Saudi operators at that time. Though 'in' with Faisal, he had no hold on the wily King. He began building bridges to 'amenable' members of the royal family and voluntarily cut some of them in. And simultaneously he was so deferential towards their reputation that he rebuked a Lockheed official who criticized an intrusive prince. He handled them so well and his sensitivity to their ways was so great that he refused to stay in Boston's Ritz Carlton Hotel with Prince Tallal in order not to be in the way and later on the same trip he ordered his wife not to wear some of her jewellery and to do without make-up in order not to upstage the Prince's wife.

Towards the companies, Khashoggi showed similar care. His awareness of potential problems over commission payments led him to create small companies in Switzerland and Liechtenstein to receive them, in order to protect the client companies from public exposure and the censure which might go with it. The especially created companies appeared with and disappeared after every deal. He went further, and in moves which betrayed an uncanny sense for the need to protect his flank, he began courting US officials and politicians whose functions might help with his business, people like CIA Middle East chief James Critchfield, CIA super-agent Kim Roosevelt and President Nixon's friend Bebe Rebozo. (They came in handy: Critchfield kept him apprised of CIA attitudes, Roosevelt organized for Northrop Corporation to pay a small bribe through Khashoggi to Saudi Air Force chief Hashem Hashem and Bebe Rebozo carried messages back and forth to Nixon.)

This was the beginning of Khashoggi the big-time arms dealer. He achieved that status in a very short time and his quick attainment of this unique position showed he was a man who totally understood the circles of power within which he operated. It was the same sensitivity to surroundings which prompted Khashoggi to focus on the Sudeiri clan within the House of Saud: the present King Fahd and his six full brothers. Khashoggi sensed their growing importance and their coming hold on power before others did and banked on them as the key to his future. There is no record of his cultivating the friendship of Princes Muhammad, Bandar and Nasir, who, according to the seniority system, should each have become king before Fahd.

Everything was going the Sudeiris' way. During the 1960s King Fahd was Minister of the Interior and Minister of Education; Prince Sultan was Minister of Defence; and their full brothers held equally important portfolios. Khashoggi dealt with each on his own terms, but he dealt with all of them. To Fahd he was the entertaining companion who introduced him to Régine's discothèque and the South of France and all that went with them, but he protected Fahd's movements and stayed out of the way. Sultan described him as a man 'who does research for the Defence Ministry', meaning someone who told them what to buy and *how*. He accommodated Minister of the Interior Prince Nayef's need for French electronic equipment for his ministry. He was quiet and unassuming in the presence of Prince Salman because that was what Salman liked, and stayed on good terms with Deputy Minister of Defence Prince Turki without offending his elder brother and boss Prince Sultan. In personal and business terms, Khashoggi was a window on the world to the Sudeiris.

As they moved towards total control of the country, the Sudeiri princes' dependence on him grew in proportion to their growing importance and needs, and he never let them down. Khashoggi was so busy that he would keep others waiting days to see him, but he was always on time to see a prince and he was always prepared. He whispered, nodded agreement and withdrew to carry out their commands. He spoke about everything under the sun except his royal friends and the nature of their relationship and to this day the record of any payments to them has never gone beyond hearsay and circumstantial evidence. It is true that Khashoggi became a very public person and a jet-setter, but, unlike Yamani, his love of the limelight has never appropriated the royal image and, by contrast with Pharoan, he never dealt behind their backs. There was never the slightest suggestion that his personal power and influence was anything but an extension of theirs.

It was in the mid-1970s when the Khashoggi the world knows, or thinks it knows, emerged on the business and social scenes and became recognized as one of the world's greatest wheeler-dealers and party givers. The origins of his reputation lie in the incredible amounts of money he made – and all in less than ten years. His $100-million commissions from Northrop Corporation were topped by $106 million from Lockheed, and there were many others, and he accounted for 80 per cent of the country's foreign procurement business. It was largesse on a scale the world had never known and is unlikely to know again and this pudgy man, five feet four inches tall and with a double chin, a receding hairline and a shy smile became the symbol of oil wealth as much as Yamani did.

People who knew Khashoggi during this period insist that he had visions of transforming Triad Holdings into one of the world's largest corporations. He created companies for construction, leisure, design, development and other subsidiaries, and staffed them with Nordic-looking graduates from America's leading universities, Harvard lawyers, Princeton architects, Stanford MBAs and Yale troubleshooters. He hired people like David Searby, a former Assistant Secretary of State for Commercial Affairs; retained the consultants McKinsey to organize his business activities and used Price Waterhouse to audit his books.

However, none of this worked because in reality Triad was a one-man show and the turnover in personnel was staggering and crippling. Organizing a company and turning it into a global enterprise – and he did open offices in 35 countries – may have been on Khashoggi's mind but it was not what he was good at. His strength lay in handling people, from asking about the family of the doorman of the building where he lived to meeting the demands of a future king. His successes in this area were an extension of his personal charm but at the same time he was failing to make sense of his by now far-flung business empire.

After the 1960s Khashoggi's fortunes ran parallel to the rising star of the Sudeiri seven and in order to maintain his position he needed to broaden his approach in line with their increasing demands on him. He fronted for them in obvious ways and some unattractive ones. He met President-to-be Richard Nixon at Paris's Rasputin nightclub and befriended him. His friendship with Prince Rainier of Monaco flourished and he got to know Prince Bernhard of the Netherlands just in case he needed something from his country. He endeared himself to King Juan Carlos of Spain and acted as a conduit for Saudi royals who built palaces in that country. He insisted on dealing directly with leaders of Third World countries which represented potential areas for investment, among others President Ja'afar Numeiri of the Sudan, Sir James Mancham of the Seychelles and Jomo Kenyatta of Kenya. But Khashoggi also exemplified the glamorous and ugly sides of fame and fortune with his dependence on Bertram Meadows of London's 21 Club, the appearances in public with Joan Collins, Sean Connery, George Hamilton IV and Elizabeth Taylor and the use of Mireille Griffon, the famous madam from the South of France, to provide girls for Arab and other visitors.

Huge wealth affected Khashoggi and the fun-loving, publicity-seeking public side of his personality began to overwhelm the discreet businessman in him. For example, his purchase of the Japanese fashion designer Kenzo Takade subordinated business to publicity. His private DC8 jet and ocean-going yacht *Nabilla* became the most talked-about toys in the world and both had Arab and Western wardrobes in them. Decorating them cost over $20 million, and gold fittings and 10-foot-wide beds seemed as important as their role as mobile business headquarters equipped with state-of-the-art electronics. Even his public quarrels with his attractive first wife, Soraya, appear to have satisfied a craving for the limelight.

Meanwhile Khashoggi's attempts at expanding his business base made a lot of headlines but did not succeed. A Saudi Government-sponsored scheme which cost hundreds of millions of dollars to turn the Sudan into the bread basket of the Middle East foundered because Triad was not organized enough to carry it out. Barrick Investment in Hong Kong was trumpeted as a major entry into the Far Eastern market but it never amounted to very much. OY Finline, a Finnish shipping company, was bought and turned into the Saudi Shipping Company, but in time the lack of depth in its management began to show and it got nowhere. One of Khashoggi's companies imported food from Brazil, but it never got the attention it deserved and success eluded it. Khashoggi's banks, travel agencies and furniture operations suffered from neglect because only one man could make decisions and Khashoggi had little time to devote to them and concentrated on the business he knew best, arms.

Khashoggi's vision far outstripped his ability to give his schemes organizational content and his 'legitimate' businesses began losing a great deal of money. Two major examples of this were the 1970s investments in 21.8 acres in downtown Houston and a 740-acre industrial park in Salt Lake City. Both were massive projects with huge potential which required considerable amounts of development money, much more even than the huge sums Khashoggi was still making out of over 20 defence contractors he was representing. In Houston, although he managed to interest many wealthy investors in joining him, Khashoggi still could not push the deal forward in the organized business fashion it deserved and he eventually gave it up. The Salt Lake City project called for an investment of $600 million. Khashoggi failed in two important respects: the development was too elaborate and expensive for Salt Lake City and he lacked the money to complete it. When he could not keep up the payments, Triad America was forced to file for bankruptcy under the USA's Chapter 11. Khashoggi's lack of organization was so widespread it covered his personal affairs: he defaulted on paying his $500,000 American Express bill and his card was temporarily withdrawn.

By the early 1980s stories about Khashoggi going bankrupt were common, and many of them originated with former employees who were promised the moon and left empty-handed. Some of his businesses had to close down, but Khashoggi still told the world that his personal expenses amounted to over $100 million a year. Funnily, both of these contradictory statements were true, for Khashoggi was having serious financial problems yet his intangible assets – his relationship with the House of Saud and several heads of state and his knowledge of the arms business – were intact, and this translated into an ability to borrow on a huge scale.

Irangate was not a Godsend or a stroke of luck; it was a case of a complex international deal finding expression in the one person who knew how to wheel and deal across international boundaries, hob-nob with heads of governments, indulge in quasi-legal deals and keep secrets. Irangate was the supersecret operation which involved the United States supplying Iran with arms secretly through Israel. It called for this transaction to be funded by Saudi Arabia in a way which would produce profits which the executive branch of the United States used in illegally funding the Contra rebels in Nicaragua. The arms in question were Tow anti-tank missiles and Hawk anti-aircraft missiles. Supplying them to Iran was contrary to avowed US policy calling for neutrality during the Iran–Iraq War and it was an insult to the American people, who were smarting from Iran's hostage-taking activities. On the other side, cooperation between Saudi Arabia and Israel amounted to an act of treason by Saudi Arabia.

Khashoggi was the father of this elaborate scheme. It began in 1983 when an Iranian arms dealer, Manachur Ghorbinfar, asked him to get him the missiles in return for the release by Iran of some of the American hostages. It was a Khashoggi-type idea and he set to work on it. In the process of organizing the deal, Khashoggi met White House aides, the present Israeli Prime Minister Yitzhak

Rabin, King Fahd and everybody in between. Over 2000 Tow missiles and an unknown number of Hawks found their way to Iran. Four countries were beholden to Khashoggi and he made millions of dollars out of the deal.

The operation was exposed by a pro-Syrian Lebanese magazine, *Al Shira*, because Syria disapproved of the secret amity developing between Iran and America. The world held its breath as the details were disclosed. White House Chief of Staff Robert McFarland, one of the architects of the American part of the deal, attempted suicide. Colonel Oliver North, a member of the National Security Council and another conspirator, appeared in front of a congressional committee and defended the right of the executive branch to conduct illegal secret operations. Discussions about impeaching President Ronald Reagan for violating the law became an everyday topic of conversation. Finally Khashoggi spoke.

To Khashoggi, all the people involved in this affair were 'friends'. His American friends wanted their hostages released; his Iranian friends were in desperate need of arms; his Saudi friends were helping their American friends and Rabin was a new friend who facilitated the whole thing. He loved every minute of it. The whole affair gave Khashoggi a chance to confirm his three major characteristics: his ability to make money, his loyalty to his friends and his love of the limelight. This time the publicity was greater than usual and there were lengthy television interviews which revealed the showman in him. Once again the emphasis was on the limelight, rather than discreet business practices.

Despite Irangate, Khashoggi is still in financial difficulties. The lifestyle he has led since the mid-1980s is a reduced one because he no longer makes as much money as before. But it is a continuation, perhaps an exaggeration, of his earlier years and it is still, for better or for worse, dependent on the Sudeiri clan. Rather than go into details I will settle for an example which demonstrates the perils of this dependence.

Irangate's circuitous sale of arms to Iran had Iraqi President Saddam Hussein hopping mad. To him, it was a betrayal by America and Saudi Arabia, but he was still in the middle of the Iran–Iraq War and could not afford to offend either country. The Iraqis therefore began thinking of punishing the chief culprit, Adnan Khashoggi. The Saudi royalty, aware of the violent nature of the Iraqi regime, were confronted by two unpalatable alternatives. Either they protected Khashoggi by saying that they themselves were behind the deal and he was nothing but a messenger, or they disowned him by claiming that he had conducted a personal deal which had nothing to do with them. The moment their interests in maintaining a friendly relationship with Iraq were threatened, Khashoggi became dispensable.

King Fahd sent to Saddam Hussein a messenger who denied Saudi official involvement in Irangate and blamed Khashoggi for everything. The King went further and asserted that Saudi Arabia would never have anything to do with Israel and that people who dealt with the Arabs' enemy should be punished. Alas, continued the message, the Saudis are not good at eliminating people, so Iraq might wish to deal with Khashoggi directly. Fahd gave Saddam Hussein a green light to kill one of his most trusted friends.

Weeks after this oral message reached Saddam Hussein, Jihad Al Khazen, the editor of the Saudi-owned, London-based daily newspaper *Al Hayat*, came to see me and told me that the Saudis had issued a warrant for Khashoggi's arrest. I gave the story to the *Mail on Sunday*, which published it. There is no way of knowing whether Al Khazen was aware that he was being used and that the story was a piece of disinformation, nothing but a Saudi attempt to clean up their image in the Arab world. But the successful attempt to plant this disinformation, along with the invitation to Iraq to eliminate Khashoggi, demonstrates yet again how the House of Saud guards its own interests and how dispensable members of its confederacy are.

Khashoggi survived Saddam's anger because it coincided with an Iraqi attempt to present a new image to the world. In 1985 Adnan Khashoggi, in all likelihood unaware of any threat to his life, gave himself a 50th birthday party in Marbella. Four hundred guests were flown to Spain at his expense from all over the world, and included Sean Connery, Shirley Bassey, Brooke Shields, George Hamilton IV and the *crème de la crème* of European society. It was a non-stop affair which lasted four days and cost several million dollars. At the end of it Khashoggi was crowned King Adnan I. His second wife, Lamia, wearing a $100,000 Chanel dress and a 21-carat diamond ring was there, but she was not crowned. Nobody asked, king of what? King of the party givers? Maybe of the wheeler-dealers? Or of the survivors? It was one of the most unwholesome demonstrations of vulgarity ever recorded.

But nothing in Khashoggi's publicity arsenal could restore his pre-eminence. In October 1988 he was arrested in Switzerland and kept in prison for 90 days. He was charged with concealing funds realized from the sale of jewellery and paintings which belonged to ex-President Marcos of the Philippines but which had a US federal claim against them. Later, he was transferred to prison in the USA, released on bail, tried and acquitted.

In 1992 fortune briefly smiled on Khashoggi. He played middle-man in a deal which saw Libya acquire a share of the UK's Metropole Hotels for £170 million. When nobody would front for Qaddafi, Khashoggi jumped in and is reported to have realized £14 million from the deal. This has provided him with a respite from hounding creditors, but the prospects are not good.

What nobody has noticed about the decline in the fortunes of Khashoggi is that it signalled an important change in how business is done in Saudi Arabia. The House of Saud no longer needs intermediaries; its members are their own middlemen. As was demonstrated by the disclosures of the Yamama 2 programme, Princes Bandar and Khalid are involved in the deal, and young Prince Abdel Aziz is implicated too. Without being able to front for the House of Saud in this unwholesome area or to provide for its personal needs, Khashoggi has no function. Once again, the corruption of the Saudi court is claiming one of its infants.

There is nothing new in the way the House of Saud views Pharoan, Yamani and Khashoggi except the temporary or per-manent circumstances under which each became dispensable. The House of Saud's ability to deal for itself internationally is a new development, but the attitude behind it is a traditional House of Saud one. Ministers, generals, ambassadors, intermediaries and pimps are appointed, hired, used, abused and fired or neglected depending on the House of Saud's need for their services. The stories I have told speak for themselves; in working for the House of Saud, Pharoan, Yamani and Khashoggi accepted the implicit conditions of the royal family's supremacy and absolutism, and these show no signs of changing. There is no dignity in working for the House of Saud – just money and perhaps glamour; it comes down to empty, unwholesome men working for stupid, unwholesome men. The way things in Saudi Arabia are going, Pharoan, Yamani and Khashoggi will one day soon have to account for their deeds to a people's court composed of justly angry men.

10

Oil, OPEC and the Overseers

'There is no such thing as known world oil reserves. If we're willing to pay $1000 a barrel, even $100 a barrel, then there is more oil in the world than we can ever use. People who speak of known world oil reserves are talking about the stuff extractable at a reasonable, affordable price, and that's when the Middle East comes in, way ahead of everywhere else.' This is how Sam Nakasian, an Armenian-American lawyer who has dealt with Middle East oil for decades explained the world energy situation to me at the height of the oil crisis of the early 1970s.

Oil extractable cheaply, available in huge quantities and sold at a low price is the background to the story told in this book. This story concerns the House of Saud's abuse of the oil wealth and how the Saudi people are denied its full benefits. At present Saudi Arabia is producing oil from only 15 fields of the 60 or so which can produce it. In other words, if the production facilities were in place Saudi Arabia would be capable of producing much more oil, perhaps more than 20 million barrels a day. Saudi Arabia's reserves have increased yearly for over 20 years and in early 1993 there was a little-noticed important announcement of the discovery of a new oilfield 150 miles north of the city of Yanbu, 1100 miles from the Dhahran area, where most of the operating Saudi oil wells are. Some geologists believe that the new find confirms the existence of another important oil reservoir in the western part of the country, which means that Saudi Arabia's oil reserves will continue to increase for the foreseeable future.

Except for greater use of gas, which also comes in large part from the Middle East, all attempts by the industrialized world to find a substitute for oil have so far failed. Even the most dramatic and unexpected discovery of a substitute, and it is not on the cards, would mean a minimum of a 30-year change-over to a new source of energy. Oil is indispensable and only two developments have kept the dependence on it from fulfilling the doomsday prophecies of the late 1970s and producing meteoric

273

price increases and a consequent transfer of wealth from the industrialized world to the oil-producing countries. The first is the progress made in the area of conservation and the second is the emergence of natural gas as an alternative energy source. New cars, planes and power stations consume 40 per cent less oil than before; the heating of buildings and the operating of everything else from refrigerators to hair-driers are consuming considerably less energy than a few years ago. And gas, cleaner and available in prodigious quantities, is now easier to transport and use and is making slow but serious inroads as a replacement for oil in several areas of consumption. The results of these two developments have balanced the supply-demand situation for over 12 years and the decreasing demand has tipped the scales in favour of the consumers (between 1979 and 1982 the demand decreased by over 4 per cent a year). The predictions of the $100 barrel of oil which everybody made in the late 1970s have not come to pass.

Saudi Arabia has gas – not as much as oil, and not as much as Qatar, Iran or Iraq – but enough to maintain its position as a major energy supplier for over 30 years after the oil is depleted. The switch to gas production and use is gaining momentum and its share of the market is already big enough for the Saudis to undertake some costly development of their resources. The high cost of developing gas fields and converting plant and equipment to use it is among the reasons for its slow progress, but time and environmental considerations point towards an acceleration of this process. For the time being, however, oil is king.

If we accept the premise that oil is behind the importance of Saudi Arabia and that, however unattractive, the House of Saud is Saudi Arabia, then the preceding chapters have correctly addressed themselves to the unwholesome results. This chapter will deal with the history of the oil companies in terms of how they abused oil, and of the oil-producing countries until the emergence of OPEC became inevitable; how the same oil companies contributed to the corruption which developed in Saudi Arabia over the years; and how members of the House of Saud interfere in the marketing of oil.

The House of Saud abuses the country's wealth at its source and subordinates its national oil policy to personal whims and greed. Furthermore, Saudi Arabia's OPEC policy, which began as a genuine expression of the wish of the country to control its only natural resource, has degenerated into a policy aimed at reducing rather than enhancing the power of this organization.

With regard to the interference of members of the House of Saud in the marketing of oil, previous chapters have dealt with the use of money and power derived from oil. This chapter focuses on the interference in the marketing of the oil itself – before it is sold for money. Inevitably, abusing oil income and tampering with its marketing overlap, but the distinction is important. Meddling with the oil as a commodity is solid proof that the House of Saud sees the country and its oil as a piece of private property. It is theft at the source, the ultimate act of corruption.

The 'Seven Sisters' is the generic nickname for the major international oil companies Exxon, Mobil, Chevron, Texaco, Gulf, Shell and British Petroleum. In the West, they are mysterious monoliths and, though the average individual associates them with monopolies, corruption and unethical lobbying and influence peddling, they are also the providers of a much-needed commodity. In the Middle East, their image is deservedly bad, for the Seven Sisters were guilty of seven major sins.

Acting in concert with and backed by their governments, the Seven Sisters have as their sole aim to maximize their profits against the interests of the oil-producing countries. Throughout the Middle East they arrogated to themselves the following rights: where to explore for oil, how much to invest in exploration, how much oil to produce, what price to charge, how to share the proceeds among themselves, how to transport the oil and what political leaders of the oil-producing countries to support or oppose. Given that oil is the primary source of livelihood for most of the oil-producing countries, the extent of influence, indeed control, the Seven Sisters exercised over the destinies of the producing countries was a unique historical situation the like of which the world is unlikely to see again. Indeed, given that in the 1940s and 50s the Seven Sisters controlled Iraq, Iran, Venezuela, Saudi Arabia, Kuwait, Nigeria, Indonesia and other countries, we are entitled to speak of an oil empire.

In the Middle East, it all began with the British oil concession in Iran in 1901. Bahrain and Iraq followed, the latter as an inheritance from Turkey after the First World War. The San Remo Treaty of 1920 recognized oil as a major strategic element and dealt with it in considerable detail. Among other things, Britain and France sought to divide the oil of the Middle East between themselves without involving American companies. The oneness of purpose between the oil companies and their governments was total, and it was the United States Government which successfully opposed this division of the spoils on behalf of Standard Oil of New Jersey. What followed in 1928 was called the Red Line Agreement, a compact between the oil companies to share the oil within a geographical line which included most of the oil-producing countries of the Middle East. This awarded the lion's share to Britain and stipulated the American share at 23.5 per cent, the same as that of France.

Throughout this period there were no consultations whatsoever with the governments of the oil-producing region, not even with independent Iran. The concessionaires made all the decisions as a single, exploitative group with the support of their governments. The American Government, beginning with the Wilson administration, supported the unjust agreements reached by the oil companies with no apparent misgivings. In any case, the agreements were signed with leaders who were appointed, supported and beholden to the victors of the First World War. This amounted to the West signing agreements with itself by proxy. In the case of ARAMCO, it went beyond that and, as will be discussed further later in this chapter, the oil companies had considerable say on how the local governments, or chiefs, used what little money they received.

Saudi Arabia emerged as an oil concession area in the 1930s, but the one-sided relationships between the oil companies and the local governments did not change until the 1950s. The British lack of interest which allowed the Americans to gain the Saudi concession meant the end of the inter-company Red Line Agreement, but the agreement between Saudi Arabia and ARAMCO subscribed to the companies' ways.

The final agreement signed by a desperately broke Ibn Saud and Lloyd Hamilton of Standard Oil of California provided the United States with a chance to support its claims that it was not a colonial power and to distance itself from Britain and France and their predatory ways. But the opportunity was not taken and the interests of Standard Oil of California superseded the avowed policy of the US Government. It was an uneven agreement signed by one of the largest corporations in the world, backed by a major power, and a destitute local chief. (Ibn Saud had already offered Karl Twitchell 10 per cent of his receipts from any oil agreement he obtained for him and later told Harry St John Philby that he was 'ready to give an oil concession for the whole country for a million pounds'.)

The Saudis who 'negotiated' the agreement, Ibn Saud and

'Minister of Everything' Abdallah Suleiman, knew nothing about international contracts. Furthermore, unlike their opposite numbers, the Saudis who gave the concession had little appreciation of the increasing importance of oil internationally, the coming reliance on their reserves or on international politics and agreed to a 60-year concession without asking for a single Saudi appointment to the board of directors. In signing the agreement in a hurry and without questioning any of its provisions, Saudi Arabia ceded part of its sovereignty without knowing it. The implementation articles called for referral in case of disputes to the International Court of Justice in the Hague with no reference to Saudi law. This surrendered Saudi Arabia's right to act to protect its rights in accordance with Saudi law.

Both sides got what they wanted: Ibn Saud used the oil income and US Government and ARAMCO loans to indulge himself, and the Americans controlled the largest oil reservoir in the world. Ibn Saud always wanted more money and he always sent his Minister of Everything to ARAMCO to get it, but he was scarcely concerned whether the money came in the form of royalty payments, grants or loans against future oil production. He felt no need to change the agreement. The Saudi people were not part of the equation; and Ibn Saud saw the agreement with ARAMCO as a personal deal – so much so that he waited until 1950 before creating a Directorate of Petroleum. For the rest of Ibn Saud's life, until 1953, the Saudis did not ask for any changes in the agreement. Even when their income from oil declined from 23.6 cents in barrel in 1940 to 17.3 cents a barrel in 1946, the overall relationship remained unaltered all the while the King's personal needs were met. But while Ibn Saud subscribed to his 'Catholic marriage' to ARAMCO, there was a lot of activity within the American camp and much of it affected America's and ARAMCO's relations with Saudi Arabia.

In 1938 the realization by Standard Oil of California of the vastness of the Saudi oilfields led it to invite Texaco, Mobil and Standard Oil of New York to take shares in its oil concession. The ARAMCO consortium was created. In addition to the four partners sharing the development cost, the new consortium had more marketing outlets and greater leverage with the State Department. Amazingly even this change in ownership did not open Ibn Saud's eyes to what was happening in his own backyard and according to the Saudi writer Tewfik Al Sheikh his response was: 'Good, more companies means more money.'

But preoccupation with the more immediate problems of the

Second World War kept what was known to oilmen and US Government officials on the back burner. To the rest of the world the size and importance of Saudi oil was a postwar discovery. Suddenly, the United States needed the oil for its European-based armed forces and the navies which supported them, and to rebuild Europe's industry. The need for Saudi oil for domestic American consumption was becoming a reality, the income from the oil was deemed important and controlling Saudi Arabia's colossal oil reserves strengthened America's position as the world's number one international trader and economic power. These vital facts, unrecognized as they were by Ibn Saud, generated much debate within the American camp.

In 1943 US Undersecretary of the Navy William Bullit, supported by none other than Secretary of the Interior Harold Ickes, proposed that the US Government acquire a majority shareholding in ARAMCO. The company, whose annual profits were nearly 200 per cent of its invested capital, rejected the offer through its shareholders. However, the debate as to who should control ARAMCO, anchored as it was in one of the most important postwar developments, produced a compromise solution. The company and the US Government agreed to coordinate their activities. The Government openly undertook to protect the company as the producer of Saudi oil, mostly against other oil companies, and the company took immediate steps to produce oil in sufficient quantities to meet America's strategic needs.

This was when ARAMCO began to behave like a state within a state. Beyond playing middleman between the United States and Saudi Arabia and thus assuming a role in the latter's external affairs, it was ARAMCO which advised the Saudis on what nationals to hire, what clothes to wear and where to dig for water wells. Within the American city of Dhahran there was a lot of booze and women in shorts and the company had its own radio station and golf clubs. Simultaneously, ARAMCO began shipping oil in substantial quantities to meet the needs of the Petroleum Reserve Corporation (PRC) and decided to build TAPLINE, the Trans-Arabian Pipeline, which carried Saudi oil across Jordan and Syria to the Lebanese port of Sidon. As its name suggests, PRC was building up US reserves of oil and TAPLINE, above all, was aimed at keeping the American navy supplied with its fuel needs. It was against this background of convergence of interest that the roles of diplomats, CIA agents and company executives became interchangeable.

The increase in Saudi oil production and ARAMCO's profits in the period following the Second World War created unanticipated problems for the company. It was still paying Saudi Arabia one-sixteenth of the selling price of a barrel of crude oil. Neighbouring countries such as Iran were openly demanding a greater share of the receipts of the oil companies. Meanwhile independent oil companies such as Getty, Conoco and Italy's ENI were making approaches to the producing countries and offering them more money. The US Government, somewhat embarrassed by the profits ARAMCO was producing and afraid of anything which might disturb the company's unique position, reacted first. Assistant Secretary of State for Near Eastern Affairs George McGhee foresaw the coming pressures on ARAMCO to pay the Saudis more money and warned its management: 'It's in your interests if you make concessions to the Saudis.' Increasing the royalty paid to the Saudis became inevitable.

In 1949, responding to the pressures for it to share its excess profits, ARAMCO broke with the rest of the oil concessionaires and offered Saudi Arabia a 50–50 agreement. This called for the company to pay the country 50 per cent of the price of a barrel of oil after deducting production and marketing costs. On the surface and compared with what the other oil companies were paying, it was a generous offer, but Saudi oil was so abundant in total and in terms of production per well that ARAMCO's profits between 1949 and 1951 still rose by 300 per cent.

Despite a new royalty agreement which was to the liking of the Saudis and ARAMCO, there were two new influences on the Middle East oil picture in the early 1950s and they both came from the outside. In 1951, in a move which stunned the oil companies and the world, Iranian Prime Minister Muhammad Mossadeq nationalized the Anglo-Iranian Oil Company. Three years later, Egyptian President Nasser, who had assumed power in his country in 1952, began referring to the Saudi oil as 'Arab oil'.

Mossadeq's move exposed the vulnerability of the oil companies as well as their strength. The mere act of nationalizing a Western oil company amounted to reclamation of a country's inalienable sovereign rights, an anti-colonialist revolution, but the oil companies conspired with their governments and paid the CIA and MI6 to overthrow Mossadeq in 1953 (Operation Ajax has been documented by several people, including Kim Roosevelt, its controller). This sent the right signal to the producing countries, for it demonstrated the ability of the companies and Western governments to respond to similar moves. Nasser's claim began three years later and it took the form of appealing to the Saudi people to demand a greater share of ARAMCO's income and to share it with fellow Arabs.

The combined effects of Mossadeq and Nasser may have been limited by the results of the Iranian experience, but they still opened the door for the leaders of the oil-producing countries to think of ways to realize more money at the expense of the oil companies. Unfortunately, it was the hapless King Saud who led the way in trying to loosen ARAMCO's control of all aspects of producing and marketing the oil of his country.

Like independent oil companies, tanker-fleet owners were always on the lookout for ways to undermine the monopoly of the oil companies. In 1954 the Greek shipping magnate Aristotle Onassis decided that he had found the right partner to do it. Using secret emissaries and middlemen, he finally convinced King Saud to become his partner in a shipping company that would transport Saudi oil to the international market. The result was the Saudi Maritime Tanker Company and the agreement creating it assigned to the company the exclusive shipping rights hitherto held by ARAMCO.

The deal represented an intelligence failure on the part of the US Government and ARAMCO, since they heard about it only after the fact. But that did not mute their response and ARAMCO, with solid US Government backing which included statements by Secretary of State John Foster Dulles, maintained that it had the right to transport all Saudi oil. When Saud resisted, the US Ambassador to Saudi Arabia, George Wadsworth, bluntly told him that the eventual American response would be to stop extracting Saudi oil, which would break Saudi Arabia financially. Saud gave in, ARAMCO maintained its monopoly on transporting oil and notice was served, as before in Iran, that the oil companies who proved their willingness to pay the producing countries more money were unwilling to cede them any control. The previous statements made by US Government officials, including trouble-shooter General Patrick Hurley's comment that 'US companies don't follow an imperialist government', were shown to be empty, directed mostly against the British. But despite the failure of Saudi Arabia to have its own tanker fleet, Mossadeq and Nasser created a popular atmosphere which was not lost on the leaders and which foreshadowed the emergence of OPEC.

The first move towards the formation of OPEC came in April

1959, appropriately enough in Cairo, where an Arab Petroleum Congress was meeting to discuss the companies' relations with Arab countries. Equally appropriately, the moving spirit behind it was a Saudi, Abdallah Tariki, the newly appointed Oil Minister. By today's standards, what was agreed was modest indeed: essentially the producers had the right to review the contractual arrangements with the companies and to be involved in the pricing of their production. But at that time these were revolutionary demands which went to the heart of the relationship, and the significance of the joint declaration was enhanced by the presence in Cairo, as an observer, of Venezuelan Oil Minister Pérez Alfonso.

Alfonso and Tariki met, liked each other and decided to coordinate Middle Eastern and Venezuelan oil production to stop the companies from manipulating the posted price of oil. The problem was to get other oil-producing countries to join them. Kuwait, still under British protection (it became independent in 1961) was happy to settle for coordinating minor aspects of the relationships with the companies. In fact, but for the preoccupation of Saud and Faisal with their personal quarrel, Saudi Arabia might not have joined in any efforts to form a cartel and Tariki himself was treading on thin ice. What the situation needed to move it forward was a dramatic demonstration that the existing contracts with the companies infringed on the rights of the producing countries. Foolishly, the companies which were dismissive of the Cairo conference, gave them a free hand.

With Esso in the lead, and with no prior consultation with the producing countries, in August 1960 the companies decided to reduce the posted price of oil by 7–9 per cent. The decision by itself would have represented a rare piece of stupidity but coming as it did after the Cairo conferees had asked for prior consultation on prices, it amounted to a challenge to their right to make such a request.

Tariki and Alfonso capitalized on the companies' move. An oil producers' meeting in Baghdad in September 1961 to discuss cooperation among them was turned into one solidly in favour of creating an organization to oversee this cooperation. It was Alfonso who suggested the name Organization of Petroleum Exporting Countries and it was adopted unanimously. The original OPEC consisted of Venezuela, Saudi Arabia, Iraq, Iran and Kuwait, with Qatar limiting itself to the role of observer. The organization's first resolution rejected the companies' right to determine prices, proceeded to create specialist departments to deal with the various aspects of the oil monopoly by the Seven Sisters and promised measures to protect the rights of the countries. Even Kuwait, which until then had been counted on to present the companies' point of view, found itself agreeing to the measures wholeheartedly.

The companies' response to the creation of OPEC confirmed that their precipitous price reduction was not an accident but part of a policy which insisted on ignoring the wishes of producing countries. They decided to ignore it and resorted to old techniques to undermine it. In 1961 the *New York Times* ran a number of stories inspired by CIA agent Bill Eveland which were dismissive of the consortium and predicted it would fall victim to internal squabbling and be short-lived. The companies and the CIA paid newspapers to run stories resurrecting old feuds between the member countries in an attempt to foment trouble and stop them cooperating. They approached individual countries with promises of increasing their production at the expense of others, in particular an attempt to prise Kuwait loose by affording it a greater share of the market at the expense of populous Iraq.

Their efforts failed. Venezuela's Pérez Alfonso was a master at educating his less knowledgeable colleagues in the long-term benefits of OPEC; Tariki's presence meant the consortium had the support of the most conservative country of them all; and Nasser's background exhortations created a popular atmosphere within the Arab countries which limited the Arab countries' ability to rescind a popular move. My reporter's notebook of 1960 includes a statement by the late eminent Lebanese oil expert and editor of the Middle East Economic Survey Fuad Ottayem: 'It [the creation of OPEC] is a popular political move, like wanting independence.' Saudi Arabia, a reluctant joiner of any organization, was caught. By the time Faisal became king in 1962, the most he could hope for was to reassert the House of Saud's control over the source of wealth of the country by firing Tariki. Tariki's departure improved relations between Saudi Arabia and ARAMCO. His replacement, Yamani, reflected Faisal's viewpoint and followed rather than led, but OPEC was already a reality and that meant Saudi Arabia had to develop policies to live within it. When that became apparent to the companies they finally recognized the organization, in 1962, three years after its creation.

The period from 1962 until the 1967 Arab–Israeli War was one of consolidation. There were many OPEC meeetings which concerned themselves with royalties and production programming;

in particular the member countries wanted their 50 per cent share to be in addition to the 'rent' per barrel the companies were paying, but very little happened. The companies would not budge on anything, and OPEC itself still had not mustered the means to force any changes; they were sparring but not fighting. Once again, it was Ottayem who described the situation accurately: 'OPEC isn't businesslike and the industry has shown no signs of imagination and flexibility.'

The outcome of the 1967 War inflamed Arab nationalism and in some cases frustration expressed itself openly, as in 1969, when Colonel Muammer Qaddafi overthrew the Government of Libya. The Arab pressure to use oil as a weapon coincided with an increase in worldwide demand and the situation placed OPEC in an excellent position to realize its demands for greater revenues and greater coordination among the producers. This was when Saudi Arabia showed its true colours and subordinated oil economics to the political interests of the House of Saud.

Because dealing with all the price increases, attempts to take over the companies and the devising of production quotas would mean rehashing all of OPEC's many meetings, outlining some of the major decisions having bearing on these elements is enough. However, it should be pointed out that oil experts are essentially agreed on the meaning of Saudi oil policy. Daniel Yergin, the author of the incomparable study of the history of oil, *The Prize*, states that there was 'a general meeting of the minds between Riyadh and Washington'. The oil-nationalist and one-time Tariki collaborator Anton Sarkis speaks of Saudi Arabia playing 'Don Quixote to protect US interests, even if it means sacrificing their interests and the rest of OPEC'. Oil affairs expert Pierre Terzian falls between the two and his record of the 1973 oil embargo and how it was thrust on Saudi Arabia, which lifted it first and forced the others to follow, is masterly.

In fact, all the oil experts are making the same point in their own way: since Tariki Saudi Arabia has never done anything except try to control the power of the OPEC cartel to suit the House of Saud and its American protectors. This is why every major OPEC meeting is preceded by Saudi–American contacts at the highest level (Reagan or Bush with Fahd) or a trip to Washington by the Saudi Oil Minister. In 1968 they advocated participation when the rest of the producing countries called for nationalization of the oil companies. It took a share in ARAMCO in 1974, a year after little Kuwait and Qatar had taken the same step and well after Iran, Iraq, Venezuela and Algeria. At one point in the early 1970s, in attempting to keep prices down, Saudi Arabia was selling oil at $14.45 a barrel when it was fetching $35 on the spot market. In 1979 Saudi Arabia lost $23 billion by sticking to its own lower price. And in 1981 Yamani told NBC News that Saudi Arabia 'organized the oil surplus' to decrease prices. Overall, Saudi Arabia gained control over its oil only when it became impossible not to do it.

The issue here is not moderation and I am a strong advocate of dialogue between the oil producers and consumers to arrive at a sensible way to price oil and maintain an economic equilibrium between the two sides. The real issue is the House of Saud's willingness to act contrary to the wishes of its people and the interests of OPEC. The Saudi taxi driver who complains about not benefiting from oil makes a valid point. The Arab who believes he should be considered a more deserving recipient of Saudi largesse makes another. Some OPEC members who cry for an increase in prices to meet their development needs are telling the truth. The House of Saud goes its own unhappy way regardless.

Another major failure of most writers who have claimed to tell the story of Saudi Arabia is exposed by the little space they have devoted to the influence of ARAMCO on Saudi life, in addition to its role as a major component of the oil industry. For four decades ARAMCO's presence affected Saudi governmental and social development in a profound way, as did its attempts to present Saudi Arabia to the world. ARAMCO is now a Saudi company; it was Saudized in 1980 as part of the changing relationship between the oil-producing countries and the oil companies. After Saudization its role changed, but there was a time when it was difficult to determine where the influence of ARAMCO and the oil companies which held all its shares stopped and the jurisdiction of the Saudi Government began.

We have seen how the oil companies prevailed on the US Government during the Second World War to rescue Ibn Saud financially and how the US Government ceded the handling of US–Saudi relations to ARAMCO during the 1950s, something which allowed a corporation driven by narrow self-interest to supervise those relations. I have also reported how the ARAMCO CIA created Islamic fundamentalist cells to counter the threat of Nasser's Arab nationalism and how they sent Saudi students to colleges thinking they were producing pro-American technocrats without much thought about the inevitable need to respond to the natural demands of educated Saudis. But ARAMCO's short-sighted policies went further and the company's influence on Saudi governmental policy, the behaviour of members of the House of Saud and the life of the average Saudi was incredibly pervasive, much greater than that of the oil companies operating in other countries.

In the 1940s and 50s it was ARAMCO rather than the US Government which used its huge resources to keep British and other non-American oil companies out of Saudi Arabia. ARAMCO was the only American presence in Saudi Arabia when Ibn Saud claimed the country's income as his own, and later the US Government found it difficult to divorce itself from the blind policies of the company. Above all, it was ARAMCO's involvement in shady and corrupt practices (direct bribes to government officials and pimping) which represented a pattern of behaviour which became a sordid tradition and contributed to the present sorry state of both Saudi Arabia and relations between the two countries.

ARAMCO's actions were the result of American lack of experience in the Middle East and fear of the British. In fact, ARAMCO's fear of the British was pathological. It behaved like an insecure upstart who believed that the British were plotting to control Saudi oil and that Britain's long experience in the Arab world gave it an advantage. The supposed mysterious British advantage, a long colonial history, was misjudged. In reality, the British were never accepted by the people of the Middle East, only by some of their leaders, and ARAMCO and the Americans missed a chance to fill a void and assume the role of a more attractive presence to the Arab people. Instead, they competed with the British on the latter's own terms and in the process opposed all British moves without analyzing them. The blind opposition led to the use of underhand methods which produced a worse colonialism and undermined US–British relations and the combined Western position in the Middle East.

ARAMCO's desire to please Ibn Saud was behind opposition to the British moves to free the slaves and introduce financial controls in Saudi Arabia. These negative reactions were followed by others which had a disastrous influence on Saudi regional and foreign policy. In 1954 ARAMCO, with US State Department backing, encouraged Saudi Arabia not to join the British-led CENTO alliance of Iraq, Turkey and Iran. It wrongly saw the alliance as a threat to its oil interests, a case of commercial interests coming first, even above strengthening an anti-Soviet pact. In the late 1950s ARAMCO went further and aided and abetted the Saudi claim to the Bureimi Oasis, the disputed oil-rich wedge of land between Saudi Arabia, the United Arab Emirates and Oman. The Saudi claim was questionable, but ARAMCO spent millions of dollars sponsoring historians and researchers who produced improvised documents which it gratuitously supplied to the Saudi Government and released to the Beirut press to fan the flames of crisis between Britain (then the governor of Oman and the Emirates) and Saudi Arabia.

It was a successful effort which led to a break in diplomatic relations between the two countries and indirectly to the strengthening of ARAMCO's position. Also, lest future historians forget, it is worth repeating that ARAMCO backed the Saudi Government's adoption of Islamic fundamentalism without much thought of the future. The same Lebanese, Syrian, Jordanian and Iraqi journalists and spies who promoted Islam attacked Britain. These moves, which corrupted the decision-making process of the country and stopped it from following sensible policies, took place against a background of aiding and abetting the corruption of its kings. Meanwhile Britain was incapable of supplanting the Americans in Saudi Arabia and the British had begrudgingly accepted the American dominance in the country and given up on the oil concession.

These huge policy errors represented the visible part of ARAMCO's policy towards the kingdom, but there was another part which was equally disastrous and that had to do with the company's attitude towards the personal behaviour of the House of Saud and the Saudi people. This was American naiveté and bungling at its worst.

ARAMCO developed the plans and supervised the development of the royal experimental farms around the town of Kharj. The purpose of the farms was to grow fresh produce for the royal tables. Water in that area is scarce, more so than in other parts of Saudi Arabia, and it should have been used for more immediate needs. But this did not stop ARAMCO's agriculturalists. The need of water for drinking and sanitation was ignored and using it agriculturally amounted to depleting a precious resource. The growing of fruits and vegetables was essentially uneconomic; it would have been more sensible, given the value of the water, to import them. Furthermore, it was ARAMCO which lent members of the House of Saud huge sums of money to build palaces and kept them in debt when schools were needed. ARAMCO's money allowed King Saud to build 40 palaces when there were fewer schools. Any important prince could borrow money from it for equally wasteful purposes. It was also ARAMCO which initiated the global whoring expeditions which saw groups of princes travel the world, misbehave and give the Arabs a bad name. ARAMCO provided them with companions who facilitated their stupid indulgences and most of the time it picked up the tab.

ARAMCO's stupidity did not stop with their mock-colonialist treatment of the royals, but extended to their overall behaviour. For the most part, the Americans who worked for the American oil consortium in Saudi Arabia during the 1940s, 50s and 60s came from the oil states of Texas, California and Oklahoma. They were 'rednecks' and called their hosts A-rabs. Everything which followed was an extension of this insulting misnomer. These people were primarily technicians who were paid over the odds, two or three times what they received for similar jobs in America. The added enticements included an exclusive, air-conditioned life full of weekend barbecues in a specially built American town, the North Camp or American Compound, part of today's Dhahran.

Little attention was paid to the way the 'natives' lived. Most of them were on hourly wages and lived in shacks and tents, and even the senior staff among them were relegated to cement cubicles with little resistance to the hot days and cold nights of the desert. The so-called 'native quarter', also purpose-built, lacked a refuse-collection service and was provided with less than a fifth the water per capita supplied to its American counterpart. The Saudis who had the competence to perform duties similar to those of some of the Americans got less than a third of their salaries and the furniture and other human comforts provided for the Saudis were considerably inferior to those of the visitors. For the Saudis, the American Compound was a no-go area.

ARAMCO, in line with its anti-British policy, openly criticized colonialism while creating a situation worse than had existed in India and other British colonies decades if not centuries before. The Americans were new to their role and it showed. The rednecks received no counselling in how to behave towards their colonials and ended up adopting a crude, superior attitude which ignored the passage of time and the basics of colonialism's civilizing mission. They did not subscribe to a separateness based on group-think or class, but treated the Saudis the way they treated the blacks in America. They considered them unfit, lazy and inferior and, instead of adopting a constructive attitude towards them, abused them.

Abdallah Tariki was among the first people to suffer from American discrimination and short-sightedness. The man who eventually became Saudi Arabia's first Oil Minister worked for ARAMCO towards the end of the 1940s, after earning a masters degree in petroleum engineering from the University of Texas. Tariki had married an American girl and, along with his college degrees and relatively important position in the company, he felt entitled to live in the American Compound, or at least somewhere comfortable. But ARAMCO's policy-makers thought otherwise and Tariki was cold-bloodedly relegated to the inferior 'native quarter' and a stark cubicle with hard beds and no refrigerator. Tariki was and is a populist and living with his own people did not faze him except for the gross insult of being discriminated against in his own country. The effect of this situation on his American wife was dislocating; denied access to fellow Americans, she found herself with nobody to talk to. Soon the Tarikis divorced and his wife left for Texas with their small son. The incident left Tariki emotionally scarred and bitter.

Tariki got his chance to pay ARAMCO back in 1959, when he was Oil Minister, a favourite of King Saud, a co-founder of OPEC and the darling of the young nationalists in his country. The Ministry in Riyadh had moved across the street to a larger and more lavish building from the first one it had occupied. A group of ARAMCO directors went to the new building to visit Tariki, for an ordinary meeting to discuss matters of mutual interest. Tariki took the opportunity to pay them back. He kept them waiting for 45 minutes, after which they were told that His Excellency would receive them in the old building. When they entered Tariki's old office, he greeted them, saying, 'This is where I receive directors of ARAMCO.' Some of the directors did not know what he was talking about, but others remembered and tried to apologize.

Tariki's treatment by ARAMCO was of course unacceptable, but his case was not unique and it reflected a larger attitude. The oilmen accused Saudi natives of being thieves and made fun of the way they prayed, their native dress and love of dates. Even the blood used for transfusions in the hospitals serving ARAMCO's American employees went through a more stringent inspection process than the blood used for Saudi nationals. Naturally, there were separate cafeterias, cinemas and athletic events, and the sight of an American woman talking to a Saudi, even her driver, amounted to a scandal.

If this was not enough to create instant anti-Americanism,

there were hidden forms of this lack of judgement and blatant discrimination which were guaranteed to produce a broader, deeper, longer-lasting resentment. Among them was the way ARAMCO selected its trainees. Training local people cost the company less than importing carpenters, drivers and fitters from other countries. It was a laudable effort and the ARAMCO propaganda machine made much of it, but the selection process was discriminatory and the people chosen were the ones who were deemed 'hip' in American terms. For example, people who observed the Muslim prayer were discriminated against and so were people who were not subservient enough during job interviews or those who liked Nasser. The ARAMCO screening process amounted to an arrogation of a right to 'Americanize' the place. The Saudis who accepted being called 'Mo' got trained, but others who objected to reducing the Prophet's name to a vulgar diminutive did not. A guy who wore jeans stood a better chance than one who wore the native dress (infinitely more comfortable in the heat). Clean-shaven men were given precedence over those with moustaches and beards. Competence counted for less than a willingness to emulate the American way of life. Chewing Wrigley's gum became a local habit.

Some of the trainees became a credit to ARAMCO and to their country, but were they on the whole representative Saudis or a new breed? Even if they were representative, there was a built-in, highly questionable insensitivity in the training process. For example, ARAMCO personnel liked Farhan Al Qahtani, so they decided to educate him at their expense. They sent him to school to study English. But the man was an illiterate and he was a Saudi and ARAMCO had the facilities to teach him Arabic. ARAMCO did not care, and Farhan mastered English while remaining illiterate in Arabic. Later he left ARAMCO to become one of their small contractors. He could read company documents and requests, but could not translate them into written Arabic for his suppliers.

Farhan made a lot of money, lost it, made it again and lost it again. The Americans always supported him more than others because they liked his ways. His contacts with ARAMCO and its personnel had enamoured him of American ways and he became fond of shouting 'a darn good idea', 'look me straight in the eye and tell me that', and 'shake it but don't break it'. Farhan was an expression of ARAMCO culture. Eventually he began complaining about his own people and found their company less agreeable than that of Americans. Conversely, the Saudis did not like Farhan any more; he was a synthetic creation – not truly one of them – and sadly for him, he never really belonged to the other side.

The damage caused by ARAMCO's short-sightedness affected the whole community of Arab workers who worked for it. Inevitably discrimination produced natural sociological and political reactions. The Saudi workers herded to live in compounds away from their families and tribes developed serious psychological problems of loneliness and depression which led them to turn to drink and drugs. The rate of suicide among them was more than 20 times the rate among the general population. Some of those who escaped these psychological problems and adopted American ways lived out of harmony with their Arab background. They developed commitments to materialism, which led to a belief in the nuclear family rather than the tribal extended family. The dissolution of family and tribal bonds caused many of them to refuse financial help to their parents in their old age.

The discriminatory policies and the sociological and psychological damage suffered by some workers produced a wider reaction. From November 1953 until 1956, non-acceptance of ARAMCO's methods and their results on occasion took the form of strikes. Rather than do something to remedy the causes of these protests, ARAMCO worked with the local province emir to punish the strikers. On one occasion they provided him with a list of 600 workers who had petitioned them to improve living conditions. The workers were imprisoned; most were tortured and many of them were never seen again. In fact it did not need a strike to eliminate what ARAMCO called troublemakers (taking time for prayer was troublemaking) and individual workers were known to disappear after they questioned their pay or their entitlement to promotion. There is no record of anybody in ARAMCO objecting to the surrender of workers to the merciless sword of Prince bin Jalawi. Perhaps this why this province of Saudi Arabia saw the greatest number of attempted coups against the Government.

It is difficult for a loyal American to admit it, but the British would have never created a Farhan. Nor were they in the business of creating imitation Britons, isolating people from their roots, putting their language above Arabic, introducing insulting diminutives or hip phrases or relying on the methods of a bloodthirsty prince. Rightly or wrongly, the British attitude on the governmental, corporate and individual levels consisted of maintaining cultural separateness and a commitment to improve the situation of the people from within the existing cultural context. ARAMCO's application of colonialist behaviour was superficial. It confused separateness with discrimination and ignored the more subtle and complicated parts that amounted to a long-term policy. Among other things, the British would have curbed bin Jalawi and seen to it that the punishment was proportionate to the crime.

The American attitude which allowed the House of Saud to view the country's income as belonging to them was part of a bigger picture which found ARAMCO and the various American contracting companies which worked with it aiding and abetting the march of Saudi corruption in many ways. The country's first Minister of Finance (the 'Minister of Everything') was bribed every time his help was needed, mostly to convince Ibn Saud of something ARAMCO wanted. Other government officials were bribed through being awarded lucrative contracts the execution of which they knew very little about – at a time when more qualified people existed. Says the Saudi writer Tewfik Al Sheikh: 'They bribed every prince, manager, judge, employee and policeman within sight.'

In addition, US efforts in the field of education suffered from misdirection and mismanagement. Unlike the scholarships the British provided in Iraq and Iran, those provided by ARAMCO always went to the sons of leading families and there was little consideration for competence and the results. I know a former Saudi student, the son of the country's first Minister of Posts and Telegraphs, who spent ten years on an ARAMCO scholarship getting a bachelor's degree, and there were many like him. Most of the time the recipients of ARAMCO scolarships chose fields of specialization which had nothing to do with their country's needs. They went to colleges where the weather was pleasant and took the easiest courses to get any degree. The British oil companies in Iran and Iraq produced engineers and doctors while many of the Saudi students danced with the football bands of the Universities of Miami, Texas and Southern California and spent the rest of their time going to nightclubs.

With the usual exceptions, the lack of supervision of what may have been well-intentioned efforts vitiated or cancelled their effectiveness and reduced them to propaganda exercises. Even efforts to promote trade between the USA and Saudi Arabia fell into the same trap. Some of the trade delegations organized by ARAMCO in the 1950s and 60s were dubbed whoring delegations. The Saudi delegates selected by the company were royals or came from good families. ARAMCO could not and would not tell them what to do and they spent their time chasing floozies and drinking champagne from their slippers. ARAMCO went further and paid the debts of gambling princes, bought useless, substandard medical and other equipment from others and indulged in outright pimping. (New York restaurateur J. M. had an ARAMCO retainer and specialized in blondes on the plump side.)

ARAMCO's corruption, when it was still an American consortium owned by the American majors, often took the form of serious acts to promote the House of Saud and its governance while undermining real and imaginary enemies and distancing themselves from the Saudi people and their needs. Not only did ARAMCO create a bogus history for the House of Saud which connected its members with the Prophet, but the company's Beirut public relations offices and its sister company TAPLINE, a large operation of over 70 people, aided the Saudi attempt to corrupt the local press by paying Lebanese journalists to write stories favourable to the royal family. The stories told phoney tales of generosity and public concern in which every school opening was the work of a prince and the money came from his personal pocket. To ARAMCO even Muhammad Twin-Evil was worthy of praise; it presented him as the democratic head of a family council. Moreover, there was a negative aspect to its influence on the mercenary Arab press, and during the early days of OPEC, ARAMCO's journalist-spies tried to get compromising pictures and information of members of the delegations of the various countries who worked to create an effective cartel. On one occasion in Beirut in 1960, members of the impecunious Egyptian delegation were given a lavish party by a Lebanese journalist whose sole aim was to get them to drink heavily and misbehave, a ridiculous response to the substantial challenge posed by Nasser.

When most of their blackmail schemes failed, ARAMCO tried old-fashioned bribery. In addition to bribing clerks and hotel chambermaids to get them copies of OPEC delegations' documents, it was another incident concerning former Oil Minister Abdallah Tariki which demonstrated the extent and depth of ARAMCO's determination to corrupt or undermine the opposition. Tariki moved to Beirut after he was fired by King Faisal in 1962. He capitalized on the city's free atmosphere and began writing articles which underlined the injustices of the Saudi oil concession agreement and other ARAMCO practices, including discrimination, extraction methods and lack of adherence to conservation practices. ARAMCO was determined to silence him and very much in character they thought they could bribe him. My journalist father, Abu Said of *Time* magazine, was a friend of Tariki and of one Joe Ellender, a senior official of ARAMCO's huge Government Relations Department. After a period of testing the water, Ellender asked my father to play intermediary with Tariki and see if he would accept $15 million in return for stopping his attacks on ARAMCO. Tariki, as my father had expected, turned down the bribe, which my father at least had never taken seriously. He went further and began sleeping in different places, just in case ARAMCO's frustration with his activities led them to consider other ways of stopping him. But why would ARAMCO offer him such a colossal bribe? What was it they were doing which deserved such a huge pay-off to a man they had already accused of being a communist, a man they called the Red Sheikh? Did Tariki know more about their misdeeds than I have been able to report? In likelihood, the answer is yes.

ARAMCO's approach reflected the attitude of the oil companies which owned it. Why did Mobil Oil conduct the most extensive business lobbying since the Second World War to promote the House of Saud and why did it oppose the airing of *Death of a Princess*? Why did the oil companies, according to the testimony of their executives in front of the House subcommittee investigating American multinational corporations, admit to paying $5 million to lobbyists? Why did they produce pamphlets, books, documentaries singing the praises of the House of Saud? Why are many American universities with departments of Near or Middle Eastern studies (such as Johns Hopkins University, the Aspen Institute, Duke University and the University of Southern California) receiving funds to re-examine history and in the process negate the purpose for their being? The answer is simple: ARAMCO equated the welfare of the House of Saud with the welfare of the Middle East. This becomes startlingly clear when one examines the closeness of the propaganda of the oil companies to the policies of the House of Saud.

In the 1950s, when the House of Saud was paying lip-service to the Palestinian problem, ARAMCO's propaganda effort addressed itself to advocating an even-handed policy between the Arabs and Israel. Later it switched direction and began promoting King Faisal's brand of Islam. While I am totally in favour of an even-handed American foreign policy on the Arab–Israeli problem, surrendering to the House of Saud and the oil companies all efforts to attain even-handedness produced a questionable approach which alienated many American people and gave the Palestinian problem a dubious Saudi face it did not deserve. The same companies which promoted Islam are now rewriting history and beginning to question the perils of adopting it. Overall, the practices of ARAMCO and the oil companies have represented an unwelcome influence on the Saudi Government and people, the Middle East and the Government and people of the USA. The only concern of the propagators of these practices was money and all else was subordinated to that, in ugly and unacceptable ways.

Until the mid 1960s, when Nasser's propaganda machine publicized it to incite the Saudi people against their rulers, the budget of the House of Saud was published and known to all. Except for periods under King Saud when it rose to over 30 per cent, most years it amounted to 15–17 per cent of the national budget. King Faisal changed all that and characteristically found ways to hide his family's colossal theft. Of the 15 people I asked the same question, not a single oil expert, journalist, former diplomat, think-tank member, Saudi merchant or opposition member was willing to discuss the process by which the budget of the House of Saud, the money paid to members of the royal family as salaries and 'benefits', is now determined. When the question was addressed to people who were speaking off the record they fidgeted and reminded me of the rules governing the interview, while the ones who were speaking on the record had a change of heart and asked that their innocent comments be kept off the record. Even with so many known misdeeds of members of the House of Saud staring us in the eye, talking about their direct theft of their country's oil wealth amounted to an uncomfortable, even criminal topic of conversation.

The facts, stitched together from previous published budgets, the brief comments of the interviewees, published records, analysis of the costs of running the royal court and comparison of published, official budget figures with calculations of the oil income based on the country's oil production, are much simpler. The House of Saud's annual budget fluctuates between $4 billion and $7 billion (excluding pay offs from regular non-oil trade and arms deals), most years still around 15 per cent of the national income. But it is no longer a budget – it is closer to a rake-off.

Initially Faisal made the family budget dependent on the level of oil income. He imposed a royal tax of so many cents per barrel of oil, which the family got regardless of the level of oil production.

But this system was discarded after a few years because the numbers and needs of the family were disproportionate to the oil income and it became difficult to balance the two. Now the family decides what its needs are and acts accordingly. The greater part of the budget, $3–5 billion, is paid to King Fahd from the oil income before it is recorded as national income. The Oil Minister subtracts money from the country's oil income and transfers it to the King's personal account and declares the rest as national income. Fahd allocates the money he receives between the various members of his family in an improvised manner. The amount of money transferred to Fahd's personal account depends on him; he tells the Oil Minister how much he needs and the minister obeys him. In addition, Petromin, the marketing arm of ARAMCO, which is now a Saudi Government-owned company, augments this rake-off in two ways.

Quantities of oil are *given* to certain members of the royal family as outright gifts and the recipients sell it on the open market and keep the proceeds. Greater quantities of oil are allocated to some of them to sell as commission agents, to market in accordance with formulas which produce huge profits for them. In the latter case, the royal beneficiaries remit money to Petromin after they subtract their commission, which is often arrived at arbitrarily. While they are always expected to pay back amounts considerably smaller than Petromin would get from selling the oil itself, they have been known to keep more than half the price in commissions. Overall, the commission level is highest when the demand for oil is high; even for commission agents the difference between official prices and spot prices is wider.

These acts of extortion (one tenth of what they receive would still make them the highest-paid royals in the world) may represent the major elements of a foggy picture. But they are not the only ones which lead to the distortion of the Saudi national income, and do not account for why what the country realizes from the sale of oil and the figure of the national budget are not compatible and why these figures change several times during any one year. There are always last-minute developments and decisions which are superimposed on the national budget and which are decided by the King alone and these have the effect of throwing the budget out of balance.

We have already seen that the King, reacting to outside and internal influences in a way aimed at creating a favourable image for himself and his family, sponsors tens of thousands of pilgrims from other countries to perform the Hajj in Mecca. This activity is increasing because Saudi Arabia is competing with Iran and militant Muslim countries and with attempts to win over the people of the Muslim republics of the former Soviet Union. Beyond that, the kingdom is always responding to crises in the Arab and Muslim worlds which affect and occasionally endanger the Saudi image as a pretender to Arab and Muslim leadership – for example, giving aid to the Muslims of Bosnia, paying Pakistan to influence Afghanistan's internal affairs or bribing Syria to continue with the Middle East peace process. In responding to unexpected external crises, King Fahd has been known to order the shipment of free oil to needy countries, on occasion to Bangladesh or Somalia when they promised to follow a Saudi policy line, and at other times he has discounted the price of oil to non-Muslim, pro-Saudi countries such as Greece and Spain. Whether it is an outright gift or discounted, the oil aid is conditional. It goes only to those who support Saudi Arabia and is not allocated on a humanitarian basis. The Sudanese get none and are allowed to starve to death because their government does not accept the Saudi interpretation of Islam.

Furthermore, in Saudi Arabia itself oil has been used to pay for costly projects without the value of the oil bartered showing in the national budget. This happens when the inclusion of these projects in the official budget reflects badly on the originally published cost figures, when there are huge cost overruns as a result of mismanagement of development schemes and when the project is supervised by an important prince who sees it as a monument to his ego (for example, the building of an Olympic-size sports city by Prince Faisal bin Fahd). Of course there are the much simpler cases of favourites of the King needing more 'pocket money'. Between 1991 and 1993 Saudi Arabia produced 200,000–300,000 barrels of oil per day to pay for a massive, questionable and unpopular project to build underground oil-storage facilities, and did something similar to pay for the purchase of unneeded oil tankers from South Korea, where members of the royal family were the commission agents, and for other grandiose but mostly uneconomic projects. The more controversial a project, the more likely it is to be paid for through the barter of oil without the figures showing in the budget, and this leads to confusion and distortion of published budget figures.

What is of most concern, however, is what happens often and on a large enough scale to underscore the House of Saud's attitude to its country's natural wealth: the marketing of oil by members of the family who believe they own it. The massive amounts of oil assigned to members of the family by Petromin are called 'princely allocations', and while the size of these allocations varies, it may well be over a million barrels a day. So, how do members of the family, princes and princesses, deal with their princely shares, who gets oil to sell, why, how much and how do they go about marketing it?

In the late 1970s and early 80s Muhammad Twin-Evil was the leading House of Saud oil seller on the international spot market. He demanded either 300,000 barrels of oil a day as a gift or to play commission agent, and his position as the family's elder statesman and tough guy meant that his demands were always obeyed. Petromin handles the marketing of Saudi oil not committed to the major oil companies, and it always placed Muhammad's requests at the top of its princely list. His use of coarse salesmen who were very like him meant that international oil traders often ignored them. Muhammad not only sold 'his share' on the open market, but when acting as a commission agent he decided his own commission and remitted the rest of the money to Petromin. Regardless of what Muhammad's primitive efforts produced, the management recorded the transactions without comment. (I myself turned down one of Muhammad's oil salesmen who came to me with a dirty piece of paper with his Highness's signature and stamp on it. Because the scribbles on the piece of paper were near-illiterate and I could not believe that someone so basic and unsophisticated would be entrusted with something so vital and substantial, I ignored him.) Muhammad's income from these transactions fluctuated, but it was in the region of $2–4 million a day. What he did with this income is anybody's guess, but his descendants are billionaires and most of his cronies became multimillionaires.

Princess Hia, a full sister of King Fahd, lacked Muhammad Twin-Evil's masculine clout, need or greed. But there was an occasion in the early 1980s when she was broke and Fahd did not have enough cash to meet her expenses. So he ordered Petromin to give her a million barrels of oil to tide her over and she sold it on the open market and pocketed the proceeds. Her transaction showed on the official Petromin files; to King Fahd the needs of a spendthrift sister who lives behind the veil were nothing to hide. In trying to determine why Hia needed $30 million, I discovered that she buys clothes from a Lebanese family who get them in Paris and Milan and sell them to her at seven to ten times the original price. She usually buys 50 dresses at a time to give them away as presents.

Princess Moudi bin Abdel Aziz, another full sister of King Fahd, was a real spender and her needs were even greater than her sister's. According to Petromin documents, she got two lots of oil to sell: one consignment of a million barrels and another of half a million. Her ineptness at realizing an easy profit from a floating fortune showed when she entrusted a Lebanese by the name of Mansour Shafique Dhahdoub with the sale of the oil. Rumour has it that he pocketed more than his generous share and this led to trouble and a court case. It is difficult to tell why a woman who lives in seclusion needed whatever money resulted from the sale of all this oil. Perhaps it is because Princess Moudi never travels without an entourage of 20 people who stay with her in the world's most expensive hotels.

Not all members of the House of Saud behave as simply as Prince Muhammad Twin-Evil or Princesses Hia and Moudi, for some are driven by greed to maximize their return in very shady ways. Prince Muhammad bin Fahd, the King's son, governor of the eastern province of the country and his father's candidate to succeed him, was involved in one particular deal which epitomized greed. In May 1981, Muhammad bin Fahd, one of his family's big billionaires, obtained his father's approval and claimed a share of Petromin oil on the pretext of selling it to a Japanese company by the name of Petromonde. On the surface, this looked like a straightforward commission transaction similar to what members of the House of Saud do every day and which was meant to produce a huge, one-off profit – like those that Muhammad got from many of the commercial deals in which he had been involved. In reality, the purchaser did not exist and a close investigation by the *Wall Street Journal* revealed that Petromonde was part of Al Bilad, an international corporation owned by none other than Prince Muhammad himself. His Highness was not content with the commission; he also wanted to control the resale of the oil to make more money, and it was estimated that his income from the deal amounted to $11 million a month for over a year.

Sometimes princely allocations of oil and paying for projects through selling it on the open market without including the receipts in the national budget come together. In the following example, it was not a prince who marketed the oil but a collection of well-placed people who got royal approval to claim part of the Petromin share. They included the son of former Oil

Minister Yamani and the Director General of Petromin, Abdel Hadi Taher.

In 1983 Petromin contracted with a company called Petrolia to build the Rhagib refinery and it was agreed that it would pay for most of the multi-billion-dollar contract by selling oil – on the face of it an old-fashioned barter deal. In this convoluted transaction, it was King Fahd's friend John Latsis, the Greek shipping magnate and oil dealer, who controlled Petrolia, and the price of oil used to barter was to be determined on a 'net back' basis (the price of refined oil minus the costs of transporting it, refining it and marketing it). But the oil was not shipped directly to Petrolia and instead was sold on the open market and the money went to the group of influential Saudis who were entrusted with paying Petrolia after claiming a commission. I have seen documents published by *Sourakia* magazine which show that Fadh personally approved the deal and the unnecessary step of including the Saudi group. The number of people involved and the complicated nature of the deal led to quarrels and legal suits in Paris, Switzerland and elsewhere. For a while, Continental Group Holdings, the company which actually sold the oil on behalf of the Saudi middlemen, was left without its share of over $13 million dollars. Continental sued and was eventually paid; the fear of a scandal led to an out-of-court settlement. Everybody involved got their share. It is an impossible deal to follow, but estimates place the share of all the participants at 30 per cent of the total value of the oil bartered.

Another deal involving Abdel Hadi Taher took place in 1979, when he tried to sell oil to the Italian state-owned company ENI. Using Europe-based intermediaries, Taher offered ENI 100,000 barrels a day for 90 days. The price was $19 a barrel, nearly half of what oil was fetching on the spot market. The deal was signed in Riyadh in the name of a Panamian company, Sophilau Inc. The oil was never delivered. The Italian press got hold of the story and the agreement fell apart because it was difficult for Taher to justify selling oil at such a low price. Meanwhile Taher and his group had been paid $17 million which, because of Saudi Government protection, ENI had no way of recovering. In Saudi Arabia there were no repercussions, for Taher was only doing what members of the House of Saud had been doing on a regular basis and he had received the necessary royal approval for the transaction.

Perhaps the two most dramatic and startling cases of the use of Saudi oil for personal gain involved Minister of Defence Prince Sultan and former Chief of Intelligence and King Faisal's brother-in-law Kamal Adham. The Sultan case was an oil barter deal involving the purchase of 10 Boeing 747s for Saudia Airlines. The size of the deal is enough to make it unique: it called for the sale on the open market of 34.5 million barrels of Saudi oil. But there was more to the deal than its size: it represented a gross manipulation of the source of the country's wealth and the subordination of its oil policy and commitments to OPEC to the whims of an individual prince.

Prince Sultan's full title is Minister of Defence and Civil Aviation and as such he controls the policies and the purchases of Saudia Airlines, the country's flag carrier and the only airline permitted to service its extensive internal routes. In 1984 Saudia, without the usual preliminaries of considering what aircraft it needed, decided to double its fleet of Boeing 747s, from 10 to 20. Nobody but Sultan knows what was behind the decision. Airline experts suggested that the aircraft were not needed, Saudia's load factor reflected the decline in business activity in the country which resulted from the decrease in oil prices and the speedy delivery schedule added to the contradiction and the mystery.

Sultan proceeded to implement the purchase with suspicious haste, and there is no doubt that the whole deal took place against a background of unsuccessful business ventures by the Prince. It has been suggested that he was the leading investor in Adnan Khashoggi's failed Salt Lake City development scheme and that other property investments in France had lost him more money.

The decision to buy the Boeing 747s was unanticipated and there was no allocation for them in the country's oil-production schedule or published budget. So Sultan decided to barter oil through a circuitous route, to pay Boeing and the engine-maker Rolls-Royce.

The two companies had no interest in the mechanics of the deal or how Sultan was manipulating it – just in receiving the agreed price for their products.

Enter Yamani. The Saudi Oil Minister had just reached an agreement with OPEC specifying the Saudi level of oil production and the ministry's income was based on this production level and already allocated. In other words, the 34.5 million barrels Sultan needed would exceed the agreed OPEC production level for Saudi Arabia. Yamani objected to the Boeing deal because a Saudi violation of the quota system would open the floodgates for other OPEC members to do the same. The Oil Minister's reputation was at stake, but his appeals to Sultan went unheeded, as did his complaints to King Fahd. The deal went through, the market was flooded with extra oil and the price of oil tumbled. Other countries followed suit and pushed the price of oil lower. The personal needs of His Highness had undermined the pricing structure of oil throughout the whole world.

The Kamal Adham deal was also startling. Until 1978 Adham headed the dreaded internal security apparatus and his brother-in-law, King Faisal, was a firm believer in its value and Adham's personal contribution. In 1961 Saudi Arabia awarded the concession for oil in the Neutral Zone between Saudi Arabia and Kuwait to a Japanese consortium who proceeded to call themselves the Arabian Oil Company. Adham, whom Faisal had used as an emissary in deals he was loath to entrust to outsiders, represented Saudi Arabia in the negotiations with the Japanese group and Faisal thought it right to reward him for his efforts.

Faisal gave Adham an incredible 2 per cent share of the price of all the oil raised by the new company. Nobody knew the eventual value of the royal gift, but the then Oil Minister, Abdallah Tariki, thought it would be in the billions of dollars. Tariki objected and made known his disapproval in a meeting of the council of ministers. A few months later, Faisal dismissed Tariki. Adham continued to get his 2 per cent for over 25 years, until the Japanese tired of Saudi ways and ceded the concession back to the Saudis.

Adham was also involved in the BCCI scandal. He settled the resulting claims on him by the United States banking regulatory authorities by paying back $115 million in one go. He could well afford it.

Having looked at enough examples of how the Saudi royals abuse their country's wealth through the direct control and sale of oil to meet their expenses or to satisfy their greed, it is only fair to state that it is the one activity in which Crown Prince Abdallah and Foreign Minister Saud Al Faisal have never indulged and the one which has met with considerable resistance from all the people who have held the oil portfolio. Abdallah Tariki, the country's first Oil Minister, made a big issue of it with King Faisal; his stand against the Boeing deal was Yamani's moment of honour and the present incumbent, Hisham Nazer, is totally opposed it it. Perhaps this is because the Saudi people feel strongly about their oil and the oil ministers know this. I remember a Saudi taxi driver telling me: 'It's not their oil, it's my oil, my oil, and I don't get a single barrel.'

The taxi driver's complaint reflects the feeling of the vast majority of Saudis. The early 1980s was the period when the price of oil was at its peak and when members of the House of Saud overindulged in selling oil on the spot market. Because the differential between the official price and the posted one was at its greatest, they stole many billions of dollars which should have gone into the treasury. By 1984 the price of oil had collapsed and with it the income of Saudi Arabia. With a lower oil income to support it, the Saudi riyal was devalued in small steps in 1984 and 1985. This devaluation undoubtedly affected our taxi driver and the millions of disadvantaged Saudis. Would the devaluation have been necessary if the money pocketed by members of the family had gone into the national coffers? It is difficult to tell, but a repeat performance may well be on the way. Now, in late 1993, King Fahd owes billions of dollars to Saudi banks – rumour has it that he owes $1.5 billion to the National Commercial Bank alone. Other members of his family owe more in total. Will they claim millions of barrels of oil to repay their debts and produce a situation that will lead to another devaluation? It is entirely possible.

11

Too Late?

Like a rotting carcass, the House of Saud is beginning to decompose. This reality is ignored by its members and, except for perfunctory and infrequent mentions of their human rights record, by their friends. As usual, the people who are the source of decay are the last to admit their inability to halt it. In the case of the House of Saud's Western friends, the creeping awareness that a crisis is approaching is balanced by a selfish desire by those governments not to identify or assume responsibility for it.

The attitudes of the House of Saud and their Western supporters aside – for the first time ever, the Saudi Government's failures, internal, regional and international, have converged to undermine it. Most significantly and dangerously, it is the irreversible internal pressures – the Saudi people's willingness to gather under an Islamic banner and their demands for substantial change in the way they are governed – which are almost out of control.

Even with its religious police acting independently and enforcing Islamic tenets harshly and indiscriminately, the House of Saud is failing to respond to the challenge of Islam expressed by recent emergence of powerful new Islamic groups such as the Committee for The Defence of The Legitimate Rights (of the Saudi people), The Advice and Reformation Committee and many militant organizations, all of which appear to command considerable popular support. And the West can provide no protection against this drift.

Nothing is happening or is being planned to stop the process of deterioration in the internal situation of the country, nothing that would remotely alter or delay its progress towards Muslim dominance. On balance, any unexpected developments, such as the death of the seriously ailing King Fahd or the collapse of one of the many major banks with doubtful balance sheets, are likely to expedite the already advanced process of decay.

There is no better way to assess the prospects for the House of Saud than to look into the not-too-distant future. The year 1997 will do; it is not too far ahead and the elements which will make it a year of crisis are already in place. By 1997 the economic and financial problems will be much worse, even if we accept the understated official figures. By then the current official Saudi debt of over $60 billion will exceed $100 billion and the country will face a serious financial crisis which will affect all aspects of everyday life. For decades, money has served to neutralize the Saudi people's anger against the House of Saud and their wish for greater freedom. The imminent financial crisis will not affect the royal family; most members of the House of Saud have hoarded huge sums of money and have demonstrated an insensitive desire to continue to live at a lavish level regardless of the effect on their people. However, to do so will simplify the social and political confrontation which already exists, and soon it will be the House of Saud versus the rest of the Saudis except for a small number of wealthy merchants. It is a classic confrontation between the haves and the have-nots. The gap between the two is already wider than anywhere else in the world.

Recent official budget figures for 1993 show a deficit of $9 billion, but there is clear evidence that the real deficit is considerably greater than the government figure. Once again the government failed to include borrowing by publicly owned companies such as ARAMCO, SABIC (Saudi Arab Basic Industries) and the electricity and telephone companies. In addition, the government failed to fund the social security system and delayed paying for construction projects. The real deficit for 1993 alone is $15–20 billion, somewhere between 30 and 40 per cent of total government income. According to officers of the International Monetary Fund who spoke on a non-attributive basis early in 1993, this is 'dangerously non-sustainable'.

At the time of writing, the prospects for 1994 are for another serious deficit. Despite a drastic 20 per cent reduction in the official budget aimed at assuaging IMF protests and objections, the Saudi Government appears unable to implement a real austerity programme and continues its game of 'creative' accounting. 1995 and 1996 promise more of the same.

As noted, by 1997 the country's debt will be well over $100 billion, more than two years' worth of its present oil income of $45–50 billion. The country's ability to borrow on the international market or locally, already in doubt, will become more difficult or disappear completely. This has been confirmed by the rescheduling of over $9 billion in foreign military sales agreed with the USA in January 1994. But the rising cost of servicing the growing debt and an annual increase of population of over 4 per cent will offset any short-term rescheduling measures and future attempts at reducing the budget.

Cuts in the budgets of all departments except defence and the royal household cannot go deeper without serious political consequences. But defence commitments, the exceptionally high salaries of military personnel, signed military contracts and the greed of commission agents preclude a meaningful reduction where it is most needed. And the family's ways are entrenched and its members' needs, however unjustified, are increasing. The continuing effects of curtailing all areas of expenditure except these two will add to the problems of Saudi business and lead to a further lowering of the standard of living – already down over 50 per cent from its 1982 high. The government will be crippled and the pervasive anti–House of Saud feeling will lead to open defiance in the souk and the street. Meanwhile, the West will be unable to help. The people of America and Europe are not prepared to pay to save a royal family which squanders its country's wealth – not when the House of Saud's wasteful habits are legend. The people of the West are already reluctant to help the truly needy in nations such as Russia and Egypt, and concealing from them the reality of the Saudi crisis, much as the unpopularity of the Shah of Iran was concealed, only makes matters worse.

By 1997 Saudi Arabia's defence expenditure, according to the Washington Institute somewhere between 42 and 96 per cent of its oil income during any of the past ten years, will become an unsustainable burden. The country has several multi-billion-dollar contracts with the United States, Britain, France, Canada and Brazil (F-15 and Tornado aircraft worth $15 billion, plus helicopters, tanks and armoured personnel carriers, warships, torpedo boats and radar systems) and there are dozens of smaller defence contracts. Even without new commitments – and amazingly negotiations with both the USA and UK to buy more hardware are in progress – the money needed to meet major contracts amounts to $29-33 billion. Along with contracts for essential everyday hardware and the inflated salaries of members of the armed forces, the cost of these major contracts will maintain the defence budget at near, or perhaps over, the present unaffordable level. And it is axiomatic that military salaries cannot be reduced during a time of crisis and internal threats to the regime.

The budget of the royal family can be reduced, but the House of Saud shows no signs of doing it or understanding the need for it, and in any case it isn't as easy as it appears. The King shows no signs of understanding what is happening, the members of the family are increasing, and more and more members of the House of Saud are coming of age and want to join the billionaire league. In addition, some of them, including the King, have incurred huge debts which must be repaid to avoid the collapse of the local banking structure, already under considerable stress because of the limited amount of funds the local banks have in the international interbank system. King Fahd reportedly owes a local bank $1.5 billion and his relatives owe further billions to other local banks. To satisfy their rapid growth in number, their greed and their debts, the House of Saud will continue to pay its members unrealistically large salaries and interfere in commerce.

Beyond defence and the royal family, the third area of potential budget reduction is that of huge government subsidies of food; petrol, telephone and electricity systems; and other public services. But the political conditions in the country render any attempt in this area dangerous and most unlikely. In fact, precedent is against such a move. There was an unsuccessful attempt to reduce these subsidies in 1992, but the resulting outcry forced King Fahd to rescind his decision before it was applied and instead he had to increase some of the subsidies to placate the people. Maintaining the present policy and current prices without adjusting them to reflect inflation means subsidies will claim a greater part of the 1995 budget than of the present one.

A fourth area where cuts could be made, aid to friendly Arab neighbours such as Syria, Lebanon and Egypt, would – if carried to an extreme – considerably endanger the governments of these countries and have adverse effects on the stability of Saudi Arabia itself. These governments, threatened by internal Islamic movements, are needed by Saudi Arabia to protect itself against Iran and the growing Islamic militancy in the Sudan and other neighbouring countries. But even if Saudi Arabia were to opt for total cutoff of aid to Arab countries, the resulting $3 billion saving would not be enough to change its overall financial situation. Moreover, the financial claims on Saudi Arabia to maintain its Arab and Muslim positions are increasing. The House of Saud's policy of trying to counter the increasing radicalization of Islam will create a need for it to lend financial assistance to new countries, such as Bosnia and the former Muslim republics of the USSR.

If substantial budget cuts are not possible, the seemingly available remedy would be to raise money through privatising public companies. This has been looked into and discounted; most public companies, including the flag carrier Saudia, are too inefficient to be acceptable to an already suspicious public. As we have seen, the drastic steps needed to bring these companies to a level of acceptability to investors are unpopular in nature, to the extent of overweighing the expected benefits.

This leaves the most obvious of all remedies, an increase in the production or the price of oil. Doing either is more complicated than it sounds. Saudi Arabia is already producing over eight million barrels of oil a day. An increase in production is not a viable solution except in tight coordination with the rest of OPEC because a mere increase in volume would be offset by an equal or greater decline in price. A large increase in the price of oil is possible through adhering to the pre-set OPEC price, which the other producers would welcome, but this would undermine the House of Saud's all-important relationship with America, the only thing it has going for it. The effects of a small, 'tolerable' increase in the price of oil would be marginal and, as a remedy, inadequate. Without taking into consideration the inevitability of Iraq's re-emergence as an oil producer – with or without Saddam Hussein – manipulating oil production and prices is not an option. Indeed there are signs that whatever the increase in the demand for oil, it is likely to be met by the conversion to gas. Along with the re-emergence of Iraq as an oil supplier, the possibility of OPEC over-production or of Russia and some of the former Soviet republics modernizing their facilities and increasing their output, though remote, is real.

The financial crisis I am talking about exists today, in miniature, and it has been reported widely in America and confirmed by Secretary of Treasury Bentsen. It will reach its climax in 1997; the worsening conditions in the country will lead to an increase in the number of sit-down and other protests which have already taken place and will alter their nature and lead to violent confrontations. The Islamic fundamentalist movement is growing stronger by the day, already prompting mass arrests of clerics and academics, hardly a long-term solution. The House of Saud is divided; there are too many contenders for the throne and they are placing their personal ambitions above the family's survival. Support from the loyal, Government-sponsored religious leaders has evaporated and their groups are moving towards militancy and making their own claims (it was these groups which forced Saudi Arabia to cancel its participation in the UN-sponsored conference on population in Cairo). The pro-Western new class is restive. Rising expectations among Saudis continue to outstrip the royal family's ability or wish to meet them, and unemployment among recent college graduates is over 25 per cent. These situations which, except for feuds within the family, reflect an intrinsic Saudi objection to absolutism and the resulting abuse, have already been exacerbated by a serious decline in the standard of living. According to the World Bank, the per capita income in Saudi Arabia declined from $14,300 in 1982 to $7,000 in 1993 and even lower in 1994. Elasticity in this area – how much more the people are willing to tolerate – is near its limit. There is no doubt that demands for political reform will be reinforced by the inevitable further decline in the standard of living. The people are already blaming the House of Saud for frittering away the country's reserves, which dwindled from $140 billion in 1982 to a $60 billion debt a decade later, and for producing this unhappy state of affairs.

In the Arab sphere, even with the GCC, the coming three years are likely to see a worsening of Arab-Saudi relations. Other GCC members' attempts to respond to their peoples' demands for greater participation in their countries' affairs and have already produced the usual stupid Saudi objections to such things as the relatively liberal charters of their consultative councils. As a result, the GCC's effectiveness has been undermined and two members, Qatar and Oman, behave as if they were in open rebellion against Saudi dominance. Syria and Egypt are bowing to internal pressures and distancing themselves from Saudi Arabia and its totally pro-Western policies. Saudi Arabia is unable to provide enough economic aid to keep Syria and Egypt in line, and they worry about its refusal to act on conditions within its territory and around it. Saudi relations with Iraq, Jordan, the PLO, the Yemen, Libya and the Sudan are already bad and those with Algeria and Tunisia are lukewarm. There is little chance of improvement in Saudi-Arab relations because that would require huge amounts of money and a change in direction; the House of Saud cannot offer more money and will not change its direction. The isolation of Saudi Arabia from the rest of the Arab nations will add to the unhappiness of its people.

The problem doesn't stop there. Saudi Arabia is fighting a rearguard action in its formerly safe redoubt, the Muslim world. The preemption of its brand of conservative pro-Western and anti-communist Islam by militant Islamic movements has turned into an immediate challenge. In particular, the Bosnian situation is making life difficult for the House of Saud: in the eyes of the average Saudi and Muslim, the Western failure to protect Bosnia's Muslims is an unfriendly act directed against all Muslims. In addition, Iran, the Sudan and militant Islamic movements in Algeria, Egypt, Tunisia, Jordan, Pakistan, Afghanistan, Malaysia and other places are opposed to the House of Saud and are gaining strength. Their appeals to the people of Saudi Arabia are meeting with greater acceptance.

Time is against the House of Saud, and it has few supporters except in the West. It is true that the West does not respond to a crisis until it is too late, and in this case, the Clinton and other administrations are reluctant to go public with their concerns and shoulder the blame for something that has been in the making for decades. Nevertheless, attributing Western support of the House of Saud exclusively to the oversight, cynicism or foolishness of Western leaders is too facile. Even Western leaders who know little about world affairs, Reagan and Clinton come to mind, have knowledgeable advisers on whose empirical judgement they rely. The consistency of Western support regardless of who is at the helm suggests that the reasons for it are beyond individual whims and shortcomings.

In the past, the Western position consisted of overlooking the House of Saud's crimes against its own people and neglecting or encouraging its attempts to weaken the Arab and Muslim worlds. Support for the House of Saud was seen as producing results which outweighed the results of withholding support. This Western position must be re-examined, not only in terms of the overwhelming and increasing human misery it causes but also by assessing it against the failure of the House of Saud's internal, Arab and Muslim policies. The overwhelming ethical considerations aside, now there are equally overwhelming practical reasons for the West to change direction.

We should examine, however, the arguments behind the Western attitude. Oil, and what might happen to it were the House of Saud to fall, underlies the argument for the West's continued support of the House of Saud. The present dependence of the West on Saudi oil – it accounts for 25 per cent of US oil imports – would have surprised even Harold Ickes, the man who first foresaw it. Not only does the House of Saud guarantee the flow of huge quantities of oil at a reasonable price, but Saudi Arabia acts as an OPEC policeman, using its colossal oil reserves and its ability to produce so much oil so cheaply to force other producers into line.

As proven by Iran's militant Islamic government, however, there is no substitute for selling oil to the industrialized world. A change in the Saudi Government therefore, even to an Islamic revolutionary one, would not result in a complete cut-off of oil. What needs to be considered is the temporarily disruptive effect a take-over of the Government of Saudi Arabia would produce and what would follow in terms of oil prices. The odds are definitely against a take-over in Saudi Arabia producing a government as accommodating as the present one, and any assumption of power by Islamic forces or a combination of forces more accommodating to Islamist thinking will produce adverse effects on prices. Moreover, the use of the oil weapon to influence the policies of the Western world would in all probability ensue. An Islamic regime or one responsive to Islamic movements would not need Western support to survive. This is why the West prefers a pliant House of Saud.

In opting to support the House of Saud, Western leaders also take into consideration how a new government might affect the stability and unity of Saudi Arabia. Some accept that the House of Saud is to blame for following policies which perpetuated regional divisions within the country but believe its members to be committed to national unity and able to assert a functional if brutal authority. By contrast, there is fear that a new leader or ideology might cause enough turmoil to lead to a splintering of the tribal and religiously divided country into troublesome smaller states.

A third consideration is what the demise of the House of Saud would do to regional stability. Western leaders view the House of Saud as a moderating influence on the whole Middle East. They equate the potential disappearance of the House of Saud with regional instability and the spread of anti-Western radical movements. Furthermore, there is awareness that no one would be able to assume Saudi Arabia's moderating role.

Fourthly, though its Muslim policies have been discredited and overtaken by independent Islamic movements (including many radical ones), the House of Saud is seen as playing within Islam a role similar to its regional Arab one. Western leaders believe that a radical Islamic regime in Saudi Arabia could use Mecca and

Medina to provide leadership the House of Saud failed to assume, with untold consequences.

Of course, the Palestinian problem, and Jerusalem in particular, and an out-of-date perception of what the absence of the House of Saud would do to reinvigorate the Arab will to do battle with Israel are major factors. The United States still believes other Arab countries would find it difficult to support any peaceful solution to the Palestinian problem or normalization of relations with Israel opposed by Saudi Arabia. In this case, they see Saudi Arabia as a swing decision-maker.

The above considerations were relevant to the West's support for the House of Saud at one time, but are they still? The simple answer is that they used to be relevant in terms of power policies but they stopped being so in 1992–3. Continuing to support the House of Saud is becoming more and more counterproductive. Time has run out on all the reasons for such support. The benefits of continuing to ignore the rights of the Saudi people and of sub-ordinating the nation's oil policy to the House of Saud's wish to stay in power are cancelled by the monumental internal pressures against its members' abusive ways and low oil prices. The House of Saud will have to respond to these pressures or be toppled. Saudi Arabia's ability to influence Arab and Muslim countries is at or near its end. The House of Saud is no longer able to provide the Arab and Muslim leadership role which guaranteed Western support in the past. Saudi Arabia's involvement and influence on the Palestinian problem is marginal.

The Saudi people are determined to participate in the running of their country, to break the royal monopoly on power, stop the waste of the country's wealth, reform the judiciary and determine foreign and other policies. They do not want their oil used to bribe the West. They want an ordinary consumer-supplier rela-tionship unencumbered by the personal interests of unpopular rulers. There is no Saudi taxi driver, teacher, religious leader, mer-chant, student or anybody else who sees the present oil policies as anything except an expression of the House of Saud's selfishness and detrimental to ordinary Saudis' welfare. The people see proper management of the country's oil resources as the way to their salvation, and the rising internal pressures on the House of Saud to change its oil policies have reached the point of no return. Either it changes them or it will face a popular uprising. The West's belief that it can keep the House of Saud in absolute power is wishful thinking. The West cannot occupy Saudi Arabia. It is not feasible and the problems it would create are greater than the ones it would solve.

The growing financial crisis will unite the people, focus their attention on these policies and create a wish to punish the leaders responsible for them. The role of the House of Saud as a unifier of the country, one of the few credits it can claim, is not enough to guarantee the loyalty of the people, and in any case many Saudis see the royal family as performing the opposite role, as a divider of the country. They see the separatist movements as protest movements against the House of Saud which would disappear with its demise. There is no way for the West to deny the legitimacy of the calls for change by the Saudi people.

The House of Saud's ability to influence Arab and Muslim policies is already a myth. The only influence it has left is with a small number of countries and this is vanishing along with the ability to afford the price of buying their loyalty. Moreover, the Saudi dependence on unpopular leaders – as demonstrated by its recent telling failure to divide the Yemen through bribing the South Yemeni leadership – has its limits. There is a lack of responsiveness to Saudi ways because the countries involved are finding it harder to resist the demands of their own people to separate themselves from the policies of the House of Saud, and its behaviour. The same is true of the Muslim world. Within a short time, unless there is a change, Islamic movements in the Arab and Muslim worlds will be in a position to help overthrow the Saudi monarchy.

The effect the overthrow of the House of Saud might have on the Palestinian problem is exaggerated. Lack of funds means it exercises little influence on the situation now, and the Palestinians themselves have accepted the principle of a reasonable, peaceful solution to the problem. Rather than worry about what might happen, the West would do better to push harder for a resolution of the details of this problem with the direct participants with the aim of eliminating it as a source of Arab-Western and Muslim-Western friction.

There are now practical reasons for Western leaders to reconcile their belief in human rights with their realpolitik interests. Continuing with present Western policies is leading to disaster. Except for John Kennedy, no Western leader has ever seen the inherent long-term damage that depending on the House of Saud causes to Western interests. Only Kennedy tried to guide the House of Saud toward more sensible policies which would guarantee its survival and make it a suitable partner and an acceptable deputy sheriff guarding Western interests. It is because the blind support provided by the West since Kennedy has backfired and been abused that the reasons for it are no longer valid. In other words, the reasons for supporting the House of Saud have destroyed themselves. Now the danger is not adopting new policies.

Because it is almost too late, the West needs to take drastic, immediate action – nothing less than a total reversal of policy. This is the only hope of stopping the assumption of power in Saudi Arabia by a militant Islamic regime that, like Khomeini's Iran, would want to punish the West for its past mistakes. And while the results of the West attempting to distance itself from, and force changes upon, the House of Saud are both far from guaranteed politically and likely to produce temporary economic discomfort, the alternatives make the gamble worth taking. Trying to change the House of Saud leaves the West with options that include building bridges and encouraging the country's moderate Islamic movements at the expense of the militancy of the others. There are major Islamic elements which advocate dialogue with the West and discoursing and finding common ground with them is preferable to the wholesale demonization of Islamic movements. The present inaction helps the militants and encourages the House of Saud to maintain its repressive policies.

Steps must be taken – in short, forced on the House of Saud – to bring the present financial chaos under control. These steps must include introducing controls on the most obvious ways the country's wealth is being abused (the colossally wasteful habits of the royal family and the Ministry of Defence) and allowing Saudi Arabia to increase its oil prices. Reducing the level of armament procurement and a higher price for oil would affect the Western economies in the short term, but they are needed to appease the Saudi people. The money realized for Saudi Arabia from these moves must be rechannelled into projects aimed at improving education and health care, seeking alternative sources of water and maintaining the infrastructure of the country.

The West must force King Fahd to form an independent consultative council or another para-parliamentary body that would have real legislative powers. This would replace the present one, which reflects his will and pays little attention to the grievances and desires of the people. Religious discrimination against the Shias must cease. The monopoly of political power by members of the royal family must cease and so must their

313

Government-supported involvement in trade. Above all, all Islamic fundamentalist movements must be dealt with as a political expression of anger rather than a collection of unreasonable fanatics whom the House of Saud and the West want to eliminate.

The process of succession must be organized and subordinated to the pressing needs for reform. The two princes in line to succeed Fahd, Abdallah and Sultan, are unfit for kingship, too old (in their 70s) to carry out the needed reform and should be forced to forgo their positions. And while the succession process after that is unclear, with many princes running for king, this potentially destabilizing situation should be manipulated. A 'Mr Clean' from within the ranks of the family, perhaps the relatively young Foreign Minister Saud Al Faisal, should be elevated to crown prince, and his ways, rather than Fahd's or the older generations', should prevail. After skipping to a representative of a new generation, the unwieldiness of the succession process must give way to a system which values talent above all other considerations.

Enforcing these measures is a tall order. Above all, it calls for massive interference in Saudi internal affairs. But this is not as novel as it sounds: the West already tells Saddam Hussein how to behave towards his Shias and Kurds and it tells Egypt and other countries how to manage their financial affairs. In addition, such interference is totally manageable, for the House of Saud cannot do without Western support nor can it resist by turning to other powers for help. Furthermore, it cannot punish the West by withholding its oil because that would hasten the financial crisis and expedite the royal family's demise. Last but not least, taking a chance with a corrective programme is a better long-term defence of the supply of oil than the present policy of securing it through a regime which threatens to self-destruct and thus engenders the prospect of having to fight the Arab and Muslim worlds for oil.

Even the implementation of some, rather than all, of these measures would improve conditions within Saudi Arabia. It would measurably enhance the image of the West with the Saudis, Arabs and Muslims and intercept the march towards an unnecessary confrontation with Islamic fundamentalism everywhere. And should any move to force reform open the floodgates and bring about the fall of the House of Saud, then the West would still be in a better position for having tried, and would find it easier to live with its replacement. If nothing is done there will be a revolution; if not in 1997, soon after. Without interception, the coming breakdown in the country's financial structure is beyond the West's ability to contain. Even if the breakdown were possible to contain, to do so without reforming what led to it would be another empty, temporary measure which would ignore the ordinary Saudi's pressing desire to reclaim his rights and dignity.

Bibliography

Books

The Holy Koran

Abdalah, King of Jordan. *Memoirs*
Abdallah, Anwar. *Petroleum and Manners* (Arabic)
Abdel Hai, Tewfik. *Death of a Princess* (Arabic)
Abdel Rahman, Awatef. *Studies in the Modern Press of the Arab World* (Arabic)
Abdel Rahman, Faiz. 'Scandals of the Oil Kings' (Arabic)
Aburish, Saïd K. *Payoff: Wheeling and Dealing in the Arab World*
Acheson, Dean. *Present at the Creation*
Adams and Franz. *A Full Service Bank: The Story of BCCI*
Al Challabi, Fadhil. *OPEC and the International Oil Industry*
Al Hajri, Yusuf. *Is Saudi Arabia Swallowing Yemen?*
Al Jamil, Rassim. *Communications in the Arab World* (Arabic)
Alireza, Marianne. *At the Drop of a Veil*
Al Sheikh, Tewfik. *Petroleum And Politics in Saudi Arabia* (Arabic)
Amer, Abdel Latif. *The Islamic Movement in the Arabian Peninsula* (Arabic)
Antonius, George. *The Arab Awakening*
H. C. Armstrong. *Lord of Arabia*
Badeau, John S. *The American Approach to the Middle East*
Badeeb, Said. *The Saudi–Egyptian Conflict in the Yemen*
Bazzaz, Sa'ad. *The Gulf War and the One After* (Arabic)
Bell, Gertrude. *Letters*
Blandford, Linda. *The Oil Sheikhs*
Cooke, Hedley. *Challenge and Response in the Middle East*
Cooley, John. *Payback: America's Long War in The Middle East*
Copeland, Miles. *The Game of Nations*
——*The Real Spy World*
Diah, Jean. *The Qwakibi Press* (Arabic)
Dickson, H. R. P. *The Arab of the Desert*
Eddy, William. *The Stories of Juha*
——*The Oil People*
Emerson, Steven. *The American House of Saud*

316

BIBLIOGRAPHY

Farah and Karudah. *Political Socialization in the Arab States*
Field, Michael. *US $100-Million a Day*
Friedman, Thomas. *From Beirut to Jerusalem*
Gahtani, Fahd. *Yemen and the House of Saud* (Arabic)
——*Struggle of the Branches* (Arabic)
——*Comments on Saudi Arabia* (Arabic)
——*The Juhyman Earthquake in Mecca* (Arabic)
Galeano, Eduardo. *The Veins of Latin America*
Gaury de, Gerald. *Faisal*
Ghazi, Abdel Aziz. *Saudi Armaments: The Illusion of Security and the Squandering of Wealth* (Arabic)
Glubb, Sir John Baggot. *Soldier with the Arabs*
——*Britain and the Arabs*
Goldberg, Jacob. *The Foreign Policy of Saudi Arabia, 1902–1918*
Haikal, Mohammad. *The Cairo Documents*
Hiro, Dillip. *Islamic Fundamentalism*
——*Inside the Middle East*
Hirst, David. *The Gun and the Olive Branch*
Hitti, Phillip. *The History of the Arabs*
Holden, David. *Farewell to Arabia*
——and Richard Johns. *The House of Saud*
Hollingworth, Claire. *The Arabs and the West*
Hook, Sidney. *The Hero in History*
Hopwood, Derek. *The Arabian Peninsula*
Horowitz, H. C. *The Struggle for Palestine*
Howarth, David. *The Desert King*
Huds, Michael C. *Arab Politics and the Search for Legitimacy*
Hurwitz, J. C. *Oil, the Arab–Israeli Dispute and the Industrial World*
Kerr, Malcolm. *The Arab Cold War: Gamal Abdel Nasser and his Rivals, 1958–1970*
Kessler, Ronald. *The Rise and Fall of the World's Richest Man*
Khadouri, Majid. *Contemporary Arabs: The Role of Leaders in Politics*
Kissinger, Henry. *The White House Years*
Lacey, Robert. *The Kingdom*
Lacqueur, Walter. *The Soviet Union and the Middle East*
——*The Struggle for the Middle East*
Leitenbergh, Milton (ed.). *The Power Intervention in the Middle East*
Levins, Hoag. *Arab Reach*
Long, David S. *The US and Saudi Arabia, Ambivalent Allies*
Mackey, Sandra. *The Saudis*
Makki, Alia. *A Woman's Diary in Saudi Prison* (Arabic)
Mallah, Rajai and Dorothea. *Saudi Arabia*
Mantel, Hilary. *8 Months on Gaza Street*
Maul, Hans and Otto Pick (eds.). *The Gulf War*

Miller, Aaron D. *Search for Security: Saudi Arabian Oil and US Foreign Policy*

Moysten, Trevor. *Iran, Iraq and the Arabian Peninsula*

Munif, Abdel Rahman. *Cities of Salt* (Arabic)

Munsen, Henry Jr. *Islam and Revolution in the Middle East*

Naqeeb, Khaldoun. *Society and State in the Gulf and Arabian Peninsula*

Ortega y Gasset, José. *History as a System*

Philby, Harry St John. *Arabian Jubilee*

——*Arabian Highlands*

Piscati, James P. *Islam in the Political Process*

Pordham, B. R. (ed.). *The Arab Gulf and the West*

Pryce-Jones, David. *The Closed Circle: An Interpretation of the Arabs*

Quandt, William. *Saudi Arabia in the 1980s*

Robinson, Jeffrey. *Yamani*

Roosevelt, Kermit. *Arabs, Oil and History*

Rugh, William. *The Arab Press*

Safran, Nedev. *The Explosion of the Saudi Regime*

Sahab, Victor. *The Crisis in Official Arab Media* (Arabic)

Said, Edward. *Orientalism*

Said, Nasser. *History of the House of Saud* (Arabic)

Salinger, Pierre. *The Gulf War Documents*

Sampson, Anthony. *The Seven Sisters*

——*The Money Lenders*

——*The Arms Bazaar*

Sandwick, John. *The Gulf Cooperation Council*

Secnec, Jean-François. *The Financial Markets of the Gulf*

Seymour, Ian. *OPEC: Instrument of Change*

Sharabi, Hisham. *The Next Arab Decade*

Skeet, Ian. *OPEC: 25 Years of Price and Politics*

Tahiri, Amir. *The Cauldron: The Middle East Behind the Headlines*

Terzian, Pierre. *OPEC: The Inside Story*

Theroux, Peter. *Sandstorm*

Timmerman, Kenneth R. *The Death Lobby*

Twitchell, K. S. *Saudi Arabia*

Vasil'yev, A. *Chapters in the History of Saudi Arabia*

Viorst, Milton. *Sands of Sorrow*

Wahbeh, Hafez. *Arabian Days*

Wynn, Wilton. *Nasser: The Search for Dignity*

Yergin, Daniel. *The Prize*

Statistical Abstracts

Who's Who in Saudi Arabia
The Future of the Arab World
Various ARAMCO publications

Press and Broadcasting

Arab world:

Arab News, ARAMCO World, Al Arab, Al Hawadess, Al Hayat, Al Jazira, Al Arabia, Al Quds Al Arabi, Al Musawar, Al Nahar, Al Tadamun, Al Yemen Al Khubra, Islamic Revolution, Khalij Times, Middle East Economic Digest, Middle East Economic Survey, Al Riyadh, Sharq Al Awsat, Sourakia, The Middle East.

Saudi underground press:

Sawt Al Masjid, Sawt Al Nass

Britain:

Banker, Economist, Daily Express, Financial Times, Guardian, Independent, Mail on Sunday, Observer, Spectator, The Times
BBC World Service, BBC Home Service, ITV

France:

International Herald Tribune, L'Express, Le Monde, Libération,

Germany:

Quick, Stern

USA

Foreign Affairs, National Geographic, Newsweek, Boston Globe, Los Angeles Times, New York Times, Philadelphia Inquirer, San Francisco Examiner, Washington Post, Time, Wall Street Journal
ABC News, CBS News, NBC News, PBS

Published Documents

Amnesty International, London
Article 19, London
Department of State, Washington DC
Foreign and Commonwealth Office Library, London
India Office Library and Records, London
Middle East Watch, New York
Minnesota Lawyers' International Human Rights Committee, Minneapolis, Minnesota
Royal Institute of International Affairs, London
Royal United Services Institute, London
Strategic Institute of International Affairs, London
US Congress, sessions 1964–89
US Congress, House Subcommittee on Multinationals.

Unpublished Documents

Iranian Foreign Office
Jordanian Foreign Office
Internal Memoranda, Time Inc.

Index

INDEX